The Heath Guide to Poetry

The Heath Guide to Poetry

David Bergman
Towson State University

Daniel Mark Epstein
Johns Hopkins University

D. C. HEATH AND COMPANY
Lexington, Massachusetts   Toronto

Cover illustration: Blue #2, 1916, by Georgia O'Keeffe. The Brooklyn Museum, Gift of Miss Mary T. Cockcroft.

Published simultaneously in Canada.

Printed in the United States of America.

International Standard Book Number: 0–669–05111–X

Library of Congress Catalog Card Number: 82–81623

For our teachers at Kenyon College

Credits

Preface

Note to the Student

If you have never studied poetry seriously, or if you wish to gain a fuller understanding of it, then this is the book for you. Using easy-to-follow language and a clear format, we will guide you to a better comprehension of this important literary form, and a lasting appreciation of it. To experience a poem fully, one must respond to it both emotionally and intellectually; in this book we will show you how poets and readers form a bond that defines, directs, and controls the poem. Unlike the many texts that treat poems as wholly separate or autonomous objects, we continually strive to show how *you*, the reader, react and help give poetry meaning. You are a necessary part of any poem, and this book will give you the tools you need to play an active role in the literature you read.

We have selected approximately four hundred works, which represent the wide spectrum of poetic form, style, and content. Unlike most introductions to poetry, this book includes chapters on narrative and dramatic poetry as well as one on lyric poetry. We have selected representative pieces from the Greek and Roman classics, and a number of works from Oriental, biblical, and native American literature. Naturally, we have chosen extensively from the full breadth of British and American poetry, and we have included numerous examples of comic poems, elegies, ballads, and song lyrics to demonstrate the variety of the genre. But for all the diversity, two criteria unite the works we present: poetic excellence and accessibility. Every poem—even those included to help you distinguish bad from good verse—deserves a reader's time and effort.

We have organized the material in fifteen separate chapters, which focus on the important elements of poetry: figures of speech, the various poetic modes and structures, and considerations of tone and quality. Many poems are followed by provocative questions that will lead you to a closer examination of a particular work's meaning and emotional force. Marginal glosses and footnotes have been judiciously added to explain unfamiliar references and to enhance your enjoyment and comprehension of poetry. At selected points, exercises and writing suggestions further check your comprehension of the poems and stimulate you to discover and understand your own responses, often asking you to relate your personal experiences to the experiences captured in the poems. Again, the emphasis here is on how you read a poem in light of your accumulated feelings, interests, and ideas.

There are readers who will wish to strike out on their own and read poetry without the aid of any editorial apparatus. For them there are poems for further study at the end of most chapters, and a rich and lengthy anthology at the close of the book.

Because many of you will be required to write essays on either the poems or the subjects suggested by the poems, we have included an appendix on writing about poetry. It contains information and advice on the writing process, on essay structure and format, and on quoting and footnoting procedure. A detailed glossary of literary terms is provided at the end of the book.

We hope you will share with us the excitement, pleasure, and rewards that poetry offers.

Note to the Instructor

The selections included in this text are a unique mix of fresh poems that are not often anthologized, and time-tested favorites. Our intention is to provide students and teachers with a wealth of familiar, "classic" works and at the same time to offer for consideration some poems that we deem interesting and accessible but that have not become stale through overexposure in the classroom. To supplement the text there is an instructor's guide, which includes numerous teaching suggestions as well as concise analyses of each of the works presented in the text.

The pedagogical program for this text is unique in one other respect. A ninety-minute cassette tape containing forty-two of the book's selections, many of them read by their famous authors, has been developed to serve as a classroom aid. Through it, students will come to appreciate more fully the oral qualities of poetry. The symbol • appears in the tables of contents and in the text beside those poems that are included on the tape. A full listing appears on page lv.

Acknowledgments

We are grateful to the many people who have helped us in the preparation of this book. It certainly would not have come to be written without the enormous help of Gordon Lester-Massman. Linda Vlasak and Sylvia Mallory helped us improve the style. We wish to thank Charles Haller and Jennifer Isaacs, who typed the manuscript and further advised us on style. Diskin Clay, Richard Howard, Hugh Kenner, and David St. John graciously answered our questions. Elaine Hedges and Donald R. Craver shared their knowledge and experience. We also wish to thank John Irwin, Mary Camerer, and Dorothy De Witt for their many kindnesses during the preparation of the manuscript.

The following persons read the manuscript and generously helped us with their suggestions: Chris Antonides, Lansing Community College; Jerald Butler, San Diego State University; Alice Carter, Ohio State University, Columbus; Joan Doggrell, Clark County Community College; Leon Gatlin, University of North Carolina, Charlotte; Ralph D. Howell, Mississippi College, Clinton; Ejner Jensen, University of Michigan, Ann Arbor; Michael Joyce, Jackson Community College; Paulino Lim, California State University, Long Beach; Phyllis Read, Bronx Community College–CUNY; Barclay M. Wheeler, Evergreen Valley College.

Finally we must acknowledge our many students, who, by their excitement, confusion, understanding, and impatience, have led us to improve ourselves as teachers and to grow as individuals.

Contents

5 Dramatic Poetry: The Poet as Actor   79

6 Images: Seeing Is Feeling   99

Chronological Contents

Medieval

Sixteenth and Seventeenth Century

Twentieth Century

The D. C. Heath Poetry Reading

W. H. AUDEN READING: "In Memory of W. B. Yeats" (1:44)

THE POETRY OF WILLIAM BLAKE: "London" (:50)
Performance by Sir Ralph Richardson

GWENDOLYN BROOKS READING HER POETRY: "Sadie and Maud" (:48)

THE POETRY OF COLERIDGE: "Kubla Khan" (3:17)
Performance by Sir Ralph Richardson

E. E. CUMMINGS READS HIS COLLECTED POETRY: "next to of course god america i" (:55), and "somewhere i have never travelled, gladly beyond" (2:18)

POEMS AND LETTERS OF EMILY DICKINSON: "Because I Could Not Stop for Death" (1:03), "Hope is the Thing with Feathers" (:30), and "I Felt a Funeral in My Brain" (:54)
Performance by Julie Harris

T. S. ELIOT READING THE LOVE SONG OF J. ALFRED PRUFROCK: "The Love Song of J. Alfred Prufrock" (8:03), and "Preludes" (2:15)

ENGLISH ROMANTIC POETRY: "John Anderson My Jo" (:56), "She Walks in Beauty" (1:04), "Ode on a Grecian Urn" (3:42), "On First Looking into Chapman's Homer" (1:04), "To Autumn" (2:28), "When I Have Fears" (1:11), and "Ode to the West Wind" (4:22)
Performances by Anthony Quayle, Frederick Worlock, and Sir Ralph Richardson

THE POETRY OF GERARD MANLEY HOPKINS: "Pied Beauty" (:50), "Spring and Fall" (:56), and "The Windhover" (1:16)
Performance by Cyril Cusack

THE POETRY AND VOICE OF TED HUGHES: "Hawk Roosting" (1:30)

PALGRAVE'S GOLDEN TREASURY OF ENGLISH POETRY: "They Flee From Me" (2:13), "The Passionate Shepherd to His Love" (1:21), "Shall I Compare Thee to a Summer's Day" (1:05), "Ode on the Death of a Favorite Cat" (1:45), and "Dover Beach" (2:10)
Performances by Eric Portman and John Neville

THE POETRY OF TENNYSON: "Ulysses" (4:52)
Performance by Sir Lewis Casson

DYLAN THOMAS READING HIS POETRY: "Do Not Go Gentle into That Good Night" (1:31), "Fern Hill" (3:51), and "The Hand That Signed the Paper (1:22)

POETRY OF WILLIAM WORDSWORTH: "The Solitary Reaper" (1:39), "Lines Composed a Few Miles above Tintern Abbey" (9:39), and "The World Is Too Much with Us" (:56)
Performance by Sir Cedric Hardwicke

THE LOVE POEMS OF JOHN DONNE: "The Flea" (1:30), and "A Valediction: Forbidding Mourning" (1:52)
Performance by Richard Burton

THE POEMS OF WILLIAM BUTLER YEATS: "Crazy Jane Talks with the Bishop" (:51), "The Lake Isle of Innisfree" (1:06), and "Sailing to Byzantium" (2:02)
Performances by Siobhan McKenna and Cyril Cusack

POETRY OF LANGSTON HUGHES: "Who But the Lord?" (:46)
Performance by Ossie Davis

ROBERT LOWELL: A READING: "Robert Frost" (1:06), and "Skunk Hour" (2:20)

The Heath Guide to Poetry

1 🌿 The Definition of Poetry

Lovers of poetry have been searching for an accurate definition of it for at least two thousand years. The ideal definition would be short. It would enable us to know a real poem when we hear it, and help us understand the power and long life of great poetry. But the search for this definition has not yielded a single description or formula to satisfy all admirers of this various art. Like most things human, poetry will not be reduced, tagged, or made to sit in one corner for very long. And there are as many ways to account for its power as there are poets.

W. H. Auden's description of poetry as "memorable speech" applies to most poetry but also to many things that are not poetry, such as advertising jingles. Matthew Arnold called poetry a "criticism of life," a characterization that is certainly true of his own poetry and discounts advertising jingles, but that is not a useful description of limericks or of nonsense poems such as Lewis Carroll's "Jabberwocky." William Wordsworth believed that poetry was "the spontaneous overflow of powerful feelings," a dramatic but broad definition, and Robert Frost viewed it as that property of speech that is "untranslatable."

All these poets would agree, however, that poetry is markedly different from the prose of legal contracts, encyclopedias, or newspapers. Poetry is more intense than other writing—more intense with feeling, and more intense in its concentration of meaning. Poetry is the true language of emotion. We have all had the experience of joy, love, or sadness so great that no matter how urgently we need to express it, words fail us. The birth of a child, the return of a friend after long absence, the death of a parent: these events can leave us speechless. At such times we might wish we were poets. For poetry succeeds where ordinary speech fails to communicate those urgent and subtle feelings that are most essentially human. That is why poetry is the most enduring form of literature.

By saying that poetry is the language of emotion, we do not mean to suggest that poetry does not engage our thoughts and ideas. Poets may praise the theories of relativity and economics as well as the colors of the sunset. Like Hamlet, they

1

may pose an abstract question: "To be, or not to be, that is the question." But if the writer does not communicate the emotion of discovering thought, we are not likely to find poetry in that writer's work.

Ezra Pound said that "literature is news that *stays* news." He must have had poetry in mind, for great poetry is eternally fresh. The poet writes what is most important in a given moment, and writes with such intensity and clarity that years later the verse can still seem important to a reader. How does a poet do this? Suiting the words and the rhythm of language perfectly to the experience, the poet says it so that we cannot imagine it being said any better.

Let us read a poem of joy and thoughtful discovery by a recent contemporary, James Wright.

JAMES WRIGHT (1927–1980)

A Blessing

Just off the highway to Rochester, Minnesota,
Twilight bounds softly forth on the grass.
And the eyes of those two Indian ponies
Darken with kindness.
5   They have come gladly out of the willows
To welcome my friend and me.
We step over the barbed wire into the pasture
Where they have been grazing all day, alone.
They ripple tensely, they can hardly contain their happiness
10   That we have come.
They bow shyly as wet swans. They love each other.
There is no loneliness like theirs.
At home once more,
They begin munching the young tufts of spring in the darkness.
15   I would like to hold the slenderer one in my arms.
For she has walked over to me
And nuzzled my left hand.
She is black and white,
Her mane falls wild on her forehead,
20   And the light breeze moves me to caress her long ear
That is delicate as the skin over a girl's wrist.
Suddenly I realize
That if I stepped out of my body I would break
Into blossom.

Our time for reading serious literature is limited. Therefore, we have every reason to ask our poets, What claim do you make on our attention? How has this poem arrived in front of us? And, now that it is here, what are we to make of it? You have noticed that poems usually have more white space around them than other literature, as if to say that they are somehow special, that they deserve extra attention. The great poems *are* special. They earn their space on the page and invite our attention.

In the case of James Wright's poem our opening questions are easily answered. How has the poem come to us? Wright and his friend turned "just off the highway" and encountered two ponies. Their beauty and affection for each other, and their delight in welcoming the two travelers, cause the poet to realize something important about himself. The poem comes to us because he wishes to share the experience and his discovery.

Is this an experience we wish to share? The title, "A Blessing," piques our curiosity, suggesting that something remarkable is about to happen. In the first lines Wright evokes a world rich with possibilities. Twilight is a charming hour, a time of day in which magic seems likely. When "twilight bounds softly forth" in the shape of two ponies, we find ourselves in a world that is both familiar and strange, and altogether enticing. The beauty of the horses, who "bow shyly as wet swans," and the warmth of their greeting add to the enchantment of the scene.

By the time Wright admits the impulse "to hold the slenderer one in my arms," we have identified with him and can share his love for these exquisite creatures. When he speaks of the pony's ear, "delicate as the skin over a girl's wrist," the comparison reveals that Wright sees the horses as nearly human in their capacity to inspire and receive love. At the same time we can understand that the skin that separates human from human, and person from animal, is a very thin one.

It is just one more stage in the poet's thought to realize that he himself is part of nature and that he might, in a single step out of his body, out of the slender confines of human life, break into blossom. Hence the great power and beauty of the last lines. It is an important revelation, perfectly expressed. Miracles are in short supply, and a poem that can provide one has earned our attention. It is indeed "A Blessing."

Not all poetry is so joyous. The next poem, Emily Dickinson's meditation on death, moves us in a quite different direction.

EMILY DICKINSON (1830–1866)

· I Felt a Funeral in My Brain

I felt a funeral in my brain,
And mourners to and fro
Kept treading, treading, till it seemed
That sense was breaking through.

5 And when they all were seated,
A service like a drum
Kept beating, beating, till I thought
My mind was going numb.

And then I heard them lift a box
10 And creak across my soul
With those same boots of lead again,
Then space began to toll,

As all the heavens were a bell,
And being but an ear,
20 And I and silence some strange race
Wrecked solitary here.

And then a plank in reason broke,
And I dropped down and down
And hit a world at every plunge,
25 And finished knowing then.

Questions

1. Where is the action of the poem really taking place?
2. Whose funeral is it? The poet's? A friend's?
3. What is in the box?
4. Would the mourners actually wear "boots of lead"? If not, why does the poet describe them that way?
5. At the end of the poem, the poet says that she "hit a world at every plunge." What sorts of worlds do you imagine?

Emily Dickinson (*Amherst College Library*)

Everyone who has lived enough to value life has had a similar curiosity and fear about death. Emily Dickinson fashioned this poem out of the richness of those feelings, and we are moved to find them so similar to our own. Notice how the poet personalizes her fear by taking the funeral out of the real world and putting it into her own brain. Next she introduces ominous sounds and makes them more frightening through repetition: the footsteps of the mourners, the beating of the drum, the tolling of the bell. Try to imagine the horror of those sounds going on inside your own head. It is not at all surprising, then, when the poet tells us that "a plank in reason broke." No one's sanity could withstand such a racket. When her reason breaks, she feels herself falling through worlds and worlds until she finally arrives where there can be no knowing. Many of us are familiar with the fear of falling. The poet is telling us that death must be like falling through some plank of reason to a place where nothing is known. This is an exciting, if fearful, way of looking at death.

The two poems we have read so far represent the more thoughtful, serious side of the muse. The Muses, nine sister goddesses in Greek mythology, presided over the creative arts. From them we get the word *music* as well as the phrase *the muse*, which has come to designate the source of all poetic genius and inspiration. The muse has many different moods, as the multiplicity of the Greek goddesses suggests. Poetry is not always as mystical as Wright's "A Blessing" or as brooding as Dickinson's "I Felt a Funeral in My Brain." It can also be erotic or comical. In the following poem by Christopher Marlowe, we see the muse at its fun-loving best, as the speaker, a shepherd, tries to persuade his lady friend to be his love.

CHRISTOPHER MARLOWE (1564–1593)

• The Passionate Shepherd to His Love

Come live with me and be my love,
And we will all the pleasures prove°   *test, evaluate*
That valleys, groves, hills, and fields,
Woods, or steepy mountain yields.

5   And we will sit upon the rocks,
Seeing the shepherds feed their flocks
By shallow rivers, to whose falls
Melodious birds sing madrigals.

And I will make thee beds of roses
10   And a thousand fragrant posies,
A cap of flowers and a kirtle°   *gown*
Embroidered all with leaves of myrtle;

A gown made of the finest wool
Which from our pretty lambs we pull;
15   Fair-lined slippers for the cold,
With buckles of the purest gold;

A belt of straw and ivy buds,
With coral clasps and amber studs.
And if these pleasures may thee move,
20   Come live with me and be my love.

The shepherds' swains shall dance and sing
For thy delight each May morning:
If these delights thy mind may move,
Then live with me and be my love.

Questions

1. Vocabulary: *posies* (10), *swains* (21).
2. What has moved the shepherd to speak? Is it the same emotion that has inspired Marlowe to write the poem?
3. Why does the shepherd take such care in describing the clothes he will make for his "love"?
4. Do you think that life with the shepherd would be as marvelous as he describes it?
5. Would the poem lend itself to music?
6. Do you think the shepherd's argument is persuasive?
7. Compare this poem with Sir Walter Raleigh's "The Nymph's Reply to the Shepherd" on page 350.

The next poem, a whimsical children's story cast in rhyme, appeals to still another appetite in us, the love of nonsense and satire. The poem was written for children. But its portraiture of the ironic bear and its gentle satire of the gushing Lady sustain reexamination by readers of all ages.

THEODORE ROETHKE (1908–1963)

The Lady and the Bear

A Lady came to a Bear by a Stream.
"O Why are you fishing that way?
Tell me, dear Bear there by the Stream,
Why are you fishing that way?"

5   "I am what is known as a Biddly Bear,—
That's why I'm fishing this way.
We Biddly's are Pee-culiar Bears,
And so,—I'm fishing this way.
"And besides, it seems there's a Law:
10   A most, most exactious Law
Says a Bear
Doesn't dare
Doesn't dare
Doesn't DARE
15   Use a Hook or a Line,
Or an old piece of Twine,

Not even the end of his Claw, Claw, Claw,
Not even the end of his Claw.
Yes, a Bear has to fish with his Paw, Paw, Paw.
20   A Bear has to fish with his Paw."

"O it's Wonderful how with a flick of your Wrist,
You can fish, out a fish, out a fish, out a fish.
If *I* were a fish I just couldn't resist
You, when you are fishing that way, that way,
25   When you are fishing that way."

And at that the Lady slipped from the Bank
And fell in the Stream still clutching a Plank,
But the Bear just sat there until she Sank;
As he went on fishing his way, his way,
30   As he went on fishing his way.

Questions

1. From the beginning of the poem, the Lady is quite complimentary to the Bear.
   From his comments in stanza 2, do you think that he appreciates her flattery, her
   presence?
2. When the Lady falls into the stream, why doesn't the Bear help her?

2 🌿 Listening in on the Poem

Distinguishing between eloquence and poetry, John Stuart Mill wrote that eloquence is heard, but poetry is overheard. This suggests a useful way to read poetry. Imagine that we have picked up a telephone to make a call. To our surprise, we hear someone talking on the other end. At first we do not understand what the person is saying, but because something in the speaker's voice interests us, we continue listening. By piecing together bits of information, we eventually come to understand the conversation. The same is true of many poems. At first we may be puzzled, but if we listen long and carefully enough, the good poets will tell us what we need to know to appreciate what they are saying.

Having the text of the poem gives us an advantage over the telephone eavesdropper. We can reread the poem in order to understand and appreciate the speaker fully. Also, the reader of a poem can look up unfamiliar words in the dictionary. Before tackling any poem, we should give ourselves time to reread it, and we should have a dictionary close at hand.

How then do we piece together the poet's conversation? One way to begin is by asking ourselves three basic questions:

1. Who is speaking?
2. To whom is he or she speaking?
3. What has prompted the speaker to talk?

Sometimes the answers to these questions will be obvious and unrevealing. But often they are necessary for understanding the poem. The following is a good example of an overheard poem.

WALTER SAVAGE LANDOR (1775–1864)

Mother, I Cannot Mind My Wheel

Mother, I cannot mind my wheel;
　My fingers ache, my lips are dry:

Oh! if you felt the pain I feel!
   But oh, who ever felt as I?

5   No longer could I doubt him true;
      All other men may use deceit:
   He always said my eyes were blue,
      And often swore my lips were sweet.

The first word of this poem provides the answer to our second question: the poem is addressed to the speaker's mother. After reading the first line, we know that the daughter is speaking, trying to explain why she cannot sit quietly at the spinning wheel, a task that requires great patience. She tells her mother that her fingers ache and her lips are dry. But in the second stanza she reveals the true reason for her restlessness—her lover has abandoned her. His abandonment is especially painful for the speaker because she had trusted him. "All other men may use deceit," but her man, she thought, was honest. Moreover, he had flattered her by admiring her blue eyes and sweet lips.

We may also infer from the poem that the speaker—or *persona*, as the speaker is called—is young and naive. She asks her mother, "But oh, who ever felt as I?" as if no one else had ever known disappointed love. Her statement is not really a question, but an exclamation. For the moment, the woman feels utterly abandoned and heartsick.

What emerges from these eight short lines is a portrait of a young woman in the throes of her first disappointed love. Landor has given us a rich, vivid picture. No word is wasted.

Perhaps you have other questions. Is the girl ugly or pretty? Rich or poor? Was the man a neighbor or a stranger? Is the mother indifferent, angry, or sympathetic? These are all good questions, but we simply cannot answer them. The poet has not given us the necessary information. Instead of speculating, we will simply remain silent. The good reader will keep to the facts of the text and refrain from making unsupported guesses. We can do nothing more than read carefully. Where the poem is silent, we must be silent too.

The Persona and the Poet

In "Mother, I Cannot Mind My Wheel," the persona—or speaker—is obviously not Walter Savage Landor. But even in poems in which the speaker is not clearly distinguished from the author, it is often useful to think of the speaker as a fictional character. Here is a personal poem in which it is unimportant whether the speaker is the author or someone else.

LINDA PASTAN (1931–)

25th High School Reunion

We come to hear the endings
of all the stories

in our anthology
of false starts:
5   how the girl who seemed
as hard as nails
was hammered into shape;
how the athletes ran
out of races;
10   how under the skin
our skulls rise
to the surface
like rocks in the bed
of a drying stream.
15   Look! We have all
turned into
ourselves.

Questions

1. What else does the speaker refer to when he or she says, "We have all/turned into/ourselves"?
2. To what might "our anthology/of false starts" refer?

The title of this poem is crucial to our understanding of it. (Titles are often important and should never be overlooked.) If we ask who the speaker is, we can say only that it is a high school graduate who has celebrated his or her twenty-fifth reunion and is, therefore, middle-aged. Linda Pastan may fit this description, but the poem does not require her to be the speaker. In fact, the speaker might be *any* middle-aged high school graduate.

The reunion has forced the speaker to reflect on how his or her classmates have changed. A tough student has been "hammered into shape." The athletes look worn out. Everyone appears to have dried up. The alumni's skulls are becoming prominent, signifying the approach of death.

The poem ends on a surprising note. The speaker turns directly to us, addressing us as fellow alumni and reminding us that we too will be middle-aged someday and will begin to show signs of approaching death.

The Importance of Context

Sometimes speakers do not refer to themselves at all in the poem; nevertheless, our appreciation of the poem may be enhanced by imagining a context for the speaker. In the following poem, "Musée des Beaux Arts" (which means "Fine Arts Museum" in French), we might find it useful to imagine the speaker as a tour guide pointing out one beautiful painting after another and commenting on the great artists—the Old Masters—who painted them.

For a moment we stop in front of Pieter Brueghel's painting *Landscape with the Fall of Icarus* in the Musée des Beaux Arts in Brussels, Belgium, which

Landscape with the Fall of Icarus, by Pieter Brueghel the Elder (*Royal Museums of Art and History, Brussels*)

Auden visited in 1939, just before he wrote this poem. Icarus was the son of Daedalus, whose name means literally "cunning worker." Father and son were imprisoned together in a tower, where Daedalus made wings out of wax and feathers so that they could escape. The device worked, but Icarus was so delighted with his wings that he flew toward the sun. The sun melted the wings, and Icarus fell to his death in the sea below. With that bit of information, you should be ready to begin to appreciate the poem.

W. H. AUDEN (1907–1973)

Musée des Beaux Arts

About suffering they were never wrong,
The Old Masters: how well they understood
Its human position; how it takes place
While someone else is eating or opening a window or just walking dully along;
5   How, when the aged are reverently, passionately waiting
For the miraculous birth, there always must be
Children who did not specially want it to happen, skating
On a pond at the edge of the wood:
They never forgot
10   That even the dreadful martyrdom must run its course
Anyhow in a corner, some untidy spot
Where the dogs go on with their doggy life and the torturer's horse
Scratches its innocent behind on a tree.

In Brueghel's *Icarus,* for instance: how everything turns away
15   Quite leisurely from the disaster; the ploughman may

Have heard the splash, the forsaken cry,
But for him it was not an important failure; the sun shone
As it had to on the white legs disappearing into the green
Water; and the expensive delicate ship that must have seen
20   Something amazing, a boy falling out of the sky,
Had somewhere to get to and sailed calmly on.

Questions

1. Vocabulary: *martyrdom* (10).
2. What is the "human position" that suffering occupies?
3. How is suffering depicted in Brueghel's *Icarus*?
4. What political events of 1939 may have prompted Auden to write about suffering?
5. Does the speaker follow the Old Masters' examples for showing suffering?
6. Do you think the matter-of-fact tone is appropriate for this poem? Would the poem be more effective if the speaker were more emotional?
7. What sort of attitude should we adopt toward the poem? Toward suffering?

The Poet as Speaker

Finally, there are poems in which the speaker is unquestionably the poet. Biographical information may be useful for appreciating such poems, but they can move us even without such knowledge. Take Ben Jonson's poem on the death of his son:

BEN JONSON (1573?–1637)

On My First Son

Farewell, thou child of my right hand, and joy;
My sin was too much hope of thee, loved boy:
Seven years thou wert lent to me, and I thee pay,
Exacted by the fate, on the just day.[1]
5   O could I lose all father now! for why
Will man lament the state he should envy,
To have so soon 'scaped world's and flesh's rage,
And, if no other misery, yet age?
Rest in soft peace, and asked, say, "Here doth lie
10   Ben Jonson his best piece of poetry."
For whose sake henceforth all his vows be such
As what he loves may never like too much.

Questions

1. To whom is the poem addressed? Does this fact suggest something about Jonson's spiritual beliefs?
2. In what sense might a man "envy" the death of a young boy?

---

[1] The boy was born in 1596 and died on his birthday in 1603.

3. Would you call Jonson a proud father? Does Jonson feel there is any connection between his fatherly pride and his son's death?
4. What is the relationship between Jonson's son and poetry?
5. What relationship does Jonson hope to develop in the future between himself and those he loves?

This poem ably conveys the feeling of grief, whether or not we know anything about Ben Jonson. Additional information will, however, help us appreciate Jonson's sorrow. For example, Jonson's son was named Benjamin after his father. The first line of the poem contains the Hebrew meaning of the boy's name: "child of the right hand."

The poem contains one complicated line, "O could I lose all father now!" Jonson means that he wishes he could forget he possessed the attributes of fatherhood; then he might regard his son's death more philosophically. He could console himself with the knowledge that by dying young the boy has escaped many hardships.

The poet can have various relationships to the persona of a poem. Sometimes the speaker is not the poet, but a fictional character. At other times the speaker could be the poet but does not necessarily have to be. At still other times the speaker does not even appear as a character in the poem. Whatever relationship the poet adopts to the speaker, we should listen closely to the speaker's words and base our assumptions on the text of the poem and the context of the speaker.

3  Narrative Poetry

The Poet as Storyteller

We commonly think that stories, like laws, are best written in prose. Yet the ancient Greeks composed their laws in verse, and the earliest known poem, *The Epic of Gilgamesh*, composed in Sumer some five thousand years ago, is a long tale about the adventures of a king.

The first narrative or storytelling poems recounted the adventures of great heroes and their relations with gods and demons. Often these poems would record a nation's origins and history. They were also an early source of entertainment. Poet-reciters called *bards* regaled courts with these long heroic tales. Later, scribes committed the narrative poems to paper, and so they are preserved today. In England the scribes were often monks, who were scolded by their superiors for taking time away from religious studies to copy down pagan poems. In the nineteenth century, scholars like Francis Child roamed the countryside collecting the ballads and stories of illiterate peasants.

Formulae

How could an illiterate bard remember a poem that might take all evening to recite? First, the rhythms of the poem helped him to remember, just as we are more likely to remember a jingle than a flat piece of prose of equal length. Also, the bards had stock phrases, or *formulae*, that they used over and over again. Similarly, little formulae help parents tell bedtime stories. In "Goldilocks and the Three Bears," for example, there are constantly reworked phrases:

"Someone's been sitting in my chair."

"Someone's been eating my porridge."

"Someone's been sleeping in my bed."

These formulae help parents tell the story each night in roughly the same words. Like parents, bards did not remember their poems perfectly, and the poems passed down through oral tradition usually appear in a number of different versions.

Let us look at a Scottish ballad, a poem composed orally and handed down from singer to singer. Like an epic, this ballad tells the story of a brave man, and it relies on the repetition of formulaic expressions. In the version that follows, most of the language has been modernized, but enough of the Scottish dialogue remains to give you a flavor of the original.

ANONYMOUS

Sir Patrick Spence

The king sits in Dumferling town
    Drinking the blood-red wine:
"O where will I get a good sailor,
    To sail this ship of mine?"

5   Up and spake an elder knight
    Sat on the king's right knee:
"Sir Patrick Spence is the best sailor,
    That sails upon the sea."

The king has written a broad letter
10   And signed it with his hand
And sent it to Sir Patrick Spence
    Was walking on the sand.

The first line that Sir Patrick read
    A loud lauch° lauched he;   *laugh*
15   The next line that Sir Patrick read
    The tear blinded his ee.°   *eye*

"O who is this has done this deed
    This ill deed done to me,
To send me out this time of the year,
20   To sail upon the sea!

"Make haste, make haste, my merry men all
    Our good ship sails the morn."
"O say not so, my master dear,
    For I fear a deadly storm.

25   "Late, late yestreen° I saw the new moon   *last evening*
    With the old moon in her arm
And I fear, I fear, my dear master
    That we will come to harm."

O our Scots nobles were rich laith°   *very loath*
30   To wet their cork-healed schoone;°   *shoes*
But long before the play was played
    Their hats they swam aboone.°   *above*

O long, long may their ladies sit,
    With their fans into their hand

35   Or e'er they see Sir Patrick Spence
        Come sailing to the land.

    O long, long may the ladies stand
        With their golden combs in their hair
    Waiting for their own dear lords
40   For they'll see them no mair.°   *more*

    Half o'er, half o'er to Aberdour,
        It's fifty fathoms deep,
    And there lies good Sir Patrick Spence,
        With the Scots lords at his feet.

"Sir Patrick Spence" is like a short story in many ways, but the differences are interesting and important. Like many short stories, it contains characters, a setting, conflict and dialogue, and a single significant action. But in "Sir Patrick Spence" these elements are more condensed. We never learn where Sir Patrick lived or how he achieved his fame. The poet tells us only that he was walking on the beach. Nor do we learn whether he is married or has children. These details would be important in a short story, but they are unimportant for the poetic narrator. Nevertheless, we do learn a good deal about Sir Patrick. He sees the foolish, vindictive, and thoughtless nature of the king's courtiers. But he is loyal and brave. He does not question his orders but immediately commands his sailors, despite their protests, to man the ship. His actions say more than words. Of course, the longer the narrative, the greater its detail. Book-length poems contain a rich supply of narrative detail.

Transitions in Narrative Poetry

"Sir Patrick Spence" illustrates another mark of the poetic narrative technique: rarely are there transitions from one scene to another. A narrative poem moves in much the same way as a film. Movie directors often shift instantaneously from one scene to another. Similarly, in "Sir Patrick Spence" we move from a scene in which Sir Patrick reads his orders to one in which he is on the deck encouraging his frightened sailors. Moreover, in a poetic narrative we do not necessarily began at the beginning of the story. For example, Charles Dickens starts his novel *David Copperfield* with the sentence "I am born." But the poetic narrator begins, as critics have noted, *in medias res*—Latin for "in the middle of things." The shorter the poem, the more concentrated the action. In the most concentrated narrative poems, the climax alone is presented.

Still another feature of the narrative poem is omission of certain scenes. In "Sir Patrick Spence," for example, the scene of the shipwreck is entirely missing. The poet shows us only the hats floating above the sunken ship, markers signaling the disaster brought by vanity. The rhythm and music of the poem provide the continuity we would have missed if this were a prose account.

The ballad form provides an excellent mode for narration. A discussion of ballad form is provided in Chapter 12. Here it is enough to point out that the

Langston Hughes (*National Portrait Gallery, Smith-sonian Institution, Washington, D.C.*)

four-line stanza, or *quatrain*, provides a handy short unit for developing a single scene. The second and fourth lines are shorter than the first and third. These shorter lines give the stanza its speed and propel the reader from stanza to stanza.

Ballads continue to be popular, especially with poets who wish to reach a wide audience. Here is a modern ballad.

LANGSTON HUGHES (1902–1967)

Sylvester's Dying Bed

I woke up this mornin'
'Bout half-past three.
All the womens in town
Was gathered round me.

5   Sweet gals was a-moanin',
"Sylvester's gonna die!"
And a hundred pretty mamas
Bowed their heads to cry.

I woke up a little later
10   'Bout half-past fo',
The doctor 'n' undertaker's
Both at ma do'.

Black gals was a-beggin',
"You can't leave us here!"
15 Brown-skins cryin', "Daddy!
Honey! Baby! Don't go, dear!"

But I felt ma time's a-comin',
And I know'd I's dyin' fast.
I seed the River Jerden
20 A-creepin' muddy past—
But I's still Sweet Papa 'Vester,
Yes, sir! Long as life do last!

So I hollers, "Com'ere, babies,
Fo' to love yo' daddy right!"
25 And I reaches up to hug 'em—
When the Lawd put out the light.

Then everything was darkness
In a great . . . big . . . night.

Questions

1. Is there anything heroic about Sylvester? How would you compare the way he approaches death with the way Sir Patrick Spence meets his fate?
2. Are there any repeated phrases or formulaic expressions in "Sylvester's Dying Bed"? How do they contribute to the story?
3. The four-line stanza pattern is broken twice in this poem. Why is stanza 5 longer than the others? Why is stanza 7 shorter?

Epic Poetry

The longest narratives are called *epics*. These poems do not simply recount a single action; they record a way of life. The Greek epics, the *Iliad* and the *Odyssey*, are among the greatest treasures of Western culture. These orally transmitted narratives are called *primary epics*. Later, poets consciously imitated these earlier works by writing epics of their own. Virgil's *Aeneid*, Dante's *Divine Comedy*, and John Milton's *Paradise Lost* are among the most famous secondary epics. Epics are too long for us to include a complete one in this book, but an excerpt from the *Odyssey* appears at the end of this chapter.

Personal History in Narrative Poems

Unlike the bards of ancient Greece or the minstrels of Scotland, contemporary poets are not responsible for recording national history, although some continue to narrate incidents of national importance. More often, however, today's poets tell personal or family histories that are more likely to be forgotten in the future. The following poem is one of several poems by Edward Field that recount his family's history.

EDWARD FIELD (1924–)

My Polish Grandmother

Grandma and the children left at night.
It was forbidden to go. In those days
the Czar and his cossacks rode through the town at whim
killing Jews and setting fire to straw roofs
5   while just down the road the local Poles
sat laughing as they drank liquor.

Grandpa had gone to America first
and earned the money for the rest of the family to come over.
So they left finally, the whole brood of them
10   with the hired agent running the show,
an impatient man, and there were so many kids
and the bundles kept falling apart
and poor grandma was frightened of him.

She gave the man all the money
15   but she couldn't round up the kids fast enough for him.
They were children after all and didn't understand
and she was so stupid and clumsy herself,
carrying food for all of them and their clothes
and could she leave behind her pots?
20   Her legs hurt already; they were always swollen
from the hard work, the childbearing, and the cold.

They caught the train and there was a terrible moment
when the conductor came by for the tickets:
The children mustn't speak or he would know they were Jewish,
25   they had no permits to travel—Jews weren't allowed.
But the agent knew how to handle it,
everybody got *shmeared*, that means money got you everywhere.

The border was the worst. They had to sneak across at night.
The children musn't make a sound, not even the babies.
30   Momma was six and she didn't want to do anything wrong
but she wasn't sure what to do.
The man led them through the woods
and beyond they could hear dogs barking from the sentry hut,
and then they had to run all of them down the ravine to the other side,
35   grandma broken down from childbearing with her bundles
and bad legs and a baby in her arms,
they ran all the children across the border
or the guards might shoot them
and if the little ones cried, the agent said he would smother them.

40   They got to a port finally.
Grandpa had arranged for cabin passage, not steerage,
but the agent cheated and put them in the hold
so they were on the low deck looking up at the rich people.
My momma told me how grandma took care of all her children,
45   how Jake didn't move anymore he was so seasick, maybe even dead,

and if people thought he was dead
they would throw him overboard like garbage, so she hid him.
The rich tossed down oranges to the poor children—
my momma had never had one before.

50   They came to New York, to the tenements,
a fearful new place, a city, country people in the city.
My momma, who had been roly-poly in slow Poland,
got skinny and pimply in zippy New York.
Everybody grew up in a new way.

55   And now my grandma is dead and my momma is old
and we her children are all scattered over the earth
speaking a different language and forgetting
why it was so important
to go to a new country.

Questions

1. Vocabulary: *cossacks* (3), *ravine* (34), *steerage* (41).
2. Why does Field feel compelled to retell this story?
3. What is worth retelling about this story? Does your family have similar stories about coming to America?
4. How does the poem reflect political history?
5. In what way does this poem start *in medias res*?
6. Compare this poem to Gary Soto's "History" on pages 439–441.

Use of Language in Narrative Poetry

There is yet another difference between the traditional prose story and the poetic narrative. The prose writer, by and large, wants to make the scene so vivid that we look beyond the words and feel that we are actually present in the scene. The poet, however, at crucial moments draws our attention to the language. In fact, the poet would like to believe that the story is happening *in* the language. In the following poem we are asked to pay particularly close attention to the last line.

DANIEL MARK EPSTEIN (1948–)

Madonna (With Child Missing)[1]

Shouts from the street, spotlights crossfire
at a third story window. The woman
stares through smoked glass at a crowd
and firemen in glazed slickers—
5   flames climbing the stairs behind her two at a time.
She lifts up the window sash with one hand,
kisses the infant and rolls it out trusting the air,
the soft knock of skull on stone in her heart.

---

[1] *Madonna* is Italian for "mother." It is often the name of works of art depicting the Virgin Mary.

Notice the last line. Would this be an acceptable ending in a prose story? If this were a prose account, wouldn't we demand to know whether the child was saved? In a poetic narrative these plot concerns are less important. For the mother, the child is both saved and injured. The sounds and rhythms of the last line imitate both the erratic beating of the mother's heart and the imagined disaster to the child. The story is secondary to the action of the language. It is this concern with language that makes a poetic narrative so memorable for both the original audience and the contemporary reader. In the poems that follow, you should try to attend not only to the engaging stories the poets write, but also to the language they use to enact the story.

Suggestions for Essayists

1. Retell in prose one of the narrative poems from this chapter. Discuss what you have gained in the translation and what you have lost.
2. Discuss how the ideas of loyalty and heroism have changed since the time of Sir Patrick Spence.
3. Narrate an episode of family history that you have either lived through or heard about and that is in danger of being forgotten.

Suggestions for Poets

1. Narrate an episode of family history that is in danger of being forgotten.
2. Find an episode in the newspaper and retell it in ballad form.

❧ Poems for Further Study

ANONYMOUS

The Wife of Usher's Well

There lived a wife at Usher's Well,
  And a wealthy wife was she;
She had three stout and stalwart sons,
  And sent them o'er the sea.

5   They hadna been a week from her,
  A week but barely ane,
When word came to the carline° wife   *peasant*
  That her three sons were gane.

They hadna been a week from her,
10 A week but barely three,
Whan word came to the carline wife
  That her sons she'd never see.

"I wish the wind may never cease,
  Nor flashes° in the flood,   *troubles*

15 Till my three sons come hame to me
  In earthly flesh and blood."

It fell about the Martinmass
  When nights are lang and mirk,
The carline wife's three sons came hame,
20   And their hats were o the birk.°   *birch*

It neither grew in syke° nor ditch,   *trench*
  Nor yet in ony sheugh;°   *furrow*
But at the gates o Paradise
  That birk grew fair eneugh.

25 "Blow up the fire, my maidens,
  Bring water from the well;
For a' my house shall feast this night
  Since my three sons are well."

And she has made to them a bed,
30   She's made it large and wide,
And she's ta'en her mantle her about,
  Sat down at the bed-side.

Up then crew the red, red cock,
  And up and crew the gray;
35 The eldest to the youngest said,
  " 'Tis time we were away."

The cock he hadna crawd but once
  And clappd his wings at a',
When the youngest to the eldest said,
40   "Brother, we must awa.

"The cock doth craw, the day doth daw,
  The channerin° worm doth chide;   *devouring*
Gin° we be mist out o our place,   *if*
  A sair pain we maun bide.

45 "Fare ye weel, my mother dear!
  Fareweel to barn and byre!°   *cattle-shed*
And fare ye weel, the bonny lass
  That kindles my mother's fire!"

DUDLEY RANDALL (1914–)

Ballad of Birmingham[2]

(On the bombing of a church in Birmingham, Alabama, 1963)

"Mother dear, may I go downtown
Instead of out to play,

---

[2] "Freedom marches" were parades organized to promote civil rights in the South during the 1950s and the 1960s.

And march the streets of Birmingham
In a Freedom March today?"

5　"No, baby, no, you may not go,
For the dogs are fierce and wild,
And clubs and hoses, guns and jails
Aren't good for a little child."

"But, mother, I won't be alone.
10　Other children will go with me,
And march the streets of Birmingham
To make our country free."

"No, baby, no, you may not go,
For I fear those guns will fire.
15　But you may go to church instead
And sing in the children's choir."

She has combed and brushed her night-dark hair,
And bathed rose petal sweet,
And drawn white gloves on her small brown hands,
20　And white shoes on her feet.

The mother smiled to know her child
Was in the sacred place,
But that smile was the last smile
To come upon her face.

25　For when she heard the explosion,
Her eyes grew wet and wild.
She raced through the streets of Birmingham
Calling for her child.

She clawed through bits of glass and brick,
30　Then lifted out a shoe.
"O, here's the shoe my baby wore,
But, baby, where are you?"

ROBERT FROST (1874–1963)

'Out, Out—'[3]

The buzz-saw snarled and rattled in the yard
And made dust and dropped stove-length sticks of wood,
Sweet-scented stuff when the breeze drew across it.
And from there those that lifted eyes could count
5　Five mountain ranges one behind the other
Under the sunset far into Vermont.
And the saw snarled and rattled, snarled and rattled,
As it ran light, or had to bear a load.
And nothing happened: day was all but done.

---

[3] The title is an allusion to Shakespeare's *Macbeth*, act 5, scene 5, in which Macbeth, hearing about his wife's death, says, "Out, out, brief candle! / Life's but a walking shadow, a poor player / That struts and frets his hour upon the stage / And then is heard no more."

10   Call it a day, I wish they might have said
      To please the boy by giving him the half hour
      That a boy counts so much when saved from work.
      His sister stood beside them in her apron
      To tell them 'Supper.' At the word, the saw,
15   As if to prove saws knew what supper meant,
      Leaped out at the boy's hand, or seemed to leap—
      He must have given the hand. However it was,
      Neither refused the meeting. But the hand!
      The boy's first outcry was a rueful laugh,
20   As he swung toward them holding up the hand
      Half in appeal, but half as if to keep
      The life from spilling. Then the boy saw all—
      Since he was old enough to know, big boy
      Doing a man's work, though a child at heart—
25   He saw all spoiled. 'Don't let him cut my hand off—
      The doctor, when he comes. Don't let him, sister!'

      So. But the hand was gone already.
      The doctor put him in the dark of ether.
      He lay and puffed his lips out with his breath.
30   And then—the watcher at his pulse took fright.
      No one believed. They listened at his heart.
      Little—less—nothing!—and that ended it.
      No more to build on there. And they, since they
      Were not the one dead, turned to their affairs.

ELIZABETH BISHOP (1911–1980)

The Fish

      I caught a tremendous fish
      and held him beside the boat
      half out of water, with my hook
      fast in a corner of his mouth.
5   He didn't fight.
      He hadn't fought at all.
      He hung a grunting weight,
      battered and venerable
      and homely. Here and there
10   his brown skin hung in strips
      like ancient wallpaper,
      and its pattern of darker brown
      was like wallpaper:
      shapes like full-blown roses
15   stained and lost through age.
      He was speckled with barnacles,
      fine rosettes of lime,
      and infested
      with tiny white sea-lice,
20   and underneath two or three

rags of green weed hung down.
While his gills were breathing in
the terrible oxygen
—the frightening gills,
25   fresh and crisp with blood,
that can cut so badly—
I thought of the coarse white flesh
packed in like feathers,
the big bones and the little bones,
30   the dramatic reds and blacks
of his shiny entrails,
and the pink swim-bladder
like a big peony.
I looked into his eyes
35   which were far larger than mine
but shallower, and yellowed,
the irises backed and packed
with tarnished tinfoil
seen through the lenses
40   of old scratched isinglass.
They shifted a little, but not
to return my stare.
—It was more like the tipping
of an object toward the light.
45   I admired his sullen face,
the mechanism of his jaw,
and then I saw
that from his lower lip
—if you could call it a lip—
50   grim, wet, and weaponlike,
hung five old pieces of fish-line,
or four and a wire leader
with the swivel still attached,
with all their five big hooks
55   grown firmly in his mouth.
A green line, frayed at the end
where he broke it, two heavier lines,
and a fine black thread
still crimped from the strain and snap
60   when it broke and he got away.
Like medals with their ribbons
frayed and wavering,
a five-haired beard of wisdom
trailing from his aching jaw.
65   I stared and stared
and victory filled up
the little rented boat,
from the pool of bilge
where oil had spread a rainbow

70   around the rusted engine
to the bailer rusted orange,
the sun-cracked thwarts,
the oarlocks on their strings,
the gunnels—until everything
75   was rainbow, rainbow, rainbow!
And I let the fish go.

EDWIN MUIR (1887–1959)

The Horses

Barely a twelvemonth after
The seven days war that put the world to sleep,
Late in the evening the strange horses came.
By then we had made our covenant with silence,
5   But in the first few days it was so still
We listened to our breathing and were afraid.
On the second day
The radios failed; we turned the knobs; no answer.
On the third day a warship passed us, heading north,
10   Dead bodies piled on the deck. On the sixth day
A plane plunged over us into the sea. Thereafter
Nothing. The radios dumb;
And still they stand in corners of our kitchens,
And stand, perhaps, turned on, in a million rooms
15   All over the world. But now if they should speak,
If on a sudden they should speak again,
If on the stroke of noon a voice should speak,
We would not listen, we would not let it bring
That old bad world that swallowed its children quick
20   At one great gulp. We would not have it again.
Sometimes we think of the nations lying asleep,
Curled blindly in impenetrable sorrow,
And then the thought confounds us with its strangeness.
The tractors lie about our fields; at evening
25   They look like dank sea-monsters couched and waiting.
We leave them where they are and let them rust:
'They'll moulder away and be like other loam'.
We make our oxen drag our rusty ploughs,
Long laid aside. We have gone back
30   Far past our father's land.

                       And then, that evening
Late in the summer the strange horses came.
We heard a distant tapping on the road,
A deepening drumming; it stopped, went on again
And at the corner changed to hollow thunder.
35   We saw the heads
Like a wild wave charging and were afraid.

We had sold our horses in our fathers' time
To buy new tractors. Now they were strange to us
As fabulous steeds set on an ancient shield
40 Or illustrations in a book of knights.
We did not dare go near them. Yet they waited,
Stubborn and shy, as if they had been sent
By an old command to find our whereabouts
And that long-lost archaic companionship.
45 In the first moment we had never a thought
That they were creatures to be owned and used.
Among them were some half-a-dozen colts
Dropped in some wilderness of the broken world,
Yet new as if they had come from their own Eden.
50 Since then they have pulled our ploughs and borne our loads,
But that free servitude still can pierce our hearts.
Our life is changed; their coming our beginning.

EDGAR ALLAN POE (1809–1849)

The Raven

Once upon a midnight dreary, while I pondered, weak and weary,
Over many a quaint and curious volume of forgotten lore,—
While I nodded, nearly napping, suddenly there came a tapping,
As of some one gently rapping, rapping at my chamber door.
5   " 'T is some visitor," I muttered, "tapping at my chamber door:
                    Only this and nothing more."

Ah, distinctly I remember it was in the bleak December,
And each separate dying ember wrought its ghost upon the floor.
Eagerly I wished the morrow;—vainly I had sought to borrow
10   From my books surcease of sorrow—sorrow for the lost Lenore,
For the rare and radiant maiden whom the angels name Lenore:
                    Nameless here for evermore.

And the silken sad uncertain rustling of each purple curtain
Thrilled me—filled me with fantastic terrors never felt before;
15   So that now, to still the beating of my heart, I stood repeating
" 'T is some visitor entreating entrance at my chamber door,
Some late visitor entreating entrance at my chamber door:
                    This it is and nothing more."

Presently my soul grew stronger; hesitating then no longer,
20   "Sir," said I, "or Madam, truly your forgiveness I implore;
But the fact is I was napping, and so gently you came rapping,
And so faintly you came tapping, tapping at my chamber door,
That I scarce was sure I heard you"—here I opened wide the door:—
                    Darkness there and nothing more.

25   Deep into that darkness peering, long I stood there wondering, fearing,
Doubting, dreaming dreams no mortal ever dared to dream before;
But the silence was unbroken, and the stillness gave no token,

And the only word there spoken was the whispered word, "Lenore?"
This I whispered, and an echo murmured back the word, "Lenore:"
30   Merely this and nothing more.

Back into the chamber turning, all my soul within me burning,
Soon again I heard a tapping somewhat louder than before.
"Surely," said I, "surely that is something at my window lattice;
Let me see, then, what thereat is, and this mystery explore;
35   Let my heart be still a moment and this mystery explore:
                          'Tis the wind and nothing more."

Open here I flung the shutter, when, with many a flirt and flutter,
In there stepped a stately Raven of the saintly days of yore.
Not the least obeisance made he; not a minute stopped or stayed he;
40   But, with mien of lord or lady, perched above my chamber door,
Perched upon a bust of Pallas[4] just above my chamber door:
                          Perched, and sat, and nothing more.

Then this ebony bird beguiling my sad fancy into smiling
By the grave and stern decorum of the countenance it wore,—
45   "Though thy crest be shorn and shaven, thou," I said, "art sure no craven,
Ghastly grim and ancient Raven wandering from the Nightly shore:
Tell me what thy lordly name is on the Night's Plutonian[5] shore!"
                          Quoth the Raven, "Nevermore."

Much I marvelled this ungainly fowl to hear discourse so plainly,
50   Though its answer little meaning—little relevancy bore;
For we cannot help agreeing that no living human being
Ever yet was blessed with seeing bird above his chamber door,
Bird or beast upon the sculptured bust above his chamber door,
                          With such name as "Nevermore."

55   But the Raven, sitting lonely on the placid bust, spoke only
That one word, as if his soul in that one word he did outpour.
Nothing further then he uttered, not a feather then he fluttered,
Till I scarcely more than muttered—"Other friends have flown before;
On the morrow *he* will leave me, as my Hopes have flown before."
60   Then the bird said, "Nevermore."

Startled at the stillness broken by reply so aptly spoken,
"Doubtless," said I, "what it utters is its only stock and store,
Caught from some unhappy master whom unmerciful Disaster
Followed fast and followed faster till his songs one burden bore:
65   Till the dirges of his Hope that melancholy burden bore
                          Of 'Never—nevermore.' "

But the Raven still beguiling all my fancy into smiling,
Straight I wheeled a cushioned seat in front of bird and bust and door;
Then, upon the velvet sinking, I betook myself to linking

---

[4] *Pallas* is Greek for "maiden" and was the epithet used to refer to Athena, the goddess of war and wisdom.
[5] *Pluto* is the god of the underworld.

70 　Fancy unto fancy, thinking what this ominous bird of yore,
　　What this grim, ungainly, ghastly, gaunt, and ominous bird of yore
　　　　　　　　Meant in croaking "Nevermore."

　　This I sat engaged in guessing, but no syllable expressing
　　To the fowl whose fiery eyes now burned into my bosom's core;
75 　This and more I sat divining, with my head at ease reclining
　　On the cushion's velvet lining that the lamp-light gloated o'er,
　　But whose velvet violet lining with the lamp-light gloating o'er
　　　　　　　　She shall press, ah, nevermore!

　　Then, methought, the air grew denser, perfumed from an unseen censer
80 　Swung by seraphim whose foot-falls tinkled on the tufted floor.
　　"Wretch," I cried, "thy God hath lent thee—by these angels he hath sent thee
　　Respite—respite and nepenthe[6] from thy memories of Lenore!
　　Quaff, oh quaff this kind nepenthe, and forget this lost Lenore!"
　　　　　　　　Quoth the Raven, "Nevermore."

85 　"Prophet!" said I, "thing of evil! prophet still, if bird or devil!
　　Whether Tempter sent, or whether tempest tossed thee here ashore,
　　Desolate yet all undaunted, on this desert land enchanted—
　　On this home by Horror haunted—tell me truly, I implore:
　　Is there—*is* there balm in Gilead?[7]—tell me—tell me, I implore!"
90 　　　　　　　　Quoth the Raven, "Nevermore."

　　"Prophet!" said I, "thing of evil—prophet still, if bird or devil!
　　By that Heaven that bends above us, by that God we both adore,
　　Tell this soul with sorrow laden if, within the distant Aidenn,[8]
　　It shall clasp a sainted maiden whom the angels name Lenore:
95 　Clasp a rare and radiant maiden whom the angels name Lenore!"
　　　　　　　　Quoth the Raven, "Nevermore."

　　"Be that word our sign of parting, bird or fiend!" I shrieked, upstarting:
　　"Get thee back into the tempest and the Night's Plutonian shore!
　　Leave no black plume as a token of that lie thy soul hath spoken!
100 　Leave my loneliness unbroken! quit the bust above my door!
　　Take thy beak from out my heart, and take thy form from off my door!"
　　　　　　　　Quoth the Raven, "Nevermore."

　　And the Raven, never flitting, still is sitting, *still* is sitting
　　On the pallid bust of Pallas just above my chamber door;
105 　And his eyes have all the seeming of a demon's that is dreaming,
　　And the lamp-light o'er him streaming throws his shadow on the floor:
　　And my soul from out that shadow that lies floating on the floor
　　　　　　　　Shall be lifted—nevermore!

---

[6] *Nepenthe* is a drug one uses to forget pain.
[7] See Jeremiah 8:22.
[8] *Aidenn* is a combination of Eden and Aden—thus, an exotic place of pleasure.

CHRISTINA ROSSETTI (1830–1894)

Goblin Market

Morning and evening
Maids heard the goblins cry,
"Come buy our orchard fruits,
Come buy, come buy:
5   Apples and quinces,
Lemons and oranges,
Plump unpecked cherries,
Melons and raspberries,
Bloom-down-cheeked peaches,
10   Swart-headed mulberries,
Wild free-born cranberries,
Crab-apples, dewberries,
Pineapples, blackberries,
Apricots, strawberries—
15   All ripe together
In summer weather—
Morns that pass by,
Fair eves that fly;
Come buy, come buy:
20   Our grapes fresh from the vine,
Pomegranates full and fine,
Dates and sharp bullaces,
Rare pears and greengages,
Damsons and bilberries,
25   Taste them and try;
Currants and gooseberries,
Bright-fire-like barberries,
Figs to fill your mouth,
Citrons from the South,
30   Sweet to tongue and sound to eye;
Come buy, come buy."

Evening by evening
Among the brook-side rushes,
Laura bowed her head to hear,
35   Lizzie veiled her blushes;
Crouching close together
In the cooling weather,
With clasping arms and cautioning lips,
With tingling cheeks and finger tips.
40   "Lie close," Laura said,
Pricking up her golden head.
"We must not look at goblin men,
We must not buy their fruits;
Who knows upon what soil they fed
45   Their hungry thirsty roots?"

"Come buy," call the goblins
Hobbling down the glen.
"Oh," cried Lizzie, "Laura, Laura,
You should not peep at goblin men."
50   Lizzie covered up her eyes,
Covered close lest they should look;
Laura reared her glossy head,
And whispered like the restless brook:
"Look, Lizzie, look, Lizzie,
55   Down the glen tramp little men.
One hauls a basket,
One bears a plate,
One lugs a golden dish
Of many pounds' weight.
60   How fair the vine must grow
Whose grapes are so luscious!
How warm the wind must blow
Through those fruit bushes!"
"No," said Lizzie, "No, no, no;
65   Their offers should not charm us,
Their evil gifts would harm us."
She thrust a dimpled finger
In each ear, shut eyes and ran.
Curious Laura chose to linger,
70   Wondering at each merchant man.
One had a cat's face,
One whisked a tail,
One tramped at a rat's pace,
One crawled like a snail,
75   One like a wombat prowled obtuse and furry,
One like a ratel° tumbled hurry-skurry.   *badgerlike animal*
She heard a voice like voice of doves
Cooing all together;
They sounded kind and full of loves
80   In the pleasant weather.

Laura stretched her gleaming neck
Like a rush-imbedded swan,
Like a lily from the beck,°   *brook*
Like a moonlit poplar branch,
85   Like a vessel at the launch
When its last restraint is gone.

Backward up the mossy glen
Turned and trooped the goblin men,
With their shrill repeated cry,
90   "Come buy, come buy."
When they reached where Laura was
They stood stock still upon the moss,
Leering at each other,
Brother with queer brother;

95   Signaling each other,
      Brother with sly brother.
      One set his basket down,
      One reared his plate;
      One began to weave a crown
100   Of tendrils, leaves, and rough nuts brown
      (Men sell not such in any town);
      One heaved the golden weight
      Of dish and fruit to offer her;
      "Come buy, come buy" was still their cry.
105   Laura stared but did not stir,
      Longed but had no money.
      The whisk-tailed merchant bade her taste
      In tones as smooth as honey,
      The cat-faced purred,
110   The rat-paced spoke a word
      Of welcome, and the snail-paced even was heard;
      One parrot-voiced and jolly
      Cried, "Pretty Goblin" still for "Pretty Polly";
      One whistled like a bird.

115   But sweet-tooth Laura spoke in haste:
      "Good folk, I have no coin;
      To take were to purloin.
      I have no copper in my purse,
      I have no silver either,
120   And all my gold is on the furze°   *a yellow-flowered bush*
      That shakes in windy weather
      Above the rusty heather."
      "You have much gold upon your head,"
      They answered all together;
125   "Buy from us with a golden curl."
      She clipped a precious golden lock,
      She dropped a tear more rare than pearl,
      Then sucked their fruit globes fair or red.
      Sweeter than honey from the rock,
130   Stronger than man-rejoicing wine,
      Clearer than water flowed that juice;
      She never tasted such before,
      How should it cloy with length of use?
      She sucked and sucked and sucked the more
135   Fruits which that unknown orchard bore;
      She sucked until her lips were sore;
      Then flung the emptied rinds away,
      But gathered up one kernel stone,
      And knew not was it night or day
140   As she turned home alone.

      Lizzie met her at the gate,
      Full of wise upbraidings:
      "Dear, you should not stay so late,

Twilight is not good for maidens;
145　Should not loiter in the glen
In the haunts of goblin men.
Do you not remember Jeanie,
How she met them in the moonlight,
Took their gifts both choice and many,
150　Ate their fruits and wore their flowers
Plucked from bowers
Where summer ripens at all hours?
But ever in the moonlight
She pined and pined away;
155　Sought them by night and day,
Found them no more, but dwindled and grew gray;
Then fell with the first snow,
While to this day no grass will grow
Where she lies low;
160　I planted daisies there a year ago
That never blow.°   bloom
You should not loiter so."
"Nay, hush," said Laura;
"Nay, hush, my sister.
165　I ate and ate my fill,
Yet my mouth waters still.
Tomorrow night I will
Buy more"; and kissed her.
"Have done with sorrow;
170　I'll bring you plums tomorrow
Fresh on their mother twigs,
Cherries worth getting;
You cannot think what figs
My teeth have met in,
175　What melons icy-cold
Piled on a dish of gold
Too huge for me to hold,
What peaches with a velvet nap,
Pellucid grapes without one seed.
180　Odorous indeed must be the mead
Whereon they grow, and pure the wave they drink
With lilies at the brink,
And sugar-sweet their sap."

Golden head by golden head,
185　Like two pigeons in one nest
Folded in each other's wings,
They lay down in their curtained bed;
Like two blossoms on one stem,
Like two flakes of new-fall'n snow,
190　Like two wands of ivory
Tipped with gold for awful kings.
Moon and stars gazed in at them,

Wind sang to them lullaby,
Lumbering owls forebore to fly,
195 Not a bat flapped to and fro
Round their nest;
Cheek to cheek and breast to breast
Locked together in one nest.

Early in the morning
200 When the first cock crowed his warning,
Neat like bees, as sweet and busy,
Laura rose with Lizzie;
Fetched in honey, milked the cows,
Aired and set to rights the house,
205 Kneaded cakes of whitest wheat,
Cakes for dainty mouths to eat,
Next churned butter, whipped up cream,
Fed their poultry, sat and sewed;
Talked as modest maidens should—
210 Lizzie with an open heart,
Laura in an absent dream,
One content, one sick in part;
One warbling for the mere bright day's delight,
One longing for the night.

215 At length slow evening came.
They went with pitchers to the reedy brook;
Lizzie most placid in her look,
Laura most like a leaping flame.
They drew the gurgling water from its deep.
220 Lizzie plucked purple and rich golden flags,
Then turning homeward said: "The sunset flushes
Those furthest loftiest crags;
Come, Laura, not another maiden lags.
No willful squirrel wags;
225 The beasts and birds are fast asleep."

But Laura loitered still among the rushes,
And said the bank was steep,
And said the hour was early still,
The dew not fall'n, the wind not chill;
230 Listening ever, but not catching
The customary cry,
"Come buy, come buy,"
With its iterated jingle
Of sugar-baited words;
235 Not for all her watching
Once discerning even one goblin
Racing, whisking, tumbling, hobbling—
Let alone the herds
That used to tramp along the glen,

240   In groups or single,
       Of brisk fruit-merchant men.

       Till Lizzie urged, "O Laura, come;
       I hear the fruit-call, but I dare not look.
       You should not loiter longer at this brook;
245   Come with me home.
       The stars rise, the moon bends her arc,
       Each glowworm winks her spark.
       Let us get home before the night grows dark,
       For clouds may gather
250   Though this is summer weather,
       Put out the lights and drench us through;
       Then if we lost our way what should we do?"

       Laura turned cold as stone
       To find her sister heard that cry alone,
255   That goblin cry,
       "Come buy our fruits, come buy."
       Must she then buy no more such dainty fruit?
       Must she no more such succous pasture find,
       Gone deaf and blind?
260   Her tree of life drooped from the root;
       She said not one word in her heart's sore ache;
       But peering through the dimness, naught discerning,
       Trudged home, her pitcher dripping all the way;
       So crept to bed, and lay
265   Silent till Lizzie slept;
       Then sat up in a passionate yearning,
       And gnashed her teeth for balked desire, and wept
       As if her heart would break.

       Day after day, night after night,
270   Laura kept watch in vain
       In sullen silence of exceeding pain.
       She never caught again the goblin cry,
       "Come buy, come buy";
       She never spied the goblin men
275   Hawking their fruits along the glen.
       But when the noon waxed bright
       Her hair grew thin and gray;
       She dwindled, as the fair full moon doth turn
       To swift decay and burn
280   Her fire away.

       One day, remembering her kernel-stone,
       She set it by a wall that faced the south;
       Dewed it with tears, hoped for a root,
       Watched for a waxing shoot,
285   But there came none.
       It never saw the sun,
       It never felt the trickling moisture run;

While with sunk eyes and faded mouth
She dreamed of melons, as a traveler sees
290 False waves in desert drouth
With shade of leaf-crowned trees,
And burns the thirstier in the sandful breeze.

She no more swept the house,
Tended the fowls or cows,
295 Fetched honey, kneaded cakes of wheat,
Brought water from the brook;
But sat down listless in the chimney-nook
And would not eat.

Tender Lizzie could not bear
300 To watch her sister's cankerous care,
Yet not to share.
She night and morning
Caught the goblin's cry:
"Come buy our orchard fruits,
305 Come buy, come buy."
Beside the brook, along the glen,
She heard the tramp of goblin men,
The voice and stir
Poor Laura could not hear;
310 Longed to buy fruit to comfort her,
But feared to pay too dear.
She thought of Jeanie in her grave,
Who should have been a bride;
But who for joys brides hope to have
315 Fell sick and died
In her gay prime,
In earliest winter time,
With the first glazing rime,°   frost
With the first snow-fall of crisp winter time.

320 Till Laura dwindling
Seemed knocking at Death's door.
Then Lizzie weighed no more
Better and worse;
But put a silver penny in her purse,
325 Kissed Laura, crossed the heath with clumps of furze
At twilight, halted by the brook,
And for the first time in her life
Began to listen and look.

Laughed every goblin
330 When they spied her peeping;
Came toward her hobbling,
Flying, running, leaping,
Puffing and blowing,
Chuckling, clapping, crowing,
335 Clucking and gobbling,

Mopping and mowing,
Full of airs and graces,
Pulling wry faces
Demure grimaces,
340 Cat-like and rat-like,
Ratel- and wombat-like,
Snail-paced in a hurry,
Parrot-voiced and whistler,
Helter-skelter, hurry-skurry,
345 Chattering like magpies,
Fluttering like pigeons,
Gliding like fishes—
Hugged her and kissed her,
Squeezed and caressed her,
350 Stretched up their dishes,
Panniers,° and plates: *wicker baskets*
"Look at our apples
Russet and dun,
Bob at our cherries,
355 Bite at our peaches,
Citrons and dates,
Grapes for the asking,
Pears red with basking
Out in the sun,
360 Plums on their twigs;
Pluck them and suck them—
Pomegranates, figs."

"Good folk," said Lizzie,
Mindful of Jeanie,
365 "Give me much and many";
Held out her apron,
Tossed them her penny.
"Nay, take a seat with us,
Honor and eat with us,"
370 They answered, grinning;
"Our feast is but beginning.
Night yet is early,
Warm and dew-pearly,
Wakeful and starry.
375 Such fruits as these
No man can carry;
Half their bloom would fly,
Half their dew would dry,
Half their flavor would pass by.
380 Sit down and feast with us,
Be welcome guest with us,
Cheer you and rest with us."—
"Thank you," said Lizzie, "but one waits
At home alone for me;

385 So without further parleying,
    If you will not sell me any
    Of your fruits though much and many,
    Give me back my silver penny
    I tossed you for a fee."—
390 They began to scratch their pates,
    No longer wagging, purring,
    But visibly demurring,
    Grunting and snarling.
    One called her proud,
395 Cross-grained, uncivil;
    Their tones waxed loud,
    Their looks were evil.
    Lashing their tails,
    They trod and hustled her,
400 Elbowed and jostled her,
    Clawed with their nails,
    Barking, mewing, hissing, mocking,
    Tore her gown and soiled her stocking,
    Twitched her hair out by the roots,
405 Stamped upon her tender feet,
    Held her hands and squeezed their fruits
    Against her mouth to make her eat.

    White and golden Lizzie stood,
    Like a lily in a flood—
410 Like a rock of blue-veined stone
    Lashed by tides obstreperously—
    Like a beacon left alone
    In a hoary, roaring sea,
    Sending up a golden fire—
415 Like a fruit-crowned orange-tree
    White with blossoms honey-sweet
    Sore beset by wasp and bee—
    Like a royal virgin town
    Topped with gilded dome and spire
420 Close beleaguered by a fleet
    Mad to tug her standard down.

    One may lead a horse to water;
    Twenty cannot make him drink.
    Though the goblins cuffed and caught her,
425 Coaxed and fought her,
    Bullied and besought her,
    Scratched her, pinched her black as ink,
    Kicked and knocked her,
    Mauled and mocked her,
430 Lizzie uttered not a word;
    Would not open lip from lip
    Lest they should cram a mouthful in;

But laughed in heart to feel the drip
Of juice that siruped all her face,
435 And lodged in dimples of her chin,
And streaked her neck which quaked like curd.
At last the evil people,
Worn out by her resistance,
Flung back her penny, kicked their fruit
440 Along whichever road they took,
Not leaving root or stone or shoot;
Some writhed into the ground,
Some dived into the brook
With ring and ripple,
445 Some scudded on the gale without a sound,
Some vanished in the distance.

In a smart, ache, tingle,
Lizzie went her way;
Knew not was it night or day;
450 Sprang up the bank, tore through the furze,
Threaded copse and dingle,
And heard her penny jingle
Bouncing in her purse—
Its bounce was music to her ear.
455 She ran and ran
As if she feared some goblin man
Dogged her with gibe or curse
Or something worse;
But not one goblin skurried after,
460 Nor was she pricked by fear;
The kind heart made her windy-paced
That urged her home quite out of breath with haste
And inward laughter.

She cried, "Laura," up the garden,
465 "Did you miss me?
Come and kiss me.
Never mind my bruises,
Hug me, kiss me, suck my juices
Squeezed from goblin fruits for you,
470 Goblin pulp and goblin dew.
Eat me, drink me, love me;
Laura, make much of me;
For your sake I have braved the glen
And had to do with goblin merchant men."

475 Laura started from her chair,
Flung her arms up in the air,
Clutched her hair:
"Lizzie, Lizzie, have you tasted
For my sake the fruit forbidden.
480 Must your light like mine be hidden,
Your young life like mine be wasted,

Undone in mine undoing,
And ruined in my ruin,
Thirsty, cankered, goblin-ridden?"—
485 She clung about her sister,
Kissed and kissed and kissed her;
Tears once again
Refreshed her shrunken eyes,
Dropping like rain
490 After long sultry drouth;
Shaking with aguish° fear, and pain,   *chilly with fever*
She kissed and kissed her with a hungry mouth.
Her lips began to scorch,
That juice was wormwood to her tongue,
495 She loathed the feast.
Writhing as one possessed, she leaped and sung,
Rent all her robe, and wrung
Her hands in lamentable haste,
And beat her breast.
500 Her locks streamed like the torch
Borne by a racer at full speed,
Or like the mane of horses in their flight,
Or like an eagle when she stems the light
Straight toward the sun,
505 Or like a caged thing freed,
Or like a flying flag when armies run.

Swift fire spread through her veins, knocked at her heart,
Met the fire smoldering there
And overbore its lesser flame;
510 She gorged on bitterness without a name—
Ah, fool, to choose such part
Of soul-consuming care!
Sense failed in the mortal strife;
Like the watch-tower of a town
515 Which an earthquake shatters down,
Like a lightning-stricken mast,
Like a wind-uprooted tree
Spun about,
Like a foam-topped waterspout
520 Cast down headlong in the sea,
She fell at last;
Pleasure past and anguish past,
Is it death or is it life?

Life out of death.
525 That night long Lizzie watched by her,
Counted her pulse's flagging stir,
Felt for her breath,
Held water to her lips, and cooled her face
With tears and fanning leaves.
530 But when the first birds chirped about their eaves,

And early reapers plodded to the place
Of golden sheaves,
And dew-wet grass
Bowed in the morning winds so brisk to pass,
535 And new buds with new day
Opened of cup-like lilies on the stream,
Laura awoke as from a dream,
Laughed in the innocent old way,
Hugged Lizzie but not twice or thrice;
540 Her gleaming locks showed not one thread of gray,
Her breath was sweet as May,
And light danced in her eyes.

Days, weeks, months, years
Afterwards, when both were wives
545 With children of their own;
Their mother-hearts beset with fears,
Their lives bound up in tender lives;
Laura would call the little ones
And tell them of her early prime,
550 Those pleasant days long gone
Of not-returning time;
Would talk about the haunted glen,
The wicked quaint fruit-merchant men,
Their fruits like honey to the throat
555 But poison in the blood
(Men sell not such in any town);
Would tell them how her sister stood
In deadly peril to do her good,
And win the fiery antidote:
560 Then joining hands to little hands
Would bid them cling together—
"For there is no friend like a sister
In calm or stormy weather;
To cheer one on the tedious way,
565 To fetch one if one goes astray,
To lift one if one totters down,
To strengthen whilst one stands."

HOMER (8th century B.C.)

From the Odyssey[9]

When the young Dawn with finger tips of rose
came in the east, I called my men together
and made a speech to them:

"Old shipmates, friends,

---

[9] The Odyssey narrates the adventures of Odysseus, or Ulysses (as he was called by the Romans).
Odysseus wandered the world for ten years before returning to his kingdom, Ithaca. He was one
of the Greek kings who defeated the Trojans. In this episode from Book IX of the Odyssey, Odysseus
recounts his visit to the Kyklopês, or Cyclops, vicious one-eyed giants, and tells how he outsmarted
them. The episode typifies many of Odysseus' exploits: he succeeds more by brains than brawn.

5   the rest of you stand by; I'll make the crossing
      in my own ship, with my own company,
      and find out what the mainland natives are—
      for they may be wild savages, and lawless,
      or hospitable and god fearing men."

10   At this I went aboard, and gave the word
      to cast off by the stern. My oarsmen followed,
      filing in to their benches by the rowlocks,
      and all in line dipped oars in the grey sea.

      As we rowed on, and nearer to the mainland,
15   at one end of the bay, we saw a cavern
      yawning above the water, screened with laurel,
      and many rams and goats about the place
      inside a sheepfold—made from slabs of stone
      earthfast between tall trunks of pine and rugged
20   towering oak trees.
                                    A prodigious man
      slept in this cave alone, and took his flocks
      to graze afield—remote from all companions,
      knowing none but savage ways, a brute
25   so huge, he seemed no man at all of those
      who eat good wheaten bread; but he seemed rather
      a shaggy mountain reared in solitude.
      We beached there, and I told the crew
      to stand by and keep watch over the ship;
30   as for myself I took my twelve best fighters
      and went ahead. I had a goatskin full
      of that sweet liquor that Euanthês' son,
      Maron, had given me. He kept Apollo's
      holy grove at Ísmaros; for kindness
35   we showed him there, and showed his wife and child,
      he gave me seven shining golden talents
      perfectly formed, a solid silver winebowl,
      and then this liquor—twelve two-handled jars
      of brandy, pure and fiery. Not a slave
40   in Maron's household knew this drink; only
      he, his wife and the storeroom mistress knew;
      and they would put one cupful—ruby-colored,
      honey-smooth—in twenty more of water,
      but still the sweet scent hovered like a fume
45   over the winebowl. No man turned away
      when cups of this came round.
                                    A wineskin full
      I brought along, and victuals in a bag,
      for in my bones I knew some towering brute
50   would be upon us soon—all outward power,
      a wild man, ignorant of civility.

      We climbed, then, briskly to the cave. But Kyklops
      had gone afield, to pasture his fat sheep,

so we looked round at everything inside:
55   a drying rack that sagged with cheeses, pens
crowded with lambs and kids, each in its class:
firstlings apart from middlings, and the "dewdrops,"
or newborn lambkins, penned apart from both.
And vessels full of whey were brimming there—
60   bowls of earthenware and pails for milking.
My men came pressing round me, pleading:

                            "Why not
take these cheeses, get them stowed, come back,
throw open all the pens, and make a run for it?
65   We'll drive the kids and lambs aboard. We say
put out again on good salt water!"

                                          Ah,
how sound that was! Yet I refused. I wished
to see the caveman, what he had to offer—
70   no pretty sight, it turned out, for my friends.
We lit a fire, burnt an offering,
and took some cheese to eat; then sat in silence
around the embers, waiting. When he came
he had a load of dry boughs on his shoulder
75   to stoke his fire at suppertime. He dumped it
with a great crash into that hollow cave,
and we all scattered fast to the far wall.
Then over the broad cavern floor he ushered
the ewes he meant to milk. He left his rams
80   and he-goats in the yard outside, and swung
high overhead a slab of solid rock
to close the cave. Two dozen four-wheeled wagons,
with heaving wagon teams, could not have stirred
the tonnage of that rock from where he wedged it
85   over the doorsill. Next he took his seat
and milked his bleating ewes. A practiced job
he made of it, giving each ewe her suckling;
thickened his milk, then, into curds and whey,
sieved out the curds to drip in withy° baskets,   *twig*
90   and poured the whey to stand in bowls
cooling until he drank it for his supper.
When all these chores were done, he poked the fire,
heaping on brushwood. In the glare he saw us.
"Strangers," he said, "who are you? And where from?
95   What brings you here by sea ways—a fair traffic?
Or are you wandering rogues, who cast your lives
like dice, and ravage other folk by sea?"

We felt a pressure on our hearts, in dread
of that deep rumble and that mighty man.
100   But all the same I spoke up in reply:

"We are from Troy, Akhaians, blown off course
by shifting gales on the Great South Sea;
homeward bound, but taking routes and ways
uncommon; so the will of Zeus would have it.
105 We served under Agamémnon, son of Atreus—
the whole world knows what city
he laid waste, what armies he destroyed.
It was our luck to come here; here we stand,
beholden for your help, or any gifts
110 you give—as custom is to honor strangers.
We would entreat you, great Sir, have a care
for the gods' courtesy; Zeus will avenge
the unoffending guest."

He answered this
115 from his brute chest, unmoved:

"You are a ninny,
or else you come from the other end of nowhere,
telling me, mind the gods! We Kyklopês
care not a whistle for your thundering Zeus
120 or all the gods in bliss; we have more force by far.
I would not let you go for fear of Zeus—
you or your friends—unless I had a whim to.
Tell me, where was it, now, you left your ship—
around the point, or down the shore, I wonder?"

125 He thought he'd find out, but I saw through this,
and answered with a ready lie:

"My ship?
Poseidon Lord, who sets the earth a-tremble,
broke it up on the rocks at your land's end.
130 A wind from seaward served him, drove us there,
We are survivors, these good men and I."

Neither reply nor pity came from him,
but in one stride he clutched at my companions
and caught two in his hands like squirming puppies
135 to beat their brains out, spattering the floor.
Then he dismembered them and made his meal,
gaping and crunching like a mountain lion—
everything: innards, flesh, and marrow bones.
We cried aloud, lifting our hands to Zeus,
140 powerless, looking on at this, appalled;
but Kyklops went on filling up his belly
with manflesh and great gulps of whey,
then lay down like a mast among his sheep.
My heart beat high now at the chance of action,
145 and drawing the sharp sword from my hip I went
along his flank to stab him where the midriff

holds the liver. I had touched the spot
when sudden fear stayed me: if I killed him
we perished there as well, for we could never
150   move his ponderous doorway slab aside.
So we were left to groan and wait for morning.

When the young Dawn with finger tips of rose
lit up the world, the Kyklops built a fire
and milked his handsome ewes, all in due order,
155   putting the sucklings to the mothers. Then,
his chores being all dispatched, he caught
another brace of men to make his breakfast,
and whisked away his great door slab
to let his sheep go through—but he, behind,
160   reset the stone as one would cap a quiver.
There was a din of whistling as the Kyklops
rounded his flock to higher ground, then stillness.
And now I pondered how to hurt him worst,
if but Athena granted what I prayed for.
165   Here are the means I thought would serve my turn:

a club, or staff, lay there along the fold—
an olive tree, felled green and left to season
for Kyklops' hand. And it was like a mast
a lugger of twenty oars, broad in the beam—
170   a deep-sea-going craft—might carry:
so long, so big around, it seemed. Now I
chopped out a six foot section of this pole
and set it down before my men, who scraped it;
and when they had it smooth, I hewed again
175   to make a stake with pointed end. I held this
in the fire's heart and turned it, toughening it,
then hid it, well back in the cavern, under
one of the dung piles in profusion there.
Now came the time to toss for it: who ventured
180   along with me? whose hand could bear to thrust
and grind that spike in Kyklops' eye, when mild
sleep had mastered him? As luck would have it,
the men I would have chosen won the toss—
four strong men, and I made five as captain.

185   At evening came the shepherd with his flock,
his woolly flock. The rams as well, this time,
entered the cave: by some sheep-herding whim—
or a god's bidding—none were left outside.
He hefted his great boulder into place
190   and sat him down to milk the bleating ewes
in proper order, put the lambs to suck,
and swiftly ran through all his evening chores.
Then he caught two more men and feasted on them.

My moment was at hand, and I went forward
195   holding an ivy bowl of my dark drink,
looking up, saying:

                            "Kyklops, try some wine.
Here's liquor to wash down your scraps of men.
Taste it, and see the kind of drink we carried
200   under our planks. I meant it for an offering
if you would help us home. But you are mad,
unbearable, a bloody monster! After this,
will any other traveller come to see you?"

He seized and drained the bowl, and it went down
205   so fiery and smooth he called for more:

"Give me another, thank you kindly. Tell me,
how are you called? I'll make a gift will please you.
Even Kyklopês know the wine-grapes grow
out of grassland and loam in heaven's rain,
210   but here's a bit of nectar and ambrosia!"

Three bowls I brought him, and he poured them down.
I saw the fuddle and flush come over him,
then I sang out in cordial tones:

                                "Kyklops,
215   you ask my honorable name? Remember
the gift you promised me, and I shall tell you.
My name is Nohbdy: mother, father, and friends,
everyone calls me Nohbdy."

                              And he said:

220   "Nohbdy's my meat, then, after I eat his friends.
Others come first. There's a noble gift, now."

Even as he spoke, he reeled and tumbled backward,
his great head lolling to one side; and sleep
took him like any creature. Drunk, hiccuping,
225   he dribbled streams of liquor and bits of men.

Now, by the gods, I drove my big hand spike
deep in the embers, charring it again,
and cheered my men along with battle talk
to keep their courage up: no quitting now.
230   The pike of olive, green though it had been,
reddened and glowed as if about to catch.
I drew it from the coals and my four fellows
gave me a hand, lugging it near the Kyklops
as more than natural force nerved them; straight
235   forward they sprinted, lifted it, and rammed it
deep in his crater eye, and I leaned on it
turning it as a shipwright turns a drill
in planking, having men below to swing

the two-handled strap that spins it in the groove.
240 So with our brand we bored that great eye socket
while blood ran out around the red hot bar.
Eyelid and lash were seared; the pierced ball
hissed broiling, and the roots popped.

                                     In a smithy
245 one sees a white-hot axehead or an adze°   *hatchet*
plunged and wrung in a cold tub, screeching steam—
the way they make soft iron hale and hard—:
just so that eyeball hissed around the spike.
The Kyklops bellowed and the rock roared round him,
250 and we fell back in fear. Clawing his face
he tugged the bloody spike out of his eye,
threw it away, and his wild hands went groping;
then he set up a howl for Kyklopês
who lived in caves on windy peaks nearby.
255 Some heard him; and they came by divers ways
to clump around outside and call:

                                 "What ails you,
Polyphêmos? Why do you cry so sore
in the starry night? You will not let us sleep.
260 Sure no man's driving off your flock? No man
has tricked you, ruined you?"

                                Out of the cave
the mammoth Polyphêmos roared in answer:
"Nohbdy, Nohbdy's tricked me, Nohbdy's ruined me!"

265 To this rough shout they made a sage reply:
"Ah well, if nobody has played you foul
there in your lonely bed, we are no use in pain
given by great Zeus. Let it be your father,
Poseidon Lord, to whom you pray."

                          Translation by Robert Fitzgerald (1910–)

4 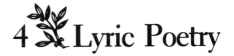 Lyric Poetry

The Solitary Singer

CATULLUS (84?–54 B.C.)

LXXXV

I hate and I love. Why? you might ask
but I can't tell. The feeling seizes me
and riddles me with pain.

Outside of literature we rarely have the opportunity to look into the hearts and minds of others. Many people are shy about themselves or feel that their language is inadequate for expressing what is most important to them. Great poets can open themselves to us in moments of crisis or discovery so that we can know their thoughts as intimately as we know our own.

The *lyric* is generally considered the most intense and personal form of poetry—indeed, of all literature. The word *lyric* comes from the Greek word for the lyre, a stringed instrument similar to a guitar and suitable for the accompaniment of a solitary singer. Like the concert of an impassioned singer, the lyric poem is a private, often visionary act of intelligence and emotion that becomes public through the music of language. Lyric poetry is also an artifact of language, capable of great beauty and excitement in its exploration of new perceptions. Language is a precious part of our heritage that is enriched by the vision and experience of each new generation of poets.

The Love Poem

Perhaps the form of lyric most familiar to us is the love poem.

WILLIAM BUTLER YEATS (1865–1939)

He Wishes for the Cloths of Heaven

Had I the heavens' embroidered cloths,
Enwrought with golden and silver light,

49

The blue and the dim and the dark cloths
Of night and light and the half-light,
5   I would spread the cloths under your feet:
But I, being poor, have only my dreams;
I have spread my dreams under your feet;
Tread softly because you tread on my dreams.

Question

1. Vocabulary: *enwrought* (2).

How does one express love? One common way is through gifts. We want the finest gift for the one we love, a gift that will be as beautiful and rare as what we feel. In this poem Yeats (or his persona) realizes that nothing he possesses would be adequate as a gift for his beloved. All he can do is wish for such a gift, the magnificent cloths he describes. If he had such cloths, he tells her, he would spread them before her as a path. But he is poor and cannot provide such a gift. Instead, he offers her his dreams. This, too, should be familiar to us. When we are in love, we want to share with those we love not only material things, but also our aspirations, our plans, our dreams. These are the finest gifts the lover can provide. When he has spread his dreams in her path, he asks her to "tread softly" because dreams are delicate, much more fragile than the cloths he described earlier.

Thus the first gift is the wish described in the poem's opening lines, and the second gift is the lover's dreams. But just as important as either of these is the gift of the poem itself.

William Butler Yeats (*Photograph by Howard Coster*)

We have considered the poem as a love lyric to a particular woman. But is it not also a gift to the reader? The "you" of the poem might be *any* reader, for as we read, we are admitted to the privacy of the poet's thoughts. We are in effect receiving a gift of his thoughts. We are being asked to read carefully, for we are treading on his dreams throughout the poem. It is as much a love poem to us as it is to a particular woman.

H. D. (HILDA DOOLITTLE) (1886–1961)

Never More Will the Wind

Never more will the wind
cherish you again,
never more will the rain.

Never more
5   shall we find you bright
in the snow and wind.

The snow is melted,
the snow is gone,
and you are flown:

10   Like a bird out of our hand,
like a light out of our heart,
you are gone.

Here is another kind of love lyric, one that expresses the anguish of loss. The poem is intensely private, for the poet is speaking to someone who is not there to listen. Maybe the one she loves has died, or perhaps he has gone to another country. The poem is not concerned with these questions. Rather, it shows us how the poet's world has changed in the absence of her beloved. Everything is emptier: the wind, the rain, the snow. Everywhere she looks, the landscape speaks of loneliness and absence. The poet clearly wishes to share this with us. She includes us in her world when she says "we" in the second stanza, and "our" in the final lines.

TED BERRIGAN (1934–)

Scorpio[1]

If I don't love you I
Won't let it show. But I'll
Make it clear, by
Never letting you know.

5   & if I love you, I will
Love you true: insofar
As Love, itself,
Will do.

---

[1] A constellation and the eighth sign of the zodiac.

& While I live, I'll be
10 Whatever I am, whose
Constant, impure, fire
Is outwardly only a man.

Questions

1. Scorpio is the speaker's astrological sign. Scorpios are thought to be intense and romantic. What other personality traits does the speaker reveal?
2. Is he honest about his feelings? How can you tell?

WILLIAM SHAKESPEARE (1564–1616)

When, in Disgrace with Fortune and Men's Eyes

When, in disgrace° with fortune and men's eyes,   *out of favor*
I all alone beweep my outcast state
And trouble deaf heaven with my bootless° cries   *useless*
And look upon myself and curse my fate,
5 Wishing me like to one more rich in hope,
Featured like him, like him with friends possess'd,
Desiring this man's art and that man's scope,°   *range of activity*
With what I most enjoy contented least;
Yet in these thoughts myself almost despising
10 Haply I think on thee, and then my state,
Like to the lark at break of day arising
From sullen earth, sings hymns at heaven's gate;
    For thy sweet love remember'd such wealth brings
    That then I scorn to change my state with kings.

Questions

1. Vocabulary: *beweep* (2), *sullen* (12).
2. Why is the speaker so upset in the first eight lines of the poem?
3. Why is he so happy in the last six lines?
4. What emotion has inspired the poem?

ANDREW MARVELL (1621–1678)

To His Coy Mistress

Had we but world enough, and time,
This coyness,° lady, were no crime.   *modesty, reluctance*
We would sit down and think which way
To walk, and pass our long love's day.
5 Thou by the Indian Ganges' side
Should'st rubies find; I by the tide
Of Humber² would complain.° I would   *sing sad songs*
Love you ten years before the Flood,

---

² The Humber is a river that passed near Marvell's home.

And you should, if you please, refuse
10 Till the conversion of the Jews.[3]
My vegetable° love should grow   *vegetative*
Vaster than empires, and more slow.
An hundred years should go to praise
Thine eyes, and on thy forehead gaze,
15 Two hundred to adore each breast,
But thirty thousand to the rest.
An age at least to every part,
And the last age should show your heart.
For, lady, you deserve this state,
20 Nor would I love at lower rate.
        But at my back I always hear
Time's winged chariot hurrying near;
And yonder all before us lie
Deserts of vast eternity.
25 Thy beauty shall no more be found,
Nor in thy marble vault shall sound
My echoing song; then worms shall try
That long preserved virginity,
And your quaint honor turn to dust,
30 And into ashes all my lust.
The grave's a fine and private place,
But none, I think, do there embrace.
        Now therefore, while the youthful hue
Sits on thy skin like morning dew
35 And while thy willing soul transpires
At every pore with instant° fires,   *immediate*
Now let us sport us while we may;
And now, like am'rous birds of prey,
Rather at once our time devour,
40 Than languish in his slow-chapped° power,   *slowly chewing*
Let us roll all our strength, and all
Our sweetness, up into one ball;[4]
And tear our pleasures with rough strife
Thorough° the iron gates of life.   *through*
45 Thus, though we cannot make our sun
Stand still, yet we will make him run.

Questions

1. Vocabulary: *conversion* (10), *vault* (26), *quaint* (29), *transpires* (35), *languish* (40).
2. Reading this poem is like overhearing a personal conversation or reading someone else's letter. What sort of lady is Marvell addressing?
3. What does he want?
4. Compare this poem with Marlowe's "The Passionate Shepherd to His Love." Which poet is more persuasive?

---

[3] According to popular belief, the Jews would be converted just before the Last Judgment.
[4] Falconers would roll fat and sinew into balls that would be thrown into the air for falcons to attack and eat.

5. This poem is considered an eloquent statement of the *carpe diem* ("seize the day") philosophy, which urges us to live for the moment, without concern for the future. What are the advantages of *carpe diem*? The disadvantages?

Curses

Less familiar but no less human is the lyric poem that expresses hatred, or vengeance.

ARCHILOCHUS (7th century B.C.)

May He Lose His Way on the Cold Sea

May he lose his way on the cold sea
And swim to the heathen Salmydessos,
May the ungodly Thracians[5] with their hair
Done up in a fright on the top of their heads
5   Grab him, that he know what it is to be alone
Without friend or family. May he eat slave's bread
And suffer the plague and freeze naked,
Laced about with the nasty trash of the sea.
May his teeth knock the top on the bottom
10   As he lies on his face, spitting brine,
At the edge of the cold sea, like a dog.
And all this it would be a privilege to watch,
Giving me great satisfaction as it would,
For he took back the word he gave in honor,
15   Over the salt and table at a friendly meal.

Translation by Guy Davenport (1927–)

The poem is a curse, written by a Greek poet in the seventh century B.C. But the sentiment is as fresh as if it had been written yesterday. Archilochos is angry at someone who has gone back on his word. The two of them were having a friendly meal, and the man made a promise. Did he promise to do a business favor, or to introduce Archilochos to a woman? We will have to live with our curiosity. The point is that the man lied, and the poet is enraged. How does he manage his rage? He imagines the most dreadful things that could befall his enemy, and then invites them to happen. More than two thousand years later we can read it with sympathy and some amusement.

Poems of Praise, Poems for the Dead

Two powerful and time-honored sources of lyric poetry are admiration of something or someone, and the impact of death. The first inspires the *encomium*,

---

[5] Inhabitants of Thrace, an ancient country that comprised what is now Bulgaria and parts of Greece and Turkey. The Athenians considered Thracians barbarians.

a poem of praise. The second inspires the *elegy*, or death song. One might argue that both of these are forms of love poetry.

Here is a poem of praise written to a woman that the poet hardly knows. Let us pretend for a moment that we are walking with the poet on a country road and that he has stopped us to listen to the reaper's singing.

WILLIAM WORDSWORTH (1770–1850)

• The Solitary Reaper[6]

Behold her, single in the field,
Yon solitary Highland Lass!
Reaping and singing by herself:
Stop here, or gently pass!
5   Alone she cuts and binds the grain,
And sings a melancholy strain;
O listen! for the Vale° profound   *valley*
Is overflowing with the sound.

No Nightingale did ever chaunt°   *chant*
10   More welcome notes to weary bands
Of travellers in some shady haunt,
Among Arabian sands:
A voice so thrilling ne'er was heard
In spring-time from the Cuckoo-bird,
15   Breaking the silence of the seas
Among the farthest Hebrides.[7]

Will no one tell me what she sings?—
Perhaps the plaintive numbers flow
For old, unhappy, far-off things,
20   And battles long ago:
Or is it some more humble lay,°   *song*
Familiar matter of to-day?
Some natural sorrow, loss, or pain,
That has been, and may be again?

25   Whate'er the theme, the Maiden sang
As if her song could have no ending;
I saw her singing at her work,
And o'er the sickle bending;—
I listened, motionless and still;
30   And, as I mounted up the hill
The music in my heart I bore,
Long after it was heard no more.

---

[6] The poem is based on a passage from Thomas Wilkinson's *Tour of Scotland*. Wilkinson describes seeing a young woman reaping in the field. She sings in Erse, the native Scottish language.
[7] The Hebrides are islands off the west coast of Scotland.

Questions

1. Vocabulary: *reap* (3), *haunt* (11), *plaintive* (18), *sickle* (28).
2. Why does the poet stop when he notices the "Highland Lass"?
3. Why does he admire her so? How does he express his admiration?
4. How is the woman's singing like poetry?
5. Is it possible that the poet is envious of the reaper?
6. In what way has Wordsworth imitated the singer in writing the poem?
7. Who is the reaper's audience? Who is Wordsworth's?

GERARD MANLEY HOPKINS (1844–1889)

• Pied Beauty

Glory be to God for dappled things—
    For skies of couple-color as a brinded° cow;   *streaked*
        For rose-moles all in stipple upon trout that swim;
Fresh-firecoal chestnut-falls; finches' wings;
5   Landscape plotted and pieced—fold, fallow, and plow;
        And áll trádes, their gear and tackle and trim.°   *equipment*

All things counter, original, spare, strange;
    Whatever is fickle, freckled (who knows how?)
      With swift, slow; sweet, sour; adazzle, dim;
10   He fathers-forth whose beauty is past change:
          Praise him.

Questions

1. Vocabulary: *pied, dappled* (1), *stipple* (3), *fallow* (5).
2. Hopkins prepares an extended list of items for which he is thankful. Are any of the items unexpected?
3. Is Hopkins thankful only for natural things?
4. How is God beautiful, according to Hopkins? How is His beauty different from that of the natural world?

Suggestion for Poets

Make a list of those special and peculiar things you are thankful for.

CHRISTOPHER SMART (1722–1771)

For I Will Consider My Cat Jeoffry

For I will consider my Cat Jeoffry.
For he is the servant of the Living God, duly and daily serving him.
For at the first glance of the glory of God in the East he worships in his way.
For is this done by wreathing his body seven times round with elegant quickness.
5   For then he leaps up to catch the musk,° which is the blessing of God upon his
      prayer.   *catnip*

For he rolls upon prank to work it in.
For having done duty and received blessing he begins to consider himself.
For this he performs in ten degrees.
For first he looks upon his fore-paws to see if they are clean.
10   For secondly he kicks up behind to clear away there.
For thirdly he works it upon stretch[8] with the fore-paws extended.
For fourthly he sharpens his paws by wood.
For fifthly he washes himself.
For sixthly he rolls upon wash.
15   For seventhly he fleas himself, that he may not be interrupted upon
      the beat.°   *patrol*
For eighthly he rubs himself against a post.
For ninthly he looks up for his instructions.
For tenthly he goes in quest of food.
For having considered God and himself he will consider his neighbor.
20   For if he meets another cat he will kiss her in kindness.
For when he takes his prey he plays with it to give it a chance.
For one mouse in seven escapes by his dallying.
For when his day's work is done his business more properly begins.
For he keeps the Lord's watch in the night against the Adversary.
25   For he counteracts the powers of darkness by his electrical skin and glaring eyes.
For he counteracts the Devil, who is death, by brisking about the life.
For in his morning orisons he loves the sun and the sun loves him.
For he is of the tribe of Tiger.
For the Cherub Cat is a term of the Angel Tiger.
30   For he has the subtlety and hissing of a serpent, which in goodness he suppresses.
For he will not do destruction if he is well-fed, neither will he spit without
      provocation.
For he purrs in thankfulness when God tells him he's a good Cat.
For he is an instrument for the children to learn benevolence upon.
For every house is incomplete without him, and a blessing is lacking in the spirit.
35   For the Lord commanded Moses concerning the cats at the departure of the
      Children of Israel from Egypt.
For every family had one cat at least in the bag.

For the English Cats are the best in Europe.
For he is the cleanest in the use of his fore-paws of any quadruped.
For the dexterity of his defense is an instance of the love of God to him exceedingly.
40   For he is the quickest to his mark of any creature.
For he is tenacious of his point.
For he is a mixture of gravity and waggery.
For he knows that God is his Savior.
For there is nothing sweeter than his peace when at rest.
45   For there is nothing brisker than his life when in motion.
For he is of the Lord's poor, and so indeed is he called by benevolence perpetually—
      Poor Jeoffry! poor Jeoffrey! the rat has bit thy throat.
For I bless the name of the Lord Jesus that Jeoffrey is better.
For the divine spirit comes about his body to sustain it in complete cat.

---

[8] "He works it upon stretch" means that he works his muscles, stretching.

For his tongue is exceeding pure so that it has in purity what it wants in music.
50   For he is docile and can learn certain things.
For he can sit up with gravity which is patience upon approbation.
For he can fetch and carry, which is patience in employment.
For he can jump over a stick which is patience upon proof positive.
For he can spraggle upon waggle at the word of command.
55   For he can jump from an eminence into his master's bosom.
For he can catch the cork and toss it again.
For he is hated by the hypocrite and miser.
For the former is afraid of detection.
For the latter refuses the charge.[9]
60   For he camels his back to bear the first notion of business.
For he is good to think on, if a man would express himself neatly.
For he made a great figure in Egypt for his signal services.
For he killed the Icneumon-rat, very pernicious by land.
For his ears are so acute that they sting again.
65   For from this proceeds the passing quickness of his attention.
For by stroking of him I have found out electricity.
For I perceived God's light about him both wax and fire.
For the electrical fire is the spiritual substance which God sends from heaven to
       sustain the bodies both of man and beast.
For God has blessed him in the variety of his movements.
70   For, though he cannot fly, he is an excellent clamberer.
For his motions upon the face of the earth are more than any other quadruped.
For he can tread to all the measures upon the music.
For he can swim for life.
For he can creep.

Questions

1. Vocabulary: *orisons* (27), *quadruped* (38), *tenacious* (41), *docile* (50), *approbation*
   (51), *pernicious* (63).
2. The repetition of a word at the beginning of several lines of poetry is called anaphora.
   Do you find it agreeable in this poem? Musical? Wearying?

Elegy

An elegy is a poem of lamentation that probably originated as the cry of mourning
at ancient funerals. In classical Greece poets were engaged to inscribe elegiac
lyrics on tombstones. The death song has evolved over the centuries into a highly
sophisticated, diverse literary form, capable of expressing not only the grief of
personal loss, but larger themes of the changes wrought by time. Here is a
modern elegy, an exquisite personal statement of grief. Elegaic poets often describe the most vital qualities and scenes from the life of the deceased in order
to emphasize their feelings of loss. Roethke also refers to the landscape, as did
H. D. in her love poem, to show how the whole world shares in his sorrow.

---

[9] "The charge" refers to the cost of feeding the cat.

THEODORE ROETHKE (1908–1963)

Elegy for Jane

My Student, Thrown by a Horse

I remember the neckcurls, limp and damp as tendrils;
And her quick look, a sidelong pickerel smile;
And how, once startled into talk, the light syllables leaped for her,
And she balanced in the delight of her thought,
5   A wren, happy tail into the wind,
Her song trembling the twigs and small branches.
The shade sang with her;
The leaves, their whispers turned to kissing;
And the mold sang in the bleached valleys under the rose.

10   Oh, when she was sad, she cast herself down into such a pure depth,
Even a father could not find her:
Scraping her cheek against straw;
Stirring the clearest water.

My sparrow, you are not here,
15   Waiting like a fern, making a spiny shadow.
The sides of wet stones cannot console me,
Nor the moss, wound with the last light.

If only I could nudge you from this sleep,
My maimed darling, my skittery pigeon.
20   Over this damp grave I speak the words of my love:
I, with no rights in this matter,
Neither father nor lover.

Questions

1. Vocabulary: *tendrils* (1), *pickerel* (2), *skittery* (19).
2. Who is the sparrow in the third section? The pigeon in the fourth?
3. T. S. Eliot says that appreciation of a poem should precede our understanding of it. Do you appreciate the emotion in the poem? Do you understand all of it?
4. In the last lines the poet says that he has no right to speak the words of his love. Do you agree?

WALT WHITMAN (1819–1892)

This Dust Was Once the Man[10]

This dust was once the man,
Gentle, plain, just and resolute, under whose cautious hand,
Against the foulest crime in history known in any land or age,
Was saved the Union of these States.

---

[10] One of Whitman's elegies for Abraham Lincoln.

ALFRED, LORD TENNYSON (1809–1892)

Dark House, by Which Once More I Stand[11]

Dark house, by which once more I stand
    Here in the long unlovely street,
    Doors, where my heart was used to beat
So quickly, waiting for a hand,

5   A hand that can be clasped no more—
        Behold me, for I cannot sleep,
        And like a guilty thing I creep
    At earliest morning to the door.

He is not here; but far away
10   The noise of life begins again,
        And ghastly through the drizzling rain
On the bald street breaks the blank day.

Questions

1. In what ways is the house dark?
2. Why do you suppose Tennyson chose to describe the street as "unlovely" instead of "ugly"?
3. What feeling do you get from the last line?
4. Why does Tennyson compare himself to "a guilty thing"? Of what offense is Tennyson guilty?

A. E. HOUSMAN (1859–1936)

To an Athlete Dying Young

The time you won your town the race
We chaired° you through the market-place;   *carried on a chair*
Man and boy stood cheering by,
And home we brought you shoulder-high.

5   Today, the road all runners come,
Shoulder-high we bring you home,
And set you at your threshold down,
Townsman of a stiller town.

Smart lad, to slip betimes away
10   From fields where glory does not stay,
And early though the laurel[12] grows
It withers quicker than the rose.

Eyes the shady night has shut
Cannot see the record cut,
15   And silence sounds no worse than cheers
After earth has stopped the ears.

---

[11] This is a section of Tennyson's long poem *In Memoriam.*
[12] Laurel wreaths were awarded to the winners of competitions.

Now you will not swell the rout
Of lads that wore their honors out,
Runners whom renown outran
20 And the name died before the man.

So set, before its echoes fade,
The fleet foot on the sill of shade,
And hold to the low lintel up
The still-defended challenge-cup.

25 And round that early-laureled head
Will flock to gaze the strengthless dead,
And find unwithered on its curls
The garland briefer than a girl's.

Question

1. Vocabulary: *betimes* (9), *rout* (17), *lintel* (23), *garland* (28).

W. H. AUDEN (1907–1973)

• In Memory of W. B. Yeats

(d. Jan. 1939)

I

He disappeared in the dead of winter:
The brooks were frozen, the airports almost deserted,
And snow disfigured the public statues;
The mercury sank in the mouth of the dying day.
5 What instruments we have agree
The day of his death was a dark cold day.

Far from his illness
The wolves ran on through the evergreen forests,
The peasant river was untempted by the fashionable quays;
10 By mourning tongues
The death of the poet was kept from his poems.

But for him it was his last afternoon as himself,
An afternoon of nurses and rumours;
The provinces of his body revolted,
15 The squares of his mind were empty,
Silence invaded the suburbs,
The current of his feeling failed; he became his admirers.

Now he is scattered among a hundred cities
And wholly given over to unfamiliar affections,
20 To find his happiness in another kind of wood[13]
And be punished under a foreign code of conscience.

_____
[13] An allusion to Dante's *Inferno*, in which he sees himself as being in a dark wood.

W. H. Auden (*Cecil Beaton Photograph/Courtesy of Sotheby's Belgravia*)

The words of a dead man
Are modified in the guts of the living.

But in the importance and noise of to-morrow
25 When the brokers are roaring like beasts on the floor of the Bourse,[14]
And the poor have the sufferings to which they are fairly accustomed,
And each in the cell of himself is almost convinced of his freedom,
A few thousand will think of this day
As one thinks of a day when one did something slightly unusual.
30 What instruments we have agree
The day of his death was a dark cold day.

II

You were silly like us; your gift survived it all:
The parish of rich women, physical decay,
Yourself. Mad Ireland hurt you into poetry.
35 Now Ireland has her madness and her weather still,
For poetry makes nothing happen: it survives
In the valley of its making where executives
Would never want to tamper, flows on south
From ranches of isolation and busy griefs,
40 Raw towns that we believe and die in; it survives,
A way of happening, a mouth.

III

Earth, receive an honoured guest:
William Yeats is laid to rest.

---

[14] The French stock exchange.

Let the Irish vessel lie
45 Emptied of its poetry.

In the nightmare of the dark
All the dogs of Europe bark,[15]
And the living nations wait,
Each sequestered in its hate;

50 Intellectual disgrace
Stares from every human face,
And the seas of pity lie
Locked and frozen in each eye.

Follow, poet, follow right
55 To the bottom of the night,
With your unconstraining voice
Still persuade us to rejoice;

With the farming of a verse
Make a vineyard of the curse,
60 Sing of human unsuccess
In a rapture of distress;

In the deserts of the heart
Let the healing fountain start,
In the prison of his days
65 Teach the free man how to praise.

Question

1. Vocabulary: *quays* (9), *sequestered* (49), *unconstraining* (56).

The Meditative Poem

All the poetry we have read so far is thoughtful. Indeed, even the simplest linguistic act, such as the naming of a flower, involves some thought. But there is a kind of poetry in which thoughts, or ideas, are so much the center of attention that it has been called *meditative* poetry. It seems to rise, as does philosophy, out of a state of meditation, doubt, or curiosity. Unlike philosophers, however, poets are not content to dwell with their doubts and curiosities exclusively in the world of ideas. The ideas of poets are sparked by the real world and must return to the world of sense and emotion to find their music in language. One of the greatest meditative poets, Stéphane Mallarmé, expressed the relationship between poetry and ideas in conversation with the painter Edgar Degas; "One makes sonnets, Degas, not with ideas, but with words."

The excitement of meditative poetry lies in seeing the poet's mind in action, raising questions, and sometimes answering them, always on the threshold of new experience. We should read such work attentively in order to broaden our own experience.

---

[15] Auden is alluding here to the imminent outbreak of World War II.

OMAR KHAYYAM (A.D. 1050?–1123?)

XXVI and XXVII, the Rubaiyat

Oh, come with old Khayyam, and leave the Wise
To talk; one thing is certain, that life flies;
   One thing is certain, and the Rest is lies:
The Flower that once has blown forever dies.

5   Myself when young did eagerly frequent
Doctor and Saint, and heard great Argument
   About it and about: but evermore
Came out by the same Door as in I went.

Translation by Edward Fitzgerald (1809–1883)

   The Sufi poet Omar Khayyam spent a lifetime pursuing Truth and what one commentator refers to as "the Awakening of the Soul." In this concise, musical passage from his meditative poem the *Rubaiyat*, Omar Khayyam sums up years of education. In his youth he listened to the wisest discourse, of "Doctors," or those schooled in the world's wisdom, and of "Saints"—those well versed in the ways of God. What did Omar learn from them? "That life flies," and that "the Flower that once has blown forever dies." Is that all? You would have to read the rest of the *Rubaiyat* to get a better idea of what Omar learned. What is more important in this passage is what he did *not* learn. Look at the last line. No matter what he heard, the poet always left by the same door he entered! With wit and certainty Omar is saying that all the high conversation did not introduce him to a new door, a new path, or a new world. The *Rubaiyat* is a meditative journey that tells us something about the limits of meditation.

   Meditative poets are usually testing the limits of their knowledge. Aristotle tells us that the desire to know is our fundamental nature. One way of reading meditative poetry is to join a poet in questioning, and then see how well the question is answered, for the poet and for us.

   The poet John Milton became blind before his fiftieth year. In this meditation he considers the meaning of his blindness.

JOHN MILTON (1608–1674)

When I Consider How My Light Is Spent

When I consider how my light is spent,
   Ere half my days in this dark world and wide,
   And that one talent which is death to hide
   Lodged with me useless, though my soul more bent
5   To serve therewith my Maker, and present
   My true account, lest He returning chide;
   "Doth God exact day-labor, light denied?"
   I fondly° ask. But Patience, to prevent   *foolishly*
That murmur, soon replies, "God doth not need

10   Either man's work or His own gifts. Who best
           Bear His mild yoke, they serve Him best. His state
     Is kingly: thousands at His bidding speed,
           And post o'er land and ocean without rest;
           They also serve who only stand and wait."

Questions

1. What is the question that Milton poses?
2. Who answers him?
3. Do you consider the answer satisfactory?

ROBERT FROST (1874–1963)

Fire and Ice

     Some say the world will end in fire,
     Some say in ice.
     From what I've tasted of desire
     I hold with those who favor fire.
5   But if it had to perish twice,
     I think I know enough of hate
     To say that for destruction ice
     Is also great
     And would suffice.

In this epigram Frost considers the end of the world. The term *epigram* comes from a classical Greek word meaning to carve or inscribe, and an epigram is any terse, witty treatment of a single thought or question. Carving letters on stone or metal is difficult: we can understand why the epigram had to get right to the point. What is Frost's major question? He is asking how the world could end. He gives us a double answer: either fire or ice will do. But his reference to love and hate makes his answers much more subtle. Fire, he likens to desire, and we all know that uncontrolled desire leads to aggression and destruction. Ice, on the other hand, he compares to hatred, which could destroy the world as easily as desire.

WALLACE STEVENS (1879–1955)

Anecdote of the Jar

     I placed a jar in Tennessee,
     And round it was, upon a hill.
     It made the slovenly wilderness
     Surround that hill.

5   The wilderness rose up to it,
     And sprawled around, no longer wild.

The jar was round upon the ground
And tall and of a port in air.

It took dominion everywhere.
10   The jar was gray and bare.
It did not give of bird or bush,
Like nothing else in Tennessee.

Question

1. Vocabulary: *slovenly* (3), *dominion* (9).

   This short poem has an enormous subject and suggests many questions. The placement of the manufactured jar on a hill in the "slovenly wilderness" becomes an occasion for the poet to consider the relation between human beings and nature. Notice that the wilderness is tamed by the jar, as if its orderly shape and dignity were more powerful than all of the nature surrounding it. The jar "took dominion everywhere," just as the human race subdues and orders the larger world. In the last sentence the poet takes his meditation a step further. Stevens considers the sculptural relations of interior and exterior, being and nonbeing. The jar is what it is because it is *like* nothing else, and because it will *admit* nothing else, neither bird nor bush.

   Perhaps the greatest form of meditative lyric is the *ode*. Again the word comes to us from the ancients, from a Greek word for song, and the first great writer of odes, Pindar, was Greek. He wrote odes of praise to statesman and winners of the Olympian games. These odes were much admired because their flattering characterization and historical perspective raised their subjects to the level of mythic heroes. Full of epigrammatic wisdom or *gnomae*, of reflections on the poet's own grace or lack of grace, the Pindaric odes became a standard of lyric excellence in treating broad themes with intelligence and musicality. The Romantic poets Shelley, Keats, and Wordsworth used the form to great advantage, extending it to meditation on ideas and objects as well as people.

   The following is among the most respected of these Romantic odes.

JOHN KEATS (1795–1821)

• Ode on a Grecian Urn[16]

Thou still unravished bride of quietness,
   Thou foster-child of silence and slow time,
Sylvan historian, who canst thus express
   A flowery tale more sweetly than our rhyme:
5   What leaf-fringed legend haunts about thy shape
     Of deities or mortals, or of both,
       In Tempe or the dales of Arcady?[17]

---

[16] The urn is decorated with a woodland, or sylvan, scene.
[17] Two valleys in Greece that represent the epitome of natural beauty.

Attic Red-Figured Urn, Four Women at
Bath *(Courtesy of the Museum of Fine
Arts, Boston, Catherine Page Perkins
Fund)*

What men or gods are these? What maidens loth?
What mad pursuit? What struggle to escape?
10   What pipes and timbrels? What wild ecstasy?

Heard melodies are sweet, but those unheard
    Are sweeter; therefore, ye soft pipes, play on;
Not to the sensual° ear, but, more endeared,   *physical*
    Pipe to the spirit ditties of no tone:
15 Fair youth, beneath the trees, thou canst not leave
    Thy song, nor ever can those trees be bare;
        Bold Lover, never, never canst thou kiss,
Though winning near the goal—yet, do not grieve,
        She cannot fade, though thou hast not thy bliss,
20   For ever wilt thou love, and she be fair!

Ah, happy, happy boughs! that cannot shed
    Your leaves, nor ever bid the Spring adieu;
And, happy melodist, unwearièd,
    For ever piping songs for ever new;
25 More happy love! more happy, happy love!
    For ever warm and still to be enjoyed,
        For ever panting, and for ever young;
All breathing human passion far above,
    That leaves a heart high-sorrowful and cloyed,
30   A burning forehead, and a parching tongue.

Who are these coming to the sacrifice?
    To what green altar, O mysterious priest,
Lead'st thou that heifer lowing at the skies,
    And all her silken flanks with garlands drest?
35 What little town by river or sea shore,
    Or mountain-built with peaceful citadel,
        Is emptied of this folk, this pious morn?
And, little town, thy streets for evermore
    Will silent be; and not a soul to tell
40   Why thou art desolate, can e'er return.

O Attic shape![18] Fair attitude! with brede°   *design*
     Of marble men and maidens overwrought,
With forest branches and the trodden weed;
     Thou, silent form, dost tease us out of thought
45   As doth Eternity: Cold Pastoral!
     When old age shall this generation waste,
          Thou shalt remain, in midst of other woe
     Than ours, a friend to man, to whom thou say'st,
Beauty is truth, truth beauty,—that is all
50   Ye know on earth, and all ye need to know.

Questions

1. Vocabulary: *sylvan* (3), *loth* (8), *timbrels* (10), *melodist* (23), *cloyed* (29), *heifer* (33), *overwrought* (42).
2. It is clear from the first passages of the poem that Keats has observed the urn closely. Why does he want to know more?
3. Why does Keats admire the piper? Why the lover? Why does he so admire the leaves in the third section?
4. In the fourth stanza, the townspeople have emptied the town in order to attend a sacrifice. They can never return, for the picture is locked in time. In what way are we too locked in time? Is their fate similar to ours?
5. Keats asks the urn many questions, and in the last lines the urn answers him. In fact, it answers a more important question than any he has asked so far. What is the question?

In the poem's opening lines the speaker is addressing the urn. Such a direct address, called an *apostrophe*, is a common poetic device. Poets have apostrophized clouds, skylarks, the moon and sun, roses, and so on. Another characteristic of this ode is that the urn, for Keats, plays a number of different roles. It is an "unravished bride of quietness," meaning, among other things, that its silence has remained unbroken and its surface unmarred. It is also a "sylvan historian," however, because it preserves the rural past. Both these phrases suggest that for Keats the urn is alive, not an ancient relic of a long-ago time.

As far as we know, Keats did not have any particular Grecian urn in mind when he wrote this poem. Rather, the urn he addresses is typical of most Grecian urns. Greek artists excelled in this form of painting, and they lavished time and craftsmanship on their urns, which depicted mythological scenes as well as scenes from daily life.

WILLIAM BUTLER YEATS (1865–1939)

Lapis Lazuli[19]

(For Harry Clifton)

I have heard that hysterical women say[20]
They are sick of the palette and fiddle-bow,

---

[18] Athenian shape—that is, possessing the Greek epitome of beauty.
[19] A deep blue stone often used by the Chinese for carving.
[20] The poem was written in 1936, when Europeans were already concerned about impending war.

Of poets that are always gay,[21]
For everybody knows or else should know
5   That if nothing drastic is done
Aeroplane and Zeppelin[22] will come out,
Pitch like King Billy bomb-balls in[23]
Until the town lie beaten flat.

All perform their tragic play,
10   There struts Hamlet, there is Lear,
That's Ophelia, that Cordelia;[24]
Yet they, should the last scene be there,
The great stage curtain about to drop,
If worthy their prominent part in the play,
15   Do not break up their lines to weep.
They know that Hamlet and Lear are gay;
Gaiety transfiguring all that dread.
All men have aimed at, found and lost;
Black out; Heaven blazing into the head:
20   Tragedy wrought to its uttermost.
Though Hamlet rambles and Lear rages,
And all the drop-scenes drop at once
Upon a hundred thousand stages,
It cannot grow by an inch or an ounce.

25   On their own feet they came, or on shipboard,
Camel-back, horse-back, ass-back, mule-back,
Old civilisations put to the sword.
Then they and their wisdom went to rack:
No handiwork of Callimachus,[25]
30   Who handled marble as if it were bronze,
Made draperies that seemed to rise
When sea-wind swept the corner, stands;
His long lamp-chimney shaped like the stem
Of a slender palm, stood but a day;
35   All things fall and are built again,
And those that build them again are gay.

Two Chinamen, behind them a third,
Are carved in lapis lazuli,
Over them flies a long-legged bird,
40   A symbol of longevity;
The third, doubtless a serving-man,
Carries a musical instrument.

Every discoloration of the stone,
Every accidental crack or dent,

---

21 In Yeats's day, the primary meaning of *gay* was "merry" or "lively."
22 A lighter-than-air flying machine.
23 King William III, who defeated James II in 1690. A ballad of the time goes, "King William threw his bomb-balls in, / And set them all on fire."
24 Characters in Shakespearean tragedies. Ophelia loves Hamlet; Cordelia is Lear's daughter.
25 Greek sculptor of the 5th century B.C.

45   Seems a water-course or an avalanche,
        Or lofty slope where it still snows
        Though doubtless plum or cherry-branch
        Sweetens the little half-way house
        Those Chinamen climb towards, and I
50   Delight to imagine them seated there;
        There, on the mountain and the sky,
        On all the tragic scene they stare.
        One asks for mournful melodies;
        Accomplished fingers begin to play.
55   Their eyes mid many wrinkles, their eyes,
        Their ancient, glittering eyes, are gay.

Questions

1. Vocabulary: *palette* (2), *longevity* (40), *discoloration* (43).
2. Why are the hysterical women angry at artists? Is their anger justified?
3. According to Yeats, how should artists respond to social disorder and war? Is there anything they can do?
4. Poets often take the position that life is short and art is eternal. Does Yeats believe that art endures forever?
5. What position do the "Chinamen" hold toward history? In what ways are their views opposite to those of the hysterical women at the beginning of the poem?
6. Would you call this poem hopeful? Why?
7. Compare this poem with W. H. Auden's "Musée des Beaux Arts", on pages 12–13. How does Auden handle a similar theme of human suffering caused by war?

❧ Poems for Further Study

E. E. CUMMINGS (1894–1962)

• somewhere i have never travelled, gladly beyond

somewhere i have never travelled, gladly beyond
any experience, your eyes have their silence:
in your most frail gesture are things which enclose me,
or which i cannot touch because they are too near

5   your slightest look easily will unclose me
        though i have closed myself as fingers,
        you open always petal by petal myself as Spring opens
        (touching skilfully, mysteriously) her first rose

or if your wish be to close me, i and
10   my life will shut very beautifully, suddenly,
        as when the heart of this flower imagines
        the snow carefully everywhere descending;

nothing which we are to perceive in this world equals
the power of your intense fragility: whose texture

15   compels me with the colour of its countries,
     rendering death and forever with each breathing

     (i do not know what it is about you that closes
     and opens; only something in me understands
     the voice of your eyes is deeper than all roses)
20   nobody, not even the rain, has such small hands

CESARE PAVESE (1908–1950)

Encounter

These hard hills which have made my body,
and whose many memories still shake me so, have revealed the miracle—
this *she* who does not know I live her and cannot understand her.

I encountered her one evening: a brighter presence
5   in the unsteady starlight, in the summer haze.
The smell of those hills was around me, everywhere,
a feeling deeper than shadow, and suddenly I heard,
as if it came from the hills, a voice at once purer
and harsher, a voice of vanished seasons.

10   Sometimes I see her, as she saw me, her presence
defined, unchangeable, like a memory.
I have never managed to hold her fast: always her reality
evades my grasp and carries me far away.
I do not know if she is beautiful. Among women she is very young:
15   when I think of her, I am surprised by a faint memory
of childhood lived among these hills,
she is so young. She is like morning. Her eyes suggest
all the distant skies of those faraway mornings.
And her eyes are firm with a purpose: the sharpest light
20   dawn has ever made upon these hills.

I created her from the ground of everything
I love the most, and I cannot understand her.

Translation by William Arrowsmith (1924–)

SYLVIA PLATH (1932–1963)

Daddy

You do not do, you do not do
Any more, black shoe
In which I have lived like a foot
For thirty years, poor and white,
5   Barely daring to breathe or Achoo.

Daddy, I have had to kill you.
You died before I had time—
Marble-heavy, a bag full of God,

Ghastly statue with one grey toe
10   Big as a Frisco seal

And a head in the freakish Atlantic
Where it pours bean green over blue
In the waters off beautiful Nauset.[26]
I used to pray to recover you.
15   Ach, du.

In the German tongue, in the Polish town
Scraped flat by the roller
Of wars, wars, wars.
But the name of the town is common.
20   My Polack friend

Says there are a dozen or two.
So I never could tell where you
Put your foot, your root,
I never could talk to you.
25   The tongue stuck in my jaw.

It stuck in a barb wire snare.
Ich, ich, ich, ich,[27]
I could hardly speak.
I thought every German was you.
30   And the language obscene

An engine, an engine
Chuffing me off like a Jew.
A Jew to Dachau, Auschwitz, Belsen.[28]
I began to talk like a Jew.
35   I think I may well be a Jew.

The snows of the Tyrol, the clear beer of Vienna
Are not very pure or true.
With my gypsy ancestress and my weird luck
And my Taroc pack and my Taroc pack
40   I may be a bit of a Jew.

I have always been scared of *you*,
With your Luftwaffe,[29] your gobbledygoo.
And your neat moustache
And your Aryan eye, bright blue.
45   Panzer-man, panzer-man,[30] O You—

Not God but a swastika
So black no sky could squeak through.
Every woman adores a Fascist,
The boot in the face, the brute
50   Brute heart of a brute like you.

---

[26] Nauset Bay in northern New England.
[27] *Ich* is German for "I."
[28] Sites of German concentration camps.
[29] The German air force.
[30] Tank driver in the German army.

You stand at the blackboard, daddy,
In the picture I have of you.
A cleft in your chin instead of your foot
But no less a devil for that, no not
55   Any less the black man who

Bit my pretty red heart in two.
I was ten when they buried you.
At twenty I tried to die
And get back, back, back at you.
60   I thought even the bones would do

But they pulled me out of the sack,
And they stuck me together with glue.
And then I knew what to do.
I made a model of you,
65   A man in black with a Meinkampf look[31]

And a love of the rack and the screw.
And I said I do, I do.
So daddy, I'm finally through.
The black telephone's off at the root,
70   The voices just can't worm through.

If I've killed one man, I've killed two—
The vampire who said he was you
And drank my blood for a year,
Seven years, if you want to know.
75   Daddy, you can lie back now.

There's a stake in your fat black heart
And the villagers never liked you.
They are dancing and stamping on you.
They always *knew* it was you.
80   Daddy, daddy, you bastard, I'm through.

JOHN CROWE RANSOM (1888–1974)

Here Lies a Lady

Here lies a lady of beauty and high degree.
Of chills and fever she died, of fever and chills,
The delight of her husband, her aunt, an infant of three,
And of medicos marveling sweetly on her ills.

5   For either she burned, and her confident eyes would blaze,
And her fingers fly in a manner to puzzle their heads—
What was she making? Why, nothing; she sat in a maze
Of old scraps of laces, snipped into curious shreds—

Or this would pass, and the light of her fire decline
10   Till she lay discouraged and cold, like a thin stalk white and blown,

---

[31] Adolf Hitler's *Mein Kampf* (two volumes, 1925–1927) stated Hitler's political views.

And would not open her eyes, to kisses, to wine;
The sixth of these states was her last; the cold settled down.

Sweet ladies, long may ye bloom, and toughly I hope ye may thole,°   *endure*
But was she not lucky? In flowers and lace and mourning,
15   In love and great honor we bade God rest her soul
After six little spaces of chill, and six of burning.

WILLIAM BLAKE (1757–1827)

To See a World in a Grain of Sand

To see a world in a grain of sand
And a heaven in a wild flower,
Hold infinity in the palm of your hand
And eternity in an hour.

WILLIAM CARLOS WILLIAMS (1883–1963)

Danse Russe[32]

If when my wife is sleeping
and the baby and Kathleen
are sleeping
and the sun is a flame-white disc
5   in silken mists
above shining trees,—
if I in my north room
dance naked, grotesquely
before my mirror
10 waving my shirt round my head
and singing softly to myself:
"I am lonely, lonely.
I was born to be lonely,
I am best so!"
15 If I admire my arms, my face,
my shoulders, flanks, buttocks
against the yellow drawn shades,—

Who shall say I am not
the happy genius[33] of my household?

SAMUEL TAYLOR COLERIDGE (1772–1834)

Frost at Midnight

The frost performs its secret ministry,
Unhelped by any wind. The owlet's cry

---

[32] *Ballet Russe*, French for "Russian ballet," is the name of the famous ballet company under the direction of Sergei Diaghilev.
[33] Genius can also mean the spirit that watches over an area or a person.

Came loud—and hark, again! loud as before.
The inmates of my cottage, all at rest,
5   Have left me to that solitude, which suits
Abstruser musings: save that at my side
My cradled infant slumbers peacefully.
'Tis calm indeed! so calm, that it disturbs
And vexes meditation with its strange
10   And extreme silentness. Sea, hill, and wood,
This populous village! Sea, and hill, and wood,
With all the numberless goings-on of life,
Inaudible as dreams! the thin blue flame
Lies on my low-burnt fire, and quivers not;
15   Only that film, which fluttered on the grate,[34]
Still flutters there, the sole unquiet thing.
Methinks, its motion in this hush of nature
Gives it dim sympathies with me who live,
Making it a companionable form,
20   Whose puny flaps and freaks the idling Spirit
By its own moods interprets, every where
Echo or mirror seeking of itself,
And makes a toy of Thought.

                                But O! how oft,
How oft, at school, with most believing mind,
25   Presageful, have I gazed upon the bars,
To watch that fluttering *stranger!* and as oft
With unclosed lids, already had I dreamt
Of my sweet birth-place,[35] and the old church-tower,
Whose bells, the poor man's only music, rang
30   From morn to evening, all the hot Fair-day,
So sweetly, that they stirred and haunted me
With a wild pleasure, falling on mine ear
Most like articulate sounds of things to come!
So gazed I, till the soothing things, I dreamt,
35   Lulled me to sleep, and sleep prolonged my dreams!
And so I brooded all the following morn,
Awed by the stern preceptor's face, mine eye
Fixed with mock study on my swimming book:
Save if the door half opened, and I snatched
40   A hasty glance, and still my heart leaped up,
For still I hoped to see the *stranger's* face,
Townsman, or aunt, or sister more beloved,
My play-mate when we both were clothed alike!

    Dear Babe, that sleepest cradled by my side,
45   Whose gentle breathings, heard in this deep calm,
Fill up the interspersèd vacancies

---

[34] The "film" to which Coleridge refers is a thin ash, which in Coleridge's day was called "a stranger" because, according to popular belief, it betokened an unexpected visitor.
[35] Coleridge was born in Devonshire but was sent to school in London after the age of nine.

And momentary pauses of the thought!
My babe so beautiful! it thrills my heart
With tender gladness, thus to look at thee,
50 And think that thou shalt learn far other lore,
And in far other scenes! For I was reared
In the great city, pent 'mid cloisters dim,
And saw nought lovely but the sky and stars.
But *thou*, my babe! shalt wander like a breeze
55 By lakes and sandy shores, beneath the crags
Of ancient mountain, and beneath the clouds,
Which image in their bulk both lakes and shores
And mountain crags: so shalt thou see and hear
The lovely shapes and sounds intelligible
60 Of that eternal language, which thy God
Utters, who from eternity doth teach
Himself in all, and all things in himself.
Great universal Teacher! he shall mould
Thy spirit, and by giving make it ask.

65 Therefore all seasons shall be sweet to thee,
Whether the summer clothe the general earth
With greenness, or the redbreast sit and sing
Betwixt the tufts of snow on the bare branch
Of mossy apple-tree, while the nigh thatch
70 Smokes in the sun-thaw; whether the eave-drops fall
Heard only in the trances of the blast,
Or if the secret ministry of frost
Shall hang them up in silent icicles,
Quietly shining to the quiet Moon.

IMAMU AMIRI BARAKA (LeROI JONES) (1934–)

Preface to a Twenty Volume Suicide Note

For Kellie Jones, Born 16 May 1959

Lately, I've become accustomed to the way
The ground opens up and envelopes me
Each time I go out to walk the dog.
Or the broad edged silly music the wind
5 Makes when I run for a bus . . .

Things have come to that.

And now, each night I count the stars,
And each night I get the same number.
And when they will not come to be counted,
10 I count the holes they leave.

Nobody sings anymore.

And then last night I tiptoed up
To my daughter's room and heard her

Talking to someone, and when I opened
15   The door, there was no one there . . .
Only she on her knees, peeking into

Her own clasped hands.

JOHN ASHBERY (1927–)

And Ut Pictura Poesis *Is Her Name*

You can't say it that way any more.
Bothered about beauty you have to
Come out into the open, into a clearing,
And rest. Certainly whatever funny happens to you
5   Is OK. To demand more than this would be strange
Of you, you who have so many lovers,
People who look up to you and are willing
To do things for you, but you think
It's not right, that if they really knew you . . .
10   So much for self-analysis. Now,
About what to put in your poem-painting:
Flowers are always nice, particularly delphinium.
Names of boys you once knew and their sleds,
Skyrockets are good—do they still exist?
15   There are a lot of other things of the same quality
As those I've mentioned. Now one must
Find a few important words, and a lot of low-keyed,
Dull-sounding ones. She approached me
About buying her desk. Suddenly the street was
20   Bananas and the clangor of Japanese instruments.
Humdrum testaments were scattered around. His head
Locked into mine. We were a seesaw. Something
Ought to be written about how this affects
You when you write poetry:
25   The extreme austerity of an almost empty mind
Colliding with the lush, Rousseau-like foliage of its desire to communicate
Something between breaths, if only for the sake
Of others and their desire to understand you and desert you
For other centers of communication, so that understanding
30   May begin, and in doing so be undone.

5 ❧ Dramatic Poetry

The Poet as Actor

How often have you wished to be someone else? Imagine leaving your body for a few hours and becoming a famous musician, a fashion model, a bank robber, or a senator. This is a common fantasy, the same one that prompts children to try on their parents' hats and shoes. One of the frustrations of being human is that we cannot escape who we are no matter how much we like or dislike ourselves. Certain poets, hypersensitive to the limits of personality, adopt someone else's voice in writing a poem. A young poet might speak in the voice of an old woman, or a rich poet in a beggar's voice. This adoption of another's voice, sometimes called a mask or persona, is the poet's effort to break out of his or her own consciousness and reach into the world of another. The result of that effort is *dramatic poetry*.

Dramatic poets are not merely ventriloquists with peculiar gifts for mimicry. They must identify with the persons they are portraying—a feat requiring a profound knowledge of character and an extraordinary degree of compassion. Dramatic poetry confirms certain constants in human nature that enable poets to understand people very different from themselves: the bishop, the queen, the murderer. For the reader, dramatic poetry provides an opportunity to hear the imagined thoughts of characters who lack the poet's gift or opportunity of expression.

The Soliloquy

The simplest form of dramatic poetry is the *soliloquy*, in which the speaker is merely overheard, talking to no one in particular.

WILLIAM CARLOS WILLIAMS (1883–1963)

The Widow's Lament in Springtime

Sorrow is my own yard
where the new grass

```
     flames as it has flamed
     often before but not
 5   with the cold fire
     that closes round me this year.
     Thirtyfive years
     I lived with my husband.
     The plumtree is white today
10   with masses of flowers.
     Masses of flowers
     load the cherry branches
     and color some bushes
     yellow and some red
15   but the grief in my heart
     is stronger than they
     for though they were my joy
     formerly, today I notice them
     and turned away forgetting.
20   Today my son told me
     that in the meadows,
     at the edge of the heavy woods
     in the distance, he saw
     trees of white flowers.
25   I feel that I would like
     to go there
     and fall into those flowers
     and sink into the marsh near them.
```

If this had been written by a widow, we might consider it a simple lyric statement of sorrow. But Williams clearly is not a widow. Why do you suppose he contrived to write in a woman's voice? Perhaps the poem grew out of a conversation with a widow he knew. Or maybe some of the statements in the poem were overheard. Whether the widow is real or imagined, the poem certainly arose out of sympathy for a woman's grief, rendered here in a manner that some men might find embarrassing. Perhaps the man has found a freedom of expression in the widow's voice he might not have felt in his own—a chance to explore a more feminine side of his nature. Whatever his motivation, Williams has treated his theme with great intimacy by entering into the widow's thoughts and adopting her voice.

This form of poem, in which the poet speaks for a single character, is also called a *dramatic monologue*. Its use suggests a modern, relativistic attitude toward experience. That is, the world can look quite different to different people depending on their character and point of view. As writers became more concerned with human individuality in the nineteenth century, the dramatic monologue served to explore extreme psychological states and differing points of view. Robert Browning wrote a book-length poem, *The Ring and the Book*, in which a murder story is told ten times, once by each of the various participants in and witnesses to the crime. The resulting picture, as rich and complex as life itself, shows that the truth of a situation cannot be known by any single witness.

We must not take the statements of a persona at face value. The dramatic poet may be portraying a liar or a deranged person who is unable to report experiences clearly.

One of Browning's shorter dramatic monologues reveals how the poet speaks for a psychopathic killer. Like a playwright, the dramatic poet sets the scene: a rainy, windy night, a cottage by the lake, the lover who is waiting for the entrance of his Porphyria. Let's see what happens.

ROBERT BROWNING (1812–1889)

Porphyria's Lover

The rain set early in to-night,
   The sullen wind was soon awake,
It tore the elm-tops down for spite,
   And did its worst to vex the lake:
5   I listened with heart fit to break.
When glided in Porphyria; straight
   She shut the cold out and the storm,
And kneeled and made the cheerless grate
   Blaze up, and all the cottage warm;
10   Which done, she rose, and from her form
Withdrew the dripping cloak and shawl,
   And laid her soiled gloves by, untied
Her hat and let the damp hair fall,
   And, last, she sat down by my side
15   And called me. When no voice replied,
She put my arm about her waist,
   And made her smooth white shoulder bare,
And all her yellow hair displaced,
   And, stooping, made my cheek lie there,
20   And spread, o'er all, her yellow hair,
Murmuring how she loved me—she
   Too weak, for all her heart's endeavour,
To set its struggling passion free
   From pride, and vainer ties dissever,
25   And give herself to me for ever.
But passion sometimes would prevail,
   Nor could to-night's gay feast restrain
A sudden thought of one so pale
   For love of her, and all in vain:
30   So, she was come through wind and rain.
Be sure I looked up at her eyes
   Happy and proud; at last I knew
Porphyria worshipped me; surprise
   Made my heart swell, and still it grew

35   While I debated what to do.
    That moment she was mine, mine, fair,
      Perfectly pure and good: I found
    A thing to do, and all her hair
      In one long yellow string I wound
40   Three times her little throat around,
    And strangled her. No pain felt she;
      I am quite sure she felt no pain.
    As a shut bud that holds a bee,
      I warily oped her lids: again
45   Laughed the blue eyes without a stain.
    And I untightened next the tress
      About her neck; her cheek once more
    Blushed bright beneath my burning kiss:
      I propped her head up as before,
50   Only, this time my shoulder bore
    Her head, which droops upon it still:
      The smiling rosy little head,
    So glad it has its utmost will,
      That all it scorned at once is fled,
55   And I, its love, am gained instead!
    Porphyria's love: she guessed not how
      Her darling one wish would be heard.
    And thus we sit together now,
      And all night long we have not stirred,
60   And yet God has not said a word!

Questions

1. Vocabulary: *sullen* (2), *vex* (4), *dissever* (24).
2. What are the "vainer ties" the speaker refers to in line 24?
3. What was "Her darling one wish," mentioned in line 57?
4. How does your attitude toward the speaker change after line 30?
5. Why does he kill her? Do you believe she felt no pain?
6. Apart from the fact that he murders Porphyria, how can you tell the speaker is insane?
7. To whom is the speaker speaking? Is the poem a soliloquy?

The most vivid dramatic monologues tell us not only the character of the persona, but also the character of an auditor, the person being addressed. The great vitality of such poetry owes much to the immediacy of the scene—it takes place before our very eyes, just like a movie or a play, or a scene glimpsed through a keyhole. To read such poems we must first identify the dramatic situation, answering the questions: Who is speaking? Who is being addressed? Where are they? What prompts the speech?

WILLIAM BLAKE (1757–1827)

The Little Vagabond

Dear mother, dear mother, the Church is cold,
But the Ale-house is healthy and pleasant and warm;

Besides I can tell where I am used well,
Such usage in Heaven will never do well.

5   But if at the Church they would give us some ale,
And a pleasant fire our souls to regale,
We'd sing and we'd pray all the livelong day,
Nor ever once wish from the Church to stray.

Then the Parson might preach, and drink, and sing,
10   And we'd be as happy as birds in the spring;
And modest Dame Lurch, who is always at church,
Would not have bandy children, nor fasting, nor birch.

And God, like a father, rejoicing to see
His children as pleasant and happy as He,
15   Would have no more quarrel with the Devil or the barrel,
But kiss him, and give him both drink and apparel.

Questions

1. Vocabulary: *regale* (6), *bandy* (12).
2. Who is the persona of the poem?
3. Who is the auditor?
4. What kind of scene is depicted?
5. Is the speaker persuasive?
6. Where do you think the speaker will end up—in church or at the ale-house?

ANNE SEXTON (1928–1974)

Unknown Girl in the Maternity Ward

Child, the current of your breath is six days long.
You lie, a small knuckle on my white bed;
lie, fisted like a snail, so small and strong
at my breast. Your lips are animals; you are fed
5   with love. At first hunger is not wrong.
The nurses nod their caps; you are shepherded
down starch halls with the other unnested throng
in wheeling baskets. You tip like a cup; your head
moving to my touch. You sense the way we belong.
10   But this is an institution bed.
You will not know me very long.

The doctors are enamel. They want to know
the facts. They guess about the man who left me,
some pendulum soul, going the way men go
15   and leave you full of child. But our case history
stays blank. All I did was let you grow.
Now we are here for all the ward to see.
They thought I was strange, although
I never spoke a word. I burst empty
20   of you, letting you learn how the air is so.

The doctors chart the riddle they ask of me
and I turn my head away. I do not know.

Yours is the only face I recognize.
Bone at my bone, you drink my answers in.
25 Six times a day I prize
your need, the animals of your lips, your skin
growing warm and plump. I see your eyes
lifting their tents. They are blue stones, they begin
to outgrow their moss. You blink in surprise
30 and I wonder what you can see, my funny kin,
as you trouble my silence. I am a shelter of lies.
Should I learn to speak again, or hopeless in
such sanity will I touch some face I recognize?

Down the hall the baskets start back. My arms
35 fit you like a sleeve, they hold
catkins of your willows, the wild bee farms
of your nerves, each muscle and fold
of your first days. Your old man's face disarms
the nurses. But the doctors return to scold
40 me. I speak. It is you my silence harms.
I should have known; I should have told
them something to write down. My voice alarms
my throat. "Name of father—none." I hold
you and name you bastard in my arms.

Anne Sexton (© *Thomas Victor* 1982)

45   And now that's that. There is nothing more
      that I can say or lose.
      Others have traded life before
      and could not speak. I tighten to refuse
      your owling eyes, my fragile visitor.
50   I touch your cheeks, like flowers. You bruise
      against me. We unlearn. I am a shore
      rocking you off. You break from me. I choose
      your only way, my small inheritor
      and hand you off, trembling the selves we lose.
55   Go child, who is my sin and nothing more.

Questions

1. Vocabulary: *pendulum* (14), *catkins* (36), *disarms* (38).
2. The title and the first line of the poem introduce us to the dramatic situation. Why is the mother saying these things to an infant? For whose benefit is she speaking?
3. Why will the baby not know her long?
4. Why does she say, "The doctors are enamel" (line 12)? What does that suggest about their sympathy?
5. Why does she call herself "a shelter of lies" (line 30)?
6. Do you believe her in the last line when she says the child is "my sin and nothing more"?

The reader of dramatic poems might wonder why these imagined speakers, who are not supposed to be poets, speak with the eloquence of poets. This is one of the central tensions of dramatic poetry—the tension between poetic, or heightened, speech and natural speech. Poets have resolved this tension in various ways, sometimes simplifying the language when a character could not be expected to speak poetry; at other times choosing a persona from a faraway time or exalted station, who seems quite comfortable with eloquence. In the following poem, Lord Tennyson's "Ulysses" comes to us from Homeric Greece, a heroic age when, it seems, anything was possible—even kings who spoke poetry.

ALFRED, LORD TENNYSON (1809–1892)

• Ulysses[1]

    It little profits that an idle king,
    By this still hearth, among these barren crags,
    Matched with an agèd wife, I mete and dole
    Unequal laws unto a savage race
5   That hoard, and sleep, and feed, and know not me.
    I cannot rest from travel; I will drink
    Life to the lees. All times I have enjoyed

---

[1] "Ulysses" is discussed at length in the Appendix.

Greatly, have suffered greatly, both with those
That loved me, and alone; on shore, and when
10   Through scudding drifts the rainy Hyades[2]
Vexed the dim sea. I am become a name;
For always roaming with a hungry heart
Much have I seen and known—cities of men
And manners, climates, councils, governments,
15   Myself not least, but honored of them all—
And drunk delight of battle with my peers,
Far on the ringing plains of windy Troy.
I am a part of all that I have met;
Yet all experience is an arch wherethrough
20   Gleams that untraveled world whose margin fades
Forever and forever when I move.
How dull it is to pause, to make an end,
To rust unburnished, not to shine in use!
As though to breathe were life! Life piled on life
25   Were all too little, and of one to me
Little remains; but every hour is saved
From that eternal silence, something more,
A bringer of new things; and vile it were
For some three suns to store and hoard myself,
30   And this grey spirit yearning in desire
To follow knowledge like a sinking star,
Beyond the utmost bound of human thought.
     This is my son, mine own Telemachus,
To whom I leave the scepter and the isle—
35   Well-loved of me, discerning to fulfill
This labor, by slow prudence to make mild
A rugged people, and through soft degrees
Subdue them to the useful and the good.
Most blameless is he, centered in the sphere
40   Of common duties, decent not to fail
In offices of tenderness, and pay
Meet adoration to my household gods,
When I am gone. He works his work, I mine.
     There lies the port; the vessel puffs her sail;
45   There gloom the dark, broad seas. My mariners,
Souls that have toiled, and wrought, and thought with me—
That ever with a frolic welcome took
The thunder and the sunshine, and opposed
Free hearts, free foreheads—you and I are old;
50   Old age hath yet his honor and his toil.
Death closes all; but something ere the end,
Some work of noble note, may yet be done,
Not unbecoming men that strove with Gods.

---

[2] The daughters of Atlas. They were transformed into a group of stars, and their rising is thought
to predict rain.

The lights begin to twinkle from the rocks;
55 The long day wanes; the slow moon climbs; the deep
Moans round with many voices. Come, my friends,
'Tis not too late to seek a newer world.
Push off, and sitting well in order smite
The sounding furrows; for my purpose holds
60 To sail beyond the sunset, and the baths
Of all the western stars, until I die.
It may be that the gulfs will wash us down;
It may be we shall touch the Happy Isles,
And see the great Achilles, whom we knew.
65 Though much is taken, much abides; and though
We are not now that strength which in old days
Moved earth and heaven, that which we are, we are—
One equal temper of heroic hearts,
Made weak by time and fate, but strong in will
70 To strive, to seek, to find, and not to yield.

Questions

1. Vocabulary: *mete* (3), *lees* (7), *burnished* (23), *prudence* (36), *smite* (58), *abides* (65).
2. *Ulysses* is the Latin name for Odysseus, hero of Homer's epic the *Odyssey*. The scene here portrayed is recounted by Dante in the *Divine Comedy*. Ulysses was a great adventurer in his youth. At what stage of his life do we encounter him in this poem?
3. What is the scene? Whom is Ulysses addressing?
4. Ulysses has accomplished a great deal in his life. What does he want now? What does he intend to do?

The Epistolary Monologue

We all enjoy reading letters, whether addressed to ourselves or to other people. Abelard's love letters to Héloise and the impassioned notes of Dietrich Bonhoeffer from prison still make compelling reading, years after they were written. Dramatic poets, taking on the guise of imagined or historical correspondents, have made good use of the *epistolary*, or letter, form. In a significant way the epistolary monologue is more natural than the forms we have seen so far: the letter is *already* literature, whereas a monologue such as the preceding one is pretending to be spoken and then recorded.

The titles of epistolary poems usually indicate the letter writer as well as the addressee. The following letter is supposed to have been written by a young woman to her husband, a merchant who has been on the road for five months. The poem is prized for its autobiographical compression and the wife's dignity in controlling her emotion. She and her husband have been deeply in love since they were children, and she misses him, but she never utters a word of resentment or reproach.

The River Merchant's Wife, A Letter

While my hair was still cut straight across my forehead
I played about the front gate, pulling flowers.
You came by on bamboo stilts, playing horse,
You walked about my seat, playing with blue plums.
5   And we went on living in the village of Chokan:
Two small people, without dislike or suspicion.

At fourteen I married My Lord you.
I never laughed, being bashful.
Lowering my head, I looked at the wall.
10   Called to, a thousand times, I never looked back.

At fifteen I stopped scowling,
I desired my dust to be mingled with yours
Forever and forever and forever.
Why should I climb the look out?

15   At sixteen you departed,
You went into far Ku-to-yen, by the river of swirling eddies,
And you have been gone five months.
The monkeys make sorrowful noise overhead.

You dragged your feet when you went out.
20   By the gate now, the moss is grown, the different mosses,
Too deep to clear them away!
The leaves fall early this autumn, in wind.
The paired butterflies are already yellow with August
Over the grass in the West garden;
25   They hurt me. I grow older.
If you are coming down through the narrows of the river Kiang,
Please let me know beforehand,
And I will come out to meet you
                As far as Cho-fu-Sa.

Translation from the Chinese by Ezra Pound (1885–1972)

Poetic Dialogues

Do you remember the folk song that goes:

Where have you been, Billie Boy, Billie Boy
Oh, where have you been, charming Billie?

I have been to see my wife,
She's the darling of my life.
She's a young thing and cannot leave her mother.

This is a popular example of a dramatic lyric employing two speakers. Sometimes the words of the primary persona in a poem call for an answer. This need makes for the lively conversation in poetry known as *dramatic dialogue*. In "Billie Boy"

John Crowe Ransom *(Rollie McKenna)*

we overhear a dialogue between a mother and her son about his bride. The mother asks questions about the bride, and Billie delivers comic answers.

The dramatic dialogue is an effective form for exploring contrasts in personality and viewpoint. We often find conflict in poetic dialogues, just as we do in plays and movies. In the following dialogue between an old man and a young lady, John Crowe Ransom sketches a brief but vivid scene. It is a moonlit night in autumn. A beautiful young lady is standing on her piazza (front porch) waiting for her lover. We do not know all this at first; we must read this poem carefully twice in order to understand the dramatic situation. Without knowing the situation, we cannot appreciate the impact of the lover's first speech. The old man has been spying on the lady through a trellis. We can imagine her surprise when he whispers the first stanza to her.

JOHN CROWE RANSOM (1888–1974)

Piazza Piece

—I am a gentleman in a dustcoat trying
To make you hear. Your ears are soft and small
And listen to an old man not at all,
They want the young men's whispering and sighing.
5   But see the roses on your trellis dying
And hear the spectral° singing of the moon;   *ghostly*
For I must have my lovely lady soon,
I am a gentleman in a dustcoat trying.

—I am a lady young in beauty waiting
10   Until my truelove comes, and then we kiss.
But what grey man among the vines is this
Whose words are dry and faint as in a dream?
Back from my trellis, Sir, before I scream!
I am a lady young in beauty waiting.

The old man wants the lovely lady, and soon. He does not have much time. The young lady, who has all the time in the world, has been waiting for her young lover. What does she get? A peeping old man. What does he get? A stern refusal.

This frustration of expectations is called *dramatic irony*, or the *irony of situation*. "Piazza Piece" is a classic example, in which the irony underscores the desperation of the old man's desire and the young woman's vanity. You may wish to reread the other dramatic poems we have studied, especially "Porphyria's Lover" and "The Little Vagabond," and look for instances of dramatic irony.

The Pastoral

An early form of literary dialogue is the *pastoral. Pastor* is the Latin word for herdsman or shepherd, and the classic pastorals were imagined dialogues between shepherds and other rural folk. Written in a high style by urban poets, pastorals express their yearning for an innocence and simplicity that have been lost in the big city. On a similar impulse the courtiers of Louis XIV costumed themselves as shepherds and milkmaids to picnic on the lawns of Versailles. Though the term *pastoral* has come to refer to any idyllic or rural poem, the earliest versions, such as Hesiod's *Works and Days* and Virgil's *Eclogues*, were written as dramatic dialogue.

The following is a dialogue between a fictional shepherd, Ametas, and his girlfriend, Thestylis. Their eloquence is subtle, but their desire is not. They are twisting hay-ropes, but it is obvious they would rather be doing something else.

ANDREW MARVELL (1621–1678)

Ametas and Thestylis Making Hay-Ropes

Ametas.   Think'st thou that this love can stand,
                Whilst thou still dost say me nay?
                Love unpaid does soon disband:
                Love binds love as hay binds hay.

5   *Thestylis.* Think'st thou that this rope would twine
                If we both should turn one way?
                Where both parties so combine,
                Neither love will twist nor hay.

Ametas.   Thus you vain excuses find,
10   Which yourself and us delay:

And love ties a woman's mind
Looser than with ropes of hay.

Thestylis.   What you cannot constant hope
Must be taken as you may.

15   *Ametas.*   Then let's both lay by our rope,
and go kiss within the hay.

Questions

1. Why is Thestylis resisting Ametas? Do you agree with her argument in the second stanza?
2. See "To His Coy Mistress" in Chapter 4. Does Ametas have a *carpe diem* philosophy?

As suggested earlier, poets choose dramatic personae not only to reveal different sides of their own natures, but also to speak for those who cannot speak for themselves. This has given rise to one of the most dramatic forms of poetry, the *posthumous monologue*—the poem spoken by the dead. These poems have an aura of mystery and terror because we know nothing about death and because the act of dying seems so frightening, even though no one has ever been able to tell us about it.

The following poem comes to us from beyond the grave, spoken by a young man killed in air combat during World War II. The first sentence tells us he is young: he went from his mother to the state (or army) like a kitten, with his fur still wet. The ball turret is the armored position on the aircraft, from which the gunner can achieve a full circle of fire.

RANDALL JARRELL (1914–1965)

The Death of the Ball Turret Gunner

From my mother's sleep I fell into the State,
And I hunched in its belly till my wet fur froze.
Six miles from earth, loosed from its dream of life,
I woke to black flak° and the nightmare fighters.   *machine gun fire*
5   When I died they washed me out of the turret with a hose.

Questions

1. What is the "dream of life" referred to in line 3?
2. The speaker mentions in line 2 that he hunched in the State's "belly" until his "wet fur froze." What does this suggest about his response to the military?

EDGAR LEE MASTERS (1869–1950)

Fiddler Jones

The earth keeps some vibration going
There in your heart, and that is you.

And if the people find you can fiddle,
Why, fiddle you must, for all your life.
5   What do you see, a harvest of clover?
Or a meadow to walk through to the river?
The wind's in the corn; you rub your hands
For beeves hereafter ready for market;
Or else you hear the rustle of skirts
10 Like the girls when dancing at Little Grove.
To Cooney Potter a pillar of dust
Or whirling leaves meant ruinous drouth;
They looked to me like Red-Head Sammy

Stepping it off, to "Toor-a-Loor."
15 How could I till my forty acres,
Not to speak of getting more,
With a medley of horns, bassoons and piccolos
Stirred in my brain by crows and robins
And the creak of a windmill—only these?
20 And I never started to plow in my life
That some one did not stop in the road
And take me away to a dance or picnic.
I ended up with forty acres;
I ended up with a broken fiddle—
25 And a broken laugh, and a thousand memories,
And not a single regret.

Questions

1. Vocabulary: *beeves* (8), *drouth* (12).
2. Why did Jones become a fiddler?
3. What did he gain from fiddling? What did he lose?
4. Do you think his was a happy life?

❧ Poems for Further Study

W. B. YEATS (1865–1939)

An Irish Airman Forsees His Death

I know that I shall meet my fate
Somewhere among the clouds above;
Those that I fight I do not hate,
Those that I guard I do not love;
5   My country is Kiltartan Cross,
My countrymen Kiltartan's poor,
No likely end could bring them loss
Or leave them happier than before.
Nor law, nor duty bade me fight,

10 Nor public men, nor cheering crowds,
    A lonely impulse of delight
    Drove to this tumult in the clouds;
    I balanced all, brought all to mind,
    The years to come seemed waste of breath,
15 A waste of breath the years behind
    In balance with this life, this death.

ANTHONY HECHT (1923–)

Tarantula or the Dance of Death

During the plague I came into my own.
It was a time of smoke-pots in the house
Against infection. The blind head of bone
                    Grinned its abuse

5   Like a good democrat at everyone.
    Runes were recited daily, charms were applied.
    That was the time I came into my own.
                        Half Europe died.

    The symptoms are a fever and dark spots
10 First on the hands, then on the face and neck,
    But even before the body, the mind rots.
                        You can be sick

    Only a day with it before you're dead.
    But the most curious part of it is the dance.
15 The victim goes, in short, out of his head.
                        A sort of trance

    Glazes the eyes, and then the muscles take
    His will away from him, the legs begin
    Their funeral jig, the arms and belly shake
20   Like souls in sin.

    Some, caught in these convulsions, have been known
    To fall from windows, fracturing the spine.
    Others have drowned in streams. The smooth head-stone,
                        The box of pine,

25 Are not for the likes of these. Moreover, flame
    Is powerless against contagion.
    That was the black winter when I came
                        Into my own.

ROBERT BROWNING (1812–1889)

My Last Duchess[3]

That's my last Duchess painted on the wall,
Looking as if she were alive. I call

---

[3] This famous monologue was inspired by Browning's first trip to Italy, in 1834. The Duke of Ferrara typifies the cruelty of the Renaissance beneath its superficial beauty. He is showing the portrait of his late wife, whom he has done away with, to a representative of the father of his intended bride.

That piece a wonder, now: Frà Pandolf's hands
Worked busily a day, and there she stands.
5 Will 't please you sit and look at her? I said
"Frà Pandolf" by design, for never read
Strangers like you that pictured countenance,
The depth and passion of its earnest glance,
But to myself they turned (since none puts by
10 The curtain I have drawn for you, but I)
And seemed as they would ask me, if they durst,
How such a glance came there; so, not the first
Are you to turn as ask thus. Sir, 't was not
Her husband's presence only, called that spot
15 Of joy into the Duchess' cheek: perhaps
Frà Pandolf chanced to say "Her mantle laps
Over my lady's wrist too much," or "Paint
Must never hope to reproduce the faint
Half-flush that dies along her throat": such stuff
20 Was courtesy, she thought, and cause enough
For calling up that spot of joy. She had
A heart—how shall I say?—too soon made glad,
Too easily impressed; she liked whate'er
She looked on, and her looks went everywhere.
25 Sir, 't was all one! My favour at her breast,
The dropping of the daylight in the West,
The bough of cherries some officious fool
Broke in the orchard for her, the white mule
She rode with round the terrace—all and each
30 Would draw from her alike the approving speech,
Or blush, at least. She thanked men,—good! but thanked
Somehow—I know not how—as if she ranked
My gift of a nine-hundred-years-old name
With anybody's gift. Who'd stoop to blame
35 This sort of trifling? Even had you skill
In speech—(which I have not)—to make your will
Quite clear to such an one, and say, "Just this
Or that in you disgusts me; here you miss,
Or there exceed the mark"—and if she let
40 Herself be lessoned so, nor plainly set
Her wits to yours, forsooth, and made excuse,
—E'en then would be some stooping; and I choose
Never to stoop. Oh sir, she smiled, no doubt,
Whene'er I passed her; but who passed without
45 Much the same smile? This grew; I gave commands;
Then all smiles stopped together. There she stands
As if alive. Will 't please you rise? We'll meet
The company below, then. I repeat,
The Count your master's known munificence
50 Is ample warrant that no just pretence

Of mine for dowry will be disallowed;
Though his fair daughter's self, as I avowed
At starting, is my object. Nay, we'll go
Together down, sir! Notice Neptune, though,
55 Taming a sea-horse, thought a rarity,
Which Claus of Innsbruck cast in bronze for me!

MICHAEL HARPER (1938–)

A Mother Speaks:
The Algiers Motel Incident, Detroit[4]

It's too dark to see black
in the windows of Woodward
or Virginia Park.
The undertaker
5 pushed his body back
into place
with plastic and gum
but it wouldn't
hold water.
10 When I looked
for marks
or lineament
or fine stitching
I was led away
15 without seeing
this plastic
face they'd built
that was not my son's.
They tied the eye
20 torn out
by shotgun
into place
and his shattered
arm cut away
25 with his buttocks
that remained.
My son's gone
by white hands
though he said
30 to his last word—
"Oh I'm so sorry,
officer, I broke your gun."

---

[4] During the night of July 25–26, 1967, while rioting was going on, three policemen killed three unarmed black men. The incident is the subject of a book by John Hersey, *The Algiers Motel Incident.*

FRANK O'HARA (1926–1966)

A True Account of Talking to the Sun at Fire Island

The Sun woke me this morning loud
and clear, saying "Hey! I've been
trying to wake you up for fifteen
minutes. Don't be so rude, you are
5   only the second poet I've ever chosen
to speak to personally
                    so why
aren't you more attentive? If I could
burn you through the window I would
10   to wake you up. I can't hang around
here all day."
             "Sorry, Sun, I stayed
up late last night talking to Hal."

"When I woke up Mayakovsky he was
15   a lot more prompt" the Sun said
petulantly. "Most people are up
already waiting to see if I'm going
to put in an appearance."
                  I tried
20   to apologize "I missed you yesterday."
"That's better" he said. "I didn't
know you'd come out." "You may be
wondering why I've come so close?"
"Yes" I said beginning to feel hot
25   wondering if maybe he wasn't burning me
anyway.
          "Frankly I wanted to tell you
I like your poetry. I see a lot
on my rounds and you're okay. You may
30   not be the greatest thing on earth, but
you're different. Now, I've heard some
say you're crazy, they being excessively
calm themselves to my mind, and other
crazy poets think that you're a boring
35   reactionary. Not me.
            Just keep on
like I do and pay no attention. You'll
find that people always will complain
about the atmosphere, either too hot
40   or too cold too bright or too dark, days
too short or too long.
               If you don't appear
at all one day they think you're lazy
or dead. Just keep right on, I like it.

45   And don't worry about your lineage
poetic or natural. The Sun shines on
the jungle, you know, on the tundra
the sea, the ghetto. Wherever you were
I knew it and saw you moving. I was waiting
50   for you to get to work.
                        And now that you
are making your own days, so to speak,
even if no one reads you but me
you won't be depressed. Not
55   everyone can look up, even at me. It
hurts their eyes."
                "Oh Sun, I'm so grateful to you!"

"Thanks and remember I'm watching. It's
easier for me to speak to you out
60   here. I don't have to slide down
between buildings to get your ear.
I know you love Manhattan, but
you ought to look up more often.
                         And
65   always embrace things, people earth
sky stars, as I do, freely and with
the appropriate sense of space. That
is your inclination, known in the heavens
and you should follow it to hell, if
70   necessary, which I doubt.
                    Maybe we'll
speak again in Africa, of which I too
am specially fond. Go back to sleep now
Frank, and I may leave a tiny poem
75   in that brain of yours as my farewell."

"Sun, don't go!" I was awake
at last. "No, go I must, they're calling
me."
      "Who are they?"
80   Rising he said "Some
day you'll know. They're calling to you
too." Darkly he rose, and then I slept.

PETER KLAPPERT (1942–)

Mail at Your New Address

I

Did your car get you to Florida?
I know you don't like me
to say so but Mrs. Wilson says
the same thing. Please tell me

5   (collegt) if you are all
       there. I hope you do not
       sleep or do anything on the road.
       In Georgia.
                    Your father
10   should see all the leaves.
       Walter has not raked
       a girlfriend up the street and wont
       rake anymore. Watch out or
       theyll have the same thing Mrs. Wilson
15   says the friend stayed and look
       what happened at Cornell?
                         Even if you changed
       college is no reason to come home.
       But get a haircut. I know
20   the dean doesn't like you
       to look like a gardener.

                    II
       There have been so many deaths
       due to carbon m. poisoning
       that this is just
25   a note to suggest you leave
       a little air come into your room. Also,

       I hope you don't get involved
       with young men or older
       or made from popies (?) and Hippy's.
30   I hope you are not letting the drugs
       get you. And don't get mixed up
       with drugs. It might spoil your change
       for getting the cert. you are working for.
       Remember, it is costing quite a lot.

35   Don't scold. I am afraid of your
       trips to and near Chicago.

6  Images

Seeing Is Feeling

Poets have traditionally admired the way pictures can "speak" to us without the use of language. In fact, many poets envy the painter's or photographer's ability to capture a moment in all its complexity, to freeze life in midcourse and render all its detail, texture, and color simultaneously.

Like painters, poets have their own images. An *image* is a group of words that records sense impressions directly. Images usually record what poets see, but they can also record sounds, tastes, and smells. For example, T. S. Eliot begins his poem "Preludes" by imagining a winter evening that "settles down/with smell of steaks in passageways." We are asked to recall the greasy, smoky cooking smells that hover in the hallways of apartment houses or in close tenement alleys. The odor is familiar and not entirely pleasant. If we concentrate, we can bring to mind the slightly bitter smell of burnt animal fat. Eliot wants us to remember that experience and all the fatigue, hunger, and unpleasantness that go along with it.

Poets use images not merely to give us sensory impressions of a person, place, or thing, but also to evoke emotions. The best poets choose images that suggest to the reader precisely the feelings they wish to convey. The best images evoke an almost magical reaction. A few words will suggest an entire picture to our minds, which in turn will elicit deep—often unexpected—feelings.

Images differ from description in subtle but important ways. A description tells us about an object; an image presents us with the object. A description gives us the information we should know; an image gives us an experience we should feel. Readers have difficulty with highly imagistic writing when they do not take time to let the image register on their imaginations and emotions. Try to picture what the poet presents, and focus on the image long enough to react to it emotionally.

Haiku

The Japanese have concentrated on the power that a single image can produce. The *haiku* often contain a single, simple event that suggests to the reader a variety of feelings and associations. Although poets can place many restrictions on themselves, the haiku generally has some distinct features. It usually contains a seasonal reference and is about seventeen syllables long (commonly with a first line of five syllables, a second of seven, and a third of five). Since the following are translations, the usual syllabic criteria have not been closely met.

> For the child who won't
> stop crying, she lights a lamp
> in the autumn dusk.
>
> —*Kawahigashi Kekigodo (1873–1937)*

> To the sun's path
> The hollyhocks lean
> in the May rains.
>
> —*Matsuo Basho (1644–1694)*

> At midnight
> a distant door is slid shut.
>
> At the dark bottom
> of a well I find my face.
>
> —*Ozaki Hosai (1885–1926)*

The first of these poems shows a mother's efforts to comfort her child by lighting a lamp as the sky grows dark. The poet calls our attention not only to the mother's care, but also to her loneliness and the futility of her actions. In the second poem we sense the natural harmony of spring as the flowers bend toward the sun. In the third poem there is something final, perhaps even sinister, in the far-off sound of a closing door. In the last poem the poet registers both surprise and foreboding as he sees his reflection in the dark well water.

The Japanese have cultivated the limited image, but most Western writers feel the need to expand images or combine them with other images or commentary. The following is an example of an expanded image.

WILLIAM CARLOS WILLIAMS (1883–1963)

The Great Figure

> Among the rain
> and lights
> I saw the figure 5
> in gold
> 5   on a red
> firetruck

moving
tense
unheeded
10   to gong clangs
siren howls
and wheels rumbling
through the dark city.

Questions

1. Vocabulary: *unheeded* (9).
2. How many senses are employed in presenting this image?
3. Eliminate the lines that refer to senses other than sight. Is the poem enhanced? Weakened? Why?
4. Is there any progression in the sensations the poem presents?
5. What do you feel when you see a speeding fire truck? Did Williams capture the experience for you? If not, what did he leave out?

William Carlos Williams makes the poem a single sentence to underscore that he is presenting a single image. Yet this is an image in constant motion. The fire truck does not stay still long enough to allow a clearly focused picture. Were this a photograph, the fire truck would be blurred as it emerges out of "the rain/ and lights" and plunges back into "the dark city." Williams is careful to record the actual way we see a fast-moving object. We do not see it whole; we see bits and pieces of it. Williams's eye catches the gold number 5 painted on the truck before he notices the truck itself.

I Saw the Figure 5 in Gold, by Charles Demuth *(The Metropolitan Museum of Art, New York, The Alfred Stieglitz Collection, 1949)*

The following poem also controls the order in which the image is revealed. What governs the order of details in the poem?

THEODORE ROETHKE (1908–1963)

Child on Top of a Greenhouse

The wind billowing out the seat of my britches,
My feet crackling splinters of glass and dried putty,
The half-grown chrysanthemums staring up like accusers,
Up through the streaked glass, flashing with sunlight,
5   A few white clouds all rushing eastward,
A line of elms plunging and tossing like horses,
And everyone, everyone pointing up and shouting!

Questions

1. Who is the speaker in the poem? Through whose eyes do we see the event?
2. What does the child feel about being on top of the greenhouse? Is he frightened, delighted, surprised, guilty, fascinated? All of these?
3. Do the spectators share the child's feelings? If not, why not?
4. Why do you think the poem is in one sentence?

Combining Images

In both "The Great Figure" and "Child on Top of a Greenhouse," the authors expand the image by adding details to a central event. But poets also like to combine very different images. The result is often like a photograph in which one image is superimposed on another so that we see both images simultaneously. "In a Station of the Metro" is such a poem; it records Ezra Pound's impression of entering the Paris subway.

EZRA POUND (1885–1972)

In a Station of the Metro

The apparition of these faces in the crowd,
Petals on a wet, black bough.

This poem is both surprising and right. The pale faces of the people emerging from a subway *do* look like petals on a tree. Yet if we think about these two images, we find that they are very different. The word *apparition* suggests the deathly and supernatural. Petals, however, are natural—signs of renewed life. How can these two images so easily share the same poem? This mystery is part of the logic of poetry, the reasonings of the heart of which, according to Pascal, the mind knows nothing.

"In a Station of the Metro" is among the most famous examples of poems by *les Imagistes*, who, despite their French title, were mostly American poets, including at times Pound, Amy Lowell, Hilda Doolittle, and William Carlos Williams. They believed in the direct treatment of objects and feelings and in using "no word that doesn't contribute to the presentation." "In a Station of the Metro" started out as a poem sixty lines long. Pound spent months whittling the poem to these two intense lines.

Arthur Symons's "Pastel" contains an imagistic effect similar to the one in Pound's short poem.

ARTHUR SYMONS (1865–1948)

Pastel

The light of our cigarettes
    Went and came in the gloom:
    It was dark in the little room.

Dark, and then, in the dark,
5   Sudden, a flash, a glow,
    And a hand and a ring I know.

And then, through the dark, a flush
    Ruddy and vague, the grace—
    A rose—of her lyric face.

Questions

1. How does Symons prepare for the image of the rose?
2. The rose is a common image. How does Symons make it fresh? Is it expected?

The poems we have read so far have all used images to evoke visual sensations. But images can also suggest any kind of sensation: taste, smell, touch. In "Sound," Jim Harrison suggests the way sound moves away from its source.

JIM HARRISON (1937–)

Sound

At dawn I squat on the garage
with snuff under a lip
to sweeten the roofing nails—
my shoes and pant cuffs
5   are wet with dew.
In the orchard the peach trees
sway with the loud
weight of birds, green fruit, yellow haze.
And my hammer—the cold head taps,

10   then swings its first full arc;
       the sound echoes against the barn,
       muffled in the loft,
       and out the other side, then lost
       in the noise of the birds
15   as they burst from the trees.

Questions

1. What senses are referred to in lines 1–5? Why do you suppose there are no references to sound in the opening?
2. Does the noise dissipate after the speaker hammers, or does the sound increase?
3. Why do you suppose Harrison bothered to record this simple occurrence? Are there any seemingly trivial events that stick in your mind as noteworthy? What is memorable about them?

Synesthesia

In "Sound" Harrison writes that the trees "sway with the loud/weight of birds." These lines may strike you as odd. In what sense can a weight be loud? A weight usually is light or heavy, not loud or quiet. This manner of speaking of one sense in terms of another is called *synesthesia*, and it is really quite common. People speak of "hot pink," a "loud necktie," "cool music," or a "spicy story." Each of these expressions is synesthetic.

ANN STANFORD (1916–)

Listening to Color

Now that blue has had its say
has told its winds, wall, sick
sky even, I can listen to white

sweet poison flowers   hedge autumn
5   under a sky white at the edges
like faded paper. My message keeps

turning to yellow where few leaves
set up first fires over branches
tips of flames only, nothing here finished yet.

Questions

1. What are the synesthetic images in the poem?
2. In what ways do colors speak to us? Can you think of ways in which colors communicate? How do they speak to Stanford?
3. In what time of year is the poem set? How does nature communicate time?
4. Why does Stanford say in line 9 that nothing is finished? How does the word *yet* modify the sense of finality? How does it reinforce the sense of finality?

Images and Commentary

The most common way in which poets use images is in combination with commentary. The poet sees things and then meditates on their significance. In the following poem a sequence of images concludes in a line of commentary.

JAMES WRIGHT (1927–1980)

Lying in a Hammock at William Duffy's Farm in Pine Island, Minnesota

Over my head, I see the bronze butterfly,
Asleep on the black trunk,
Blowing like a leaf in green shadow.
Down the ravine behind the empty house,
5   The cowbells follow one another
Into the distances of the afternoon.
To my right,
In a field of sunlight between two pines,
The droppings of last year's horses
10 Blaze up into golden stones.
I lean back, as the evening darkens and comes on.
A chicken hawk floats over, looking for home.
I have wasted my life.

Questions

1. Is there any order to the observations? Or are they merely random?
2. Does Wright see anything unusual? If not, is that important to the poem?
3. Is the poem self-pitying? Do you feel sorry for Wright? Has he wasted his life?

Readers coming to this poem for the first time are often startled by the last line, which seems terribly out of place. At first it appears that Wright means that watching nature is a waste of time. On a closer reading, however, we realize that Wright means just the opposite: everything other than observing the beauties of nature is a waste. The poem records his sad recognition that he has not spent enough time lying in hammocks, looking at the world around him.

Wright's poem also illustrates two important ways poets make their work vivid: (1) by giving details rather than generalized pictures, and (2) by being specific about the details. For example, Wright gives us not a general picture of the landscape, but briefly worded details about particular things: the butterfly, the leaf, the cowbells. Because we see these small things so clearly, we have a sense of seeing the entire picture clearly. Second, Wright is specific about details. He writes not merely that a bird floats over, but, "A chicken hawk floats over, looking for home." By giving us the precise term, he makes the scene more vivid. Well-chosen, specific details are more powerful than general descriptions, both emotionally and imagistically.

There is a limit, however, to the amount of detail that is useful. If Wright had written, "I see a monarch butterfly with a wing span of three inches and a length of an inch and three quarters," he would certainly have been more specific, but he would not have been more vivid. We can easily imagine a bronze butterfly, but we cannot picture something as specific as one with a certain wing span. By giving too much information, a writer can make an image more difficult to imagine and thereby sacrifice the emotional impact of the scene. The great writers have an instinct for the appropriate detail to make a scene vivid.

The techniques Wright uses have been used by poets throughout the centuries. "The Soote Season" was written in the sixteenth century by Henry Howard, Earl of Surrey, the son of the wealthiest man in England. Like Wright's poem, it also concludes with a surprising last line.

HENRY HOWARD, EARL OF SURREY (1517–1547)

The Soote° Season

sweet

The soote season, that bud and bloom forth brings,	
With green hath clad the hill and eke° the vale;	_also_
The nightingale with feathers new she sings;	
The turtle° to her make° hath told her tale.	_turtle dove_ _mate_
5 Summer is come, for every spray now springs;	
The hart hath hung his old head on the pale;	
The buck in brake his winter coat he flings,	
The fishes float with new repairéd scale;	
The adder all her slough away she slings,	
10 The swift swallow pursueth the fliés small;	
The busy bee her honey now she mings.°	_mingles_
Winter is worn, that was the flowers' bale.°	_harm_
And thus I see among these pleasant things,	
Each care decays, and yet my sorrow springs.	

Questions

1. Vocabulary: _vale_ (2), _adder_ (9).
2. Why do you suppose the speaker is sad?
3. Has summer arrived, as the poet proclaims in line 5? If not, why does he say so?
4. Are there any unexpected or unusual images in his catalogue? If so, how do they relate to the others?

Landscapes

Occasionally a friend or relative is so closely associated with a particular place or scene that, when we see the scene again, all our feelings and memories of the person revive. In "Neutral Tones" Thomas Hardy describes his former friend in terms of a landscape.

Thomas Hardy *(Dorset County Museum, Dorchester, England)*

THOMAS HARDY (1840–1928)

Neutral Tones

We stood by a pond that winter day,
And the sun was white, as though chidden of God,
And a few leaves lay on the starving sod;
    —They had fallen from an ash, and were gray.

5   Your eyes on me were as eyes that rove
Over tedious riddles of years ago;
And some words played between us to and fro
    On which lost the more by our love.

The smile on your mouth was the deadest thing
10   Alive enough to have strength to die;
And a grin of bitterness swept thereby
    Like an ominous bird a-wing. . . .

Since then, keen lessons that love deceives,
And wrings with wrong, have shaped to me
15   Your face, and the God-curst sun, and a tree,
    And a pond edged with grayish leaves.

Questions

1. Vocabulary: *chidden* (2), *rove* (5), *tedious* (6), *ominous* (12).
2. Whom is the poet addressing?
3. Why is he speaking to her? What has happened between them?

4. What is the speaker's feeling toward the woman? Does he express his feelings directly or indirectly?
5. How do you think the woman might respond?

Poets have also used landscapes as a starting point for meditation. You may have had a similar experience while sitting beside a lake or ocean, or looking out across a valley or mountain range. At first you were attentive to the world around you, but soon you lost yourself in thought. Sometimes we meditate so deeply that we do not "return to reality" for a long time; and, when we do, reality seems to have changed. M. H. Abrams has called the kind of poem that records this process "the greater romantic lyric" because so many poets of the early nineteenth century wrote poems of this sort. Typically, these lyrics have three sections. The first section presents the landscape; the second section is the meditation; and the third section recreates the landscape in light of the poet's intervening insights. "Dover Beach" is a classic lyric of this sort. It records Matthew Arnold's visit to Dover, a seaside resort and the point in England closest to France.

MATTHEW ARNOLD (1822–1888)

• Dover Beach

The sea is calm tonight.
The tide is full, the moon lies fair
Upon the straits—on the French coast the light
Gleams and is gone; the cliffs of England stand,
5   Glimmering and vast, out in the tranquil bay.
Come to the window, sweet is the night air!
Only, from the long line of spray
Where the sea meets the moon-blanched land,
Listen! you hear the grating roar
10   Of pebbles which the waves draw back, and fling,
At their return, up the high strand,
Begin, and cease, and then again begin,
With tremulous cadence slow, and bring
The eternal note of sadness in.

15   Sophocles[1] long ago
Heard it on the Aegean,[2] and it brought
Into his mind the turbid ebb and flow
Of human misery;[3] we
Find also in the sound a thought,
20   Hearing it by this distant northern sea.

The Sea of Faith
Was once, too, at the full, and round earth's shore

---

[1] Sophocles was a Greek playwright of the fifth century B.C.
[2] Aegean Sea, the waters between Greece and Asia Minor.
[3] See Sophocles' *Antigone*, lines 583 ff.

Lay like the folds of a bright girdle° furled.   *sash*
But now I only hear
25 Its melancholy, long, withdrawing roar,
Retreating, to the breath
Of the night wind, down the vast edges drear
And naked shingles° of the world.   *beach pebbles*

Ah, love, let us be true
30 To one another! for the world, which seems
To lie before us like a land of dreams,
So various, so beautiful, so new,
Hath really neither joy, nor love, nor light,
Nor certitude, nor peace, nor help for pain;
35 And we are here as on a darkling plain
Swept with confused alarms of struggle and flight,
Where ignorant armies clash by night.

Questions

1. Vocabulary: *straits* (3), *blanched* (8), *tremulous* (13), *cadence* (13), *turbid* (17), *furled* (23), *certitude* (34).
2. Compare the opening description (lines 1–14) with the closing (lines 35–37). What accounts for the difference? Which images are most powerful?
3. Is the sadness Arnold feels a modern sadness or one that has always been with humankind?
4. According to Arnold, how can humanity avoid feelings of despair? Does he hold much hope for these methods?
5. Anthony Hecht has imagined, in his poem "The Dover Bitch" (page 410), how a woman might react to this poem if she received it. How would you respond?
6. Do you think conditions of life have changed since 1851, when Arnold wrote this poem?

Meanings of Words

Poets signal how we should respond to an image not only through commentary, but also by their choice of words. Most words have two messages: *denotative* and *connotative*. The denotative meaning is the dictionary meaning: what the word objectively signifies. But words also have connotations: associations with, for instance, social class, values, or historical periods.

We might call the same building a home, a residence, a mansion, or an estate. Each word carries a similar denotative meaning, but the words have various connotations. For example, *mansion* is a much more formal word than *home*. The word *home* evokes images of a family enjoying a television program or conversing in the kitchen, their car parked in the driveway. The word *mansion* suggests a book-lined study, quiet talks over sherry, a limousine in the garage.

Words also suggest attitudes or values. If we speak of someone's attitude as "devil-may-care," we might approve of it. If we call the same attitude "irresponsible," we appear to disapprove.

Exercise

The following are groups of roughly synonymous words. State how the connotations of the words differ, and use each word in a sentence that highlights its connotative meaning.

 1. loaded with money, very rich, very wealthy
 2. front door, entrance, portal
 3. bushes, undergrowth, shrubbery
 4. say yes, agree, state in the affirmative
 5. ending, finishing, concluding
 6. sailor, seaman, mariner
 7. letter, correspondence, epistle
 8. without sound, quiet, silent
 9. wet, damp, moist
10. backside, rear end, behind

In the following poem we have italicized a number of key words whose connotative meaning directs our response to the images. Although the poem is mostly images—the overt commentary is confined to the first two lines—the poet's attitude is anything but neutral.

HENRY DAVID THOREAU (1817–1862)

Pray to What Earth Does This Sweet Cold Belong

Pray to what earth does this *sweet* cold belong,
Which asks no duties and no conscience?
The moon goes up by leaps her *cheerful* path
In some far summer stratum of the sky,
5   While stars with their *cold* shine *bedot* her way.
The fields *gleam mildly* back upon the sky,
And far and near upon the *leafless* shrubs
The snow dust still *emits* a *silver* light.
Under the hedge, where *drift* banks are their screen,
10   The titmice now pursue their *downy* dreams,
As often in the *sweltering* summer nights
The bee doth drop asleep in the flower cup,
When evening overtakes him with his load.
By the brooksides, in the *still genial* night,
15   The more *adventurous* wanderer may hear
The *crystals* shoot and form, and winter slow
Increase his rule by *gentlest* summer means.

Questions

1. What is Thoreau's attitude toward the winter?
2. Why is he surprised that an earthly winter is so sweet?
3. In what sense does the winter ask neither duties nor conscience?

4. Is there any order to these images? Why does the image of the moon precede the image of the frozen brook? Does this order condition our response to the scene?

An easy way to observe how the poet manipulates the reader's attitude is to eliminate or alter the key words of the poem. Consider how our attitude would change had Thoreau written:

> The fields *reflect* the sky,
> And far and near upon the *barren* shrubs
> The snow dust still *gives off* a *metallic* light.

Exercise

In the following poem, underline the key words whose connotative meaning directs the reader's attitude. Eliminate or alter them to suggest a different or opposite attitude.

GARY SNYDER (1930–)

Oil

soft rainsqualls on the swells
south of the Bonins,[4] late at night. Light
from the empty mess-hall
throws back bulky shadows
5   of winch and fairlead
over the slanting fantail where I stand.

but for men on watch in the engine room,
the man at the wheel, the lookout in the bow.
the crew sleeps in cots on deck
10   or narrow iron bunks down drumming
passageways below.

the ship burns with a furnace heart
steam veins and copper nerves
quivers and slightly twists and always goes—
15   easy roll of the hull and deep
vibration of the turbine underfoot

bearing what all these
crazed, hooked nations need:
steel plates and
20   long injections of pure oil.

Surrealistic Imagery

Sometimes the images a poet asks us to picture are not strictly those we see in the actual world. When Gary Snyder writes, "Light/from the empty mess-hall/

---

[4] Island group in the western Pacific.

throws back bulky shadows," we can easily imagine the actual scene. If someone were present, he or she might be able to photograph it. In Blake's "London," however, we are invited to picture things that could not be photographed, such as "mind-forg'd manacles."

WILLIAM BLAKE (1757–1827)

• London

I wander thro' each charter'd⁵ street,
Near where the charter'd Thames does flow,
And mark in every face I meet
Marks of weakness, marks of woe.

5 In every cry of every Man,
In every Infant's cry of fear,
In every voice, in every ban,
The mind-forg'd manacles I hear.

How the Chimney-sweeper's cry
10 Every blackning Church appalls;
And the hapless Soldier's sigh
Runs in blood down Palace walls.

But most thro' midnight streets I hear
How the youthful Harlot's curse
15 Blasts the new-born Infant's tear,
And blights with plagues the Marriage hearse.

Questions

1. Vocabulary: *manacles* (8), *hapless* (11).
2. What does Blake mean in lines 1–2 when he calls the streets and river "charter'd"? What feelings do these details evoke?
3. What does Blake mean by "mind-forg'd manacles"? Can you think of any way in which you handcuff your own actions?
4. In what sense does the chimney sweeper's cry appall the church?
5. How does the harlot blast the child's tear? Why does she curse?

Although Blake wrote "London" nearly two hundred years ago, he used a technique we think of as modern. In lines 11–12 he wrote:

And the hapless Soldier's sigh
Runs in blood down Palace walls.

The image is more complicated than the synesthetic images we have observed in other poems. He is speaking not of a watery sigh, but of a sigh that "runs in blood." The image contains the kind of concentration (and perhaps illogic) that

⁵ For a lengthy discussion of this word, see the Appendix, pages 452–453.

occurs in dreams. It is almost as if the soldier had been shot in front of the palace, but we do not see the execution. Rather, we hear the sigh and see the bloodstain, or, more precisely, we experience the two merged together. This dreamlike concentration of image, known as *surrealistic imagery*, is one of the techniques used in surrealistic poetry. Why do poets use such techniques? We might as well wonder why dream images are so condensed. In highly emotional states, fine distinctions become blurred; the sigh and the blood become one experience, not separated by time.

PIERRE REVERDY (1889–1960)

Departure

The horizon lowers
   The days lengthen
   Voyage
 A heart hops in a cage
5   A bird sings
   At the edge of death
Another door is about to open
   At the far end of the corridor
   Shines
10   One star
 A dark lady
  Lantern on a departing train

Translation by Michael Benedikt (1935–)

Questions

1. What dreamlike elements are present in this poem?
2. What sort of emotions does this poem evoke?
3. What is the significance of the door about to be opened in line 7?

Notice how this poem contains the type of confusion that occurs in dreams. It is not the *bird* that hops in a cage and the *heart* that is at the edge of death. They have exchanged places.

Poets use images for a number of purposes: to place us in a landscape or a dream, to present familiar people to us, to bring us to unknown lands. Images can be realistic, a mixture of sensory experiences, or dreamlike. But whatever the kinds of image, the poet always uses imagery to evoke emotions more fully and more powerfully than could mere statements of feelings.

Suggestions for Essayists

1. Discuss how images in popular culture (in magazines, films, and advertisements) control our emotions and ideas.

2. Describe a place where you have been and the meditations it evoked.
3. Compare Matthew Arnold's "Dover Beach" with Anthony Hecht's "The Dover Bitch" on page 410.

Suggestions for Poets

1. Select a series of different emotions. Then write one image for each emotion that will evoke the feeling for the reader.
2. Evoke a landscape in images.
3. Suggest your feelings toward a person by evoking the landscape that most typifies that person.

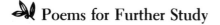 Poems for Further Study

WILLIAM WORDSWORTH (1770–1850)

• Lines Composed a Few Miles above Tintern Abbey

Composed a Few Miles above Tintern Abbey on Revisiting the Banks of the Wye during a Tour. July 13, 1798

     Five years have passed; five summers, with the length
Of five long winters! and again I hear
These waters, rolling from their mountain-springs
With a soft inland murmur. Once again

5   Do I behold these steep and lofty cliffs,
That on a wild secluded scene impress
Thoughts of more deep seclusion; and connect
The landscape with the quiet of the sky.
The day is come when I again repose

10   Here, under this dark sycamore, and view
These plots of cottage ground, these orchard tufts,
Which at this season, with their unripe fruits,
Are clad in one green hue, and lose themselves
'Mid groves and copses. Once again I see

15   These hedgerows, hardly hedgerows, little lines
Of sportive wood run wild; these pastoral farms,
Green to the very door; and wreaths of smoke
Sent up, in silence, from among the trees!
With some uncertain notice, as might seem

20   Of vagrant dwellers in the houseless woods,
Or of some Hermit's cave, where by his fire
The Hermit sits alone.

                  These beauteous forms,
Through a long absence, have not been to me
As is a landscape to a blind man's eye;

25   But oft, in lonely rooms, and 'mid the din
Of towns and cities, I have owed to them,
In hours of weariness, sensations sweet,

Felt in the blood, and felt along the heart;
And passing even into my purer mind,
30   With tranquil restoration—feelings too
Of unremembered pleasure; such, perhaps,
As have no slight or trivial influence
On that best portion of a good man's life,
His little, nameless, unremembered, acts
35   Of kindness and of love. Nor less, I trust,
To them I may have owed another gift,
Of aspect more sublime; that blessed mood,
In which the burthen of the mystery,
In which the heavy and the weary weight
40   Of all this unintelligible world,
Is lightened—that serene and blesséd mood,
In which the affections gently lead us on—
Until, the breath of this corporeal frame
And even the motion of our human blood
45   Almost suspended, we are laid asleep
In body, and become a living soul;
While with an eye made quiet by the power
Of harmony, and the deep power of joy,
We see into the life of things.
                       If this
50   Be but a vain belief, yet, oh! how oft—
In darkness and amid the many shapes
Of joyless daylight; when the fretful stir
Unprofitable, and the fever of the world,
Have hung upon the beatings of my heart—
55   How oft, in spirit, have I turned to thee,
O sylvan Wye! thou wanderer through the woods,
How often has my spirit turned to thee!

    And now, with gleams of half-extinguished thought
With many recognitions dim and faint,
60   And somewhat of a sad perplexity,
The picture of the mind revives again;
While here I stand, not only with the sense
Of present pleasure, but with pleasing thoughts
That in this moment there is life and food
65   For future years. And so I dare to hope,
Though changed, no doubt, from what I was when first
I came among these hills; when like a roe
I bounded o'er the mountains, by the sides
Of the deep rivers, and the lonely streams,
70   Wherever nature led—more like a man
Flying from something that he dreads than one
Who sought the thing he loved. For nature then
(The coarser pleasures of my boyish days,
And their glad animal movements all gone by)
75   To me was all in all.—I cannot paint

What then I was. The sounding cataract
Haunted me like a passion; the tall rock,
The mountain, and the deep and gloomy wood,
Their colors and their forms, were then to me
80 An appetite; a feeling and a love,
That had no need of a remoter charm,
By thought supplied, nor any interest
Unborrowed from the eye.—That time is past,
And all its aching joys are now no more,
85 And all its dizzy raptures. Not for this
Faint° I, nor mourn nor murmur; other gifts   *lose heart*
Have followed; for such loss, I would believe,
Abundant recompense. For I have learned
To look on nature, not as in the hour
90 Of thoughtless youth; but hearing oftentimes
The still, sad music of humanity,
Nor harsh nor grating, though of ample power
To chasten and subdue. And I have felt
A presence that disturbs me with the joy
95 Of elevated thoughts; a sense sublime
Of something far more deeply interfused,
Whose dwelling is the light of setting suns,
And the round ocean and the living air,
And the blue sky, and in the mind of man:
100 A motion and a spirit, that impels
All thinking things, all objects of all thought,
And rolls through all things. Therefore am I still
A lover of the meadows and the woods,
And mountains; and of all that we behold
105 From this green earth; of all the mighty world
Of eye, and ear—both what they half create,
And what perceive; well pleased to recognize
In nature and the language of the sense
The anchor of my purest thoughts, the nurse,
110 The guide, the guardian of my heart, and soul
Of all my moral being.
                                        Nor perchance,
If I were not thus taught, should I the more
Suffer my genial spirits[6] to decay:
For thou art with me here upon the banks
115 Of this fair river; thou my dearest Friend,[7]
My dear, dear Friend; and in thy voice I catch
The language of my former heart, and read
My former pleasures in the shooting lights
Of thy wild eyes. Oh! yet a little while
120 May I behold in thee what I was once,
My dear, dear Sister! and this prayer I make,

---

[6] Genius, a spirit that watches over a place or person.
[7] Wordsworth's sister, Dorothy.

Knowing that Nature never did betray
The heart that loved her; 'tis her privilege,
Through all the years of this our life, to lead
125   From joy to joy: for she can so inform
The mind that is within us, so impress
With quietness and beauty, and so feed
With lofty thoughts, that neither evil tongues,
Rash judgments, nor the sneers of selfish men,
130   Nor greetings where no kindness is, nor all
The dreary intercourse of daily life,
Shall e'er prevail against us, or disturb
Our cheerful faith, that all which we behold
Is full of blessings. Therefore let the moon
135   Shine on thee in thy solitary walk;
And let the misty mountain winds be free
To blow against thee: and, in after years,
When these wild ecstasies shall be matured
Into a sober pleasure; when thy mind
140   Shall be a mansion for all lovely forms,
Thy memory be as a dwelling place
For all sweet sounds and harmonies; oh! then,
If solitude, or fear, or pain, or grief
Should be thy portion, with what healing thoughts
145   Of tender joy wilt thou remember me,
And these my exhortations! Nor, perchance—
If I should be where I no more can hear
Thy voice, nor catch from thy wild eyes these gleams
Of past existence—wilt thou then forget
150   That on the banks of this delightful stream
We stood together; and that I, so long
A worshiper of Nature, hither came
Unwearied in that service; rather say
With warmer love—oh! with far deeper zeal
155   Of holier love. Nor wilt thou then forget,
That after many wanderings, many years
Of absence, these steep woods and lofty cliffs,
And this green pastoral landscape, were to me
More dear, both for themselves and for thy sake!

SAMUEL TAYLOR COLERIDGE (1772–1834)

• Kubla Khan

In Xanadu did Kubla Khan
A stately pleasure dome decree:
Where Alph, the sacred river, ran
Through caverns measureless to man
5   Down to a sunless sea.
So twice five miles of fertile ground
With walls and towers were girdled round:

And there were gardens bright with sinuous rills,
Where blossomed many an incense-bearing tree;
10 And here were forests ancient as the hills,
Enfolding sunny spots of greenery.

But oh! that deep romantic chasm which slanted
Down the green hill athwart a cedarn cover!
A savage place! as holy and enchanted
15 As e'er beneath a waning moon was haunted
By woman wailing for her demon lover!
And from this chasm, with ceaseless turmoil seething,
As if this earth in fast thick pants were breathing,
A mighty fountain momently was forced:
20 Amid whose swift half-intermitted burst
Huge fragments vaulted like rebounding hail,
Or chaffy grain beneath the thresher's flail:
And 'mid these dancing rocks at once and ever
It flung up momently the sacred river.
25 Five miles meandering with a mazy motion
Through wood and dale the sacred river ran,
Then reached the caverns measureless to man,
And sank in tumult to a lifeless ocean:
And 'mid this tumult Kubla heard from far
30 Ancestral voices prophesying war!
      The shadow of the dome of pleasure
      Floated midway on the waves;
      Where was heard the mingled measure
      From the fountain and the caves.
35 It was a miracle of rare device,
A sunny pleasure dome with caves of ice!

      A damsel with a dulcimer
      In a vision once I saw:
      It was an Abyssinian maid,
40   And on her dulcimer she played,
      Singing of Mount Abora.
Could I revive within me
Her symphony and song,
To such a deep delight 'twould win me,
45 That with music loud and long,
I would build that dome in air,
That sunny dome! those caves of ice!
And all who heard should see them there,
And all should cry, Beware! Beware!
50 His flashing eyes, his floating hair!
Weave a circle round him thrice,
And close your eyes with holy dread,
For he on honeydew hath fed,
And drunk the milk of Paradise.

ALFRED, LORD TENNYSON (1809–1892)

The Eagle: A Fragment

He clasps the crag with crooked hands;
Close to the sun in lonely lands,
Ringed with the azure world, he stands.

The wrinkled sea beneath him crawls:
5   He watches from his mountain walls,
And like a thunderbolt he falls.

AMY LOWELL (1874–1925)

Chinoiseries

Reflections

When I looked into your eyes,
I saw a garden
With peonies, and tinkling pagodas,
And round-arched bridges
5   Over still lakes.
A woman sat beside the water
In a rain-blue, silken garment.
She reached through the water
To pluck the crimson peonies
10   Beneath the surface,
But as she grasped the stems,
They jarred and broke into white-green ripples;
And as she drew out her hand,
The water-drops dripping from it
15   Stained her rain-blue dress like tears.

Falling Snow

The snow whispers about me,
And my wooden clogs
Leave holes behind me in the snow.
But no one will pass this way
20   Seeking my footsteps,
And when the temple bell rings again
They will be covered and gone.

Hoar-Frost

In the cloud-grey mornings
I heard the herons flying;
25   And when I came into my garden,
My silken outer-garment
Trailed over withered leaves.
A dried leaf crumbles at a touch,
But I have seen many Autumns

30   With herons blowing like smoke
        Across the sky.

PHILLIPPE SOUPAULT (1897–)

Sunday

The aircraft are weaving the telegraph wires
and the waterfall is singing the exact same song
At the coachmen's hangout the aperitifs are all orange
but locomotive engineers all have white eyes
5   the lady has lost her smile in the woods

Translation by Michael Benedikt (1935–)

WILLIAM CARLOS WILLIAMS (1883–1963)

The Red Wheelbarrow

so much depends
upon

a red wheel
barrow

5   glazed with rain
water

beside the white
chickens.

H. D. (HILDA DOOLITTLE) (1886–1961)

Sea Rose

Rose, harsh rose,
marred and with stint of petals,
meagre flower, thin,
sparse of leaf,

5   more precious
than a wet rose,
single on a stem—
you are caught in the drift.

Stunted, with small leaf,
10   you are flung on the sand,
you are lifted
in the crisp sand
that drives in the wind.

Can the spice-rose
15   drip such acrid fragrance
hardened in a leaf?

T. S. ELIOT (1888–1965)

• Preludes

I

The winter evening settles down
With smell of steaks in passageways.
Six o'clock.
The burnt-out ends of smoky days.
5   And now a gusty shower wraps
The grimy scraps
Of withered leaves about your feet
And newspapers from vacant lots;
The showers beat
10   On broken blinds and chimney-pots,
And at the corner of the street
A lonely cab-horse steams and stamps.

And then the lighting of the lamps.

II

The morning comes to consciousness
15   Of faint stale smells of beer
From the sawdust-trampled street
With all its muddy feet that press
To early coffee-stands.

With the other masquerades
20   That time resumes,
One thinks of all the hands
That are raising dingy shades
In a thousand furnished rooms.

III

You tossed a blanket from the bed,
25   You lay upon your back, and waited;
You dozed, and watched the night revealing
The thousand sordid images
Of which your soul was constituted;
They flickered against the ceiling.
30   And when all the world came back
And the light crept up between the shutters
And you heard the sparrows in the gutters,
You had such a vision of the street
As the street hardly understands;
35   Sitting along the bed's edge, where
You curled the papers from your hair,
Or clasped the yellow soles of feet
In the palms of both soiled hands.

IV

His soul stretched tight across the skies
40   That fade behind a city block,
Or trampled by insistent feet

At four and five and six o'clock;
And short square fingers stuffing pipes,
And evening newspapers, and eyes
45   Assured of certain certainties,
The conscience of a blackened street
Impatient to assume the world.

I am moved by fancies that are curled
Around these images, and cling:
50   The notion of some infinitely gentle
Infinitely suffering thing.

Wipe your hand across your mouth, and laugh;
The worlds revolve like ancient women
Gathering fuel in vacant lots.

ROBERT LOWELL (1917–1977)

• Skunk Hour

(For Elizabeth Bishop)

Nautilus Island's hermit
heiress still lives through winter in her Spartan° cottage;   *austere*
her sheep still graze above the sea.
Her son's a bishop. Her farmer
5   is first selectman in our village;
she's in her dotage.

Thirsting for
the hierarchic privacy
of Queen Victoria's century,
10   she buys up all
the eyesores facing her shore,
and lets them fall.

The season's ill—
we've lost our summer millionaire,
15   who seemed to leap from an L. L. Bean
catalogue. His nine-knot yawl
was auctioned off to lobstermen.
A red fox stain covers Blue Hill.

And now our fairy
20   decorator brightens his shop for fall;
his fishnet's filled with orange cork,
orange, his cobbler's bench and awl;
there is no money in his work,
he'd rather marry.

25   One dark night,
my Tudor Ford climbed the hill's skull;
I watched for love-cars. Lights turned down,

they lay together, hull to hull,
where the graveyard shelves on the town. . . .
30   My mind's not right.

A car radio bleats,
"Love, O careless Love. . . ." I hear
my ill-spirit sob in each blood cell,
as if my hand were at its throat. . . .
35   I myself am hell;
nobody's here—

only skunks, that search
in the moonlight for a bite to eat.
They march on their soles up Main Street:
40   white stripes, moonstruck eyes' red fire
under the chalk-dry and spar spire
of the Trinitarian Church.

I stand on top
of our back steps and breathe the rich air—
45   a mother skunk with her column of kittens swills the garbage pail.
She jabs her wedge-head in a cup
of sour cream, drops her ostrich tail,
and will not scare.

ETHERIDGE KNIGHT (1933–)

Haiku

1
Eastern guard tower
glints in sunset; convicts rest
like lizards on rocks.

2
The piano man
5   is sting at 3 am
his songs drop like plum.

3
Morning sun slants cell.
Drunks stagger like cripple flies
On Jailhouse floor.

4
10   To write a blues song
is to regiment riots
and pluck gems from graves.

5
A bare pecan tree
slips a pencil shadow down
15   a moonlit snow slope.

6

The falling snow flakes
Can not blunt the hard aches nor
Match the steel stillness.

7

Under moon shadows
A tall boy flashes knife and
Slices star bright ice.

8

In the August grass
Struck by the last rays of sun
The cracked teacup screams.

9

Making jazz swing in
Seventeen syllables AIN'T
No square° poet's job.   *straitlaced*

7 ❧ The Dance of the Mind

Metaphor and Simile

Poetry must attempt extraordinary leaps of both association and logic to achieve its heights of emotion and its provocative thoughts. We can easily distinguish these verbal flights from ordinary speech, as when someone says, fearfully, "She is taking her life in her hands!"; or, in admiration, "He is a diamond in the rough." Although these expressions are quite worn with use, we continue to use them because they are truly poetic. If the speaker were not animated by emotion, such statements might be dismissed as lies. The abstraction "life" cannot be held in the hands, and a man obviously is not a diamond. These expressions are true to feelings rather than to facts. Emotion has set the mind of the speaker dancing and has inspired what is known as a *figure of speech*.

The Metaphor

CHARLES SIMIC (1938–)

Watermelons

Green Buddhas
On the fruit stand.
We eat the smile
And spit out the teeth.

What has happened to the watermelons? The poet has seen them displayed on a fruit stand in their round wholeness. He has seen them cut into edible wedges. To his mind the uncut watermelons become Buddhas, godlike as they rest peacefully on the fruit stand. The tasty wedges of fruit become smiles as he thinks of eating them. And the seeds, as he recalls spitting them out, become teeth that he imagines in the red mouth of the smile. The watermelon, in short, has been transformed to express the poet's delight in all its shapes.

The transformation of one thing or idea into another is called *metaphor*. It is the most powerful figure of speech and very likely the most essential act of poetic intelligence. Metaphor is personal and visionary, requiring no allegiance to facts. A metaphor may seem quite sensible, as when someone says, "My house is a prison," or it may at first seem bizarre: "My house is a dark road." But the statements are equally metaphorical. Each is poetically true insofar as it conveys the mood of the speaker.

WALT WHITMAN (1819–1892)

From Leaves of Grass

A child said What is the grass? fetching it to me with full hands;
How could I answer the child? I do not know what it is anymore than he.

I guess it must be the flag of my disposition, out of hopeful green stuff woven.

Or I guess it is the handkerchief of the Lord,
5   A scented gift and remembrancer designedly dropt,
Bearing the owner's name someway in the corners, that we may see and remark,
    and say Whose?

Or I guess the grass is itself a child, the produced babe of the vegetation.

Or I guess it is a uniform hieroglyphic,
And it means, Sprouting alike in broad zones and narrow zones,

Walt Whitman (*National Portrait Gallery, Smithsonian Institution, Washington, D.C.*)

10   Growing among black folks as among white,
Kanuck, Tuckahoe, Congressman, Cuff, I give them the same, I receive them the same.

And now it seems to me the beautiful uncut hair of graves.

Metaphor is commonly thought of as a sort of comparison, but such a definition seriously limits our appreciation of this powerful figure of speech. A metaphor *may* arise out of a comparison, as when, noticing that buttercups and sunlight are both a certain shade of yellow, we call the sunlight a buttercup. But when Walt Whitman says that the grass is "the beautiful uncut hair of graves" or "the handkerchief of the Lord," his imagination has overwhelmed any similarities between grass and hair or handkerchiefs. His delight has transformed the grass.

As easily as metaphor can turn one thing into another, it can transform an idea into a thing. Here Emily Dickinson begins with the abstract noun *Hope*, a complex idea without visual properties. Then she transforms hope into a bird so that we can see, hear, and better appreciate it.

EMILY DICKINSON (1830–1886)

• Hope Is the Thing with Feathers

Hope is the thing with feathers
That perches in the soul,
And sings the tune without the words,
And never stops at all,

5   And sweetest in the gale is heard;
And sore must be the storm
That could abash the little bird
That kept so many warm.

I've heard it in the chillest land,
10   And on the strangest sea;
Yet, never, in extremity,
It asked a crumb of me.

Question

1. Vocabulary: *abash* (7), *extremity* (11).

In the first line, by mentioning feathers, Dickinson emphasizes the bird's lightness. In line 4 she suggests that the creature's consoling music is constant. She further characterizes Hope in the second stanza, when she tells us the peculiar bird sings most sweetly during storms, warming us in adversity. As her final compliment to the bird's nature, she tells us that Hope does its comforting work free of charge. We need not offer it so much as a crumb in order to receive its benefits.

H. D. (HILDA DOOLITTLE) (1886–1961)

Oread°   *mountain nymph*

Whirl up, sea—
whirl your pointed pines,
splash your great pines
on our rocks,
5   hurl your green over us,
cover us with your pools of fir.

Questions

1. How does the poet transform the sea?
2. What emotion or mood is evoked by the metaphor?

HART CRANE (1899–1932)

My Grandmother's Love Letters

There are no stars to-night
But those of memory.
Yet how much room for memory there is
In the loose girdle° of soft rain.   *sash*

5   There is even room enough
For the letters of my mother's mother,
Elizabeth,
That have been pressed so long
Into a corner of the roof
10 That they are brown and soft,
And liable to melt as snow.

Over the greatness of such space
Steps must be gentle.
It is all hung by an invisible white hair.
15 It trembles as birch limbs webbing the air.

And I ask myself:

"Are your fingers long enough to play
Old keys that are but echoes:
Is the silence strong enough
20 To carry back the music to its source
And back to you again
As though to her?"

Yet I would lead my grandmother by the hand
Through much of what she would not understand;
25 And so I stumble. And the rain continues on the roof
With such a sound of gently pitying laughter.

Hart Crane (*National Portrait Gallery, Smithsonian Institution, Washington, D.C.*)

Questions

1. This nostalgic lyric relies heavily on metaphor for its effects. There are two metaphors in the first stanza. What are they?
2. In the third stanza Crane mentions an invisible white hair. The hair is a metaphor representing something very important to Crane. What does it represent? What is hanging from the hair?
3. In lines 17 and 18 Crane asks himself if he can "play / Old keys that are but echoes." He has metaphorically imagined himself as a pianist, and the letters as the piano keys. Why does he imagine the keys as echoes?
4. What is the metaphor of the last line?
5. Why is the rain laughing? Does that relate to the "loose girdle" metaphor in line 4?

BILL KNOTT (1940–)

Hair Poem

Hair is heaven's water flowing eerily over us
Often a woman drifts off down her long hair and is lost

Questions

1. What mood or emotion do you suppose triggered the transformation of hair into "heaven's water?"
2. Is there a metaphor implied in line 2?

CHARLES HENRI FORD (1913–)

Somebody's Gone

There may be a basement to the Atlantic
but there's no top-storey
to my mountain of missing you.

I must say your deportment took a hunk
5 out of my peach of a heart.
 . I ain't insured against torpedoes!
My turpentine tears would fill a drugstore.

May I be blindfolded before you come my way again
if you're going to leave dry land like an amphibian;
10 I took you for some kind of ambrosial bird
with no thought of acoustics.

Maybe it's too late to blindfold me ever:
I'm just a blotter crisscrossed with the ink
of words that remind me of you.

15 Bareheaded aircastle,
you were as beautiful as a broom made of flesh and hair.

When you first disappeared
I couldn't keep up with my breakneck grief,
and now I know how grief can run away with the mind,
20 leaving the body desolate as a staircase.

Questions

1. Vocabulary: *deportment* (4), *amphibian* (9), *ambrosial* (10).
2. What do you suppose is the relationship of the poet to the "you" of the poem?
3. By suggesting there "may be a basement to the Atlantic," how is the poet transforming the ocean?
4. How does the poet express frustration in lines 13 and 14?
5. Why did Ford write this poem?

Exercise

You might try some metaphors of your own in order to discover the great power of this figure of speech. Look at the objects in your classroom, and transform them imaginatively. Write: *The desk is a desert. The blackboard is a door to night.* Transform a friend or an enemy: *John is a flagpole. Linda is a violin.* It does not take long to discover that every metaphor has emotional potential. In fact, it is difficult to make one that does not convey feeling as well as thought. Concentrate on a single object and transform it into as many other things as you can think of, trying for the greatest range of emotions.

The Simile

The simile is a more modest figure of speech. The common qualities of differing things may prompt a metaphor: "the sun is a buttercup," or "his ambition is a bubble." Having registered the similarity, however, a metaphor insists on total mental transformation of the one thing into the other. The simile, on the other hand, simply compares two different things on the basis of some shared quality.

> His head was as hairless as an egg.
> —*Anonymous*

> Her dress was as plain as an umbrella cover.
> —*Joseph Conrad*

> Thine eyes are like the deep, blue boundless heaven.
> —*William Shakespeare*

The charm of the simile comes from the observed likeness. Someone's eyes might be exactly the shade of the sky. The simile's force arises out of the differences between the things compared—by comparing someone's eyes to heaven, we attribute divine qualities to a mere mortal. But if we compare one person's eyes to another's or one tree to another, we are not making a figure of speech at all; we are simply writing prose.

Similes are easy to recognize, for they always declare their intentions by using the qualifiers *like* and *as:* "Debt is like a millstone about a person's neck" (Anon); "Childhood shows the man, as the morning shows the day" (John Milton). It is important to be able to recognize similes as we come upon them in our reading. It is even more important to appreciate the feelings and correspondences that inspire them. Let us examine a few similes with that in mind.

> A secret in his mouth is like
> a wild bird in a cage,
> whose door no sooner opens,
> than 'tis out.
> —*Ben Jonson*

The elements of the comparison are the "secret in his mouth" and the "wild bird in a cage." What is the similarity? Both the secret and the wild bird cannot resist the temptation to escape. What has inspired the figure of speech? Distrust. Ben Jonson is passing a harsh judgment on the man by means of his ingenious simile.

> Like to the moon am I, that cannot shine alone.
> —*Michelangelo*

Michelangelo, the great painter and sculptor, also wrote inspired poetry. What is the basis of comparison between the artist and the moon? He tells us that both require a light besides their own; they "cannot shine alone." The great force and emotion of this simile occur to us when we consider the great height and brilliance of the moon, the enormity of its loneliness when it cannot shine. The moon relies on the sun for its light; the artist needs love, the light of the world's approval, and inspiration. By comparing himself to the moon, Michelangelo is measuring himself on a grand scale indeed, suggesting the enormity of his needs and the grandeur of their satisfactions.

T. E. HULME (1883–1917)

Autumn

A touch of cold in the Autumn night—
I walked abroad,
And saw the ruddy moon lean over a hedge
Like a red-faced farmer.
5   I did not stop to speak, but nodded,
And round about were the wistful stars
With white faces like town children.

Questions

1. Vocabulary: *wistful* (6).
2. What does the moon have in common with the farmer? How does the idea of a moon with a farmer's face strike you? Is it frightening? Amusing?
3. What do the stars have in common with town children?
4. What mood is inspired by the last lines?

BILL KNOTT (1940–)

Death

Going to sleep, I cross my hands on my chest.
They will place my hands like this.
It will look as though I am flying into myself.

Questions

1. Who are "they" in line 2? Does the title give you a clue?
2. The final line is a striking image achieved through simile. What is being compared to what?

THOMAS MERTON (1915–1968)

The Regret

When cold November sits among the reeds like an unlucky fisher

And ducks drum up as sudden as the wind
Out of the rushy river,
We slowly come, robbed of our rod and gun,
5   Walking amid the stricken cages of the trees.

The stormy weeks have all gone home like drunken hunters,
Leaving the gates of the grey world open to December.

But now there is no speech of branches in these broken jails.
Acorns lie over the earth, no less neglected
10   Than our unrecognizable regret:

And here we stand as senseless as the oaks,
As dumb as elms.

And though we seem as grave as jailers, yet we did not come to wonder
Who picked the locks of the past days, and stole our summer.
15 (We are no longer listeners for curious saws, and secret keys!)

We are indifferent to seasons,
And stand like hills, deaf.
And never hear the last of the escaping year
Go ducking through the bended branches like a leaf.

Questions

1. This brooding meditation treats an old theme with a brilliant range of similes and metaphors. The theme is our neglect of nature, which is also a neglect of ourselves. Of all the similes, which one comes closest to summarizing that theme?
2. Why does Merton compare the stormy weeks to drunken hunters? What do they have in common?
3. Why does he compare the escaping year to a leaf in the last line?

The Conceit

A simile or metaphor that carries out a comparison in great detail is called a *conceit*.

> Beauty, like the fair Hesperian[1] tree,
> Laden with blooming gold, hath need the guard
> Of dragon watch, with unenchanted eye,
> To save her blossoms and defend her fruit
> From the rash hand of bold incontinence°   *inchastity*
> —John Milton

This decorative figure of speech, which calls attention to the writer's ingenuity, was a popular mannerism of the Renaissance. Several seventeenth-century writers, sometimes called *metaphysical poets*, seem to try to outdo each other in the elaborateness of their figures. The following love poem elaborates a single comparison, between the loved one and a summer's day. Notice how the lover is flattered by the comparison and how wittily the poet takes credit for it in the last line.

WILLIAM SHAKESPEARE (1564–1616)

• Shall I Compare Thee to a Summer's Day?

Shall I compare thee to a summer's day?
Thou art more lovely and more temperate.
Rough winds do shake the darling buds of May,

---

[1] In Greek literature Hesperus is a mythic treasure island.

And summer's lease hath all too short a date.
5   Sometime too hot the eye of heaven shines,
And often is his gold complexion dimmed;
And every fair from fair sometime declines,
By chance, or nature's changing course, untrimmed.
But thy eternal summer shall not fade,
10   Nor lose possession of that fair thou ow'st;°   *possess*
Nor shall death brag thou wand'rest in his shade,
When in eternal lines to time thou grow'st.
So long as men can breathe or eyes can see,
So long lives this, and this gives life to thee.

Questions

1. Vocabulary: *temperate* (2).
2. What does the speaker emphasize about a summer's day? Could he find more flattering things to say about it?
3. What does the speaker's beloved have that the summer's day does not?

The following poem, a meditation on one of the Virgin's tears, is often cited for its overelaborate conceits. The poem survives despite the criticism, or perhaps because of it. We will leave it to the reader to judge the poem's effectiveness.

RICHARD CRASHAW (1613?–1649)

The Tear

What bright soft thing is this,
    Sweet Mary, thy fair eyes' expense?
A moist spark it is,
    A wat'ry diamond; from whence
5   The very term, I think, was found,
The water of a diamond.

Oh! 'tis not a tear,
    'Tis a star about to drop
From thine eye, its sphere;
10   The Sun will stoop and take it up.
Proud will his sister be to wear
This thine eye's jewel in her ear.

Oh! 'tis a tear,
    Too true a tear; for no sad eyne,
15   How sad soe'er,
    Rain so true a tear as thine;
Each drop, leaving a place so dear,
Weeps for itself, is its own tear.

Such a pearl as this is,
20   (Slipped from Aurora's° dewy breast)   *dawn's*

The rose-bud's sweet lip kisses;
    And such the rose itself, when vexed
With ungentle flames, does shed,
Sweating in too warm a bed.

25   Such the maiden gem
    By the wanton Spring put on,
Peeps from her parent stem,
    And blushes on the manly Sun:
This wat'ry blossom of thy eyne,
30   Ripe, will make the richer wine.

Fair drop, why quak'st thou so?
    'Cause thou straight must lay thy head
In the dust? Oh no;
    The dust shall never be thy bed:
35   A pillow for thee will I bring,
Stuffed with down of angel's wing.

Thus carried up on high,
    (For to heaven thou must go)
Sweetly shalt thou lie,
40   And in soft slumbers bathe thy woe;
Till the singing orbs awake thee,
And one of their bright chorus make thee.

There thyself shalt be
    An eye, but not a weeping one;
45   Yet I doubt of thee,
    Whither th'hadst rather there have shone
An eye of Heaven; or still shine here
In th' Heaven of Mary's eye, a tear.

Questions

1. Vocabulary: *wanton* (26).
2. By what line of the poem has the tear become a distinct image?
3. By what line has the image of the tear become a metaphor? How many metaphors does Crashaw develop from the tear?
4. When do you sense that the figures have evolved into conceits?
5. Do the conceits become wearisome? Do they seem obsessive?

The Spanish philosopher José Ortega y Gasset refers to poetry as the "higher mathematics of literature." By that he means that poetry anticipates more popular movements in literature, and also that poetry is capable of great precision in expressing subtle states of the mind and heart. In those subtle areas no devices are more accurate in expression than metaphors and similes. If they cause us difficulty at first, we must be patient, for these figures produce some of the greatest riches in poetry. John Donne, in the following masterwork of similes and conceits, achieves extraordinary delicacy. He is treating a difficult subject:

the different kinds of love, and how lovers are affected by separation. Donne composed this poem for his wife on the eve of his departure on a long trip. In the first two stanzas he urges her to help him take his leave with silence and dignity, like "virtuous men" at the hour of death. In the third stanza he compares the lovers to celestial bodies, "the spheres," which may move apart, or irregularly, without evil consequences. Pay close attention to the gold simile in stanza 6 and to the simile of the compass that concludes the poem.

JOHN DONNE (1572–1631)

• A Valediction: Forbidding Mourning

As virtuous men pass mildly away,
    And whisper to their souls to go,
Whilst some of their sad friends do say
    The breath goes now, and some say no:

5   So let us melt, and make no noise,
    No tear-floods, nor sigh-tempests move;
'Twere profanation of our joys
    To tell the laity our love.

Moving of th' earth brings harms and fears;
10   Men reckon what it did and meant;
But trepidation of the spheres,[2]
    Though greater far, is innocent.

Dull sublunary lovers' love
    (Whose soul is sense) cannot admit
15 Absence, because it doth remove
    Those things which elemented it.

But we, by a love so much refined
    That ourselves know not what it is,
Inter-assurèd of the mind,
20   Care less, eyes, lips, and hands to miss.

Our two souls, therefore, which are one,
    Though I must go, endure not yet
A breach, but an expansion,
    Like gold to airy thinness beat.

25 If they be two, they are two so
    As stiff twin compasses are two:[3]
Thy soul, the fixed foot, makes no show
    To move, but doth, if th' other do.

And though it in the center sit,
30   Yet when the other far doth roam,

---

[2] Because of the movement of the earth, other planets appear to wobble or stand still. The odd movements were called the "trepidation of the spheres."
[3] Donne is referring to the compass used to draw circles.

It leans and harkens after it,
    And grows erect as that comes home.

Such wilt thou be to me, who must,
    Like th' other foot, obliquely run;
35   Thy firmness makes my circle just,
    And makes me end where I begun.

Question

1. Vocabulary: *valediction, profanation* (7), *trepidation* (11), *sublunary* (13).

Poems for Further Study

In reading the following poems, pay special attention to the metaphors and similes. Where you find a metaphor, determine what feelings have caused the transformation of images. Where you find a simile, look for the correspondences between the elements compared, and see how the elements complement each other by their differences.

A. E. HOUSMAN (1859–1936)

With Rue My Heart Is Laden

With rue my heart is laden
    For golden friends I had,
For many a rose-lipt maiden
    And many a lightfoot lad.

5   By brooks too broad for leaping
    The lightfoot boys are laid;
The rose-lipt girls are sleeping
    In fields where roses fade.

THOMAS MERTON (1915–1968)

Elegy for the Monastery Barn

As though an aged person were to wear
Too gay a dress
And walk about the neighborhood
Announcing the hour of her death,

5   So now, one summer day's end,
At suppertime, when wheels are still,
The long barn suddenly puts on the traitor, beauty,
And hails us with a dangerous cry,
For: "Look!" she calls to the country,
10   "Look how fast I dress myself in fire!"

Had we half guessed how long her spacious shadows
Harbored a woman's vanity
We would be less surprised to see her now
So loved, and so attended, and so feared.

15 She, in whose airless heart
We burst our veins to fill her full of hay,
Now stands apart.
She will not have us near her. Terribly,
Sweet Christ, how terribly her beauty burns us now!

20 And yet she has another legacy,°   *inheritance*
More delicate, to leave us, and more rare.

Who knew her solitude?
Who heard the peace downstairs
While flames ran whispering among the rafters?
25 Who felt the silence, there,
The long, hushed gallery
Clean and resigned and waiting for the fire?

Look! They have all come back to speak their summary:
Fifty invisible cattle, the past years
30 Assume their solemn places one by one.
This is the little minute of their destiny.
Here is their meaning found. Here is their end.

Laved° in the flame as in a Sacrament   *bathed*
The brilliant walls are holy
35 In their first-last hour of joy.

Fly from within the barn! Fly from the silence
Of this creature sanctified by fire!
Let no man stay inside to look upon the Lord!
Let no man wait within and see the Holy
40 One sitting in the presence of disaster
Thinking upon this barn His gentle doom!

N. SCOTT MOMADAY (1934–)

The Delight Song of Tsoai-Talee[4]

I am a feather on the bright sky
I am the blue horse that runs in the plain
I am the fish that rolls, shining, in the water
I am the shadow that follows a child
5 I am the evening light, the lustre of meadows
I am an eagle playing with the wind

---

[4] N. Scott Momaday's Indian name, which means "Rock-Tree Boy."

I am a cluster of bright beads
I am the farthest star
I am the cold of the dawn
10 I am the roaring of the rain
I am the glitter on the crust of the snow
I am the long track of the moon in a lake
I am a flame of four colors
I am a deer standing away in the dusk
15 I am a field of sumac and the pomme blanche
I am an angle of geese in the winter sky
I am the hunger of a young wolf
I am the whole dream of these things

You see, I am alive, I am alive
20 I stand in good relation to the earth
I stand in good relation to the gods
I stand in good relation to all that is beautiful
I stand in good relation to the daughter of *Tsen-tainte*[5]
You see, I am alive, I am alive

Compare with W.E.B. DuBois's "The Song of the Smoke," pages 380–381.

EZRA POUND (1885–1972)

The Bath Tub

As a bathtub lined with white porcelain,
When the hot water gives out or goes tepid,
So is the slow cooling of our chivalrous passion,
O my much praised but-not-altogether-satisfactory lady.

DYLAN THOMAS (1914–1953)

• Fern Hill

Now as I was young and easy under the apple boughs
About the lilting house and happy as the grass was green,
    The night above the dingle[6] starry,
      Time let me hail and climb
5   Golden in the heydays of his eyes,
And honoured among wagons I was prince of the apple towns
And once below a time I lordly had the trees and leaves
      Trail with daisies and barley
    Down the rivers of the windfall light.

---

[5] White Horse.
[6] A *dingle* is a narrow wooded valley.

10　And as I was green and carefree, famous among the barns
　　About the happy yard and singing as the farm was home,
　　　　　In the sun that is young once only,
　　　　　　　Time let me play and be
　　　　　Golden in the mercy of his means,
15　And green and golden I was huntsman and herdsman, the calves
　　Sang to my horn, the foxes on the hills barked clear and cold,
　　　　　And the sabbath rang slowly
　　　　　In the pebbles of the holy streams.

　　All the sun long it was running, it was lovely, the hay
20　Fields high as the house, the tunes from the chimneys, it was air
　　　　　And playing, lovely and watery
　　　　　　　And fire green as grass.

　　　　　And nightly under the simple stars
　　As I rode to sleep the owls were bearing the farm away,
25　All the moon long I heard, blessed among stables, the nightjars
　　　　　Flying with the ricks, and the horses
　　　　　　　Flashing into the dark.

　　And then to awake, and the farm, like a wanderer white
　　With the dew, come back, the cock on his shoulder: it was all
30　　　　Shining, it was Adam and maiden,
　　　　　The sky gathered again
　　　　　And the sun grew round that very day.
　　So it must have been after the birth of the simple light
　　In the first, spinning place, the spellbound horses walking warm
35　　　　Out of the whinnying green stable
　　　　　On to the fields of praise.

　　And honoured among foxes and pheasants by the gay house
　　Under the new made clouds and happy as the heart was long,
　　　　　In the sun born over and over,
40　　　　　　I ran my heedless ways,
　　　　　My wishes raced through the house high hay
　　And nothing I cared, at my sky blue trades, that time allows
　　In all his tuneful turning so few and such morning songs
　　　　　Before the children green and golden
45　　　　　　Follow him out of grace,

　　Nothing I cared, in the lamb white days, that time would take me
　　Up to the swallow thronged loft by the shadow of my hand,
　　　　　In the moon that is always rising,
　　　　　　　Nor that riding to sleep
50　　　　I should hear him fly with the high fields
　　And wake to the farm forever fled from the childless land.
　　Oh as I was young and easy in the mercy of his means,
　　　　　Time held me green and dying
　　　　Though I sang in my chains like the sea.

The Pond

Night covers the pond with its wing.
Under the ringed moon I can make out
your face swimming among minnows and the small
echoing stars. In the night air
5   the surface of the pond is metal.

Within, your eyes are open. They contain
a memory I recognize, as though
we had been children together. Our ponies
grazed on the hill, they were gray
10   with white markings. Now they graze
with the dead who wait
like children under their granite breastplate
lucid and helpless:

The hills are far away. They rise up
15   blacker than childhood.
What do you think of, lying so quiet
by the water? When you look that way I want
to touch you, but do not, seeing
as in another life we were of the same blood.

WILLIAM SHAKESPEARE (1564–1616)

Let Me Not to the Marriage of True Minds

Let me not to the marriage of true minds
Admit impediments. Love is not love
Which alters when it alteration finds,
Or bends with the remover° to remove.   *faithless lover*
5   O, no! it is an ever-fixèd mark
That looks on tempests and is never shaken;
It is the star to every wand'ring bark,
Whose worth's unknown, although his height be taken.
Love's not Time's fool, though rosy lips and cheeks
10   Within his bending sickle's compass come;
Love alters not with his brief hours and weeks,
But bears it out even to the edge of doom.
     If this be error and upon me proved,
     I never writ, nor no man ever loved.

PERCY BYSSHE SHELLEY (1792–1822)

Fragment: Thoughts Come and Go in Solitude

My thoughts arise and fade in solitude,
   The verse that would invest them melts away

Like moonlight in the heaven of spreading day:
How beautiful they were, how firm they stood,
5   Flecking the starry sky like woven pearl!

DAVID ST. JOHN (1949–)

Hush

For My Son

The way a tired Chippewa woman
Who's lost a child gathers up black feathers,
Black quills & leaves
That she wraps & swaddles in a little bale, a shag
5   Cocoon she carries with her & speaks to always
As if it were the child,
Until she knows the soul has grown fat & clever,
That the child can find its own way at last;
Well, I go everywhere
10   Picking the dust out of the dust, scraping the breezes
Up off the floor & gather them into a doll
Of you, to touch at the nape of the neck, to slip
Under my shirt like a rag—the way
Another man's wallet rides above his heart. As you
15   Cry out, as if calling to a father you conjure
In the paling light, the voice rises, instead, in me.
Nothing stops it, the crying. Not the clove of moon,
Not the woman raking my back with her words. Our letters
Close. Sometimes, you ask
20   About the world; sometimes, I answer back. Nights
Return you to me for a while, as sleep returns sleep
To a landscape ravaged
& familiar. The dark watermark of your absence, a hush.

JOHN DONNE (1572–1631)

• The Flea

Marke but this flea, and marke in this,
How little that which thou deny'st me is;
It suck'd me first, and now sucks thee,
And in this flea, our two bloods mingled bee;
5   Thou know'st that this cannot be said
A sinne, nor shame, nor losse of maidenhead,
   Yet this enjoyes before it wooe,
   And pamper'd swells with one blood made of two,
   And this, alas, is more than wee would doe.

10   Oh stay, three lives in one flea spare,
Where wee almost, yea more than maryed° are.   *married*

This flea is you and I, and this
  Our mariage bed, and mariage temple is;
Though parents grudge, and you, w'are met,
15 And cloysterd in these living walls of Jet.
    Though use make you apt to kill mee,
    Let not to that, selfe murder added bee,
    And sacrilege, three sinnes in killing three.

Cruell and sodaine,° hast thou since   *sudden*
20 Purpled thy naile, in blood of innocence?
Wherein could this flea guilty bee,
Except in that drop which it suckt from thee?
Yet thou triumph'st, and saist that thou
Find'st not thy selfe, nor mee the weaker now;
25   'Tis true, then learne how false, feares bee;
    Just so much honor, when thou yeeld'st to mee,
    Will wast, as this flea's death tooke life from thee.

JOHN DONNE (1572–1631)

The Extasie

Where, like a pillow on a bed,
  A Pregnant banke swel'd up, to rest
The violets reclining head,
  Sat we two, one anothers best.
5 Our hands were firmely cimented
  With a fast balme, which thence did spring,
Our eye-beames twisted, and did thred
  Our eyes, upon one double string;
So to'entergraft our hands, as yet
10   Was all the meanes to make us one,
And pictures in our eyes to get
  Was all our propagation.°   *increase, begetting*
As 'twixt two equall Armies, Fate
  Suspends uncertaine victorie,
15 Our soules, (which to advance their state,
  Were gone out,) hung 'twixt her, and mee.
And whil'st our soules negotiate there,
  Wee like sepulchrall statues lay;
All day, the same our postures were,
20   And wee said nothing, all the day.
If any, so by love refin'd,
  That he soules language understood,
And by good love were growen all minde,
  Within convenient distance stood,
25 He (though he knew not which soul spake,
  Because both meant, both spake the same)
Might thence a new concoction take,

And part farre purer than he came.
This Extasie doth unperplex°   *simplify*
30   (We said) and tell us what we love,
Wee see by this, it was not sexe,
        Wee see, we saw not what did move:
But as all severall soules containe
        Mixture of things, they know not what,
35 Love, these mixt soules, doth mixe againe,
        And makes both one, each this and that.
A single violet transplant,
        The strength, the colour, and the size,
(All which before was poore, and scant,)
40   Redoubles still, and multiplies.
When love, with one another so
        Interinanimates° two soules,   *vitalizes by mingling*
That abler soule, which thence doth flow,
        Defects of lonelinesse controules.
45 Wee then, who are this new soule, know,
        Of what we are compos'd, and made,
For, th'Atomies of which we grow,
        Are soules, whom no change can invade.
But O alas, so long, so farre
50   Our bodies why doe wee forbeare?
They are ours, though they are not wee, Wee are
        The intelligences,[7] they the spheares.
We owe them thankes, because they thus,
        Did us, to us, at first convay,
55 Yeelded their forces, sense, to us,
        Nor are drosse to us, but allay.°   *alloy*
On man heavens influence workes not so,
        But that it first imprints the ayre,[8]
Soe soule into the soule may flow,
60   Though it to body first repaire.
As our blood labours to beget
        Spirits, as like soules as it can,
Because such fingers need to knit
        That subtile knot, which makes us man:
65 So must pure lovers soules descend
        T'affections, and to faculties,°   *powers*
Which sense may reach and apprehend,
        Else a great Prince in prison lies.
To'our bodies turne wee then, that so
70   Weake men on love reveal'd may looke;
Loves mysteries in soules doe grow,
        But yet the body is his booke.
And if some lover, such as wee,
        Have heard this dialogue of one,

---

[7] *Intelligences* were the forces that medieval astronomers believed guided the stars.
[8] Astrological influences were thought to work through the air surrounding a person.

75   Let him still marke us, he shall see
        Small change, when we'are to bodies gone.

FEDERICO GARCIA LORCA (1898–1936)

Half Moon

The moon goes over the water.
How tranquil the sky is!
She goes scything slowly
the old shimmer from the river;
5   meanwhile a young frog
takes her for a little mirror.

Translation by W. S. Merwin (1927–)

8  The Idea Dresses Up

Personification, Allegory, Symbol

Philosophers and mathematicians are generally more comfortable with abstractions than are poets. Mathematicians will talk about "infinite sets" or "imaginary numbers," and philosophers of "reason," "liberty," or "epistemes." Poets, however, feel more comfortable with what they can touch, see, hear, smell, or taste. Consequently, poets have developed a number of ways to make abstractions more concrete and familiar.

Personification

One of the simplest ways to make ideas concrete is *personification:* the granting of human attributes to things that are not human. Children's literature contains many examples of talking animals, trees, and stars. There are two primary reasons for the use of personification. First, we are better able to recognize attributes when they are given to an animal. An owl can be wiser, a cricket sillier, and a lion braver than a human could be. Second, we take a certain delight in such a transformation. On a basic, perhaps primitive level, we delight when unfamiliar experiences are made commonplace, and commonplace experiences are made unfamiliar.

Here, for example, is a short poem by the Greek poet Sappho. She wishes to convey the experience of being startled by the dawn. But "dawn" is a rather general condition. To gain the emotional intensity she desires, she has condensed the characteristics of daybreak into a personified figure.

SAPPHO (7th century B.C.)

Then

In gold sandals
dawn like a thief
fell upon me.

Translation by Willis Barnstone (1927–)

This poem is complicated by yet another factor. For the Greeks, Dawn is a goddess. Sappho is startled not only by the furtive sun, but also by a beautiful goddess who arrives on golden sandals. The scene, therefore, is doubly mysterious and awesome but also familiar and intimate.

Poets personify not only conditions and animals, but also abstract concepts like Freedom and Good Sense. In the following poem, Love, that often vague, abstract emotion, becomes a rich, generous, and distant patron.

MURIEL RUKEYSER (1913–1981)

Song: Love in Whose Rich Honor

Love
in whose rich honor
I stand looking from my window
over the starved trees of a dry September
5   Love
deep and so far forbidden
is bringing me
a gift
to claw at my skin
10   to break open my eyes
the gift longed for so long
The power
to write
out of the desperate ecstasy at last
15   death and madness

Questions

1. Where is the speaker of the poem? What is she looking at? What is the relationship between what the speaker sees and what she says?
2. Why should the gift claw at her skin and break open her eyes? Is Love's gift always gentle and kind, or is it sometimes cruel and painful?
3. What does the speaker mean by "desperate ecstasy" in line 14? To be in ecstasy means literally to be "beside oneself." In what sense is the speaker "beside herself"?
4. How has personifying Love made the poem more mysterious and intimate?

This poem concerns itself with a rather special question: can authors write with intensity on such subjects as death and madness from which others shy away? How can authors face those dreaded conditions not with philosophic detachment, but with joy? The persona of this poem answers that love gives her the power to write. But it is not merely an abstract love that enriches her. It is an almost godlike love, one that is "deep and so far forbidden." Rukeyser has taken a philosophical problem and turned it into a scene in which the mysterious figure of Love visits her with a gift of power.

Allegory

Emily Dickinson uses the personification of abstractions to explore the condition of death. Here again, the result is a poem that treats the subject with both familiarity and awe, mystery and intimacy.

EMILY DICKINSON (1830–1866)

• Because I Could Not Stop for Death

Because I could not stop for Death—
He kindly stopped for me—
The Carriage held but just Ourselves—
And Immortality.

5   We slowly drove—He knew no haste
And I had put away
My labor and my leisure too,
For His Civility—

We passed the School, where Children strove
10   At Recess—in the Ring—
We passed the Fields of Gazing Grain—
We passed the Setting Sun—

Or rather—He passed Us—
The Dews drew quivering and chill—
15   For only Gossamer, my gown—
My Tippet—only Tulle—

We paused before a House that seemed
A Swelling of the Ground—
The Roof was scarcely visible—
20   The Cornice—in the Ground—

Since then—'tis Centuries—and yet
Feels shorter than the Day
I first surmised the Horses' Heads
Were toward Eternity—

Questions

1. Vocabulary: *civility* (8), *gossamer* (15), *tippet* (16), *tulle* (16), *cornice* (20).
2. What is the persona's attitude toward Death? Is he a fearsome creature or a politely stiff gentleman? How does the persona treat him?
3. What is the house they visit? Does it look like any structure you have ever seen?
4. Has the journey ended for the speaker? Has she arrived at Eternity? What can we say about the speaker's view of immortality?

Unlike Sappho or Rukeyser, Dickinson employs a number of abstractions in telling her story. Immortality is Death's traveling companion, and they are both headed toward Eternity. Dickinson has done something very complicated; she has made a small allegory. She has turned abstract ideas into people and places and then woven them into a story. Yet as complicated as this process sounds, the results are easy to understand. In fact, we often use allegory to explain complicated ideas to small children. Instead of trying to discuss in scientific terms the need for good oral hygiene, parents or dentists will tell children stories about Mr. Toothdecay, who enjoys drilling holes in new white teeth until Mr. Toothbrush comes to the rescue. The allegory is simpler, more immediate, and certainly more entertaining than a lecture. Finally, the allegory is more persuasive than charts, tables, and other means of convincing an audience.

George Herbert understood the value of allegory as a means of communicating complex notions in a lively, simple way. He left Cambridge University, where he had been elected public orator, to minister to a country parish. As public orator he had had to give flowery speeches in Latin to scholars at the university. But as a parish minister he had to persuade his poorly educated congregation to be better Christians. One of his allegorical poems follows.

GEORGE HERBERT (1593–1633)

The Pilgrimage

I traveled on, seeing the hill where lay
   My expectation.
  A long it was and weary way.
  The gloomy cave of desperation
5 I left on th'one, and on the other side
   The rock of pride.

 And so I came to fancy's meadow, strowed
   With many a flower;
  Fain would I here have made abode,
10 But I was quickened by my hour.
 So to care's copse I came, and there got through
   With much ado.

 That led me to the wild of passion, which
   Some call the wold°—   *treeless plain*
15 A wasted place but sometimes rich.
  Here I was robbed of all my gold
 Save one good angel,[1] which a friend had tied
   Close to my side.

 At length I got unto the gladsome hill
20   Where lay my hope,
  Where lay my heart; and, climbing still,
  When I had gained the brow and top,
 A lake of brackish waters on the ground
   Was all I found.

---

[1] "Good angel" refers to a gold coin as well as to a guardian angel.

25   With that abashed, and struck with many a sting
               Of swarming fears,
        I fell, and cried, "Alas, my king!
        Can both the way and end be tears?"
    Yet taking heart I rose, and then perceived
30   I was deceived:

My hill was further; so I flung away,
               Yet heard a cry,
        Just as I went: *None goes that way*
        And lives: "If that be all," said I,
35   "After so foul a journey, death is fair,
               And but a chair."

Questions

1. Vocabulary: *copse* (11), *brackish* (23), *abashed* (25).
2. What is the significance of the "lake of brackish waters" in line 23 and the "good angel" in line 17?
3. What does the speaker feel in lines 25–30?
4 Does the speaker enjoy the pilgrimage? Is he supposed to?
5. What is the relationship between the life we live and our attitude toward death?
6. Is the pilgrim's life different from anyone else's?

Herbert's "pilgrimage" is another version of the "journey of life" on which we meet many difficulties. We must avoid the "cave of desperation" and "the rock of pride" and progress through "fancy's meadow," "care's copse," and "the wild of passion." The persona's destination is the "gladsome hill," which will be beautiful and refreshing, but as the voice informs him, *"None goes that way/ And lives."* Death is the only means of reaching the goal. But the speaker is not discouraged by the news. Dying seems a small price to pay for eternal happiness. Indeed, he is quite happy to die; he compares death to a sedan chair, like those on which the rich were comfortably carried about by servants.

Herbert's poem illustrates an important characteristic of allegory: the allegorical figures are not independent of one another. One understands the significance of the "rock of pride" in relation to the "gladsome hill" or the "cave of desperation." Moreover, the general pattern for life's journey illuminates all the allegorical figures. Each one helps us see the entire pattern, and it is the pattern that is most important in allegory.

Allegory often makes use of a dialogue in which the speaking is not colloquial. Here is such an allegorical scene.

AURELIAN TOWNSHEND (c. 1583–1643)

A Dialogue Betwixt Time and a Pilgrim

PILGRIM.   Aged man, that mows these fields.
TIME.   Pilgrim speak, what is thy will?

PILGRIM.	Whose soil is this that such sweet Pasture yields?
	Or who art thou whose Foot stands never still?
5	Or where am I? TIME. In love.
PILGRIM.	His Lordship lies above.
TIME.	Yes and below, and round about
	Where in all sorts of flow'rs are growing
	Which as the early Spring puts out,
10	Time falls as fast a mowing.
PILGRIM.	If thou art Time, these Flow'rs have Lives,
	And then I fear
	Under some Lily she I love
	May now be growing there.
15 TIME.	And in some Thistle or some spire of grass,
	My scythe thy stalk before hers come may pass.
PILGRIM.	Wilt thou provide it may? TIME. No.
PILGRIM.	Allege the cause.
TIME.	Because Time cannot alter but obey Fate's laws.
20 CHORUS.	Then happy those whom Fate, that is the stronger,
	Together twists their threads, and yet draws hers the longer.

Questions

1. Where does this meeting occur? How does the allegorical setting shape the dialogue?
2. How is Time portrayed? Is this a traditional view of Time?
3. Who is "His Lordship" in line 6? Why is he "below, and round about"?
4. What is the Chorus's moral?

Townshend, like Herbert, uses the figure of the pilgrim. We are all pilgrims on life's journey. He dramatizes a scene in which the pilgrim wanders into love even before he meets the object of his affection. Townshend uses the allegorical dialogue to explore the relationships among Love, Mortality, and Fate. The dialogue presents these ideas more simply and economically than could a lecture on the subject.

The allegory is particularly useful in describing inner conflicts. Sometimes we talk silently to ourselves. The rash part of our personality might argue with the more restrained part. When two or more parts of the self engage in conflict, the work is called a *psychomachy*, meaning a "conflict of the soul."

THOMAS HARDY (1840–1928)

Memory and I

"O Memory, where is now my youth,
Who used to say that life was truth?"

"I saw him in a crumbled cot
    Beneath a tottering tree;
5 That he as phantom lingers there
    Is only known to me."

"O Memory, where is now my joy,
Who lived with me in sweet employ?"

"I saw him in gaunt gardens lone,
10   Where laughter used to be;
That he as phantom wanders there
        Is known to none but me."

"O Memory, where is now my hope,
Who charged with deeds my skill and scope?"

15   "I saw her in a tomb of tomes,
        Where dreams are wont to be;
That she as spectre haunteth there
        Is only known to me."

"O Memory, where is now my faith
20   One time a champion, now a wraith?"

"I saw her in a ravaged aisle,
        Bowed down on bended knee;
That her poor ghost outflickers there
        Is known to none but me."

25   "O Memory, where is now my love,
That rayed me as a god above?"

"I saw her in an ageing shape
        Where beauty used to be;
That her fond phantom lingers there
30   Is only known to me."

Questions

1. Why is the "I" talking to Memory? Is Memory the most appropriate one to question? Why?
2. Youth, Joy, Hope, Faith, and Love are all placed in specific settings. Are the settings appropriate? What do they tell us about the "I" of the poem?

Fable

The fable, which is closely related to the allegory, is typically a story in which animals are given human attributes and represent certain moral qualities or philosophical positions. Most of the fables we know are derived from Aesop, a legendary Greek poet. The most famous, perhaps, is the story of the turtle and the rabbit who race one another. The moral or lesson of the story is: slow, steady work will triumph over impulsiveness.

Fables can be political as well. George Orwell's *Animal Farm* is a long prose allegorical fable about the rise of dictatorships. But Orwell was not the first author to write a political fable; he was participating in a long tradition, whose origins are buried in the distant past. "The Lion, the Fox, and Geese," a fable written by John Gay in the eighteenth century, still has relevance today.

JOHN GAY (1685–1732)

The Lion, the Fox, and Geese

A Lion, tired with state affairs,
Quite sick of pomp, and worn with cares,
Resolv'd (remote from noise and strife)
In peace to pass his latter life.
5   It was proclaim'd; the day was set;
Behold the gen'ral council met.
The Fox was Viceroy nam'd. The crowd
To the new Regent humbly bow'd
Wolves, bears, and mighty tygers bend,
10 And strive who most shall condescend.
He strait assumes a solemn grace,
Collects his wisdom in his face,
The crowd admire his wit, his sense:
Each word hath weight and consequence.
15 The flatt'rer all his art displays:
He who hath power, is sure of praise.
A Fox stept forth before the rest,
And thus the servile throng addrest.
      How vast his talents, born to rule,
20 And train'd in virtue's honest school!
What clemency his temper sways!
How uncorrupt are all his ways!
Beneath his conduct and command,
Rapine shall cease to waste the land.
25 His brain hath stratagem and art;
Prudence and mercy rule his heart;
What blessings must attend the nation
Under this good administration!
      He said. A Goose who distant stood,
30 Harangu'd apart the cackling brood.
      Whene'er I hear a knave commend,
He bids me shun his worthy friend.
What praise! what mighty commendation!
But 'twas a Fox who spoke th'oration.
35 Foxes this government might prize,
As gentle, plentiful, and wise;
If they enjoy the sweets, 'tis plain
We Geese must feel a tyrant reign.
What havock now shall thin our race,
40 When ev'ry petty clerk in place,
To prove his taste and seem polite,
Will feed on Geese both noon and night!

Questions

1. Vocabulary: *pomp* (2), *viceroy* (7), *Regent* (8), *servile* (18), *clemency* (21), *stratagem* (25), *harangued* (30).

2. If the Lion represents "true kingship," what does the Fox represent?
3. Why is the Goose afraid of the Fox? Whom does the Goose represent? Are the Goose's fears justified?
4. Can you think of any political events to which this allegory might apply?

In Gay's time the Lion referred not just to any king but to King George II. The Fox was Sir Robert Walpole (1676–1745), whom historians generally consider the first prime minister in English history, a controversial figure who was greatly feared. The fables gave Gay an opportunity to make his political points and yet avoid imprisonment and the accusation of treason. Under tyranny, fables become a popular form of political expression.

Symbol

The term *symbol* refers to a large variety of literary practices, and it is important to distinguish among the various uses of the term. Allegory makes use of symbols. In Herbert's "Pilgrimage" the "gladsome hill" is a symbol for heaven; the "brackish lake" is a symbol of worldly difficulties. Indeed, we might define allegory as the narrative orchestration of a number of symbols into a coherent pattern.

In its broadest sense a symbol is any object or action that signifies more than itself. For example, the badge an officer wears is not merely a decorative silvery pin; it refers to, or symbolizes, legal authority. The candles on a birthday cake are not placed there primarily to light the room or to keep the cake warm. They symbolize the number of years the person has lived. The clothes you wear do not simply keep you comfortable and warm; they also communicate your values. You may have an embroidered alligator, Greek letters, or a numeral on your shirt or blouse. Each of these symbols has its social significance.

How are symbols formed? There are people who do nothing but design symbols intended to advertise products. But symbols appear to be a natural function of every mind. Psychiatrists tell us that our dreams are complicated allegories through which we work out our feelings. Our waking lives are no less involved with symbols. The following poem by D. H. Lawrence tells us about the formation of a symbol.

D. H. LAWRENCE (1885–1930)

Sorrow

Why does the thin grey strand
Floating up from the forgotten
Cigarette between my fingers,
Why does it trouble me?

5   Ah, you will understand;
When I carried my mother downstairs,
A few times only, at the beginning
Of her soft-foot malady,

I should find, for a reprimand
10   To my gaiety, a few long grey hairs
On the breast of my coat; and one by one
I watched them float up the dark chimney.

Questions

1. What specific words link the cigarette smoke to his mother's hair?
2. In what other senses are the hairs on his coat "a reprimand/To [his] gaiety"?
3. In line 12, what does the "dark chimney" symbolize?
4. Does the poem give you a logical explanation of why the smoke troubles the speaker? If not, why not?

Lawrence's poem shows how very different sensations become associated in our minds, especially during periods of emotional intensity. During his mother's final illness, the speaker had carried her about the house, and her hair had fallen on his clothing. Now the "thin grey strand" of cigarette smoke symbolizes the speaker's complex feelings about his mother's death.

One of the differences between the symbol of the cigarette smoke and that of the Lion in John Gay's fable is the number of associations the symbols have. The symbols in allegory and fable are relatively limited in reference. The Lion represents "natural leadership," "kingship," and—most specifically—King George II. These various references are closely related. But the cigarette smoke is associated with a complex and varied series of events, emotions, and ideas. It symbolizes the mother, her death, the speaker's continued existence. Symbols can also refer to other symbols. The cigarette smoke symbolizes the mother's hair, which in turn is "a reprimand/To [his] gaiety." The forgotten cigarette symbolizes the speaker's forgetfulness of his dying mother; it symbolizes his guilt.

One problem with symbols is that we sometimes recognize them without understanding their significance. Have you ever attended a religious ceremony of a different faith and been confused by the actions and symbols used in the ceremony, although you may have found them perfectly and even beautifully fitting? In "I Saw in Louisiana a Live-Oak Growing," Walt Whitman encounters a symbol that he finds difficult to comprehend.

WALT WHITMAN (1819–1892)

I Saw in Louisiana a Live-Oak Growing

I saw in Louisiana a live-oak growing.
All alone stood it and moss hung down from the branches.
Without any companion it grew there uttering joyous leaves of dark green,
And its look, rude, unbending, lusty, made me think of myself.
5   But I wonder'd how it could utter joyous leaves standing alone there without its
    friend near, for I knew I could not,
And I broke off a twig with a certain number of leaves upon it, and twined around
    it a little moss

And brought it away, and I placed it in sight in my room,
It is not needed to remind me as of my own dear friends,
(For I believe lately I think of little else than them.)
10   Yet it remains to me a curious token, it makes me think of manly love;
For all that, and though the live-oak glistens there in Louisiana solitary in a wide
    flat space,
Uttering joyous leaves all its life without a friend a lover near,
I know very well I could not.

Questions

1. In what way does the tree symbolize Whitman? In what ways does it not?
2. Why does the tree make Whitman think of "manly love"?
3. Why does he break off a twig?
4. Do you ever collect things in your travels? Why do you do it? Do they ever come to symbolize something for you?

ROBERT FROST (1874–1963)

For Once, Then, Something

Others taunt me with having knelt at well-curbs
Always wrong to the light, so never seeing
Deeper down in the well than where the water
Gives me back in a shining surface picture
5   Me myself in the summer heaven, godlike,
Looking out of a wreath of fern and cloud puffs.

Robert Frost *(Rollie McKenna)*

Once, when trying with chin against a well-curb,
I discerned, as I thought, beyond the picture,
Through the picture, a something white, uncertain,
10 Something more of the depths—and then I lost it.
Water came to rebuke the too clear water.
One drop fell from a fern, and lo, a ripple
Shook whatever it was lay there at bottom,
Blurred it, blotted it out. What was that whiteness?
15 Truth? A pebble of quartz? For once, then, something.

Questions

1. A Greek proverb says that "truth lies in the bottom of wells." How is this truth symbolized?
2. What does the "something" seen symbolize? Would the symbol be clearer if we were told what the speaker saw?
3. Does the whole action take on larger significance? Why does the speaker look into wells? What is peculiar about the way he does it?
4. At the poem's end, has the speaker lost the "godlike" feeling he had in line 5?

Traditional Symbols

The cigarette smoke, the live-oak, and the "whiteness" in the well are all unusual symbols, peculiar to the poets and to the poems in which they appear. Some symbols, however, are traditional. The cross symbolizes Christ's sacrifice; the unicorn is a symbol of purity; the apple represents forbidden knowledge. Poets often use traditional symbols in their work. The following song by Edmund Waller employs two traditional symbolic meanings of the rose: the rose is a symbol of love and of beauty's frailty.

EDMUND WALLER (1606–1687)

Go, Lovely Rose

Go, lovely Rose,
Tell her that wastes her Time and me,
    That now she knows,
When I resemble° her to thee,   *compare*
5 How sweet and fair she seems to be.

    Tell her that's Young,
And shuns to have her Graces spy'd,
    That hadst thou sprung
In Desarts, where no Men abide,
10 Thou must have uncommended dy'd.

    Small is the Worth
Of Beauty from the Light retir'd;
    Bid her come forth,

Suffer her self to be desir'd,
15 And not blush so to be admir'd.

        Then die, that she
The common Fate of all Things rare
        May read in thee:
How small a Part of Time they share,
20 That are so wond'rous sweet and fair.

Questions

1. How is personification used in this poem?
2. If you received this rose, how would you feel? What is the speaker's reason for addressing the rose?

Yeats was fond of the rose symbol. Notice how he relies on its traditional associations with love and beauty in this poem.

W. B. YEATS (1865–1939)

The Rose of Peace

If Michael, leader of God's host,[2]
When Heaven and Hell are met,
Looked down on you from Heaven's door-post
He would his deeds forget.

5   Brooding no more upon God's wars
In his divine homestead,
He would go weave out of the stars
A chaplet° for your head.   *wreath*

And all folk seeing him bow down,
10 And white stars tell your praise,
Would come at last to God's great town,
Led on by gentle ways;

And God would bid His warfare cease,
Saying all things were well;
15 And softly make a rosy peace,
A peace of Heaven with Hell.

Questions

1. Why would Michael forget his deeds?
2. What about the rose makes it bring peace?
3. How would this poem be different in feeling if it were about the "orchid of peace"? Is it important that the symbol be traditional?

---

[2] The archangel Michael.

Symbols are everywhere in poetry, as in the world around us, but one must be careful of them. Not everything is a symbol, though everything may contain the potential to become one. Before you interpret anything symbolically, you should try to find out if it is a traditional symbol or if the context in which it appears indicates its symbolic meaning. By being aware of context and tradition, you will become a seasoned reader able to distinguish well-chosen detail from symbol.

Suggestions for Essayists

1. With what sorts of symbols do you surround yourself? What message do you hope to convey about yourself?
2. Discuss the meanings of the symbols associated with a religious or secular holiday or ritual, such as Easter or Thanksgiving.
3. In the poems you have read, what sort of symbols have you found the most powerful? Why?

Suggestions for Poets

1. Carry on a discussion between two parts of your personality.
2. Speak to a traditional symbol, such as the rose. What do you want to tell it?
3. Retell a fable in your own words.

✍ Poems for Further Study

THOMAS HARDY (1840–1928)

The Subalterns

I

"Poor wanderer," said the leaden sky,
 "I fain would lighten thee,
But there are laws in force on high
 Which say it must not be."

II

5 —"I would not freeze thee, shorn one," cried
 The North, "knew I but how
To warm my breath, to slack my stride;
 But I am ruled as thou."

III

—"To-morrow I attack thee, wight,"
10 Said Sickness. "Yet I swear
I bear thy little ark no spite,
 But am bid enter there."

IV

—"Come hither, Son," I heard Death say;
    "I did not will a grave

15 Should end thy pilgrimage to-day,
    But I, too, am a slave!"

V

We smiled upon each other then,
    And life to me had less
Of that fell look it wore ere when

20   They owned their passiveness.

VERNON WATKINS (1906–1967)

The Lady with the Unicorn

About this lady many fruitful trees.
There the chaste unicorn before her knees
Stares in a glass to purify her sight.
At her right hand a lion sits,
5 And through the foliage, in and out, there flits
Many a bird; then hounds, with deer in flight:
Light is her element; her tapestry is light.

There is her mediaeval music met.
On the high table-top, with damask set
10 To charm, between the chaste beast and the strong,
An organ which her fingers play
Rests, and her pretty servant's hands obey
Those pipes with bellows to sustain their song
Attuned to distant stars, making their short life long.

15 This ended, gathered from some leafy way,
That servant brings her flowers upon a tray.
She lifts them to inhale their magic breath.
Caught in that breath's elusive maze,
She marvels. On a stool a monkey plays
20 With flowers from wicker trailing, strewn beneath,
A heaven of fragrance breathing through their mask of death.

Next, her right hand upholds that coat-of-arms
Seeming love's guardian against war's alarms,
And with her left she grips the upright horn.
25 This touch, while birds through branches peer,
Consecrates all the beasts as they appear,
Frisking among dark foliage to adorn
Her fingers that caress the constant unicorn.

A lion rampant grips the upright pole.
30 Her serving-maid now proffers her a bowl
Of peaches, damsons, almonds, grapes, and sweets.

Cluny Tapestry, *The Lady and the Unicorn (Editorial Photocolor Archives/Alinari)*

This lady savours one, and sees
How white of almonds, red of mulberries,
Is each a praise no other tree repeats,
35 Now strangely on love's tree engrafted while she eats.

The senses leave a chain upon her tongue.
That place is hushed, from which the light is sprung.
Curtains are hung, embroidered with strange art.
The letters 'TO MY SOLE DESIRE'
40 Crown that pavilion with a band of fire
Whose folds the unicorn and lion part,
Revealing in their midst her love-awakened heart.

O sovereign balm to heal all mortal illness:
Long let him look, and still he will find stillness,
45 Her one betrothed, who sees her museful face.
This lady, with her flowers and hounds,
Woven in light, in air, in wooded grounds,
Transmits a glory wrought about her grace,
Caught in a sacred bond within the encircling space.

50 Let him look softly, with some seventh sense
Breaking that circle's hushed magnificence,
And see what universe her love controls,
Moving with hushed, divine intent
Through the five senses to their sacrament

55   Whose Eden turns between two silent poles,
      Creating with pure speed that harmony of souls.

      Where is the heart of mathematic space?
      Throned on a mystery in that leafy place,
      This lady's fingers hold, where distance flies,
60   The Past and Future like a skein
      For her betrothed to wind, and loose again.
      Lion and unicorn forbid disguise.
      He looks, and she looks forth: there are no other eyes.

MAY SARTON (1912–)

The Lady and the Unicorn

The Cluny Tapestries

      I am the unicorn and bow my head
      You are the lady woven into history
      And here forever we are bound in mystery
      Our wine, Imagination, and our bread,
5   And I the unicorn who bows his head.

      You are all interwoven in my history
      And you and I have been most strangely wed
      I am the unicorn and bow my head
      And lay my wildness down upon your knee
10   You are the lady woven into history.

      And here forever we are sweetly wed
      With flowers and rabbits in the tapestry
      You are the lady woven into history
      Imagination is our bridal bed:
15   We lie ghostly upon it, no word said.

      Among the flowers of the tapestry
      I am the unicorn and by your bed
      Come gently, gently to bow down my head,
      Lay at your side this love, this mystery,
20   And call you lady of my tapestry.

      I am the unicorn and bow my head
      To one so sweetly lost, so strangely wed:

      You sit forever under a small formal tree
      Where I forever search your eyes to be

25   Rewarded with this shining tragedy
      And know your beauty was not cast for me,

      Know we are woven all in mystery,
      The wound imagined where no one has bled,

      My wild love chastened to this history
30   Where I before your eyes, bow down my head.

ROBINSON JEFFERS (1887–1962)

Rock and Hawk

Here is a symbol in which
Many high tragic thoughts
Watch their own eyes.

This gray rock, standing tall
5   On the headland, where the seawind
Lets no tree grow,

Earthquake-proved, and signatured
By ages of storms: on its peak
A falcon has perched.

10   I think, here is your emblem
To hang in the future sky;
Not the cross, not the hive,

But this; bright power, dark peace;
Fierce consciousness joined with final
15   Disinterestedness;

Life with calm death; the falcon's
Realist eyes and act
Married to the massive

Mysticism of stone,
20   Which failure cannot cast down
Nor success make proud.

DELMORE SCHWARTZ (1913–1966)

The Heavy Bear Who Goes with Me

"the withness of the body"
          —Whitehead[3]

The heavy bear who goes with me,
A manifold honey to smear his face,
Clumsy and lumbering here and there,
The central ton of every place,
5   The hungry beating brutish one
In love with candy, anger, and sleep,
Crazy factotum, dishevelling all,
Climbs the building, kicks the football,
Boxes his brother in the hate-ridden city.
10   Breathing at my side, that heavy animal,
That heavy bear who sleeps with me,
Howls in his sleep for a world of sugar,
A sweetness intimate as the water's clasp,

---

[3] Alfred North Whitehead (1861–1947), English mathematician and philosopher.

Howls in his sleep because the tight-rope
15   Trembles and shows the darkness beneath.
      —The strutting show-off is terrified,
      Dressed in his dress-suit, bulging his pants,
      Trembles to think that his quivering meat
      Must finally wince to nothing at all.

20   That inescapable animal walks with me,
      Has followed me since the black womb held,
      Moves where I move, distorting my gesture,
      A caricature, a swollen shadow,
      A stupid clown of the spirit's motive,
25   Perplexes and affronts with his own darkness,
      The secret life of belly and bone,
      Opaque, too near, my private, yet unknown,
      Stretches to embrace the very dear
      With whom I would walk without him near,
30   Touches her grossly, although a word
      Would bare my heart and make me clear,
      Stumbles, flounders, and strives to be fed
      Dragging me with him in his mouthing care,
      Amid the hundred million of his kind,
35   The scrimmage of appetite everywhere.

D. H. LAWRENCE (1885–1930)

Snake

      A snake came to my water-trough
      On a hot, hot day, and I in pyjamas for the heat,
      To drink there.

      In the deep, strange-scented shade of the great dark carob tree
5   I came down the steps with my pitcher
      And must wait, must stand and wait, for there he was at the trough before me.

      He reached down from a fissure in the earth-wall in the gloom
      And trailed his yellow-brown slackness soft-bellied down, over the edge of the stone
          trough
      And rested his throat upon the stone bottom,
10   And where the water had dripped from the tap, in a small clearness,
      He sipped with his straight mouth,
      Softly drank through his straight gums, into his slack long body,
      Silently.

      Someone was before me at my water-trough,
15   And I, like a second comer, waiting.

      He lifted his head from his drinking, as cattle do,
      And looked at me vaguely, as drinking cattle do,
      And flickered his two-forked tongue from his lips, and mused a moment,
      And stooped and drank a little more,

20   Being earth-brown, earth-golden from the burning bowels of the earth
    On the day of Sicilian July, with Etna[4] smoking.

    The voice of my education said to me
    He must be killed,
    For in Sicily the black, black snakes are innocent, the gold are venomous.

25   And voices in me said, If you were a man
    You would take a stick and break him now, and finish him off.

    But must I confess how I liked him,
    How glad I was he had come like a guest in quiet, to drink at my water-trough
    And depart peaceful, pacified, and thankless,
30   Into the burning bowels of this earth?

    Was it cowardice, that I dared not kill him?
    Was it perversity, that I longed to talk to him?
    Was it humility, to feel so honoured?
    I felt so honoured.

35   And yet those voices:
    If you were not afraid, you would kill him!

    And truly I was afraid, I was most afraid,
    But even so, honoured still more
    That he should seek my hospitality
40   From out the dark door of the secret earth.

    He drank enough
    And lifted his head, dreamily, as one who has drunken,
    And flickered his tongue like a forked night on the air, so black,
    Seeming to lick his lips,
45   And looked around like a god, unseeing, into the air,
    And slowly turned his head,
    And slowly, very slowly, as if thrice adream,
    Proceeded to draw his slow length curving round
    And climb again the broken bank of my wall-face.

50   And as he put his head into that dreadful hole,
    And as he slowly drew up, snake-easing his shoulders, and entered farther,
    A sort of horror, a sort of protest against his withdrawing into that horrid black
       hole,
    Deliberately going into the blackness, and slowly drawing himself after,
    Overcame me now his back was turned.

55   I looked around, I put down my pitcher,
    I picked up a clumsy log
    And threw it at the water-trough with a clatter.

    I think I did not hit him,
    But suddenly that part of him that was left behind convulsed in undignified haste,
60   Writhed like lightning, and was gone

---

[4] Mt. Etna, a volcano in Sicily.

Into the black hole, the earth-lipped fissure in the wall-front,
At which, in the intense still noon, I stared with fascination.

And immediately I regretted it.
I thought how paltry, how vulgar, what a mean act!
65 I despised myself and the voices of my accursed human education.

And I thought of the albatross,[5]
And I wished he would come back, my snake.

For he seemed to me again like a king,
Like a king in exile, uncrowned in the underworld,
70 Now due to be crowned again.

And so, I missed my chance with one of the lords
Of life.
And I have something to expiate;
A pettiness.

CHRISTOPHER SMART (1722–1771)

The Ant and the Caterpillar

As an ant, of his talents superiorly vain,
Was trotting with consequence over the plain,
A worm, in his progress, remarkably slow,
Cry'd, "Bless your good worship, wherever you go?
5 "I hope your great mightiness won't take it ill,
"I pay my respects from an hearty good will."

With a look of contempt, and ineffable pride,
"Begone you vile reptile," his antship reply'd:
"But first— look at me —see—my limbs how complete:
10 "I guide all my motions with freedom and ease;
"I run back and forward, and turn when I please.
"Of nature (grown weary) thou shocking essay!°   *trial specimen*
"I spurn you thus from me;—crawl out of my way."

The reptile insulted, and vex'd to the soul,
15 Crept onwards, and hid himself close in his hole;
But nature determin'd to end his distress,
Soon sent him abroad in a butterfly dress.

Ere long the proud ant was repassing the road,
(Fatigued from the harvest, and tugging his load)
20 The beau on a violet bank he beheld,
Whose vesture in glory, a monarch excell'd;
His plumage expanded!—'twas rare to behold
So lovely a mixture of purple and gold;
The ant, quite amaz'd at a figure so gay,
25 Bow'd low with respect, and was trudging away:

---

[5] In Coleridge's "Rime of the Ancient Mariner," the sailor brings a curse upon himself and his ship by senselessly killing an albatross.

"Stop, friend," says the butterfly, "don't be surprised;
"I once was the reptile you spurn'd and despis'd;
"But now, I can mount—in the sun-beams I play,
"While you must, forever, drudge on in your way."

The Moral: A *wretch that to-day is o'erloaded with
sorrow, May soar above those that oppressed him
tomorrow.*

JEAN DE LA FONTAINE (1621–1695)

The Rat and the Oyster

A rat, a field rat, a feeble-minded rat,
one day decided he was weary of home—
abandoned thereupon his fields and sheaves,
wandered the countryside, leaving his hole
5   behind. No sooner were familiar surroundings
out of sight, than the world, he said, was wide:
"There are the Apennines, and here the Caucasus!"[6]
Every molehill was a mountain to his eyes.
After some days' travel, the creature came
10   to a certain district where upon the shore
Thetis had deposited a great bed of oysters.[7]
And our rat, at his first sight, assumed
the shellfish were a fleet of ships.
"What a pathetic figure my father cut,"
15   he mused, "never daring to see the world,
timid to the last. Now I have seen the sea,
crossed deserts, though without a drop to drink."
The rat had acquired this information, so to speak,
from a certain professor, and spoke as he ran,
20   not being one of those rats who, chewing books,
become thereby knowledgeable to the teeth!
Among so many tight-shut oysters there was one
that lay open, gaping in the sunshine,
flattered by a gentle breeze, and taking
25   the air as if it asked for nothing better:
white, plump, and evidently of matchless savor.
No sooner had the rat caught sight of this
yawning bivalve than he exclaimed (to himself):
"What do I see? It is some delicacy—and if
30   the color of the creature does not deceive me,
today (or never) I shall dine gastronomically!"
Thereupon our rat, filled with eager hope,
approached the gaping shell, stuck out his
neck, and thereupon was caught fast, as in a trap,

---

[6] Two mountain ranges. The Apennines form a chain down central Italy. The Caucasus are in Russia between the Black and the Caspian seas.

[7] Thetis was the daughter of Nereus, a sea god, and the mother of Achilles.

35 for the oyster straightway closed fast upon
    the victim of his own ignorance, the rat.

    This fable affords more than one moral—
    first of all we discern that those who have
    no experience of the world are astonished
40 by the merest trifles, and then we may learn
    how potential captors may themselves be caught.

Translation by Richard Howard (1929–)

GEORGE HERBERT (1593–1633)

Love (III)

Love bade me welcome: yet my soul drew back,
    Guilty of dust and sin.
But quick-eyed Love, observing me grow slack
    From my first entrance in,
5 Drew nearer to me, sweetly questioning
    If I lacked anything.

"A guest," I answered, "worthy to be here":
    Love said, "You shall be he."
"I, the unkind, ungrateful? Ah, my dear,
10   I cannot look on thee."
Love took my hand, and smiling did reply,
    "Who made the eyes but I?"

"Truth, Lord; but I have marred them; let my shame
    Go where it doth deserve."
15 "And know you not," says Love, "who bore the blame?"
    "My dear, then I will serve."
"You must sit down," says Love, "and taste my meat."
    So I did sit and eat.

ROBERT SOUTHWELL (1561–1595)

The Burning Babe

As I in hoary winter's night stood shivering in the snow,
Surprised I was with sudden heat which made my heart to glow;
And lifting up a fearful eye to view what fire was near,
A pretty babe all burning bright did in the air appear;
5 Who, scorchéd with excessive heat, such floods of tears did shed
As though his floods should quench his flames which with his tears were fed.
"Alas," quoth he, "but newly born in fiery heats I fry,
Yet none approach to warm their hearts or feel my fire but I!
My faultless breast the furnace is, the fuel wounding thorns,
10 Love is the fire, and sighs the smoke, the ashes shame and scorns;
The fuel justice layeth on, and mercy blows the coals,

The metal in this furnace wrought are men's defiléd souls,
For which, as now on fire I am to work them to their good,
So will I melt into a bath to wash them in my blood."
15 With this he vanished out of sight and swiftly shrunk away,
And straight I calléd unto mind that it was Christmas day.

EDMUND SPENSER (1552–1599)

One Day As I Unwarily Did Gaze

One day as I unwarily did gaze
On those fayre eyes, my loves immortall light;
The whilest my stonisht hart stood in amaze,
Through sweet illusion of her lookes delight;
5 I mote perceive how, in her glauncing sight,
Legions of Loves with little wings did fly;
Darting their deadly arrows, fyry bright,
At every rash beholder passing by.
One of those archers closely I did spy,
10 Ayming his arrow at my very hart:
When suddenly, with twincle of her eye,
The Damzell broke his misintended dart.
    Had she not so doon, sure I had bene slayne;
    Yet as it was, I hardly scap't with paine.

9 ❧ More Figures of Speech

Hyperbole

What do we do when we see something more beautiful than we have ever seen? So ugly we can hardly bear to look at it? How do we respond when we hear Pavarotti sing an aria more beautifully than we could have imagined, or see an outfielder make a seemingly impossible catch? Sportswriters, theater reviewers, and poets often respond with a figure of speech called *hyperbole*.

> The man was so fast he could kiss a bullet.
>
> He was so delicate he was knocked unconscious by a snowflake.
>
> The engine was as noisy as a living skeleton having a fit on a hardwood floor.

Hyperbole is an exaggeration, a statement that something has either much more or much less of a quality than it actually has. *Hyperbole*, from the Greek, literally means "to overshoot the mark." Since exaggeration is a principle of comedy, hyperbole is often comic:

> My belly is as cold as if I had swallowed
> snowballs for pills to cool the veins.
> —*William Shakespeare*

Although exaggeration is usually achieved through simile and metaphor, there are other forms of hyperbole. For example, we are familiar with hyperbole in the tall tale, a popular American entertainment from the time of the early settlers. Notice the narrative imagery of the following poem. The images are drawn to prove how extreme is the quality to be exaggerated: the hinges on the skyscraper "to let the moon go by" attest to its height. We can picture two or more "liars" sitting around a stove, each trying to come up with the most outlandish exaggerations.

CARL SANDBURG (1878–1967)

They Have Yarns

They have yarns
Of a skyscraper so tall they had to put hinges
On the two top stories so to let the moon go by,
Of one corn crop in Missouri when the roots
5   Went so deep and drew off so much water
The Mississippi riverbed that year was dry,
Of pancakes so thin they had only one side,
Of "a fog so thick we shingled the barn and six feet out on the fog,"
Of Pecos Pete straddling a cyclone in Texas and riding it to the west coast where "it rained out under him,"
10   Of the man who drove a swarm of bees across the Rocky Mountains and the Desert "and didn't lose a bee,"
Of a mountain railroad curve where the engineer in his cab can touch the caboose and spit in the conductor's eye,
Of the boy who climbed a cornstalk growing so fast he would have starved to death if they hadn't shot biscuits up to him,
Of the old man's whiskers: "When the wind was with him his whiskers arrived a day before he did,"
Of the hen laying a square egg and cackling, "Ouch!" and of hens laying eggs with the dates printed on them,
15   Of the ship captain's shadow: it froze to the deck one cold winter night,
Of mutineers on that same ship put to chipping rust with rubber hammers,
Of the sheep counter who was fast and accurate: "I just count their feet and divide by four,"
Of the man so tall he must climb a ladder to shave himself,
Of the runt so teeny-weeny it takes two men and a boy to see him,
20   Of mosquitoes: one can kill a dog, two of them a man,
Of a cyclone that sucked cookstoves out of the kitchen, up the chimney flue, and on to the next town,
Of the same cyclone picking up wagon-tracks in Nebraska and dropping them over in the Dakotas.

Questions

1. What characters of tall tales has Sandburg alluded to in this poem?
2. How has Sandburg exaggerated sizes and heights?
3. How have these exaggerations captured the vastness and vitality of the American spirit?
4. What sorts of exaggerations do you use when bragging to friends about your exploits?

CECCO ANGIOLIERI (c. 1260–c. 1312)

In Absence from Becchina

My heart's so heavy with a hundred things
    That I feel dead a hundred times a-day;
Yet death would be the least of sufferings,

For life's all suffering save what's slept away;
5   Though even in sleep there is no dream but brings
From dream-land such dull torture as it may.
And yet one moment would pluck out these stings,
If for one moment she were mine to-day
Who gives my heart the anguish that it has.
10   Each thought that seeks my heart for its abode
Becomes a wan and sorrow-stricken guest:
Sorrow has brought me to so sad a pass
That men look sad to meet me on the road;
Nor any road is mine that leads to rest.

Translation by Dante Gabriel Rossetti (1828–1882)

Questions

1. Is it possible to "feel dead"? Is the poet exaggerating his pain in line 2?
2. What other hyperbole do you find in this poem?

RANDALL JARRELL (1914–1965)

The Mockingbird

Look one way and the sun is going down,
Look the other and the moon is rising.
The sparrow's shadow's longer than the lawn.
The bats squeak: "Night is here"; the birds cheep: "Day is gone."
5   On the willow's highest branch, monopolizing
Day and night, cheeping, squeaking, soaring,
The mockingbird is imitating life.

All day the mockingbird has owned the yard.
As light first woke the world, the sparrows trooped
10   Onto the seedy lawn: the mockingbird
Chased them off shrieking. Hour by hour, fighting hard
To make the world his own, he swooped
On thrushes, thrashers, jays, and chickadees—
At noon he drove away a big black cat.

15   Now, in the moonlight, he sits here and sings.
A thrush is singing, then a thrasher, then a jay—
Then, all at once, a cat begins meowing.
A mockingbird can sound like anything.
He imitates the world he drove away
20   So well that for a minute, in the moonlight,
Which one's the mockingbird? which one's the world?

Questions

1. Granted that shadows lengthen as the sun sets, is it possible that "the sparrow's shadow's longer than the lawn"? If not, why does the speaker exaggerate?
2. Does the mockingbird really "monopolize" day and night? Has he really "owned the

yard"? What does this hyperbole suggest about the importance of the bird to the speaker?

3. What other hyperbole do you find in the poem?
4. Does Jarrell exaggerate the significance of the mockingbird by suggesting he cannot distinguish it from the world?

Understatement

Understatement, or the deliberate avoidance of emphasis in description, is sometimes considered a figure of speech related to hyperbole. In the following excerpt from T. S. Eliot's poem "Aunt Helen" we find an amusing instance of understatement.

> Miss Helen Slingsby was my maiden aunt,
> And lived in a small house near a fashionable square
> Cared for by servants to the number of four.
> Now when she died there was silence in heaven
> And silence at her end of the street.
> The shutters were drawn and the undertaker wiped his feet—
> He was aware this sort of thing had occurred before.

Aware? The undertaker is not only "aware" of death, he is immersed in it, a veritable merchant of death. The delight of understatement is in the effect of verbal irony—we expect the writer to say something extreme, and he surprises us by saying something subtle. Thus understatement is not so much a figure of speech as a tone of voice. We will look at it again in our discussion of tone.

Synecdoche, Metonymy, Allusion, and Paradox

One of the things that distinguishes poetry from prose is the level of concentration of the language. Ezra Pound has written that "great literature is simply language charged with meaning to the utmost possible degree," and that poetry "is the most concentrated form of verbal expression."[1] In the effort to say more with less language, poets sometimes use a word or several words to suggest other words or some larger context of meaning.

Synecdoche

Synecdoche is a figure of speech in which part of a thing is mentioned to suggest the whole thing, or a larger concept is mentioned to suggest something specific. Either way there is a correspondence of information between part and whole that enriches our view of both. Everyday speech is full of synecdoche. When the car breaks down we may say we need "new wheels," although new wheels, without the rest of the car, would be useless. "New wheels" is a livelier expression than "car." When we refer to a sluggish person as "lazybones," we suggest the depth of his or her indolence. When the captain says, "All hands on deck," we

---

[1] Ezra Pound, *The ABC of Reading* (New York: New Directions, 1934).

know he wants the men as well as their hands, but the word "hands" tells us more about what he wants from them. And when, in despair over the loss of her mail, someone says, "My whole world is lost," she is not merely exaggerating; she is using synecdoche, expressing a specific misfortune in terms of a more general one. Robert Frost used to refer to himself as a "synecdochist," meaning that his own little *part* of life was valuable in relation to the *whole* of life.

In the following poem synecdoche is used both to specify poignant incidents and to broaden the implications of detail. The poem is addressed to an old man, presumably a close friend, who is leaving the speaker.

PO CHU-I (A.D. 772–846)

Seeing Hsia Chan Off by River

Because you are old and departing I have wetted my handkerchief,
You who are homeless at seventy, belonging to the wilderness.
Anxiously I watch the wind rising as the boat sails away,
A white-headed man amid white-headed waves.

Translation by Ching Ti

Questions

1. How does the speaker use synecdoche in line 1 to show that he wept?
2. In what way is the phrase "white-headed man" a synecdoche? Would "white-haired man" be synecdoche?
3. What is the emotional force of juxtaposing the white-headed man and the white-headed waves? Does the juxtaposition make the old man look strong? Vulnerable?

RALPH WALDO EMERSON (1803–1882)

Letters

Every day brings a ship,
Every ship brings a word;
Well for those who have no fear,
Looking seaward well assured
5   That the word the vessel brings
Is the word they wish to hear.

Question

1. How does this poem use synecdoche?

Metonymy

Metonymy is a figure of speech in which the name of a person, place, or thing calls forth a more complex structure of things and ideas that the name signifies.

Ralph Waldo Emerson
(Harvard College Library)

Place names work that way. "Vermont" calls forth an image of gentle green hills, maple trees hung with sap buckets, and vivid foliage. When we talk of "New England weather," we may mean clear, cool summer nights, or snowy Januaries. "Texas" evokes flat, windy plains, ten-gallon hats, and oil wells. If you said that someone's manners were "pure Boston prep," people would have a good idea of what you meant. When the television commentator reports on the activities of "Washington," we know he is not merely telling us about the District of Columbia, but about the U.S. government. Likewise, "the Church" signifies the whole complex of organized religion, just as "the crown" signifies the entire government of a monarchy. These are all examples of metonymy, whereby a single name is used as shorthand, for its vividness or sound.

In the following ironic protest poem, practically every noun is used metonymically. We call the poem ironic because the speaker clearly hates what he is praising.

WILLIAM BUTLER YEATS (1865–1939)

The Great Day

Hurrah for revolution and more cannon-shot!
A beggar upon horseback lashes a beggar on foot.
Hurrah for revolution and cannon come again!
The beggars have changed places, but the lash goes on.

Questions

1. What complex of actions and emotions is suggested by the metonymy of "cannon-shot"?
2. What social position is signified by the "beggar upon horseback"? The "beggar on foot"?

3. Is the phrase "on foot" an instance of metonymy, synecdoche, or both?
4. What is the significance of the lash?

The following poem achieves terrific concentration through the skillful use of synecdoche and metonymy. It is a meditation on religion and history—how civilizations rise and fall regardless of religion, and how the sense of religion survives history. By using metonymy, Lowell can include a vast range of civilizations in a relatively short poem. By using synecdoche, he creates an atmosphere of super-real detail.

ROBERT LOWELL (1917–1980)

Beyond the Alps

(On the train from Rome to Paris. 1950, the year Pius XII
defined the dogma of Mary's bodily assumption.)

Reading how even the Swiss had thrown the sponge
in once again and Everest[2] was still
unscaled, I watched our Paris Pullman[3] lunge
mooning across the fallow Alpine snow.
5   *O bella Roma!*[4] I saw our stewards go
forward on tiptoe banging on their gongs.
Life changed to landscape. Much against my will
I left the City of God[5] where it belongs.
There the skirt-mad Mussolini[6] unfurled
10   the eagle of Caesar.[7] He was one of us
only, pure prose. I envy the conspicuous
waste of our grandparents on their grand tours—
long-haired Victorian sages bought the universe,
while breezing on their trust funds through the world.

15   When the Vatican made Mary's Assumption dogma,[8]
the crowds at San Pietro screamed *Papá.*[9]
The Holy Father dropped his shaving glass,
and listened. His electric razor purred,
his pet canary chirped on his left hand.
20   The lights of science couldn't hold a candle
to Mary risen—at one miraculous stroke,

---

[2] Mount Everest, the tallest mountain in the world.
[3] A train with sleeping accommodations. Lowell is traveling from Rome to Paris.
[4] *O bella Roma* is Italian for "Oh beautiful Rome."
[5] St. Augustine's phrase, used to refer to Rome under the popes.
[6] Italian dictator during World War II; also called *Il Duce*, "the leader."
[7] The eagle, Caesar's insignia, was also used by Mussolini.
[8] Not until the twentieth century was there a papal declaration that Mary, mother of Jesus, ascended into heaven after her death.
[9] *Papá* is the Italian term of endearment for the pope. San Pietro is St. Peter's Square, outside the Vatican.

Robert Lowell (© *Thomas Victor 1982*)

angel-wing'd, gorgeous as a jungle bird!
But who believed this? Who could understand?
Pilgrims still kissed Saint Peter's brazen sandal.[10]
25   The Duce's lynched, bare, booted skull still spoke.
God herded his people to the *coup de grâce*[11]—
the costumed Switzers sloped their pikes to push,
O Pius,[12] through the monstrous human crush. . . .

Our mountain-climbing train had come to earth.
30   Tired of the querulous hush-hush of the wheels,
the blear-eyed ego kicking in my berth
lay still, and saw Apollo[13] plant his heels
on terra firma through the morning's thigh . . .
each backward, wasted Alp, a Parthenon,[14]
35   fire-branded socket of the Cyclops' eye.
There were no tickets for that altitude
once held by Hellas,[15] when the Goddess[16] stood,
prince, pope, philosopher and golden bough,
pure mind and murder at the scything prow—
40   Minerva,[17] the miscarriage of the brain.

---

[10] In the Vatican stands a statue of St. Peter, its foot worn smooth from the kisses of pilgrims who believe it to have healing properties.
[11] The finishing stroke.
[12] The pope.
[13] The Greek god whose brilliant chariot was the sun.
[14] The great temple in Athens dedicated to Athena.
[15] Classical Greece.
[16] Athena, goddess of wisdom.
[17] The Latin name for Athena. She is said to have sprung full-grown from the head of her father, Zeus.

Now Paris, our black classic, breaking up
like killer kings on an Etruscan[18] cup.

Questions

1. Vocabulary: *fallow* (4), *conspicuous* (11), *querulous* (30).
2. In line 1, is Lowell referring to all of "the Swiss"? To whom is he referring? Does line 2 give you a clue?
3. In line 4, is Lowell looking merely at the snow, or at the whole landscape? Is this an example of synecdoche?
4. Can you find an example of synecdoche in line 6?
5. "City of God" is a phrase that was first used by St. Augustine to refer to an ideal holy city. Later it was generally used to refer to Rome during papal rule. What figure of speech is Lowell employing here?
6. Can you find a synecdoche in line 9?
7. When the poet refers to "Caesar" in line 10, does he mean a specific man, or a kind of government? Is this synecdoche or metonymy?
8. Explain the references of the following metonymies: "the Vatican," "Hellas," "The Holy Father."
9. The meaning of the last two lines is obscure, although our appreciation of the poem does not depend on it. Is there metonymical significance to the phrase "black classic"? If so, what is Lowell suggesting? What is *really* breaking up?

JAMES DICKEY (1923–)

Buckdancer's Choice

So I would hear out those lungs,
The air split into nine levels,
Some gift of tongues of the whistler

In the invalid's bed: my mother,
5   Warbling all day to herself
The thousand variations of one song;

It is called Buckdancer's Choice.
For years, they have all been dying
Out, the classic buck-and-wing men

10   Of traveling minstrel shows;
With them also an old woman
Was dying of breathless angina,[19]

Yet still found breath enough
To whistle up in my head
15   A sight like a one-man band,

Freed black, with cymbals at heel,
An ex-slave who thrivingly danced
To the ring of his own clashing light

---

[18] A pre-Roman civilization in Italy.
[19] A painful heart disease.

Through the thousand variations of one song
20   All day to my mother's prone music,
The invalid's warbler's note,

While I crept to the wall
Sock-footed, to hear the sounds alter,
Her tongue like a mockingbird's break

25   Through stratum after stratum of a tone
Proclaiming what choices there are
For the last dancers of their kind,

For ill women and for all slaves
Of death, and children enchanted at walls
30   With a brass-beating glow underfoot,

Not dancing but nearly risen
Through barnlike, theatrelike houses
On the wings of the buck and wing.

Questions

1. Vocabulary: *stratum* (25).
2. How many synecdoches can you find in the first stanza?
3. The buck-and-wing is a solo tap dance with a lot of angular arm movement and spring in the knees. The name itself tends to describe the dance. What figure of speech is it?
4. What other examples of synecdoche can you find? Do they make the poem more vivid?
5. Find two examples of metonymy.

Allusion

When American soldiers and sportsmen shout "Remember the Alamo," they are using a form of verbal economy called *allusion*. The Alamo was a mission in Texas that Americans defended with unparalleled valor and persistence during a war with Mexico. Most of us have learned about this in school. Think how awkward it would be for soldiers, in the heat of combat, to cry out, "Remember the mission in Texas that Americans defended with unparalleled valor and persistence. . . ." The allusion conserves energy.

By now we have seen several instances of allusion among our examples of synecdoche and metonymy, for in the general sense an allusion is any reference by word or phrase to something other than the literal meaning. For example, "the lash" is an allusion to tyranny. Robert Lowell's poem "Beyond the Alps" is rich in historical allusion owing to his skillful use of metonymy. But the term *allusion* is most commonly used in connection with literary references and references to special or technical knowledge. Appropriate allusion deepens the background of a poem—as long as the reader understands the allusion. A poet might add a level of meaning to his poem by introducing it with a fragment from Dante's *Inferno*. But if we have not read the *Inferno*, the poet's scholarship may be lost on us. Poets can educate us if we let them, and it is often worth our while to research their allusions.

ALEXANDER POPE (1688–1744)

Intended for Sir Isaac Newton

Nature and Nature's laws lay hid in night:
God said, "Let Newton be!" and all was light.

This short poem turns on two important allusions. First, there is the allusion to the "laws" of Sir Isaac Newton, the eighteenth-century mathematician who invented calculus and formulated laws of motion that served scientists until the twentieth century. During Pope's time Newton commanded as much awe as Einstein inspires today. Second, there is the allusion to the book of Genesis: "God said, let there be light, and there was light." If you fail to recognize these allusions, the poem's high praise and subtle irony are lost.

Poets do not use allusion simply to show off their special knowledge. Allusion is a way of achieving intimacy by referring the reader to the world from which the poem comes. In the following poem for blues singer Ray Charles, Bob Kaufman evokes the mood and history of Charles's music through allusions to songs and other blues singers. The reference to Kilimanjaro, a mountain in eastern Africa, is an allusion to the African roots of blues music. *I Got a Woman* is one of Ray Charles's most popular songs. "Bessie" is Bessie Smith, the great blues singer, who was killed in an auto accident. Line 6 is literally allusion, referring us to the birth of Athena from the skull of Zeus. The parenthetic " 'way cross town" is a phrase from *I Got a Woman*.

BOB KAUFMAN (1935–)

Blues Note

For Ray Charles's birthday
N.Y.C./1961

Ray Charles is the black wind of Kilimanjaro,
Screaming up-and-down blues,
Moaning happy on all the elevators of my time.

Smiling into the camera, with an African symphony
5   Hidden in his throat, and (*I Got a Woman*) wails, too.

He burst from Bessie's crushed black skull
One cold night outside of Nashville, shouting,
And grows bluer from memory, glowing bluer, still.

At certain times you can see the moon
10   Balanced on his head.

From his mouth he hurls chunks of raw soul.
He separated the sea of polluted sounds
And led the blues into the Promised Land.

Ray Charles is a dangerous man ('way cross town),
15   And I love him.

Questions

1. How does the poet use metaphor in line 1?
2. How does he use allusion in line 13?
3. Does the poet's use of allusion help you to understand his affection for Ray Charles?

Paradox

I may be blind
but I got my eye on you.
                —*Paul Shapiro*

Paradox is a statement that at first seems self-contradictory or illogical, but that actually transcends logic to assert a greater truth. The idea of a blind man with his eye on you is bizarre and seems senseless until we consider that many sightless people are highly observant, and that the phrase "I got my eye on you" suggests something more important than literal vision.

Twenty men crossing a bridge,
Into a village
Are twenty men crossing twenty bridges,
Into twenty villages,
Or one man
Crossing a single bridge into a village.
                —*Wallace Stevens*

You may readily accept this sentence as a metaphor. But it is also a paradox, rich in philosophical implications. Literally, the sentence seems false. But if we think of it from the viewpoints of twenty men, each one crossing his own bridge, then the first part of the sentence begins to make sense. If each man sees the bridge, that makes twenty viewed bridges. If we think of the *common* vision of the twenty men, then the second part of the paradox begins to make sense—that they are "one man/Crossing a single bridge into a village." This is a sophisticated paradox that explores nothing less than the nature of consciousness, which is both shared and singular.

As an exercise of metaphysical wit, the paradox was very popular during the sixteenth and seventeenth centuries. The clown in Shakespeare's *As You Like It* strikes at the heart of human folly when he says, "The fool doth think he is wise, but the wise man knows himself to be a fool." The world is full of apparent contradictions; paradox is one figure of speech that resolves and delights in them.

GEORGE HERBERT (1593–1663)

Bitter-Sweet

Ah, my dear angry Lord,
Since Thou dost love, yet strike;
Cast down, yet help afford;
Sure I will do the like.

5   I will complain, yet praise;
I will bewail, approve:
And all my sour-sweet days
I will lament, and love.

This poem resolves the paradoxes of fortune in religious terms, returning in prayer the mixture of love and wrath that the speaker finds in life. The second line appears illogical until we consider the writer's religious conviction—the Lord strikes him out of love, not to make him suffer but to chasten him. Life must be "bitter-sweet." The phrases "bitter-sweet" and "sour-sweet" are figures of speech called *oxymorons*. An oxymoron, which combines two seemingly contradictory elements, is a form of condensed paradox. Jaques, the great cynic in *As You Like It*, speaks of his "humorous sadness." Shakespeare's sonnets likewise are full of oxymorons; he speaks of "sightless view," the "profitless usurer," and "unseeing eyes." Let us look for paradoxes in one of the sonnets.

WILLIAM SHAKESPEARE (1564–1616)

When Most I Wink, Then Do Mine Eyes Best See

When most I wink, then do mine eyes best see,
For all the day they view things unrespected;°   *unregarded, unseen*
But when I sleep, in dreams they look on thee,
And darkly bright are bright in dark directed.
5   Then thou, whose shadow shadows doth make bright,
How would thy shadow's form form happy show
To the clear day with thy much clearer light,
When to unseeing eyes thy shade shines so!
How would, I say, mine eyes be blessed made
10   By looking on thee in the living day,
When in dead night thy fair imperfect shade
Through heavy sleep on sightless eyes doth stay!
    All days are nights to see till I see thee,
    And nights bright days when dreams do show thee me.

Questions

1. Does the first line appear to be true? How is the paradox made sensible in lines 2–4?
2. Can you find an oxymoron in line 8? How does it make sense?

3. What is the paradox in the final couplet? How does it seem false? What makes it true?

SIMONIDES (c. 556–c. 468 B.C.)

For the Spartan Dead at Plataia (479 B.C.)

These men clothed their land with incorruptible
Glory when they assumed death's misty cloak.
They are not dead in death; the memory
Lives with us, and their courage brings them back.

Translation by Peter Jay

Questions

1. Vocabulary: *incorruptible* (1).
2. Where do you find paradox in this elegy?
3. What other figures of speech can you find in the poem?

MARK STRAND (1934–)

Keeping Things Whole

In a field
I am the absence
of field.
This is
5   always the case.
Wherever I am
I am what is missing.

When I walk
I part the air
10   and always
the air moves in
to fill the spaces
where my body's been.

We all have reasons
15   for moving.
I move
to keep things whole.

Questions

1. How do lines 6 and 7 seem false? How are they true?
2. What other paradoxes can you find?

🌿 Poems for Further Study

ANTHONY HECHT (1923–)

Lizards and Snakes

On the summer road that ran by our front porch
        Lizards and snakes came out to sun.
It was hot as a stove out there, enough to scorch
        A buzzard's foot. Still, it was fun
5   To lie in the dust and spy on them. Near but remote,
        They snoozed in the carriage ruts, a smile
In the set of the jaw, a fierce pulse in the throat
Working away like Jack Doyle's after he'd run the mile.

Aunt Martha had an unfair prejudice
10   Against them (as well as being cold
Toward bats.) She was pretty inflexible in this,
        Being a spinster and all, and old.
So we used to slip them into her knitting box.
        In the evening she'd bring in things to mend
15 And a nice surprise would slide out from under the socks.
It broadened her life, as Joe said. Joe was my friend.

But we never did it again after the day
        Of the big wind when you could hear the trees
Creak like rockingchairs. She was looking away
20   Off, and kept saying, "Sweet Jesus, please
Don't let him near me. He's as like as twins.
        He can crack us like lice with his fingernail.
I can see him plain as a pikestaff. Look how he grins
And swinges the scaly horror of his folded tail."

ANONYMOUS (18th century)

Grief of a Girl's Heart

O Donal Oge, if you go across the sea,
Bring myself with you and do not forget it;
And you will have a sweetheart for fair days and market days,
And the daughter of the King of Greece beside you at night.

5   It is late last night the dog was speaking of you;
The snipe was speaking of you in her deep marsh.
It is you are the lonely bird through the woods;
And that you may be without a mate until you find me.

You promised me, and you said a lie to me,
10   That you would be before me where the sheep are flocked;
I gave a whistle and three hundred cries to you,
And I found nothing there but a bleating lamb.

You promised me a thing that was hard for you,
A ship of gold under a silver mast;
15   Twelve towns with a market in all of them,
And a fine white court by the side of the sea.

You promised me a thing that is not possible,
That you would give me gloves of the skin of a fish;
That you would give me shoes of the skin of a bird;
20   And a suit of the dearest silk in Ireland.

O Donal Oge, it is I would be better to you
Than a high, proud, spendthrift lady:
I would milk the cow; I would bring help to you;
And if you were hard pressed, I would strike a blow for you.

25   You have taken the east from me; you have taken the west from me,
You have taken what is before me and what is behind me;
You have taken the moon, you have taken the sun from me,
And my fear is great that you have taken God from me!

Translation from the Irish by Lady Augusta Gregory (1852–1932)

DYLAN THOMAS (1914–1953)

• The Hand That Signed the Paper

The hand that signed the paper felled a city;
Five sovereign fingers taxed the breath,
Doubled the globe of dead and halved a country;
These five kings did a king to death.

5   The mighty hand leads to a sloping shoulder,
The finger joints are cramped with chalk;
A goose's quill has put an end to murder
That put an end to talk.

The hand that signed the treaty bred a fever,
10   And famine grew, and locusts came;
Great is the hand that holds dominion over
Man by a scribbled name.

The five kings count the dead but do not soften
The crusted wound nor stroke the brow;
15   A hand rules pity as a hand rules heaven;
Hands have no tears to flow.

JOHN CROWE RANSOM (1888–1974)

Winter Remembered

Two evils, monstrous either one apart,
Possessed me, and were long and loath at going:

A cry of Absence, Absence, in the heart,
And in the wood the furious winter blowing.

5 Think not, when fire was bright upon my bricks,
And past the tight boards hardly a wind could enter,
I glowed like them, the simple burning sticks,
Far from my cause, my proper heat and center.

Better to walk forth in the frozen air
10 And wash my wound in the snows; that would be healing;
Because my heart would throb less painful there,
Being caked with cold, and past the smart of feeling.

And where I walked, the murderous winter blast
Would have this body bowed, these eyeballs streaming,
15 And though I think this heart's blood froze not fast
It ran too small to spare one drop for dreaming.

Dear love, these fingers that had known your touch,
And tied our separate forces first together,
Were ten poor idiot fingers not worth much,
20 Ten frozen parsnips hanging in the weather.

ROBERT BROWNING (1812–1889)

How We Brought the Good News from Ghent to Aix

I

I sprang to the stirrup, and Joris, and he;
I galloped, Dirck galloped, we galloped all three;
"Good speed!" cried the watch, as the gate-bolts undrew;
"Speed!" echoed the wall to us galloping through;
5 Behind shut the postern, the light sank to rest,
And into the midnight we galloped abreast.

2

Not a word to each other; we kept the great pace
Neck by neck, stride by stride, never changing our place;
I turned in my saddle and made its girths tight,
10 Then shortened each stirrup, and set the pique right,
Rebuckled the cheek-strap, chained slacker the bit,
Nor galloped less steadily Roland a whit.

3

'T was moonset at starting; but while we drew near
Lokeren, the cocks crew and twilight dawned clear;
15 At Boom, a great yellow star came out to see;
At Düffeld, 't was morning as plain as could be;
And from Mecheln church-steeple we heard the half-chime,
So, Joris broke silence with, "Yet there is time!"

4

At Aershot, up leaped of a sudden the sun,
20 And against him the cattle stood black every one,

To stare thro' the mist at us galloping past,
And I saw my stout galloper Roland at last,
With resolute shoulders, each butting away
The haze, as some bluff river headland its spray:

5

25 And his low head and crest, just one sharp ear bent back
For my voice, and the other pricked out on his track;
And one eye's black intelligence,—ever that glance
O'er its white edge at me, his own master, askance!
And the thick heavy spume-flakes which aye and anon
30 His fierce lips shook upwards in galloping on.

6

By Hasselt, Dirck groaned; and cried Joris, "Stay spur!
Your Roos galloped bravely, the fault's not in her,
We'll remember at Aix"—for one heard the quick wheeze
Of her chest, saw the stretched neck and staggering knees,
35 And sunk tail, and horrible heave of the flank,
As down on her haunches she shuddered and sank.

7

So, we were left galloping, Joris and I,
Past Looz and past Tongres, no cloud in the sky;
The broad sun above laughed a pitiless laugh,
40 'Neath our feet broke the brittle bright stubble like chaff;
Till over by Dalhem a dome-spire sprang white,
And "Gallop," gasped Joris, "for Aix is in sight!

8

How they'll greet us!"—and all in a moment his roan
Rolled neck and croup over, lay dead as a stone;
45 And there was my Roland to bear the whole weight
Of the news which alone could save Aix from her fate,
With his nostrils like pits full of blood to the brim,
And with circles of red for his eye-sockets' rim.

9

Then I cast loose my buffcoat, each holster let fall,
50 Shook off both my jack-boots, let go belt and all,
Stood up in the stirrup, leaned, patted his ear,
Called my Roland his pet-name, my horse without peer;
Clapped my hands, laughed and sang, any noise, bad or good,
Till at length into Aix Roland galloped and stood.

10

55 And all I remember is, friends flocking round
As I sat with his head 'twixt my knees on the ground;
And no voice but was praising this Roland of mine,
As I poured down his throat our last measure of wine,
Which (the burgesses voted by common consent)
60 Was no more than his due who brought good news from Ghent.

WELDON KEES (1914–1955)

Aspects of Robinson

Robinson at cards at the Algonquin; a thin
Blue light comes down once more outside the blinds.
Gray men in overcoats are ghosts blown past the door.
The taxis streak the avenues with yellow, orange, and red.
5   This is Grand Central, Mr. Robinson.

Robinson on a roof above the Heights; the boats
Mourn like the lost. Water is slate, far down.
Through sounds of ice cubes dropped in glass, an osteopath,
Dressed for the links, describes an old Intourist tour.
10   —Here's where old Gibbons jumped from, Robinson.

Robinson walking in the Park, admiring the elephant.
Robinson buying the *Tribune*, Robinson buying the *Times*, Robinson
Saying, "Hello. Yes, this is Robinson. Sunday
At five? I'd love to. Pretty well. And you?"
15   Robinson alone at Longchamps, staring at the wall.

Robinson afraid, drunk, sobbing Robinson
In bed with a Mrs. Morse. Robinson at home;
Decisions: Toynbee[20] or luminol? Where the sun
Shines, Robinson in flowered trunks, eyes toward
20   The breakers. Where the night ends, Robinson in East Side bars.

Robinson in Glen plaid jacket, Scotch-grain shoes,
Black four-in-hand and oxford button-down,
The jeweled and silent watch that winds itself, the brief-
Case, covert topcoat, clothes for spring, all covering
25   His sad and usual heart, dry as a winter leaf.

SAMUEL TAYLOR COLERIDGE (1772–1834)

Pity

Sweet Mercy! how my very heart has bled
    To see thee, poor Old Man! and thy grey hairs
    Hoar with the snowy blast: while no one cares
To clothe thy shrivell'd limbs and palsied head.
5   My Father! throw away this tatter'd vest
    That mocks thy shivering! take my garment—use
    A young man's arm! I'll melt these frozen dews
That hang from thy white beard and numb thy breast.
My Sara too shall tend thee, like a child:
10   And thou shalt talk, in our fireside's recess,
    Of purple Pride, that scowls on Wretchedness.—
He did not so, the Galilaean mild,

---

[20] Arnold Joseph Toynbee, a twentieth-century Catholic historian and educator.

Who met the Lazars° turn'd from rich men's doors   *lepers*
And call'd them Friends, and heal'd their noisome sores!

CHIDIOCK TICHBORNE (1558?—1586)

Elegy, Written with His Own Hand in the Tower Before His Execution

My prime of youth is but a frost of cares,
   My feast of joy is but a dish of pain,
My crop of corn is but a field of tares,°   *weeds*
   And all my good is but vain hope of gain:
5   The day is past, and yet I saw no sun,
And now I live, and now my life is done.

My tale was heard, and yet it was not told,
   My fruit is fall'n, and yet my leaves are green,
My youth is spent; and yet I am not old,
10   I saw the world, and yet I was not seen:
My thread is cut, and yet it is not spun,
And now I live, and now my life is done.

I sought my death, and found it in my womb,
   I looked for life, and saw it was a shade,
15   I trod the earth, and knew it was my tomb,
   And now I die, and now I was but made:
My glass is full, and now my glass is run,
And now I live, and now my life is done.

10 ❧ The Music of Poetry

To the best of our knowledge, the earliest poetry was sung or chanted—by priestesses and priests in the temple, by bards in the court, and by actors on stage. In fact, the separation of poetry from music is a relatively recent phenomenon in the long history of literature. Surely poetry and melody arise from similar impulses. Ezra Pound has observed the historical interaction of these arts: "Music begins to atrophy when it departs too far from dance; poetry begins to atrophy when it gets too far from music."

All language is musical to some degree, from the vendor's street cry to the lawyer's plea to the orations of senators. All language has rhythm and pitch. But the rhythm and pitch of poetry is so intensified that it contributes an entire dimension of meaning to the language. The music of poetry can be so powerful and precise that some listeners can feel the basic emotion of a poem in a foreign language, even if they have no previous knowledge of that language.

Rhythm

The human voice is a musical instrument of great range and sensitivity. As we pronounce words and sentences, the voice rises and falls, growing louder and softer according to what is being communicated, and its urgency. In this the voice resembles all rhythmic movements in nature—the crests and hollows of waves, the rise and fall of daylight, the beating of the heart. The force gathers, exerts itself, and then subsides. In poetry, rhythm comes from a certain regularity of stress on syllables. Notice how regularly the stresses occur in this memorable nursery rhyme.

> Péter, Péter, púmpkin éater,
> Hád a wífe and couldn't kéep her.

For the sake of contrast let us read a sentence of editorial prose, marking the stresses.

> As thís is wrítten, Wáll Stréet hás the jítters.
> It máy be a pássing pháse and soón cúred.

Of course, most poetry is not as regular as a nursery rhyme, nor is all prose as haphazard in its rhythms as the editorial excerpt suggests. But it is apparent that in the more musical passage the stresses occur more regularly.

Accent and Emphasis

Two kinds of stress occur in speech: the stress of accents within a word, and the stress of emphasis on a word within a sentence. Thus in the nursery rhyme the stress on the first syllable of *Peter* is a stress of accent. The stress on the word *had* in the second line is due to emphasis on the word in the whole sentence.

As you listen to conversations, you will notice that usually the words and syllables that carry the most meaning are stressed, whereas the other syllables are relatively obscure. There is a good reason for this. The prominent syllable of a word is stressed because it usually contains the main idea. Thus: in-débt-ed-ness. Here the accented syllable, *debt*, is the root idea of the word. Our attention, though directed to this syllable, must also carry the other syllables that modify its meaning. This same principle applies to words in a sentence. Certain words are more important than others and are emphasized by the stress of voice, but we must not lose the meaning of the unstressed words.

Listening to the strong, important syllables and words and to the weak ones at the same time requires effort. This effort has its limits. For instance, it is difficult to hear more than two unaccented syllables attached to a stressed one, either before or after it. Poets are keenly aware of these limits, and a poet with a good ear places the stresses in his lines with great care for the listener's attention.

Scansion is the designation of stressed and unstressed syllables in a poem.

> Ĭ stóod ĭn Vénicĕ, oń thĕ Brídge ŏf Síghs;
> Ă pálăce ănd ă prísŏn ón eăch hánd:
> Ĭ sáw frŏm oút thĕ wávе hĕr strúctŭres rísе
> Ăs frŏm thĕ strókе ŏf thĕ enchántĕr's wánd . . .

Scanning a poem is a way of determining what kind of rhythm the poem has. The stresses of accent are determined by the usage of the time, so we may look in the dictionary to find out which syllables to accent within a word. But the stress of emphasis on words depends on the voice of the poet and the reader. Not all of us will scan a particular poem in the same way. For instance, in the last line just scanned, we did not stress the word *the* preceding *enchanter's*. Another reader might have stressed it. When scanning a poem, it is helpful to read it aloud in your most natural voice, in order to hear where the stresses fall.

Exercise

Scan the following fragments of poetry, reading them aloud as you mark the stresses.

1. We sweetly curtsied each to each
   And deftly danced a saraband.

2. When the game began between them for a jest,
   He played king and she played queen to match the best;
   Laughter soft as tears, and tears that turned to laughter,
   These were things she sought for years and sorrowed after.

3. Simple and fresh and fair from winter's close emerging,
   As if no artifice of fashion, business, politics, had ever been,
   Forth from its sunny nook of sheltered grass—
         innocent, golden, calm as the dawn,
   The spring's first dandelion shows its trustful face.

Questions

1. Which of the foregoing passages has the most regular rhythm? The least?
2. In scanning the lines, you see that some have more stresses due to accent, whereas others have more stresses due to emphasis. Which passage depends more on accents for its rhythm? Which depends more on the emphasis on words?

Meter

When stresses occur with sufficient regularity in a poem, the result is called *meter*. Meter is the measuring of stresses in a line of verse, determining their number and placement.

The unit of meter is called a *foot*. A metrical foot usually consists of a stressed syllable and one or two unstressed syllables that precede or follow it. A line with a single foot is called *monometer*. A line with two feet is called *dimeter*; with three, *trimeter*; with four, *tetrameter*; with five, *pentameter*; with six, *hexameter*; with seven, *heptameter*; and with eight feet, *octometer*.

There are four principal kinds of feet in American and English verse. The most common is the *iambic* foot, where the stressed syllable is preceded by one unstressed, as in the word *surprise*.

> Tŏ óne | whŏ hás | bĕen lóng | ĭn cí | tў pént,
> 'Tĭs vé | rў swéet | tŏ lóok | ĭntó | thĕ fáir
> Ănd ó | pĕn fáce | ŏf héa | vĕn.

The foregoing verses by Keats are written in *iambic pentameter*, which has been called the staff of English verse. Unrhymed iambic pentameter is also called *blank verse*. Iambics are steady and natural, and a great deal of spoken and written English—prose as well as poetry—falls easily into iambic rhythm.

When the stress comes first, followed by an unaccented syllable, the foot is called a *trochee*:

Spláshĭng
Dáshĭng.

These two lines illustrate trochaic monometer. Here is an example of trochaic
tetrameter:

Hé wăs | próudĕr | thán thĕ | dévĭl:
Hów hĕ | múst hăve | cúrsed oŭr | révĕl!

The trochee is livelier than the iamb—the effect of putting the stressed syllable
first is sometimes described as *falling rhythm*, because one "falls" more quickly
from a point of stress to an unaccented syllable. It is slightly more of an effort
for the voice to move from unstressed to stressed syllables, which is why iambic
rhythm is called "rising rhythm."

The *anapest* is a foot with two unstressed syllables followed by a stressed one,
as in the word *intervene*. The anapest is a rising rhythm, but it is more rapid
than the iamb because of the greater number of unstressed syllables. Here is a
sample of anapestic trimeter:

Frŏm thĕ cén | tĕr aĺl roŭnd | tŏ thĕ séa
Ĭ ăm lórd | ŏf thĕ fówl | ănd thĕ brúte.

You may remember the galloping rhythms of Browning's poem "How We
Brought the Good News from Ghent to Aix," which depend on the anapest for
their speed and strength. The following is a description of the hero's horse:

And his low head and crest, just one sharp ear bent back
For my voice, and the other pricked out on his track;
And one eye's black intelligence,—ever that glance
O'er its white edge at me, his own master, askance!

The *dactyl* is a foot that begins with a stressed syllable, followed by two
unstressed syllables, as in the word *délĭcăte*. It is a falling rhythm, the most rapid
and lively of English meters.

SONG
Heŕe's tŏ thĕ | máid ŏf | báshfŭl fíf | téen;
Heŕe's tŏ thĕ | wídŏw ŏf | fíftў;
Heŕe's tŏ thĕ | fláuntĭng éx | trávăgănt | quéen
Ănd heŕe's | tŏ thĕ hoŭse | wífe thăt's | thríftў.

Notice that the poem is not all dactyls, but the dactylic foot is prominent and
gives the poem its momentum. The same is true for the following lines:

Cléarlў thĕ blúe rívĕr chímes ĭn ĭts flówĭng
    Úndĕr mу́ eýe;
Wármlў ănd bróadlў thĕ sóuth wĭnds ăre blówĭng
    óvĕr thĕ ský.

In addition to the four principal feet—the iamb, the trochee, the anapest, and the dactyl—there are two other feet worth mentioning. The *spondee* is a unit of rhythm of double movement, in which both syllables are accented, as in the word *ámén*.

Róll ón | thóu deép | and dárk blúe ocean, róll.

The spondee is a rhythmic unit of great weight and solemnity.

Because of the frequency of particles in English grammar, the unit of rhythm occasionally loses its stress. When that happens, we get the *pyrrhic* foot.

Ĭ wór | shĭpped thĕ | ĭnvís | ĭblĕ | alóne.

All this terminology is useful in describing poetic rhythm. But it is more important to understand a few principles of metrics that underlie centuries of versification. Since poetry is not a science, these generalizations have their exceptions; but they will be useful in comprehending why the different feet are used.

Generally, the more stresses in a metric line, the slower the line moves. That is why the spondee creates a mood of gravity.

Breák, breák, breák
On thy cóld gráy stónes, Ó séa!

That is a good rhythm for a stately meditation—but not for a wedding celebration. For a mirthful poem the poet will have fewer stresses per line, a faster rhythm with dactyls or anapests.

Ríde ă cóck-hórse tŏ Bánbŭry Cróss
Tŏ sée ăn óld wómăn gĕt úp ŏn hĕr hórse.
Ríngs ŏn hĕr fíngĕrs, ănd bélls ŏn hĕr tóes,
Shĕ shăll háve músĭc wherévĕr shĕ góes.

Of course, most poetry is neither funereal nor merry. That explains the predominance of the iambic and trochaic lines, with their balance between stressed and unstressed syllables.

The so-called falling rhythms—trochaic and dactylic—are more rapid, respectively, than the rising rhythms—iambic and anapestic. As we have observed, this is the result of greater ease in moving from stressed to unstressed syllables.

Since we tend to pause at the end of a line of poetry, the shorter the lines, the slower the movement of the poem. All other things being equal, dimeter puts much more stress on individual words than does tetrameter, and pentameter slightly more than hexameter.

In the following lines, notice how Tennyson changes the line length and foot to vary rhythm. He poses the question of the first section with deliberate spondees and forceful dactyls. The dimeter of this section makes for a constrained opening, which breaks into lively trochaic and anapestic tetrameter in the second section.

ALFRED, LORD TENNYSON (1809–1892)

The Mermaid

I

Who would be
A mermaid fair,
Singing alone,
Combing her hair
5   Under the sea,
In a golden curl
With a comb of pearl,
On a throne?

II

    I would be a mermaid fair;
10   I would sing to myself the whole of the day;
With a comb of pearl I would comb my hair;
And still as I comb'd I would sing and say,
"Who is it loves me? who loves not me?"
I would comb my hair till my ringlets would fall,
15   Low adown, low adown,
From under my starry sea-bud crown
         Low adown and around
And I should look like a fountain of gold
         Springing alone
20   With a shrill inner sound,
         Over the throne
         In the midst of the hall;
Till that great sea-snake under the sea
From his coiled sleeps in the central deeps
25   Would slowly trail himself sevenfold
Round the hall where I sate, and look in at the gate
With his large calm eyes for the love of me.
And all the mermen under the sea
Would feel their immortality
30   Die in their hearts for the love of me.

III

But at night I would wander away, away,
    I would fling on each side my low-flowing locks,
And lightly vault from the throne and play
    With the mermen in and out of the rocks;
35   We would run to and fro, and hide and seek,
    On the broad sea-wolds° in the crimson shells,   *sea hills*
     Whose silvery spikes are nighest the sea.
But if any came near I would call, and shriek,
And adown the steep like a wave I would leap
40   From the diamond-ledges that jut from the dells;
For I would not be kiss'd by all who would list,
Of the bold merry mermen under the sea;

They would sue° me, and woo me, and flatter me,   *pay suit to*
In the purple twilights under the sea;
45   But the king of them all would carry me,
Woo me, and win me, and marry me,
In the branching jaspers under the sea;
Then all the dry pied° things that be   *many-colored*
In the hueless mosses under the sea
50   Would curl round my silver feet silently,
All looking up for the love of me.
And if I should carol aloud, from aloft
All things that are forked, and horned, and soft
Would lean out from the hollow sphere of the sea,
55   All looking down for the love of me.

Samuel Taylor Coleridge composed the following lines as an aid to memory of the metrical units:

Trochee trips from long to short;°   *stressed to unstressed*
From long to long in solemn sort
Slow Spondee stalks, strong foot, yet ill able
Ever to come up with Dactyl trisyllable.
Iambics march from short to long;
With a leap and a bound the swift Anapests throng.

If you scan these lines you will see that each one illustrates the metrical unit it describes.

Students of meter should bear in mind that meter does not create the rhythms of poetry. The rhythms arise out of the poet's emotion, just as do images and figures of speech. Metrical scansion is the measuring of regular rhythms after they have occurred, and consciousness of meter is not a prerequisite for composition.

Exercise

Scan the following lines. Describe the line length as monometer, dimeter, trimeter, and so on. Then characterize the metrical units as iambic, trochaic, anapestic, dactylic, spondaic, and pyrrhic. Which lines are liveliest? Most forceful? Which lines seem most solemn? Which are the most sprightly? What other words can you use to describe the moods rhythm instills?

1. Come live with me and be my love
   And we will all the pleasures prove
   That valleys, groves, hills and fields
   Woods or steepy mountain yields.

2. Let us swear an oath and keep it with an equal mind.

3. Dear my friend and fellow student, I would lean my spirit o'er you.

4. If they rob us of name and pursue us with beagles,
   Give their roof to the flame and their flesh to the eagles.

5. And now the storm-blast came, and he
   Was tyrannous and strong;
   He struck with his o'ertaking wings
   And chased us south along.

6. Has any here an old gray Mare
   With three legs all her store,
   O put it to her Buttocks bare
   And straight she'll run on four.

7. Just for a handful of silver he left us,
   Just for a riband° to stick in his coat—   *ribbon of honor*
   Found the one gift of which fortune bereft us,
   Lost all the others she lets us devote . . .

8. Solomon Grundy
   Born on Monday,
   Christened on Tuesday,
   Married on Wednesday,
   Took ill on Thursday,
   Worse on Friday,
   Died on Saturday,
   Buried on Sunday.
   This is the end
   Of Solomon Grundy.

9. If I did take your kingdom from your sons,
   To make amends, I'll give it to your daughter.
   If I have killed the issue of your womb,
   To quicken your increase I will beget
   Mine issue of your blood upon your daughter:
   A grandam's name is little less in love
   Than in the doting title of a mother . . .

The Line and Line Endings

One of the more obvious features of poetry is that it is usually written in lines, or verses, and that each line functions as a rhythmic and sense unit. Charles Olson has suggested that the line length corresponds to the poet's breathing; thus Walt Whitman and Homer wrote long lines because they had prodigious energy and took deep breaths before uttering their epic verses. Whatever the case, the line certainly provides rhythmic opportunities unavailable in prose. We have already observed that shorter lines concentrate our attention on individual words and images.

> There is a spell, for instance
> in every sea-shell.
> —H. D. (Hilda Doolittle)

We have also remarked that the way lines begin—with stressed or unstressed syllables—often determines the thrust of the line, as we naturally move more quickly from a stressed to an unstressed syllable.

The line ending is equally important in controlling the poem's rhythmic movement. Lines that end with a stressed word or syllable, sometimes called a *masculine ending*, come to a more resolute pause than those that end with an unstressed syllable or *feminine ending*. In the following verses, notice that the masculine endings seem to gather up the sense of the line, contain it, and pause before the poem moves on. The feminine endings leave us with a slight sense of irresolution that urges us on to the next line.

ALGERNON CHARLES SWINBURNE (1837–1909)

Rococo

Take hand and part with laughter;
    Touch lips and part with tears;
Once more and no more after,
    Whatever comes with years.
5 We twain° shall not remeasure   *two*
    The ways that left us twain;
Nor crush the lees° of pleasure   *dregs*
    From sanguine grapes of pain.

We twain once well in sunder,°   *separated*
10   What will the mad gods do
For hate with me, I wonder,
    Or what for love with you?
Forget them till November,
    And dream there's April yet,
15 Forget that I remember,
    And dream that I forget.

Time found our tired love sleeping,
    And kissed away his breath;
But what should we do weeping,
20   Though light love sleep to death?
We have drained his lips at leisure,
    Till there's not left to drain
A single sob of pleasure,
    A single pulse of pain.

25 Dream that the lips once breathless
    Might quicken if they would;
Say that the soul is deathless;
    Dream that the gods are good;
Say March may wed September,
30   And time divorce regret;
But not that you remember,
    And not that I forget.

We have heard from hidden places
    What love scarce lives and hears:
35 We have seen on fervent faces

The pallor of strange tears:
We have trod the wine-vats treasure,
   Whence ripe to steam and stain,
Foams round the feet of pleasure
40   The blood-red must° of pain.   *juice*

Remembrance may recover
   And time bring back to time
The name of your first lover,
   The ring of my first rhyme;
45 But rose-leaves of December
   The frosts of June shall fret,
The day that you remember,
   The day that I forget.

The snake that hides and hisses
50   In heaven we twain have known;
The grief of cruel kisses,
   The joy whose mouth makes moan;
The pulses pause and measure,
   Where in one furtive vein
55 Throbs through the heart of pleasure
   The purpler blood of pain.

We have done with tears and treasons
   and love for treason's sake;
Room for the swift new seasons,
60   The years that burn and break,
Dismantle and dismember
   Men's days and dreams, Juliette;
For love may not remember,
   But time will not forget.

65 Life treads down love in flying,
   Time withers him at root;
Bring all dead things and dying,
   Reaped sheaf and ruined fruit,
Where, crushed by three days' pressure
70   Our three days' love lies slain;
And earlier leaf of pleasure,
   And latter flower of pain.

Breathe close upon the ashes,
   It may be flame will leap;
75 Unclose the soft close lashes,
   Lift up the lids and weep.
Light love's extinguished ember,
   Let one tear leave it wet
For one that you remember
80   And ten that you forget.

Swinburne is often praised for his mastery of classical meters and the lilting, songlike ease of his versification. This lies as much in his imaginative variations as in his adherence to the pattern. The line length is fairly strict trimeter. It is the fashioning of line openings and endings, the alternation of rising and falling rhythms, that give the poem its life. A poem with only masculine endings, or unrelieved trochaic trimeter, would be monotonous and slow by comparison.

Reading the poem aloud, you will notice that the lines usually end where the sense of the sentence requires a pause. If the poem were printed as prose, the reader would naturally pause in those places. Many of those pauses coincide with commas, semicolons, and periods. Any line that ends where the sentence calls for a grammatical pause is called an *end-stopped* line. The first four lines of "Rococo" are end-stopped:

> Take hands and part with laughter;
> Touch lips and part with tears;
> Once more and no more after,
> Whatever comes with years.

A line that ends before the sentence does, or before a pause is demanded by the sense, is called a *run-on* line. There is an example in lines 5 and 6 of "Rococo":

> We twain shall not remeasure
> The ways that left us twain;

This running over of the sense unit from line to line is called *enjambment*. Again, this offers pleasant relief in a poem in which most of the lines are end-stopped.

When a poem is composed of long lines, there is sometimes a natural pause *within* the line.

> Gone—faded out of the story, | | the sea-faring friend I remember?
> Gone for a decade, they say: | | never a word or a sign.
> Gone with his hard red face | | that only his laughter could wrinkle,
> Down where men go to be still, | | by the old way of the sea.

Caesura is a grammatical or natural pause occuring within a line of poetry. The hexameters in the preceding poem might have been broken down into trimeters. But the poet, Edwin Arlington Robinson, has chosen the longer line with caesura to hasten the telling of his story.

EDNA ST. VINCENT MILLAY (1892–1950)

Recuerdo

> We were very tired, we were very merry—
> We had gone back and forth all night on the ferry.
> It was bare and bright, and smelled like a stable—

But we looked into a fire, we leaned across a table,
5   We lay on a hill-top underneath the moon;
And the whistles kept blowing, and the dawn came soon.

We were very tired, we were very merry—
We had gone back and forth all night on the ferry;
And you ate an apple, and I ate a pear,
10   From a dozen of each we had bought somewhere;
And the sky went wan, and the wind came cold,
And the sun rose dripping, a bucketful of gold.

We were very tired, we were very merry,
We had gone back and forth all night on the ferry.
15   We hailed, "Good morrow, mother!" to a shawl-covered head.
And bought a morning paper, which neither of us read;
And she wept, "God bless you!" for the apples and pears,
And we gave her all our money but our subway fares.

Questions

1. Scan the poem, indicating the caesuras.
2. Which lines have masculine endings? Which have feminine endings? Do you see a pattern? If so, how does it contribute to the music of the poem?
3. What is the basic line length? Is it consistent?
4. From the number of caesuras, do you think one might cast the poem in shorter lines? How would that alter the rhythm?

Syllabic Verse

In an effort to break out of the strictures of traditional metrics without wholly abandoning predictable form, certain poets have adopted a metrical system called *syllabic verse*. Originating in Oriental and French poetry, syllabic verse counts syllables instead of accents in a line. From Chapter 6, you are familiar with the haiku, the Japanese syllabic form with seventeen syllables—five in the first line, seven in the second, and five again in the third.

> I must go begging
> for water . . . morning glories
> have captured my well.
> —From *Cricket Songs: Japanese Haiku*

By counting syllables, the poet gives shape to the poem without relying on strong rhythmic emphasis. The result is a quieter, more syncopated rhythm that still has a certain predictability of line length.

MARIANNE MOORE (1887–1972)

The Wood-Weasel

emerges daintily, the skunk—
don't laugh—in sylvan black and white chipmunk

Marianne Moore (*National Portrait Gallery, Smithsonian Institution, Washington, D.C.*)

regalia. The inky thing
adaptively whited with glistening
5   goat fur, is wood-warden. In his
ermined well-cuttlefish-inked wool, he is
determination's totem. Out-
lawed? His sweet face and powerful feet go about
in chieftain's coat of Chilcat cloth.
10   He is his own protection from the moth,

noble little warrior. That
otter-skin on it, the living polecat,
smothers anything that stings. Well,
this same weasel's playful and his weasel
15   associates are too. Only
wood-weasels shall associate with me.

Questions

1. Vocabulary: *sylvan* (2), *regalia* (3).
2. Count the number of syllables in each line. What is the basic pattern of line length?
3. What lines break the pattern? In the two lines that do break the pattern, do you see a justification in the meaning?

Rhyme

Many great poems do not use rhyme. Languages that are rich in rhyme words, such as French and Italian, use rhyme frequently; the classical Latin and Greek poets used it rarely, if at all. Verses that have little to offer *except* rhyme, such as greeting card sentiments and advertising jingles, are not dignified by the term poetry. We call them *doggerel*.

Poems that use rhyme depend on the rhyme words for structure, resolution, and tonal effects. The similarity of sounds is striking to the ear and serves as an aid to memory as well as an incitement of the reader's expectations.

ROBERT CREELEY (1926–)

If You

If you were going to get a pet
what kind of animal would you get.

A soft bodied dog, a hen—
feathers and fur to begin it again.

5   When the sun goes down and it gets dark
I saw an animal in a park.

Bring it home, to give it to you.
I have seen animals break in two.

You were hoping for something soft
10   and loyal and clean and wondrously careful—

a form of otherwise vicious habit
can have long ears and be called a rabbit.

Dead. Died. Will die. Want.
Morning, midnight. I asked you

15   if you were going to get a pet
what kind of animal would you get.

These intimate and deceptively simple verses by Robert Creeley have a remark-able appeal to readers of all ages. Much of this appeal can be attributed to the charm of rhyme. The first two lines rhyme at the end; this is called *end rhyme*. When a poem begins thus, with a rhymed couplet, the poem has created an expectation of rhyme. This expectation is satisfied in line 4, with the end rhyme of *again* with *hen*. By the time we get to line 5, a *rhyme scheme* has been established; the poem leads us on by our curiosity to discover the next rhyme word. This anticipation is not entirely conscious, for we are probably more concerned with the poem's sense. It is a musical anticipation, and the more effective because it works partly on an unconscious level.

Creeley breaks the pattern in line 10. We are waiting for the rhyme to come in line 10, but it doesn't. Why not? Look at the sense of lines 9 and 10.

You were hoping for something soft,
and loyal and clean and wondrously careful—

He is talking about hope, and creating a mystery in these lines. The reader is waiting for an answer. What kind of animal are we hoping for? We are denied the resolution of rhyme because we are also being denied the answer to the question. This is a perfect adaptation of form to content. We get the rhyme when we get the answer.

> a form of otherwise vicious habit
> can have long ears and be called a rabbit.

When the rhyme at last comes, it is a more elaborate, outrageous rhyme than we have yet heard, and well worth the wait. All the other rhymes have been *masculine rhymes*, with the similarity of sounds falling to the last syllable. This last is a *feminine rhyme*, one where the similarity of sounds is in both of the last two syllables. Feminine rhyme is a good deal louder than masculine rhyme and is often used to develop a comic tone (see Chapter 11 on tones of voice).

Lines 13 and 14 challenge the rhyme scheme again, and again we see the connection of form and content. The tone of the poem has turned suddenly grave, from a discussion of pets to a meditation on death, and the lack of an immediate rhyme word suits the tone change. Also notice that line 14 has a rhyming antecedent in lines 7 and 8. The poet has not wholly abandoned rhyme, but he has attenuated its resolution in these lines. Thus the resolution is all the more satisfying when it comes in the closing couplet.

The best rhymes come naturally and seem inevitable without losing a certain freshness or surprise.

W. H. AUDEN (1907–1973)

Fleet Visit

The sailors come ashore
Out of their hollow ships,
Mild-looking middle class boys
Who read the comic strips;
5   One baseball game is more
To them than fifty Troys.

They look a bit lost, set down
In this unamerican place
Where natives pass with laws
10   And futures of their own;
They are not here because
But only just-in-case.

The whore and ne'er-do-well
Who pester them with junk
15   In their grubby ways at least
Are serving the Social Beast;
They neither make nor sell—
No wonder they get drunk.

But their ships on the vehement° blue   *powerful*
20   Of this harbour actually gain
     From having nothing to do;
     Without a human will
     To tell them whom to kill
     Their structures are humane

25   And, far from looking lost,
     Look as if they were meant
     To be pure abstract design
     By some master of pattern and line,
     Certainly worth every cent
30   Of the billions they must have cost.

The characterization of these young sailors, in the first stanza, is cast in rhymes
as original and fresh as the context in which Auden sees them. Emerging from
the "hollow ships" (an allusion to Greek vessels), the boys remind Auden of the
great classical mariners. Yet they are still boys, readers of comic strips. Thus we
hear the rhyming and concomitant association of *ships* and *strips*, *boys* and
Troys—fresh unpredictable rhymes that are nevertheless natural in the context,
seemingly effortless.

Rhyme is reflexive. It joins not only words with similar sounds, but the things
and ideas to which the words refer. Notice the witty closing of stanza 2 and how
the rhyme words reinforce the meaning.

     They look a bit lost, set down
     In this unamerican place
     Where natives pass with laws
     And futures of their own;
     They are not here because
     But only just-in-case.

The natives have their own futures and *laws*. Yet the sailors are not here *because*
of any specific destiny or lawful purpose. The navy does not belong in this
unamerican place. They are here *just-in-case* they are needed. The rhymes—
laws and *because*, *place* and *just-in-case*—are surprising ones that underscore
the anomaly of the sailors' presence.

In "Fleet Visit" Auden employs both *exact rhyme* and *near rhyme*. Exact
rhyme occurs when rhyme words have the same vowel sounds, and the consonant
ending, if there is one, is identical. *Blue* and *do*, in stanza 4, are exact rhymes,
as are *will* and *kill*, *gain* and *humane*. Near rhyme, also called *off rhyme* and
partial rhyme, occurs when the vowel sound is different but the consonant is
identical, as in *down* and *own*, *laws* and *because*. Near rhyme is not a defect,
but a pleasant variation of rhyme.

Most rhyme comes at the end of lines and is called *end rhyme*. All the rhymes
in "Fleet Visit" are end rhymes. When rhymes fall within the line, they are
called *internal rhymes*.

Come live within me, said the waterfall.
There is a chamber of black stone
High and dry behind my stunning life,
Stay here a year or two, a year or ten,
Until you've heard it all,
The inside story deafening but true.

       —James Merrill

The internal rhyming of *high* and *dry* in line 3 and of *here* and *year* in line 4 helps to establish the resonance of the waterfall. Notice how smoothly Robert Frost uses end rhyme in the following poem.

ROBERT FROST (1874–1963)

The Road Not Taken

Two roads diverged in a yellow wood,
And sorry I could not travel both
And be one traveler, long I stood
And looked down one as far as I could
5 To where it bent in the undergrowth;

Then took the other, as just as fair,
And having perhaps the better claim,
Because it was grassy and wanted wear;
Though as for that the passing there
10 Had worn them really about the same,

And both that morning equally lay
In leaves no step had trodden black.
Oh, I kept the first for another day!
Yet knowing how way leads on to way,
15 I doubted if I should ever come back.

I shall be telling this with a sigh
Somewhere ages and ages hence:
Two roads diverged in a wood, and I—
I took the one less traveled by,
20 And that has made all the difference.

Questions

1. At what point in the poem do you notice that a rhyme scheme has developed?
2. Does the poem ever depart from the rhyme scheme?
3. Are the rhymes in the poem masculine or feminine?
4. Is there any near rhyme in the poem? Internal rhyme?
5. Suppose the poem were written in rhymed couplets. Would that be as suitable to the poem's theme? How does Frost's rhyme scheme relate to his subject?

Alliteration and Assonance

By now you have noticed that repetition is a principle of music in language. It forges connections between words and phrases, creates expectations, and is pleasing in itself. We have seen the repetition of accent patterns in rhythm and of word endings in rhyme, and how both contribute to the mood and movement of the poem. *Alliteration* is the repetition of consonant sounds. Like rhyme, it binds together words with similar sounds. In the heat of emotion we have a tendency to use words with the same initial consonant: "You *d*irty *d*og!" Many proverbs are composed in this manner, for emphasis as well as memory: "*T*ime and *t*ide wait for no man." "When the *w*ine is in, the *w*it is out." Judging from some current newspaper headlines, alliteration is as popular a mode of expression as ever.

Assonance is the repetition of vowel sounds.

> Be near me when my light is low,
>> When the blood creeps, and the nerves prick
>> And tingle and the heart is sick,
> And all the wheels of Being slow.
>> *—Alfred, Lord Tennyson*

The repetition of the *ē* sound in lines 1, 2, and 4 draws attention to the opening and helps to slow the phrase "wheels of Being." Assonance, like alliteration, attracts the reader to certain words and can create strong resonances.

MARGARET WALKER (1915–)

Lineage

My grandmothers were strong.
They followed plows and bent to toil.
They moved through fields sowing seed.
They touched earth and grain grew.
5   They were full of sturdiness and singing.
My grandmothers were strong.

My grandmothers are full of memories.
Smelling of soap and onions and wet clay
With veins rolling roughly over quick hands
10   They have many clean words to say.
My grandmothers were strong.
Why am I not as they?

Questions

1. Find an example of alliteration in stanza 1. Find an example of assonance. How do the techniques affect the meaning of the stanza?

2. What phrases in the second stanza stand out because of alliteration? Do those phrases deserve special attention? Why?

Alliteration and assonance sometimes imitate sounds of the things to which they refer. This is called *onomatopoeia* and is the purest relation of sound and meaning in poetry. The words *pop*, *sizzle*, and *crash* are onomatopoetic. Through the repetition of vowel or consonant sounds, an entire line may become onomatopoetic, as when Tennyson speaks of

> The moan of doves in immemorial elms,
> And murmuring of innumerable bees.

The repetition of the consonant *m* mimics the moaning and murmuring to which the lines refer. Shakespeare, in *Venus and Adonis*, fills Venus's lines with *s*'s just as she is playing the serpent in tempting young Adonis.

> Here come and sit, where never serpent hisses,
> And being set, I'll smother thee with kisses . . .

One of the greatest studies in alliteration, assonance, and onomatopoeia in American poetry is Edgar Allan Poe's "The Bells." Its effects are ingenious and excessive; the poem has been praised, ridiculed, imitated, and parodied.

EDGAR ALLAN POE (1809–1849)

The Bells

I

Hear the sledges with the bells—
    Silver bells!
What a world of merriment their melody foretells!
    How they tinkle, tinkle, tinkle,
5   In the icy air of night!
While the stars that oversprinkle
All the heavens, seem to twinkle
    With a crystalline delight;
    Keeping time, time, time,
10   In a sort of runic rhyme,
To the tintinnabulation that so musically wells
    From the bells, bells, bells, bells,
      Bells, bells, bells—
From the jingling and the tinkling of the bells.

II

15   Hear the mellow wedding bells—
      Golden bells!
What a world of happiness their harmony foretells!
    Through the balmy air of night
    How they ring out their delight!—
20   From the molten-golden notes,
      And all in tune,
    What a liquid ditty floats
To the turtledove that listens, while she gloats
    On the moon!

25   Oh, from out the sounding cells,
What a gush of euphony voluminously wells!
     How it swells!
     How it dwells
    On the future!—how it tells
30   Of the rapture that impels
   To the swinging and the ringing
      Of the bells, bells, bells—
    Of the bells, bells, bells, bells,
     Bells, bells, bells—
35 To the rhyming and the chiming of the bells!

III

   Hear the loud alarum bells—
    Brazen bells!
What a tale of terror, now, their turbulency tells!
    In the startled ear of night
40   How they scream out their affright!
     Too much horrified to speak,
     They can only shriek, shriek,
      Out of tune,
In a clamorous appealing to the mercy of the fire,
45 In a mad expostulation with the deaf and frantic fire,
     Leaping higher, higher, higher,
     With a desperate desire,
    And a resolute endeavor
    Now—now to sit, or never,
50   By the side of the pale-faced moon.
    Oh, the bells, bells, bells!
    What a tale their terror tells
     Of despair!
   How they clang, and clash, and roar!
55   What a horror they outpour
On the bosom of the palpitating air!
     Yet the ear, it fully knows
      By the twanging
      And the clanging,
60   How the danger ebbs and flows;
   Yet the ear distinctly tells,
      In the jangling
      And wrangling,
   How the danger sinks and swells,
65 By the sinking or the swelling in the anger of the bells—
      Of the bells,—
    Of the bells, bells, bells, bells,
     Bells, bells, bells—
In the clamor and the clangor of the bells!

IV

70   Hear the tolling of the bells—
     Iron bells!

What a world of solemn thought their monody compels!
      In the silence of the night,
      How we shiver with affright
75 At the melancholy menace of their tone!
      For every sound that floats
      From the rust within their throats
         Is a groan.
      And the people—ah, the people—
80 They that dwell up in the steeple,
         All alone,
      And who tolling, tolling, tolling,
        In that muffled monotone,
      Feel a glory in so rolling
85   On the human heart a stone—
      They are neither man nor woman—
      They are neither brute nor human—
        They are ghouls:—
        And their king it is who tolls:—
90   And he rolls, rolls, rolls,
         Rolls
      A paean from the bells!
      And his merry bosom swells
      With the paean of the bells!
95 And he dances, and he yells;
      Keeping time, time, time,
      In a sort of runic rhyme,
        To the paean of the bells—
        Of the bells—
100 Keeping time, time, time,
      In a sort of runic rhyme,
        To the throbbing of the bells—
        Of the bells, bells, bells—
        To the sobbing of the bells;
105 Keeping time, time, time,
        As he knells, knells, knells,
      In a happy runic rhyme,
        To the rolling of the bells—
        Of the bells, bells, bells:—
110   To the tolling of the bells—
      Of the bells, bells, bells, bells,
        Bells, bells, bells—
  To the moaning and the groaning of the bells.

Questions

1. Vocabulary: *euphony* (26), *voluminously* (26), *turbulency* (38), *monody* (72), *paean* (92), *runic* (97).
2. Underline or list all examples of alliteration, assonance, and onomatopoeia of words and phrases in stanza 1.

3. Find an example of interior rhyme in stanza 2.
4. What vowel sound is most frequent in lines 39–44? To what extent is that assonance onomatopoetic?
5. How does the poem's mood change from stanza 1 to stanza 4? How is that change reflected in the assonances of stanza 4?
6. It has been claimed that Poe's poetry has more ardent fans in France than in the United States. Perhaps one reason is that the musical effects we find excessive seem less prominent to a foreign ear. Do you find the great elaboration of sound effects pleasing? Exhilarating? Frightening?

Vowel Tones

English is rich in vowel sounds, from the wide and resonant *ah* sound to the piercing long *ē*. Our vowels are formed to reflect various emotional states and tensions through changes of pitch. The riders on a roller coaster scream the *ē* sound when the train takes a dive, and they sigh *ah* when the ride is over and the tension is released. Many words illustrate this connection between emotion and vowel tone. In "The Bells," notice that Poe's pleasant description of the bells in stanza 2 uses rich, open vowel sounds in words like "mellow," "golden," "harmony," and "molten-golden." But when he describes the "alarum bells" in stanza 3 he uses pinched, shrill vowels to express danger: "brazen," "scream," "affright," "shriek," and "leaping."

Generally the lower-register vowel sounds—the *aw* (awe), *oo* (doom), and *ō* (woe)—are effective in conveying horror, grief, solemnity, and great magnitude. The shorter vowel sounds—the *i* in little, the *e* in pet, the *a* in rattle—lend themselves to rapid movement, smallness, and gaiety. We have seen how, in the merry first stanza of "The Bells," Poe uses a preponderance of short vowels in words like "merriment," "tinkle," "crystalline," and "tintinnabulation"; and how in the horror of the last stanza he moves to the lower register, in words like "rolling," "tolling," "moaning," and "groaning." Listen to the short vowel sounds in Shakespeare's description of the tiny Queen Mab, from *Romeo and Juliet*, act 1, scene 4:

> She is the fairies' midwife and she comes
> In shape no bigger than an agate stone . . .
> Drawn with a team of little atomies . . .
> Her whip, of cricket's bone; the lash, of film . . .

There are vowel tones of lower register as well, but they are there to set off the diminutive sounds of "little atomies," "whips," and "cricket." Now listen to King Lear in the last act of Shakespeare's great tragedy, when he enters carrying his dead daughter.

> Howl, howl, howl, howl! O you are men of stones:
> Had I your tongues and eyes, I'd use them so
> That heaven's vault should crack. She's gone forever.
> I know when one is dead and when one lives . . .

The passage is dominated by the low vowel sounds ō, o͞o, and *aw*, to render the magnitude of Lear's grief.

The metrics of the classical Greek and Latin poets depended on the duration of vowels, rather than accents, for its rhythm. Instead of accented and unaccented syllables, there were long and short syllables. This is called *quantitative meter*. Although our metrics is based primarily on accent, the duration of vowels also plays its part, as will be seen in the following selections.

Exercise

Explain the relation between vowel tones and meaning in the following lines.

1. You do not do, you do not do
   Any more, black shoe
   In which I have lived like a foot
   For thirty years, poor and white,
   Barely daring to breathe or Achoo.

   —*Sylvia Plath*

2. Roll on, thou deep and dark blue ocean, roll.

   —*George Gordon, Lord Byron*

3.   The brittle fleet
   Touch'd, clink'd, and clashed, and vanished.

   —*Alfred, Lord Tennyson*

4. The stoned dogs crawl back through the blood . . .

   —*Weldon Kees*

5. I dared not meet the daffodils
   For fear their yellow gown
   Would pierce me with a fashion
   So foreign to my own.

   —*Emily Dickinson*

6. He from forth the closet brought a heap
   Of candied apple, quince, and plum, and gourd;
   With jellies sooter° than the creamy curd   *sweeter*
   And lucent syrops, tinct° with cinnamon . . .   *flavored*

   —*John Keats*

7. A sudden little river crossed my path
   As unexpected as a serpent comes.

   —*Robert Browning*

Now that we have developed a working knowledge and a vocabulary of musical techniques, let us read some poems with ears attuned to rhythm, rhyme, and the relation of form and content. Read each poem aloud, exaggerating the rhythms, alliterations, and vowel tones.

WILLIAM BUTLER YEATS (1865–1939)

• The Lake Isle of Innisfree

I will arise and go now, and go to Innisfree,
And a small cabin build there, of clay and
    wattles° made: *poles interwoven with branches*
Nine bean-rows will I have there, a hive for the honey-bee,
And live alone in the bee-loud glade.

5   And I shall have some peace there, for peace comes dropping slow,
Dropping from the veils of the morning to where the cricket sings;
There midnight's all a glimmer, and noon a purple glow,
And evening full of the linnet's wings.

I will arise and go now, for always night and day
10   I hear lake water lapping with low sounds by the shore;
While I stand on the roadway, or on the pavements gray,
I hear it in the deep heart's core.

Questions

1. At what line do you notice that a rhyme scheme has been established? Having established the scheme, does Yeats alter it?
2. Does the poem use internal rhyme? If so, what resonances are thereby created?
3. Scan the third stanza. Does it differ metrically from stanza 1? If so, does the meaning justify the difference?
4. Find an example of spondees in stanza 3. How does it affect our reading of the line in which it is found? Does it focus attention? Diffuse it?
5. Discuss the effect of short syllables on the movement of stanza 2.

Innisfree is a kind of Shangri-la for Yeats—a paradise of simplicity, peace, and solitude. The speaker is filled with longing and delight in contemplating this haven. The rhythm he has chosen in the first three lines is heptameter, with a caesura after the fourth foot. These lines have considerable momentum before the caesura and a peaceful resolution after it. The shorter fourth line achieves the most dramatic resolution, with its three spondees at the end. Notice that the basic movement of the lines in the stanza is rising rhythm, moving from unstressed to stressed syllables in an effective rhythmic expression of yearning. But see what happens in lines 5 and 6, when he imagines the dream attained:

And Ĭ shắll hăve sŏme peáce thére, fŏr peáce cŏmes dróppĭng slów,
Dróppĭng frŏm thĕ veĭls ŏf thĕ mórnĭng tŏ whĕre thĕ crĭckĕt sĭngs;

The rhythm shifts radically from a rising to a falling rhythm, with a pyrrhic foot in line 6. This line is as light and ecstatic as his dream of peace.

Peasants Dancing, by Pieter Brueghel the Elder *(Kunsthistorisches Museum, Vienna)*

WILLIAM CARLOS WILLIAMS (1883–1963)

The Dance

In Breughel's great picture, The Kermess,
the dancers go round, they go round and
around, the squeal and the blare and the
tweedle of bagpipes, a bugle and fiddles
5   tipping their bellies (round as the thick-
sided glasses whose wash they impound)
their hips and their bellies off balance
to turn them. Kicking and rolling about
the Fair Grounds, swinging their butts, those
10   shanks must be sound to bear up under such
rollicking measures, prance as they dance
in Breughel's great picture, The Kermess.

Questions

1. Vocabulary: *impound* (6).
2. How many instances of onomatopoeia can you find in this poem?
3. Scan the poem. Are there more stressed syllables or unstressed ones? How does that affect the movement of the poem?

4. Which lines are end-stopped? Which lines are enjambed? How does enjambment contribute to the movement from line to line?
5. Does the rhythm of the poem remind you of any particular dance rhythm?

Songs

We began our discussion with the observation that poetry and songs have a common root in our emotions, and that literary, or unsung, poetry is a relatively new development in the history of literature. Since the Renaissance the distinction between song and literary poetry may be drawn along the following general lines. First, most songs demand greater adherence to regular rhythm and rhyme than does spoken poetry. We are accustomed to hearing rhyme and regular rhythm in our songs, and we are dissatisfied when it is lacking. Second, because songs are composed to be heard rather than studied, songwriters usually avoid the concentration of images and figures that strengthen literary poetry. They use them, but in less profusion, and in such a way that they may be grasped on first hearing. Songwriters have melodies to charge their lines with emotion, so their language can relax.

This is not to minimize the power of poetry in songwriting. The United States has been fortunate in its extraordinary poet-lyricists: the anonymous singers of ballads and spirituals, troubadours Woody Guthrie and Bob Dylan, urban songwriters Billie Holiday and Huddie Ledbetter, and the countless writers of Broadway show tunes. These composers have created a tradition of lyric poetry of wit, beauty, and power.

Perhaps one of the true tests of a good song is that it loses its essential power when committed to cold type. If you have recordings of the following songs, you should listen to them before and after studying them as literature.

ANONYMOUS

Frankie and Albert

Frankie was a good girl,
As everybody knows.
She paid a hundred dollars
For Albert's suit of clothes.
5   He was her man and he done her wrong.

Frankie went down to the corner saloon,
Wasn't goin' to be there long.
Asked the bartender had he seen her Albert,
'Cause he done been home and gone.
10   He was her man and he done her wrong.

Well, the bartender he told Frankie,
Can't lie to you if I try.
Old Albert been here an hour ago
And gone home with Alice Fry.
15   He was her man and he done her wrong.

Frankie went down to Albert's house,
Only a couple of blocks away,
Peeped in the keyhole of his door,
Saw Albert lovin' Alice Fry.
20   He was her man and he done her wrong.

Frankie called out to Albert,
Albert said I don't hear.
If you don't come to the woman you love
Goin' to haul you out of here.
25   He was her man and he done her wrong.

Frankie she shot old Albert,
And she shot him three or four times.
Said I'll hang around a few minutes
And see if Albert's dyin'.
30   He was my man and he done me wrong.

An iron-tired wagon
With ribbons all hung in black
Took old Albert to the buryin' ground
And it didn't bring him back.
35   He was her man and he done her wrong.

Frankie told the sheriff
What goin' to happen to me?
Said looks like from the evidence
Goin' to be murder first degree.
40   He was your man and he done you wrong.

Judge heard Frankie's story,
Heard Albert's mother testify.
Judge said to Frankie,
You goin' to be justified.
45   He was your man and he done you wrong.

Dark was the night,
Cold was the ground,
The last words I heard Frankie say,
I done laid old Albert down.
50   He was my man and he done me wrong.

Last time I heard of Frankie
She was settin' in her cell,
Sayin' Albert done me wrong
And for that I sent him to hell.
55   He was my man and he done me wrong.

I aint goin' to tell no stories,
I aint goin' to tell no lies.
The woman who stole Frankie's Albert
Was the girl they call Alice Fry.
60   He was her man and he done her wrong.

1. If you were to classify "Frankie and Albert" as a genre of poetry, how would you classify it? As lyric? Dramatic? Narrative?
2. Is the imagery of the song denser than that of most lyric poems? Less dense? Do you find it at all difficult to follow?
3. Can you find many instances of near rhyme? Is it graceful, or is it awkward in print? Do you suppose these rhymes would be more pleasing if you heard them sung?

BILLIE HOLIDAY (1915–1959)

God Bless the Child

Them that's got shall get, Them that's not shall lose;
So the Bible said, and it still is news;
Moma may have, Papa may have, but,
God bless the child that's got his own; That's got his own.

5   Yes, the strong gets more, while the weak ones fade.
Empty pockets don't ever make the grade;
Moma may have, Papa may have, but
God bless the child that's got his own! That's got his own.

Money, you got lots o' friends, crowdin' 'round the door.
10   When you're gone, and spendin' ends, they don't come no more.
No. No. No.

Rich relations give, crust of bread and such.
You can help yourself, but don't take too much!
Moma may have, Papa may have, but
15   God bless the child that's got his own! That's got his own.

Questions

1. Find an example of allusion in stanza 1. How does it enrich the song?
2. Find an instance of synecdoche in stanza 2. Another in stanza 4.
3. The line repeated at the end of stanzas 1, 2, and 4 is the song's *refrain*. Why does she repeat it?

BOB DYLAN (1941–)

Boots of Spanish Leather

Oh, I'm sailin' away my own true love,
I'm sailin' away in the morning.
Is there something I can send you from across the sea,
From the place that I'll be landing?

5   No, there's nothin' you can send me, my own true love,
There's nothin' I wish to be ownin'.
Just carry yourself back to me unspoiled,
From across the lonesome ocean.

Oh, but I just thought you might want something fine
10   Made of silver or of golden,
Either from the mountains of Madrid
Or from the coast of Barcelona.

Oh, but if I had the stars from the darkest night
And the diamonds from the deepest ocean,
15   I'd foresake them all for your sweet kiss,
For that's all I'm wishin' to be ownin'.

That I might be gone a long time
And it's only that I'm askin',
Is there something I can send you to remember me by,
20   To make your time more easy passin'.

Oh, how can, how can you ask me again,
It only brings me sorrow.
The same thing I want from you today,
I would want again tomorrow.

25   I got a letter on a lonesome day,
It was from her ship a-sailin',
Saying I don't know when I'll be comin' back again,
It depends on how I'm a-feelin'.

Well, if you, my love, must think that-a-way,
30   I'm sure your mind is roamin'.
I'm sure your heart is not with me,
But with the country to where you're goin'.

So take heed, take heed of the western wind,
Take heed of the stormy weather.
35   And yes, there's something you can send back to me,
Spanish boots of Spanish leather.

Questions

1. How many personae do you hear in the song? Is it a monologue? A dialogue?
2. What are the most vivid images in the poem? Are there stanzas without images?
3. Find an example of metonymy. Find an example of hyperbole.

COLE PORTER (1893–1964)

My Heart Belongs to Daddy

I used to fall
In love with all
Those boys who maul
Refined ladies.
5   But now I tell
Each young gazelle
To go to hell—

I mean, hades,
For since I've come to care
10   For such a sweet millionaire.

While tearing off
A game of golf
I may make a play for the caddy.
But when I do
15   I don't follow through
'Cause my heart belongs to Daddy.

If I invite
A boy, some night,
To dine on my fine finnan haddie,°   *smoked haddock*
20   I just adore
His asking for more,
But my heart belongs to Daddy,
Yes, my heart belongs to Daddy.
So I simply couldn't be bad.
25   Yes, my heart belongs to Daddy,
Da-da, da-da-da, da-da-da, dad!
So I want to warn you, laddie,
Tho' I know you're perfectly swell,
That my heart belongs to Daddy
30   'Cause my Daddy, he treats me so well.
He treats it and treats it,
And then he repeats it,
Yes, Daddy, he treats it so well.

Saint Patrick's day,
35   Although I may
Be seen wearing green with a paddy,
I'm always sharp
When playing the harp,
'Cause my heart belongs to Daddy.
40   Though other dames
At football games
May long for a strong undergraddy,
I never dream
Of making the team
45   'Cause my heart belongs to Daddy.
Yes, my heart belongs to Daddy,
So I simply couldn't be bad.
Yes, my heart belongs to Daddy,
Da-da, da-da-da, da-da-da, dad!
50   So I want to warn you, laddie,
Tho' I simply hate to be frank,
That I can't be mean to Daddy
'Cause my Da-da-da-daddy might spank.
In matters artistic
55   He's not modernistic
So Da-da-da-daddy might spank.

11 ❧ Tones of Voice

There is more to speech than the literal meaning of words. We may mean what we say, or we may mean something quite different. In conversation our tone of voice indicates how we feel about what we are communicating. Even in privacy, we shout good news and whisper condolences. We sneer sarcasm. When your mother said, "Don't speak to me in that tone of voice," you may have been saying something quite agreeable in itself. You may have been saying, "Sure, I'll take out the garbage," but in such a bitter tone that it came out sounding like, "Sure, I'll take out the garbage (and spread it all over the lawn)."

Tone is the way writers or speakers indicate their attitudes and feelings toward the subject. Of course, it is difficult to capture on the printed page the qualities of the spoken voice. Through their rhythms, images, and word choices, poets can subtly suggest their underlying sentiments. How do we know when people are lying to us? The content of what they say may be perfectly believable, but something in the rhythm—perhaps it is too regular, too pat, too rehearsed—indicates that the speaker is insincere. Poets perfect their language, but they usually wish to achieve the spontaneity of a sincere expression. Most of the poems we have read are quite sincere, and you will notice in their music a sustained immediacy that is hard to fake.

The Range of Tones

Let us begin with a poem whose tone is subtle, almost neutral.

WILLIAM CARLOS WILLIAMS (1883–1963)

The Young Housewife

At ten A.M. the young housewife
moves about in negligee behind

William Carlos Williams *(Rollie McKenna)*

the wooden walls of her husband's house.
I pass solitary in my car.

5   Then again she comes to the curb
to call the ice-man,[1] fish-man, and stands
shy, uncorseted, tucking in
stray ends of hair, and I compare her
to a fallen leaf.

10   The noiseless wheels of my car
rush with a crackling sound over
dried leaves as I bow and pass smiling.

To determine the tone of a poem, first consider the poet's attitude toward the subject. How does Williams feel about the housewife? He seems so cool and unperturbed that we must scrutinize his *observations* for a clue. He mentions that she wears a negligee and is uncorseted. He notices her "tucking in/stray ends of hair." These observations suggest that Williams finds the woman attractive. But he does not say, "Look at the beautiful housewife!" He does not rhapsodize about her charms. In the only figure of speech he permits himself, he simply compares her to a fallen leaf. The tone of the poem is masterful in its restraint.

    The following poem is equally masterful, in its lack of restraint. The subject is similar: a man is describing a woman. But Lawrence's admiration for this

---

[1] Before the advent of the home refrigerator, blocks of ice were delivered to homes by icemen.

woman is unembarrassed, and his enthusiasm drives the rhythms and figures of speech. The resulting tone is racy, ebullient.

D. H. LAWRENCE (1885–1930)

Gloire de Dijon[2]

When she rises in the morning
I linger to watch her;
She spreads the bath-cloth underneath the window
And the sunbeams catch her
5   Glistening white on the shoulders,
While down her sides the mellow
Golden shadow glows as
She stoops to the sponge, and her swung breasts
Sway like full-blown yellow
10   Gloire de Dijon roses.

She drips herself with water, and her shoulders
Glisten as silver, they crumple up
Like wet and falling roses, and I listen
For the sluicing of their rain-dishevelled petals.
15   In the window full of sunlight
Concentrates her golden shadow
Fold on fold, until it glows as
Mellow as the glory roses.

Here nothing is held back. The similes are sensual and fulsome. Notice how the lines tumble over one another in the excitement of long sentences, and how the speaker features the long ō vowel in "shadow glows" and "roses" at the ends of both stanzas. That ō sound is the sound of wonderment. The poem is an articulate "wow" from beginning to end. Since distinctive tone in poetry often results from rhythm and the arrangement of vowels, we will refer to the music of poetry again in our discussions of tone.

Irony

Although the tones of the foregoing poems differ in intensity, they share an important quality: they are both sincere. Nothing in the tone of either speaker would lead us to suspect that he does not mean what he says. When poets mean the opposite of what they say, they use the tone known as *irony*. This tone of voice is unmistakable in conversation. The compliment "That's a lovely hat" can become an ironic jibe if we overemphasize the word *lovely*. We often use irony to tease each other.

---

[2] *Gloire de Dijon* is French for "glory of Dijon." Dijon is a city in eastern France, also famous for its mustard.

Translating the ironic tone into literature is likewise done by overemphasis and understatement. Lacking the speaker's control of pitch and volume, the poet must rely on posturing, surprising diction, and excessive imagery to set the tone.

The following protest poem is a veritable test pattern of ironic tones. Whitman is describing a military parade. At first his irony is so subtle we might think he really admires "the show." But by the time he describes the phantom soldiers, "bandaged and bloodless," his repetition of "this is indeed a show" is downright bitter. The first time he calls the parade a "show," we think he means entertainment. He does not mean that at all: he hates it.

WALT WHITMAN (1819–1892)

A Boston Ballad

To get betimes in Boston town I rose this morning early,
Here's a good place at the corner, I must stand and see the show.

Clear the way there Jonathan!
Way for the President's marshal—way for the government cannon!
5   Way for the Federal foot and dragoons,
     (and the apparitions° copiously° tumbling.)   *phantoms   plentifully*

I love to look on the Stars and Stripes,
    I hope the fifes will play Yankee Doodle.

How bright shine the cutlasses of the foremost troops!
10   Every man holds his revolver, marching stiff through Boston town.

A fog follows, antiques of the same come limping,
Some appear wooden-legged, and some appear bandaged and bloodless.

Why this is indeed a show—it has called the dead out of the earth!
The old graveyards of the hills have hurried to see!
15   Phantoms! phantoms countless by flank and rear!
Cock'd hats of mothy mould—crutches made of mist!
Arms in slings—old men leaning on young men's shoulders.

What troubles you Yankee phantoms? what is all this chattering
    of bare gums?
Does the ague° convulse your limbs? do you mistake your crutches   *fever*
    for firelocks and level them?

20   If you blind your eyes with tears you will not see the President's marshal,
If you groan such groans you might balk the government cannon.

For shame old maniacs—bring down those toss'd arms,
    and let your white hair be,
Here gape your great grandsons, their wives gaze at them from the windows,
25   See how well dress'd, see how orderly they conduct themselves.

Worse and worse—can't you stand it? are you retreating?
Is this hour with the living too dead for you?

Retreat then—pell-mell!
To your graves—back—back to the hills old limpers!
30   I do not think you belong here anyhow.

But there is one thing that belongs here—shall I tell you what it is,
    gentlemen of Boston?

I will whisper it to the Mayor, he shall send a committee to England,
They shall get a grant from the Parliament, go with a cart to the royal vault,
Dig out King George's coffin, unwrap him quick from the grave-clothes,
35   box up his bones for a journey,
Find a swift Yankee clipper—here is freight for you, black-bellied clipper,
Up with your anchor—shake out your sails—steer straight toward Boston bay.

Now call for the President's marshal again, bring out the government cannon,
Fetch home the roarers from Congress, make another procession,
40   guard it with foot and dragoons.
This centre-piece for them;
Look, all orderly citizens—look from the windows, women!

The committee open the box, set up the regal ribs, glue those that will not stay,
Clap the skull on top of the ribs, and clap a crown on top of the skull.

45   You have got your revenge, old buster—the crown is come to its own,
    and more than its own.

Stick your hands in your pockets, Jonathan—you are a made man from this day,
You are mighty cute—and here is one of your bargains.

The phantom veterans remind us of the deeper meaning of military shows. They symbolize war and suffering. Whitman's description of the phantoms' maimed decrepitude, their weeping and groaning in the presence of the orderly parade, emphasizes the reality of war and the proud ignorance of the young dragoons. When he finally dismisses the phantoms, saying, "I do not think you belong here anyhow," the line resonates with bitterness and irony. It is classic understatement.

Then comes the most ironic image of all. What *does* belong in the midst of this show of nationalism and militarism is the corpse of King George, whose tyranny the phantom veterans died to depose. When Whitman says to Jonathan, the gawking spectator, "here is one of your bargains," and "you are a made man from this day," he cannot be taken literally. Whitman's vision of a militarized United States is grim, and his tone is pure sarcasm. The drumbeat rhythms of the poem underscore his sarcasm.

ALAN DUGAN (1923–)

Morning Song

Look, it's morning, and a little water gurgles in the tap.
I wake up waiting, because it's Sunday, and turn twice more

than usual in bed, before I rise to cereal and comic strips.
I have risen to the morning danger and feel proud,

5   and after shaving off the night's disguises, after searching
close to the bone for blood, and finding only a little,
I shall walk out bravely into the daily accident.

Questions

1. How does the speaker feel about the morning? Are the phrases "morning danger" and "the daily accident" accurate descriptions of the day, or are they excessive?
2. How does the speaker feel about his own response to the morning? Are the words "proud" and "bravely" sincere or excessive?
3. To what degree is the poem ironic in tone?

ANNE STEVENSON (1933–)

Pregnant

When we loved
it was as if we created each other.
As if in my body two zeros,
two embryos
5   curved in the well of my sex.

But then you detached yourself,
you receded, transposed into pure sound—
a bell sharpening itself on its distance,
a blade honing itself to tremulous thinness—
10   while the mirror held me dumbly—my woman's face,
my body like a globe
nourishing its stray curl of flesh,
my huge breasts and body bound,
bound to the shape of this world.

Questions

1. What is the speaker's attitude toward her lover? Toward herself?
2. Do the metaphors of lines 8 and 9 ring true? Does the metaphor of the globe in line 11 sound sincere?
3. Is there any suggestion of irony in the poem?

Didactic Poetry

The Latin poet Horace, in a great didactic poem called "The Art of Poetry," said that the purpose of poetry is to teach or to delight. Sometimes it is both. Didactic poetry aims to teach; poems have been written to teach physics, bee-keeping, even the art of love. The didactic tone is distinctive. The poet's attitude toward the subject is: I know about this, and now I'm going to let you in on it.

This is also the attitude of doctors, moralists, and a few teachers. The didactic tone can be charming, or it can be presumptuous. We are most familiar with it in little rhymes that help us remember important facts.

Thirty days hath September,
April, June and November . . .

Red sky at night:
Sailor's delight.
Red sky at morning:
Sailors take warning.

Oysters into milk
Go smooth as silk.

In all of literature no didactic speech has been more frequently quoted than the advice of Polonius to his son, from Shakespeare's *Hamlet*.

And these few precepts in thy memory
Look thou charácter. Give thy thoughts no tongue,
Nor any unproportion'd thought his act.
Be thou familiar, but by no means vulgar;
Those friends thou hast, and their adoption tried,
Grapple them unto thy soul with hoops of steel;
But do not dull thy palm with entertainment
Of each new-hatch'd, unfledg'd comráde. Beware
Of entrance to a quarrel, but, being in,
Bear 't that th' opposed may beware of thee.
Give every man thy ear, but few thy voice;
Take each man's censure, but reserve thy judgment.
Costly thy habit as thy purse can buy,
But not express'd in fancy; rich, not gaudy;
For the apparel oft proclaims the man,
And they in France of the best rank and station
Are of a most select and generous clef° in that.   *sort*
Neither a borrower, nor a lender be;
For loan oft loses both itself and friend,
And borrowing dulleth edge of husbandry.°   *household management*
This above all: to thine own self be true,
And it must follow, as the night the day,
Thou canst not then be false to any man.
Farewell; my blessing season this in thee!

Polonius, a professional advisor, has saved up the best advice for his son. He is a master of the didactic tone, and his instructions ring with confidence and conviction. They do not invite questions; they represent an end of questioning, the treasury of an old man's wisdom. In this certainty the didactic distinguishes itself from the meditative tone.

There is comedy in the tone as well. What begins as a "few precepts" runs on to twenty-four lines of moral disquisition, more than any young man could absorb or believe. Even the wisest advice is a little silly if there is too much of it.

At its best the didactic tone is both convincing and modest. Advice is easiest to hear when it seems hard won and is offered with humility.

EMILY DICKINSON (1830–1886)

Success Is Counted Sweetest

Success is counted sweetest
By those who ne'er succeed.
To comprehend a nectar
Requires sorest need.

5   Not one of all the purple host
Who took the flag to-day
Can tell the definition,
So clear, of victory,

As he, defeated, dying,
10   On whose forbidden ear
The distant strains of triumph
Break, agonized and clear.

The poem is organized like a simple lesson—a general proposition followed by a corollary and an illustration. Dickinson states the proposition so plainly that it seems incontestable. Should we be tempted to quibble, the example of the battle is so apt and moving that it disarms us. Unlike Polonius, Dickinson does not weary us with her wisdom.

English poets of the eighteenth century had greater confidence in reason and human perfectibility than those of any other period in history. To Alexander Pope any problem worth solving would yield to reason. Being supremely reasonable, Pope found the didactic tone natural. His verse is a model of clarity and balance, its tone even and assured, its rhythms highly regular. Such a tone is the mark of secure faith, a system that leaves little room for doubt.

ALEXANDER POPE (1688–1744)

From An Essay on Man (Epistle IV)

Honour and shame from no condition rise;
Act well your part, there all the honour lies.
Fortune in men has some small diff'rence made,
One flaunts in rags, one flutters in brocade;
5   The cobbler aproned, and the parson gowned,
The friar hooded, and the monarch crowned.
"What differ more (you cry) than crown and cowl?"
I'll tell you, friend; a wise man and a fool.

You'll find, if once the monarch acts the monk,
10 Or, cobbler-like, the parson will be drunk,
Worth makes the man, and want of it, the fellow;
The rest is all but leather or prunella.°   *a woolen fabric*
    Stuck o'er with titles and hung round with strings,
That thou mayest be by kings, or whores of kings.
15 Boast the pure blood of an illustrious race,
In quiet flow from Lucrece° to Lucrece;   *a virtuous Roman woman*
But by your fathers' worth if yours you rate,
Count me those only who were good and great.

Questions

1. What is more important to the speaker—apparel or character?
2. Do you agree with the ideas expressed in lines 9–12?
3. What is the meter of the poem? Does it suit the didactic tone?

Toughness

Many readers tend to think of poets as soft-hearted creatures who bruise easily and have the most exquisite sympathy for all living things, but they are not. As evidence of this misconception, certain poets adopt a tone of toughness. There is a little of Mae West or Humphrey Bogart in all of us, an attitude that life is hard, kid, so you may as well brace up and plow through it. This poetry is not sighed or sung. It is spoken straight.

PHILIP LEVINE (1928–)

To a Child Trapped in a Barber Shop

You've gotten in through the transom
        and you can't get out
till Monday morning or, worse,
        till the cops come.

5   That six-year-old red face
        calling for mama
is yours; it won't help you
        because your case

is closed forever, hopeless.
10   So don't drink
the Lucky Tiger,° don't   *hair tonic*
        fill up on grease

because that makes it a lot worse,
        that makes it a crime
15 against property and the state
        and that costs time.

We've all been here before,
          we took our turn
     under the electric storm
20   of the vibrator

     and stiffened our wills to meet
          the close clippers
     and heard the true blade mowing
          back and forth

25   on a strip of dead skin,
               and we stopped crying.
     You think your life is over?
               It's just begun.

Questions

1. How serious is the child's predicament?
2. Does the speaker care about the child? What phrases suggest that he does?
3. The speaker is feeling both sympathy and distance from his side of the glass. How does the tone reveal these conflicting feelings?
4. Will the speaker try to rescue the child?

CHARLES BUKOWSKI (1920–)

Yellow

Seivers was one of the hardest running backs[3] since
Jimmy Brown, and lateral motion too,
like a chorus girl, really, until one day he got hit on
the blind side by Basil Skronski; we carried Seivers off the field
5   but Skronski had gotten one rib and cracked another.

the next year Seivers wasn't even good in practice, gun shy as a
squirrel in deer season; he stopped contact, fumbled, couldn't even
hold a look-in pass or a handoff—all that wasted and he could go the 100 in 9.7[4]

I'm 45 years old, out of shape, too much beer, but one of the best
10   assistant coaches in the pro game, and I can't stand to see a man
jaking° it. I got him in the locker room the other day when the whole   *shirking*
squad was in there. I told him, "Seivers, you used to be a player
but now you're chickenshit!"

"you can't talk that way to me, Manny!" he said, and I turned him
15   around, he was lacing on a shoe, and I right-cracked him
right on the chin. he fell against a locker
and then he began to cry—the greatest since Brown,
crying there against the locker, one shoe off, one on.

"come on, men, let's get outa here!" I told the gang, and we ran
20   on out, and when we got back he had cleared out, he was gone, his

---

[3] In football, a backfield ball carrier.
[4] The hundred-yard dash in 9.7 seconds.

gear was gone. we got some kid from Illinois running his spot now,
head down, knees high, he don't care where he's going.

guys like Seivers end up washing dishes for a buck an hour
and that's just what they deserve.

Questions

1. What is the speaker's attitude toward Seivers?
2. What figures of speech reveal this attitude in the first two stanzas?
3. Try to say the line "I can't stand to see a man/jaking it," in the speaker's voice. Do you hear the tone? What attitude does it express toward Seivers? Toward the game of football?
4. What does the speaker care more about—Seivers's feelings, or football?
5. Do you feel sorry for Seivers?
6. Would you like the speaker to be your coach? How would you like him to be your father?

The Comic Tone

When poets adopt a comic attitude toward a subject we sometimes can hear it in rollicking or off-beat rhythms, in clownish imagery and diction. The subject may or may not be funny—the tone is what makes us laugh.

ANONYMOUS

Miss Bailey's Ghost

A captain bold, in Halifax, who dwelt in country quarters,
Seduced a maid, who hang'd herself, one morning, in her garters,
His wicked conscience smited him, he lost his stomach daily,
He took to drinking ratafee,° and thought upon Miss Bailey.   *an almond liqueur*
5   Oh, Miss Bailey! unfortunate Miss Bailey.

One night betimes he went to rest, for he had caught a fever,
Says he, "I am a handsome man, but I'm a gay deceiver";
His candle just at twelve o'clock began to burn quite palely,
A ghost stepp'd up to his bedside, and said, "behold Miss Bailey."
10   Oh, Miss Bailey! unfortunate Miss Bailey.

"Avaunt, Miss Bailey," then he cried, "your face looks white and mealy,"
"Dear Captain Smith," the ghost replied, "you've used me ungenteely;
The Crowner's Quest goes hard with me, because I've acted fraily,
And parson Biggs won't bury me, though I am dead Miss Bailey."
15   Oh, Miss Bailey! unfortunate Miss Bailey.

"Dear Corpse," said he, "since you and I accounts must once for all close,
I've really got a one pound note in my regimental small clothes;
'Twill bribe the sexton for your grave."—The ghost then vanish'd gaily,
Crying "Bless you, wicked Captain Smith, remember poor Miss Bailey."
20   Oh, Miss Bailey! unfortunate Miss Bailey.

The situation itself is not very funny. Poe would have made a nightmare of it, Tennyson a dirge. But the rhyme of *quarters* and *garters* is so unexpected and silly that it quickly deflates the seriousness of the hanging. Likewise the captain's excessive stomach trouble and his vanity, as confessed in line 7. The dance-hall rhythm is so unsuited to the macabre events that its very inappropriateness is comic.

Max Beerbohm has observed that all humor is the result of exaggeration or incongruity. Comic poems usually make fun not only of their subjects but of poetry as well, either by exaggerating its techniques or misapplying them.

EDMUND CLERIHEW BENTLEY (1875–1956)

Lord Clive

What I like about Clive
Is that he is no longer alive.
There is a great deal to be said
For being dead.

Does poetry have to rhyme? All right then, says the comic poet, I'll make it rhyme to the most awkward rhythm. "Lord Clive" is not only a burlesque of rhythm and rhyme. It is a takeoff on the elegy, which is usually quite serious.

Verses that rhyme not only the last syllable, but the last two, are called feminine rhymes. Perhaps as a result of a sort of tonal overkill, the effect of feminine rhyme is often comic.

ANONYMOUS

There Was a King

There was a King and he had three daughters,
And they all lived in a basin of water;
    The basin bended,
    My story's ended.
5   If the basin had been stronger,
My story would have been longer.

The comic charm of this poem depends on its tone, induced by eccentric rhythms and feminine rhymes. Its wit would be lost in prose.

Two popular tricks in the comic poet's repertoire are the *pun* and the *spoonerism*. The pun is a play on words with similar sounds or on a single word with different meanings: "I stuck my finger in the pie and meringue came off." That's a terrible pun. Here is a better one:

HILAIRE BELLOC (1870–1953)

On His Books

When I am dead, I hope it may be said
"His sins were scarlet, but his books were read."

Read: red. Get it? Roman audiences 2000 years ago acknowledged puns by groaning, and that response has not changed.

A spoonerism is a slip of the tongue that exchanges the parts of two words. Thus, "Let's sit by the fire and spin" becomes "Let's spit by the fire and sin." William Spooner once told one of his students: "You have hissed all of my mystery lessons and completely tasted two whole worms." (Translation: You have missed all of my history lessons and completely wasted two whole terms.)

Diction Levels

Some poets use unfamiliar words and complex literary sentences, whereas others never depart from plain speech. Customarily we refer to formal, literary language as *high diction* and to street language as *low diction*. We associate the former with pulpit, courtroom, and college, and the latter with racetrack and locker room. The poet's level of diction is an element of tone indicating both an attitude toward the subject and a regard for the reader. High diction suggests acuity, demands scholarship, and promises to reward it. Simple diction is humbler, more relaxed and inviting.

We have seen a range of diction levels, from the heights of "An Essay on Man" (pages 228–229) to the idiomatic force of Bukowski's "Yellow" (pages 230–231). Emily Dickinson's poem "Success Is Counted Sweetest" is neither as high toned as "An Essay on Man" nor as low as "Yellow." How would you rank the diction level of Emily's poem, in relation to Philip Levine's (pages 229–230)?

Ford Madox Ford, an English essayist, set a limit to the artificiality of diction. He said that a poet should not write anything that he could not, under the stress of some emotion, actually *say*. Modern poets have taken his advice to heart, but there is still a great range of diction levels, owing to our diverse educations and personalities. This makes for a lively variety of tones.

One of our more formal poets is Richard Wilbur.

RICHARD WILBUR (1921–)

The Death of a Toad

A toad the power mower caught,
Chewed and clipped of a leg, with a hobbling hop has got
To the garden verge, and sanctuaried him
Under the cineraria° leaves, in the shade   *exotic flowering plant*

Of the ashen heartshaped leaves, in a dim,
    Low, and a final glade.

  The rare original heartsblood goes,
Spends on the earthen hide, in the folds and wizenings, flows
  In the gutters of the banked and staring eyes. He lies
10 As still as if he would return to stone,
    And soundlessly attending, dies
      Toward some deep monotone,

    Toward misted and ebullient seas
And cooling shores, toward lost Amphibia's emperies.°   *empires*
15 Day dwindles, drowning, and at length is gone
  In the wide and antique eyes, which still appear
    To watch, across the castrate lawn,
      The haggard daylight steer.

Questions

1. Vocabulary: *sanctuaried* (3), *wizenings* (8), *ebullient* (13), *castrate* (17).
2. How would you describe the diction of the poem? Did it send you to the dictionary? How often?
3. Have you ever heard anyone talk like the speaker of this poem? Is there a single sentence or phrase that you could imagine someone saying?
4. What is Wilbur's attitude toward his subject? Serious? Frivolous?
5. Suppose the poet had used more natural speech. What subtleties might be lost? What music?

LANGSTON HUGHES (1902–1967)

• Who But the Lord?

I looked and I saw
That man they call the Law.
He was coming
Down the street at me!
5 I had visions in my head
Of being laid out cold and dead,
Or else murdered
By the third degree.

I said, *O, Lord, if you can,*
10 *Save me from that man!*
Don't let him make a pulp out of me!
But the Lord he was not quick.
The Law raised up his stick
And beat the living hell
15 Out of me!

Now, I do not understand
Why God don't protect a man

From police brutality.
Being poor and black,
20   I've no weapon to strike back
So who but the Lord
Can protect me?

Questions

1. How would you describe the diction of this poem? Literary? Conversational?
2. The poet's attitude toward his subject is clearly serious. Why, then, has he chosen such common diction? What does this suggest about his attitude toward his reader? Intimacy? Distance?

Dialects

In many cultures the line between the literary tradition and the popular culture has been sharply drawn. There are some poems meant to be read by scholars and others that are meant for a popular audience. Where there is a significant difference between the written and the spoken language, some poets strive to capture the accents of the vernacular. Some of the most popular poets, such as Robert Burns, James Russell Lowell, and Paul Laurence Dunbar, have written in dialect. Unfortunately, the popularity of poetry in dialect is often as short-lived and local as the dialect itself.

ROBERT BURNS (1759–1796)

• John Anderson My Jo

John Anderson my jo,° John,	*a term of endearment*
When we were first acquent,	
Your locks were like the raven,	
Your bonnie brow was brent;°	*smooth*
5 But now your brow is beld,° John,	*bald*
Your locks are like the snow;	
But blessings on your frosty pow,°	*head*
John Anderson, my jo.	
John Anderson my jo, John,	
10 We clamb the hill thegither;	
And mony a canty° day, John,	*cheerful*
We've had wi' ane anither:	
Now we maun° totter down, John,	*must*
And hand in hand we'll go,	
15 And sleep thegither at the foot,	
John Anderson, my jo.	

Questions

1. What is the speaker's attitude toward John?
2. Would she be able to achieve such intimacy without her dialect?

3. Are you familiar with the Scots accent? If so, read the poem aloud, first with the Scots accent and then in your own. Which sounds better?

PAUL LAURENCE DUNBAR (1872–1906)

In the Morning

'Lias! 'Lias! Bless de Lawd!
Don' you know de day's erbroad?
Ef you don't git up, you scamp,
Dey'll be trouble in dis camp.
5   T'ink I gwine to let you sleep
W'ile I meks yo' boa'd an' keep?
Dat's a putty howdy-do—
Don' you hyeah me, 'Lias—you?

Bet ef I come crost dis flo'
10 You won' fin' no time to sno'.
Daylight all a-shinin' in
W'ile you sleep—w'y hit's a sin!
Ain't de can'le-light enough
To bu'n out widout a snuff,
15 But you go de mo'nin' thoo
Bu'nin' up de daylight too?

'Lias, don' you hyeah me call?
No use tu'nin' to'ds de wall;
I kin hyeah dat mattuss° squeak;   *mattress*
20 Don' you hyeah me w'en I speak?
Dis hyeah clock done struck off six—
Ca'line, bring me dem ah sticks!
Oh, you down, suh; huh, you down—
Look hyeah, don' you daih to frown.

25 Ma'ch° yo'se'f an' wash yo' face,   *march*
Don' you splattah all de place;
I got somep'n else to do,
'Sides jes' cleanin' aftah you.
Tek dat comb an' fix yo' haid—
30 Looks jes' lak a feddah baid.°   *feather bed*
Look hyeah, boy, I let you see
You sha'n't roll yo' eyes at me.

Come hyeah; bring me dat ah strap!
Boy, I'll whup you 'twell you drap;
35 You done felt yo'se'f too strong,
An' you sholy° got me wrong.   *surely*
Set down at dat table thaih;
Jes' you whimpah ef you daih!
Evah mo'nin' on dis place,
40 Seem lak I mus' lose my grace.

Paul Laurence Dunbar
(Ohio Historical Society)

Fol' yo' han's an' bow yo' haid—
Wait ontwell de blessin' 's said;
"Lawd, have mussy on ouah souls—"
(Don' you daih to tech dem rolls—)
45   "Bless de food we gwine to eat—"
(You set still—I *see* yo' feet;
You jes' try dat trick again!)
"Gin us peace an' joy. Amen!"

Questions

1. This is one of the most popular poems ever written in America. It has been memorized and recited by thousands of schoolchildren. Can you explain its popularity?
2. Without the aid of the marginal glosses, could you have understood the poem?
3. Translate one of the stanzas into literary English, making as few changes as possible. What does the poem lose in translation? How much of the tone survives?

12 🌿 The Poem's Shape I

The everyday words we use become literature when they are given expressive shape. No literature is without shape. A playwright, for example, cannot merely tape-record a lively conversation and call it a play. A dialogue must be molded so that the conversation has a beginning and an end. Even interviewers shape a conversation by asking prepared questions and by carefully editing the transcript after the interview is over.

Why is shape necessary? Shape gives a work of literature unity and completeness. By *unity* we mean that everything in the poem belongs in it and is connected to everything else. In conversation, all sorts of extraneous and unconnected statements arise. In literature, the writer limits him- or herself to what contributes to the overall meaning and effectiveness of the work. By *completeness* we mean that everything needed by the poem is present, in its proper place. In conversation we often forget what we intended to say or later think of what we ought to have said. A good poem, however, contains everything it needs to be effective, and nothing extra. Its shape both highlights and determines the poem's unity and completeness.

We speak of shape in poetry in two general ways: form and structure. By *form* critics usually mean the outward container that shapes the work. By *structure* they mean the inner framework around which the work amasses. It might help to think of the shape of our bodies. The flesh gives the body outward form; bones give it inner structure. Of course, form and structure are not separate. In a poem, as in the body, form and structure work toward the same end—expressive efficiency.

The Structure of Free Verse

We generally think of a poem's shape in terms of rhyme schemes, yet the earliest English poetry did not rhyme. In fact, rhyme is an unusually late device imported to England from France and Italy, whose languages are much richer in rhyme words than is English. Some of the greatest poetry, not only in English but also in other languages, does not rhyme at all. The Psalms, for example, are unrhymed but are organized through meaning. Each line has two parts, which are in parallel structure either to each other or to the line that follows. In this brief psalm watch for the ways in which ideas are repeated or mirrored.

Psalm 121: A Song of Degrees

I will lift up mine eyes unto the hills: from whence cometh my help.
My help cometh from the Lord: which made heaven and earth.
He will not suffer thy foot to be moved: he that keepeth thee will not slumber.
Behold, he that keepeth Israel; shall neither slumber nor sleep.
5 The Lord is thy keeper: the Lord is thy shade, upon thy right hand.
The sun shall not smite thee by day; nor the moon by night.
The Lord shall preserve thee from all evil; he shall preserve thy soul.
The Lord shall preserve thy going out, and thy coming in: from this time forth
    and even for evermore.

Questions

1. What is the parallel concept in lines 5, 6, and 8? How is line 8 more complex than the others?
2. Are the lines linked together in other ways? What connections exist between lines 2 and 3 and lines 4 and 5?

Line 1 has two ideas: hills and the coming of help. Line 2 speaks of the coming of help and of heaven and earth, a mirroring of the opening lines. Lines 3 and 4 mirror each other even more clearly. The two parts of line 7 repeat the same idea. Moreover, there is an overall structure to the poem. It begins by looking for help, and it ends by finding it.

Free verse is poetry that is unrhymed and lacks a regular metrical unity. Free verse is not free of shape, however. Indeed, one may say it dispenses with outward formal devices to give full range to internal structures.

DENISE LEVERTOV (1923–)

The Ache of Marriage

The ache of marriage:

thigh and tongue, beloved,
are heavy with it,
it throbs in the teeth

5 We look for communion
and are turned away, beloved,
each and each

It is leviathan° and we   *Biblical sea beast*
in its belly
10   looking for joy, some joy
not to be known outside it

two by two in the ark of
the ache of it.

Questions

1. How are the first and last lines related? Do you have a sense of completeness? How do they correspond to the self-enclosed feeling of marriage?
2. How are the allusions to "leviathan" and "the ark" related?
3. How is the belly image in stanza 4 related to the images in stanza 2?
4. Are there any words or images that seem out of place in the poem? Do all the words seem closely connected?

Notice that "The Ache of Marriage" is divided into units, or what are called *stanzas*. A stanza is any group of lines that make up a division of the poem, but it can sometimes be a single line. In "The Ache of Marriage" these units are of irregular length, both in meter and in number of lines. Frequently, the stanzas in a poem are determined by length, meter, or rhyme scheme.

The stanzas work like paragraphs by bringing together similar ideas or images. Levertov uses a period only at the end of the poem, but stanzas 2, 3, and 4 approximate sentences.

Because structure is internal, it is often less noticeable than rhyme as a shaping device. But a free verse poem is not free of shape, and a reader should pay strict attention to what joins the parts of the poem and gives them a sense of unity. Although the rest of this chapter will be concerned with verse forms, we wish to emphasize the fundamental nature of structure. Poets may dispense with rhyme; they may dispense with a clear metrical unity, with imagery and other devices. But poets can never give up internal structure. Without structure, there is no poem.

Some Traditional English Forms
The Ballad

One of the most popular literary forms is the *ballad*. The ballad is built from four-line stanzas, or *quatrains*, in which the second and fourth lines must rhyme. Usually the first and third lines have four feet, and the other two lines have three feet; but there are variant scansions. The ballad is an excellent form for narrative poetry because the shortened second and fourth lines give the stanza an unusual sense of propulsion (see the discussion in Chapter 3). "Incident" is an example of a short "literary" ballad; unlike traditional ballads, it has a known author.

COUNTEE CULLEN (1903–1946)

Incident

(For Eric Walrond)

Once riding in old Baltimore,
   Heart-filled, head-filled with glee,
I saw a Baltimorean
   Keep looking straight at me.

5   Now I was eight and very small,
   And he was no whit bigger,
And so I smiled, but he poked out
   His tongue, and called me, "Nigger."

I saw the whole of Baltimore
10   From May until December;
Of all the things that happened there
   That's all that I remember.

Questions

1. Does the poem have a sense of completeness? What gives the poem unity?
2. Why is the information in line 2 important for the poem? How does it set the stage for what follows?
3. Why would Cullen remember only this incident? What feeling do you take away from the poem?

The Couplet

A *couplet* is any two consecutive lines, usually ones that rhyme and have the same meter. Couplets appear in many different languages. In English, however, the couplet has had enormous influence, especially a specialized form of couplet, the *heroic couplet*, which dominated the poetry of the eighteenth century. A heroic couplet is in iambic pentameter, and the second line is end-stopped; thus each couplet is not only a metrical unit but a grammatical unit as well. Consequently, couplets on the same subject can be gathered into *verse paragraphs*, long poetic passages that function like prose paragraphs by grouping couplets that discuss the same topic. Occasionally three successive rhymed lines, called a *triplet*, were permitted in the verse paragraphs to give the passage variety.

John Dryden was an early champion of the heroic couplet. In the following poem, he mourns a fellow poet who had died young.

JOHN DRYDEN (1631–1700)

To the Memory of Mr. Oldham

Farewell, too little, and too lately known,
Whom I began to think and call my own;

For sure our souls were near allied, and thine
Cast in the same poetic mold with mine.
5   One common note on either lyre did strike,
And knaves and fools we both abhorred alike.
To the same goal did both our studies drive;
The last set out the soonest did arrive.
Thus Nisus[1] fell upon the slippery place,
10   While his young friend performed and won the race.
O early ripe! to thy abundant store
What could advancing age have added more?
It might (what nature never gives the young)
Have taught the numbers° of thy native tongue.   metrics
15   But satire needs not those, and wit will shine
Through the harsh cadence of a rugged line:[2]
A noble error, and but seldom made,
When poets are by too much force betrayed.
Thy generous fruits, though gathered ere their prime,
20   Still showed a quickness; and maturing time
But mellows what we write to the dull sweets of rhyme.
Once more, hail and farewell; farewell, thou young,
But ah too short, Marcellus[3] of our tongue;
Thy brows with ivy, and with laurels bound;[4]
25   But fate and gloomy night encompass thee around.

Questions

1. Vocabulary: *knaves* (6), *abhorred* (6), *cadence* (16), *encompass* (25).
2. How does the reference to ivy and laurel relate to the opening lines? Is it an appropriate allusion? Does it give the poem a sense of unity?
3. Does the metaphor of fruit (lines 11–21) fit the poem?
4. Is the alexandrine in line 21 fitting?
5. Is there a sense that the poem has concluded? How does Dryden achieve that sense of completeness?

The poets of the eighteenth century felt the heroic couplet possessed the grace, dignity, and flexibility they admired in the classical meters of Virgil and Homer. The heroic couplet is still used today. In "Moly" it suggests the "heroic" and classical origins of Gunn's subject.

---

[1] In Virgil's *Aeneid* (Book 5, lines 315–339) Nisus slipped in a pool of blood during a footrace.
[2] Dryden believed, as did Renaissance theorists, that satire should be in rough meter.
[3] Marcellus was heir to the Roman Empire when he died at the age of twenty.
[4] The traditional crown for poets.

THOM GUNN (1929–)

Moly[5]

Nightmare of beasthood, snorting, how to wake.
I woke. What beasthood skin she made me take?

Leathery toad that ruts for days on end,
Or cringing dribbling dog, man's servile friend,

5   Or cat that prettily pounces on its meat,
Tortures it hours, then does not care to eat:

Parrot, moth, shark, wolf, crocodile, ass, flea.
What germs, what jostling mobs there were in me.

     These seem like bristles, and the hide is tough.
10   No claw or web here: each foot ends in hoof.

Into what bulk has method disappeared?
Like ham, streaked. I am gross—grey, gross, flap-eared.

The pale-lashed eyes my only human feature.
My teeth tear, tear. I am the snouted creature

15   That bites through anything, root, wire, or can.
If I was not afraid I'd eat a man.

Oh a man's flesh already is in mine.
Hand and foot poised for risk. Buried in swine.

     I root and root, you think that it is greed,
20   It is, but I seek out a plant I need.

Direct me, gods, whose changes are all holy,
To where it flickers deep in grass, the moly:

Cool flesh of magic in each leaf and shoot,
From milky flower to the black forked root.

25   From this fat dungeon I could rise to skin
And human title, putting pig within.

I push my big grey wet snout through the green,
Dreaming the flower I have never seen.

Questions

1. Vocabulary: *servile* (4), *jostling* (8).
2. How does the dream in the final line contrast with the nightmare of the opening?
3. How does the persona contrast the human with the bestial?
4. How do the verse paragraphs emphasize the progress of the poem?
5. To what extent are we all part human and part beast? Can we ever become completely human, according to the persona?
6. Does this poem have a sense of completeness? What more would you say if you were the persona?

---

[5] *Moly* was a magic herb given by Hermes to Odysseus, whose men had been turned into swine by the enchantress Circe.

Italian Forms
The Sonnet

No other form has had the nearly universal appeal of the sonnet. Originating in Sicily, it took root on the Italian mainland, from which it spread as far as Russia to the east and the United States to the west. Since its arrival in England in the sixteenth century, the sonnet has found consistent favor.

The *Italian* or *Petrarchan* sonnet is a fourteen-line poem divided between an opening *octave* (eight lines) and a concluding *sestet* (six lines). It is rhymed *abba abba cdc cdc*.[6] The form is demanding, since it requires three endings to rhyme four times each. In Italian, where almost every word ends in a vowel, rhymes are plentiful. In English, however, the form is usually slightly altered to give the poet some freedom.

JOHN KEATS (1795–1821)

• On First Looking into Chapman's Homer

Much have I traveled in the realms of gold,
   And many goodly states and kingdoms seen;
   Round many western islands have I been
Which bards in fealty° to Apollo[7] hold.   *allegiance*
5 Oft of one wide expanse had I been told
   That deep-browed Homer ruled as his demesne;
   Yet did I never breathe its pure serene°   *atmosphere*
Till I heard Chapman[8] speak out loud and bold:
Then felt I like some watcher of the skies
10   When a new planet swims into his ken;
Or like stout Cortez[9] when with eagle eyes
   He stared at the Pacific—and all his men
Looked at each other with a mild surmise—
   Silent, upon a peak in Darien.

Questions

1. Vocabulary: *fealty* (4), *desmesne* (6), *ken* (10).
2. Has Keats altered the rhyme scheme?
3. Has he preserved the distinction between octave and sestet? What sort of change occurs between the parts?

---

[6] Throughout this chapter and the next, we will refer to rhymed forms in a schematic way. Each rhyme ending is designated by a letter, starting with *a*. These schemes do not refer to the length of the lines.

[7] Apollo is the god of poetry.

[8] George Chapman (1559?–1634), English poet and translator of Homer.

[9] Hernando Cortez (1485–1534), Spanish conqueror of Mexico. Keats is historically inaccurate, however. The first European to see the Pacific was Vasco de Balboa, who viewed it from Darien, Panama.

4. Keats wrote this poem after his discovery of Chapman's translation, which revealed the splendor of Homer to him for the first time. Have you ever experienced a joyous discovery? How did you feel? Does Keats capture a similar experience?

The sonnet has maintained its popularity for a number of reasons. First, like all performers, poets enjoy doing the difficult with apparent ease. Sonnets are poets' high-wire acts, their perfect figure-eights. Second, the sonnet's length is attractive. It is long enough to tackle serious subjects but still short enough to require all of the poet's economy, exactitude, and grace.

In English the sonnet has been dominated by Shakespeare and the rhyme scheme he employed. Shakespeare divided the sonnet into three quatrains and a couplet. The *Shakespearean* or *English* sonnet is rhymed *abab cdcd efef gg*.

WILLIAM SHAKESPEARE (1564–1616)

That Time of Year Thou Mayst in Me Behold

That time of year thou mayst in me behold
When yellow leaves, or none, or few, do hang
Upon those boughs which shake against the cold,
Bare ruined choirs, where late the sweet birds sang.
5   In me thou see'st the twilight of such day
As after sunset fadeth in the west,
Which by and by black night doth take away,
Death's second self that seals up all in rest.
In me thou see'st the glowing of such fire,
10   That on the ashes of his youth doth lie,
As the deathbed whereon it must expire,
Consumed with that which it was nourished by.
This thou perceiv'st, which makes thy love more strong,
To love that well which thou must leave ere long.

Questions

1. What is the relationship among the three quatrains? What unites them? How are they individually organized?
2. What is the relationship between the quatrains and the final couplet?
3. Does the couplet give the poem a sense of completeness? Is there anything more that needs to be said?
4. Why does Shakespeare order line 2 as he does? What can you tell about the speaker from line 2?
5. If you were addressed in such a way, how would you feel about the speaker? About yourself?

Love and mortality are traditional themes of the sonnet. The following is a modern sonnet about a circumstance similar to Shakespeare's.

EDNA ST. VINCENT MILLAY (1892–1950)

Pity Me Not Because the Light of Day

Pity me not because the light of day
At close of day no longer walks the sky;
Pity me not for beauties passed away
From field and thicket as the year goes by;
5   Pity me not the waning of the moon,
Nor that the ebbing tide goes out to sea,
Nor that a man's desire is hushed so soon,
And you no longer look with love on me.
This have I known always: Love is no more
10   Than the wide blossom on which the wind assails,
Than the great tide that treads the shifting shore,
Strewing fresh wreckage gathered in the gales:
Pity me that the heart is slow to learn
What the swift mind beholds at every turn.

Questions

1. What is the relationship between the first two quatrains and the third? Is the internal structure more typical of the Shakespearean or the Italian sonnet?
2. What is the relationship between the quatrains and the couplet?
3. Does the couplet give the poem a sense of completion? Does anything more need to be said?
4. What is the difference between Shakespeare's attitude toward old age and Millay's attitude?
5. How would you describe the tone of the speaker in the sonnets of Shakespeare and Millay?

Although poets traditionally have used the sonnet as a love poem, they have also found it appropriate for theological meditation and political denunciation. Indeed, the brevity of the form makes it particularly useful for passionate cries of any kind. For example, John Milton, while secretary for Prime Minister Oliver Cromwell, wished to protest the slaughter of the Waldenses, members of a heretical sect who lived in the Piedmont valleys of northern Italy. The Waldenses were similar to the Protestants in that they forbade graven images in their church. Along with several angry letters to papal authorities, Milton composed the following poem of denunciation.

JOHN MILTON (1608–1674)

On the Late Massacre in Piedmont

Avenge, O Lord, thy slaughtered saints, whose bones
    Lie scattered on the Alpine mountains cold,

Even them who kept thy truth so pure of old
When all our fathers worshiped stocks and stones,
5   Forget not: in thy book record their groans
Who were thy sheep and in their ancient fold
Slain by the bloody Piemontese that rolled
Mother with infant down the rocks. Their moans
The vales redoubled to the hills, and they
10   To Heaven. Their martyred blood and ashes sow
O'er all th' Italian fields where still doth sway
The triple tyrant;[10] that from these may grow
A hundredfold, who having learnt thy way
Early may fly the Babylonian woe.[11]

Questions

1. Vocabulary: *redoubled* (9).
2. Is this a Shakespearean or a Petrarchan sonnet?
3. Has Milton preserved the division between the octave and the sestet?
4. What is the poem's predominant vowel sound? Why is it used so frequently?
5. What is Milton's attitude toward the Piemontese? Toward the Waldenses?

In 1919 Claude McKay, a Jamaican who had settled in Harlem, wrote "If We Must Die" in response to riots and the suppression of black intellectuals after World War I.

CLAUDE McKAY (1890–1948)

If We Must Die

If we must die, let it not be like hogs
Hunted and penned in an inglorious spot,
While round us bark the mad and hungry dogs,
Making their mock at our accursed lot.
5   If we must die, O let us nobly die,
So that our precious blood may not be shed
In vain; then even the monsters we defy
Shall be constrained to honor us though dead!
O kinsmen! we must meet the common foe!
10   Though far outnumbered let us show us brave,
And for their thousand blows deal one deathblow!
What though before us lies the open grave?
Like men we'll face the murderous, cowardly pack,
Pressed to the wall, dying, but fighting back!

Questions

1. Vocabulary: *constrained* (8).

---

[10] The pope.
[11] Catholicism. Protestants saw the Catholic Church as the whore of Babylon.

2. What kind of sonnet is "If We Must Die"? Has McKay retained the internal structure of the sonnet?
3. Is McKay's poem optimistic? Does he believe his people will prevail?
4. Winston Churchill used this poem to rally the British against Nazi Germany in World War II. Can you identify any quality in this poem that would make it a powerful rallying cry?

Like most popular forms, the sonnet has been adapted to the uses of many writers. Shakespeare, Sidney, and Spenser collected them into sonnet series or sequences. One of the great masterpieces of Russian literature, *Eugene Onegin* by Alexander Pushkin, is a verse novel in sonnets. George Meredith, in his sonnet series *Modern Love*, employed a sixteen-line sonnet of his own creation. Although longer than the traditional sonnet, it deserves the name because it deals with the same material and has the same economy and force.

GEORGE MEREDITH (1828–1909)

In Our Old Shipwrecked Days There Was an Hour

In our old shipwrecked days there was an hour,
When in the firelight steadily aglow,
Joined slackly, we beheld the red chasm grow
Among the clicking coals. Our library-bower
5   That eve was left to us: and hushed we sat
As lovers to whom Time is whispering.
From sudden-opened doors we heard them sing:
The nodding elders mixed good wine with chat.
Well knew we that Life's greatest treasure lay
10   With us, and of it was our talk. "Ah, yes!
Love dies!" I said: I never thought it less.
She yearned to me that sentence to unsay.
Then when the fire domed blackening, I found
Her cheek was salt against my kiss, and swift
15   Up the sharp scale of sobs her breast did lift:—
Now am I haunted by that taste! that sound!

Questions

1. Vocabulary: *chasm* (3), *bower* (4).
2. Do you see any similarity between the rhyme scheme of Meredith's poem and the traditional sonnet?
3. Where does the scene take place? Is the setting significant?
4. What is the significance of the burning coal?
5. What is the speaker's attitude toward the incident? Toward his life?

Robert Lowell, in the last decade of his life, wrote hundreds of fourteen-line, unrhymed poems. These poems, which he arranged in various ways, covered any number of subjects and situations. In the following poem he portrays the poet Robert Frost.

ROBERT LOWELL (1917–1977)

• Robert Frost

Robert Frost at midnight, the audience gone
to vapor, the great act laid on the shelf in mothballs,
his voice musical, raw and raw—he writes in the flyleaf:
"Robert Lowell from Robert Frost, his friend in the art."
5   "Sometimes I feel too full of myself," I say.
And he, misunderstanding, "When I am low,
I stray away. My son wasn't your kind. The night
we told him Merrill Moore[12] would come to treat him,
he said, 'I'll kill him first.' One of my daughters thought things,
10 knew every male she met was out to make her;
the way she dresses, she couldn't make a whorehouse."
And I, "Sometimes I'm so happy I can't stand myself."
And he, "When I am too full of joy, I think
how little good my health did anyone near me."

Questions

1. Do any parts of this poem correspond to the structure of a Shakespearean sonnet? In what way do the last two lines act as a couplet?
2. How does this private image of Frost compare with the public one?
3. What is Lowell's attitude toward Frost?
4. What are their attitudes about the joy of life?
5. In what sense is this a love poem?

Terza Rima

Although Italy's most successful export to English poetry has been the sonnet, that country has contributed other verse forms as well. One of the most attractive and demanding is the *terza rima*, the verse form Dante used in *The Divine Comedy*. Terza rima is made up of three-line stanzas or *tercets* interlocked by rhymes so that the inner rhyme of one tercet becomes the outer rhyme of the subsequent tercet. In schematic terms, terza rima is rhymed *aba bcb cdc.* . . . Because terza rima requires triple rhymes for each ending, most English practitioners use occasional near rhymes and assonance instead of true rhymes.

One aspect that draws poets to terza rima is the possibility of an unbroken chain of language. A poem in terza rima can continue indefinitely, without being forced to a close by the rhyme scheme. Another valuable aspect of terza rima is that its use is a kind of allusion. The poet cannot use it without suggesting

---

[12] Merrill Moore (1903–1957) was a poet and psychoanalyst and Frost's friend. Frost's son committed suicide.

Dante or the Renaissance Italy in which he lived. In "The Death of Vitellozzo Vitelli," Irving Feldman writes not only about an incident in Italy's history, but also about the force of destiny—one of Dante's constant themes. Vitelli was a nobleman and soldier who at first aided the ruthless Cesare Borgia's conquest of Italy and then secretly conspired against Borgia. The scene in the poem shows Vitelli on his way to Borgia, who had Vitelli strangled in 1502. Rome is a center of Borgia's strength.

IRVING FELDMAN (1928–)

The Death of Vitellozzo Vitelli

Vitelli rides west toward Fano,[13] the morning sun
Has spread his shadow before him, his head is cast
Upon the road beyond the horse, and now in vain

He works his spurs and whip. For all his speed, his past
5   Like a heavy wind has thrown his death far before
Him, and not till midday shall he fill the waste

Of light he has made with the goldness of his spur
And the greenness of his cape. Then shall he stand
At last by the bridge at Fano and know no more

10   His way than the farmer at noon who looks from his land
To his heart and knows not where next to turn his plow;
Or lovers who have stayed abed and reach a hand

And yet have turned away, even as they do so,
To move their legs and sigh, wearied of their embrace
15   —Yet nothing else seems worth their while. His road shall go

Before him, having broken itself in two ways:
One goes to Borgia in Fano, and one toward Rome.
But his shadow hurries from his feet to his face.

Questions

1. How has Feldman accentuated the unbroken character of terza rima? To what extent are the tercets independent units?
2. Why does Vitelli hesitate at the bridge? Does Vitelli himself know?
3. In what way is Vitelli a farmer? Is the comparison ironic?
4. In what way is he a lover? Is the comparison ironic?
5. Does Vitelli have any choices? How would you describe his fate?

Perhaps the most famous example of terza rima in English is Percy Bysshe Shelley's "Ode to the West Wind." Shelley, however, chose to break the terza rima periodically with a couplet. The result is five fourteen-line sections that

---

[13] A small town in central Italy.

resemble sonnets. In a sense, Shelley's ode is a combination of terza rima and sonnet sequence.

PERCY BYSSHE SHELLEY (1792–1822)

• Ode to the West Wind

I

O wild West Wind, thou breath of Autumn's being,
Thou, from whose unseen presence the leaves dead
Are driven, like ghosts from an enchanter fleeing,

Yellow, and black, and pale, and hectic red,
5   Pestilence-stricken multitudes: O Thou,
Who chariotest to their dark wintry bed

The winged seeds, where they lie cold and low,
Each like a corpse within its grave, until
Thine azure sister of the Spring shall blow

10   Her clarion o'er the dreaming earth, and fill
(Driving sweet buds like flocks to feed in air)
With living hues and odours plain and hill:

Wild Spirit, which art moving everyhere;
Destroyer and Preserver; hear, O hear!

II

15   Thou on whose stream, 'mid the steep sky's commotion,
Loose clouds like Earth's decaying leaves are shed,
Shook from the tangled boughs of Heaven and Ocean,

Angels of rain and lightning: there are spread
On the blue surface of thine aery surge,
20   Like the bright hair uplifted from the head

Of some fierce Mænad,[14] even from the dim verge
Of the horizon to the zenith's height,
The locks of the approaching storm. Thou Dirge

Of the dying year, to which this closing night
25   Will be the dome of a vast sepulchre,
Vaulted with all thy congregated might

Of vapours, from whose solid atmosphere
Black rain and fire and hail will burst: O hear!

III

Thou who didst waken from his summer dreams
30   The blue Mediterranean, where he lay,
Lulled by the coil of his chrystalline streams,

Beside a pumice isle in Baiæ's bay,[15]

---

[14] A nymph attendant on the god Dionysus.
[15] A bay in Naples around which kings built castles.

And saw in sleep old palaces and towers
Quivering within the wave's intenser day,

35 All overgrown with azure moss and flowers
So sweet, the sense faints picturing them! Thou
For whose path the Atlantic's level powers

Cleave themselves into chasms, while far below
The sea-blooms and the oozy woods which wear
40 The sapless foliage of the ocean, know

Thy voice, and suddenly grow grey with fear,
And tremble and despoil themselves: O hear!

IV

If I were a dead leaf thou mightest bear;
If I were a swift cloud to fly with thee;
45 A wave to pant beneath thy power, and share

The impulse of thy strength, only less free
Than thou, O Uncontrollable! If even
I were as in my boyhood, and could be

The comrade of thy wanderings over Heaven,
50 As then, when to outstrip thy skiey speed
Scarce seemed a vision; I would ne'er have striven

As thus with thee in prayer in my sore need.
Oh! lift me as a wave, a leaf, a cloud!
I fall upon the thorns of life! I bleed!

55 A heavy weight of hours has chained and bowed
One too like thee: tameless, and swift, and proud.

V

Make me thy lyre,[16] even as the forest is:
What if my leaves are falling like its own!
The tumult of thy mighty harmonies

60 Will take from both a deep, autumnal tone,
Sweet though in sadness. Be thou, Spirit fierce,
My spirit! Be thou me, impetuous one!

Drive my dead thoughts over the universe
Like withered leaves to quicken a new birth!
65 And, by the incantation of this verse,

Scatter, as from an unextinguished hearth
Ashes and sparks, my words among mankind!
Be through my lips to unawakened Earth

The trumpet of a prophecy! O Wind,
70 If Winter comes, can Spring be far behind?

---

[16] The Aeolian harp, or wind harp.

Questions

1. Vocabulary: *pestilence* (5), *multitudes* (5), *azure* (9), *clarion* (10), *zenith* (23), *sepulchre* (26), *pumice* (34), *chasms* (40), *harmonics* (63).
2. How does stanza 4 unify the three stanzas that precede it?
3. Why does Shelley want to be lifted by the wind? How does he feel about his adult experiences?
4. What does Shelley wish the wind to do to him in stanza 5?
5. In what sense is the poem optimistic? How does the concluding line recollect the opening one?
6. Does this poem have unity? Does it stand as a whole?

French Forms

Perhaps the greatest inventors of forms were the *troubadour* poets of southern France, who lived between the eleventh and thirteenth centuries. A troubadour could be a king—Richard the Lion-hearted was one—or a traveling adventurer. Usually the poets attached themselves to a court or noble family who acted as patrons of their art. The troubadours delighted in elaborate poetic forms and the skillful employment of complicated word games. Occasionally they were accompanied by an apprentice, called a *jongleur*, who might set their poems to music.

The Ballade

The most popular form troubadours used was the *ballade*, which should not be confused with the *ballad*. Because of the demands of the rhyme scheme, it has not found as much favor with English poets. The ballade consists of three seven-line stanzas and an *envoi*, which is a concluding statement. The stanzas are rhymed *ababbcc*, and the rhymes are the same throughout the poem. The *envoi* can be of various lengths and rhyme schemes.

    Poor in his old age, Geoffrey Chaucer, the first great poet in English, apparently sent "The Complaint of Chaucer to His Purse" to the newly crowned king, Henry IV. In response to the poem, Henry raised Chaucer's pension.

GEOFFREY CHAUCER (1340?–1400)

The Complaint of Chaucer to His Purse

To yow, my purse, and to noon other wight°   *person*
Complayne I, for ye be my lady dere!
I am so sory, now that ye been lyght;
  For certes,° but° ye make me hevy chere,   *surely unless*
5 Me were as leef° be layd upon my bere;   *I would like to be*
For which unto your mercy thus I crye:
Beth hevy ageyn, or elles moote° I dye!   *must*

Now voucheth sauf° this day, or° yt be nyght,   *vouchsafe before*
That I of yow the blisful soun° may here,   *sound*

10   Or see your colour lyk the sonne bryght,
That of yelownesse hadde never pere.
Ye be my lyf, ye be myn hertes stere,°   *guide*
Quene of comfort and of good companye:
Beth hevy ageyn, or elles moote I dye!

15   Now purse, that ben to me my lyves lyght
And saveour, as° doun in this world here,   *while*
Out of this toune helpe me thurgh your myght,
Syn that ye wole nat ben my tresorere;
For I am shave as nye° as any frere.°   *close*   *friar*
20   But yet I pray unto your curtesye:
Beth hevy ageyn, or elles moote I dye!

Lenvoy de Chaucer:

O conquerour of Brutes° Albyon,°   *Brutus's*   *England*
Which that by lyne and free eleccion[17]
Been verray° kyng, this song to yow I sende;   *true*
25   And ye, that mowen° alle our harmes amende,   *can*
Have mynde upon my supplicacion!

Questions

1. What is the tone of the refrain? Is Chaucer actually going to die?
2. What figure of speech has Chaucer utilized throughout this poem? How does he address his purse?
3. Why does Chaucer mention that he is as closely shaved as a friar in line 19? To what extent is this a mock religious poem? A mock love poem?
4. If you were Henry IV, would you give Chaucer more money?

Villanelle

A form that has attracted much more attention in English is the *villanelle*, which contains five tercets and a concluding quatrain. What makes the villanelle special is that the first and third lines become the closing refrain of alternate tercets and reappear as the concluding two lines of the poem. Thus the form has remarkable unity of structure. The echoing and reechoing of the refrains give the villanelle a plaintive, delicate beauty that some poets find irresistible.

However, the villanelle is not without its difficulties. Since it has only two rhyme endings, the poem can easily become monotonous. The risk of monotony is increased by the incessant appearance of the refrains that constitute eight of the poem's nineteen lines—nearly half of the poem. The skilled author of the villanelle, thus, is careful to achieve the maximum tonal range and to fit the

---

[17] Henry IV, though a usurper, claimed the throne because he was the grandson of Edward II and thus was in the line of succession, and also because he had been placed on the throne by an act of Parliament—therefore, by "free eleccion."

Dylan Thomas
(Rollie McKenna)

refrain lines as naturally as possible into the logic of the poem. Despite these
difficulties, there are a number of excellent villanelles.

DYLAN THOMAS (1914–1953)

• Do Not Go Gentle into That Good Night

Do not go gentle into that good night,
Old age should burn and rave at close of day;
Rage, rage against the dying of the light.

Though wise men at their end know dark is right,
5   Because their words had forked no lightning they
Do not go gentle into that good night.

Good men, the last wave by, crying how bright
Their frail deeds might have danced in a green bay,
Rage, rage against the dying of the light.

10   Wild men who caught and sang the sun in flight,
And learn, too late, they grieved it on its way,
Do not go gentle into that good night.

Grave men, near death, who see with blinding sight
Blind eyes could blaze like meteors and be gay,
15   Rage, rage against the dying of the light.

And you, my father, there on the sad height,
Curse, bless, me now with your fierce tears, I pray.
Do not go gentle into that good night.
Rage, rage against the dying of the light.

Questions

1. How are the middle stanzas of the poem organized? Is the relationship between them and the rest of the poem clear?
2. How has Thomas sought rhythmic variety? How has he integrated the refrains into the flow of the poem?
3. In line 8, what does Thomas mean by saying the deeds "might have danced in a green bay"?
4. What does he mean by "sang the sun in flight" (line 10)?

THEODORE ROETHKE (1908–1963)

The Waking

I wake to sleep, and take my waking slow.
I feel my fate in what I cannot fear.
I learn by going where I have to go.

We think by feeling. What is there to know?
5   I hear my being dance from ear to ear.
I wake to sleep, and take my waking slow.

Of those so close beside me, which are you?
God bless the Ground! I shall walk softly there,
And learn by going where I have to go.

10   Light takes the Tree; but who can tell us how?
The lowly worm climbs up a winding stair;
I wake to sleep, and take my waking slow.

Great Nature has another thing to do
To you and me; so take the lively air,
15   And, lovely, learn by going where to go.

This shaking keeps me steady. I should know.
What falls away is always. And is near.
I wake to sleep, and take my waking slow.
I learn by going where I have to go.

Questions

1. How has Roethke sought rhythmic variety? How has he altered and integrated the refrains in order to unify the poem?
2. What is the relationship in this poem between the inevitability of the refrains and Roethke's sense of destiny?
3. What is the connection between the speaker and nature?
4. What is the relationship between the speaker and God?
5. What does Roethke mean by "I wake to sleep"?

Sestina

Those who believe that the difficulty of a form is the result of rhyming will be surprised by the *sestina*. Often considered the most demanding of verse forms, the sestina—originated by the great Provençal poet, Arnaut Daniel—does not rhyme at all. The sestina consists of six six-line stanzas and a concluding stanza of three lines. The last word (or *talon*) of each line in stanza 1 is used as the talon for the remaining stanzas. In the concluding stanza the words are used in the middle and end of each line. The order of the talons is different for each stanza. Because the sestina requires the constant repetition of a small vocabulary, the poem can become very rigid and boring. Sestina writers have little opportunity to change subjects, since they are drawn back to the same vocabulary. Thus the sestina can suffer from a peculiar claustrophobia. In the hands of a fine writer, however, a sestina can have both breath and breadth. Elizabeth Bishop has used the inherent liabilities of the sestina to create a fascinating psychological portrait. Raised in the Maritime provinces of northern Canada, she knew the restraints of its harsh winters.

ELIZABETH BISHOP (1911–1980)

Sestina

September rain falls on the house.
In the failing light, the old grandmother
sits in the kitchen with the child
beside the Little Marvel Stove,
5   reading the jokes from the almanac,
laughing and talking to hide her tears.

She thinks that her equinoctial tears
and the rain that beats on the roof of the house
were both foretold by the almanac,
10   but only known to a grandmother.
The iron kettle sings on the stove.
She cuts some bread and says to the child,

It's time for tea now; but the child
is watching the teakettle's small hard tears
15   dance like mad on the hot black stove,
the way the rain must dance on the house.
Tidying up, the old grandmother
hangs up the clever almanac

on its string. Birdlike, the almanac
20   hovers half open above the child,
hovers above the old grandmother
and her teacup full of dark brown tears.
She shivers and says she thinks the house
feels chilly, and puts more wood in the stove.

25   *It was to be*, says the Marvel Stove.
I know what I know, says the almanac.
With crayons the child draws a rigid house
and a winding pathway. Then the child

puts in a man with buttons like tears
30   and shows it proudly to the grandmother.

But secretly, while the grandmother
busies herself about the stove,
the little moons fall down like tears
from between the pages of the almanac
35   into the flower bed the child
has carefully placed in the front of the house.

Time to plant tears, says the almanac.
The grandmother sings to the marvellous stove
and the child draws another inscrutable house.

Questions

1. Vocabulary: *equinoctial* (7), *foretold* (9), *inscrutable* (39).
2. How does Bishop achieve variety in the poem? Are the vowel sounds of the various talons similar?
3. The almanac tries to predict the unpredictable. How does the scheme of the sestina support the work of the almanac? Could you predict the end of the poem from the outset? How are the events of the poem surprising?
4. In what other ways is the almanac symbolic?
5. In what way is the child's drawing symbolic? Why does Bishop call the house in the picture "rigid"?
6. In what way is the whole poem "inscrutable"?

Perhaps the chapter could end in no better way than with Swinburne's "Sestina." Algernon Charles Swinburne was a poet fascinated by formal difficulties. In this sestina he not only rhymes the talons, but uses only two rhymes in the entire poem! For another astounding formal feat, see Sir Philip Sidney's "Ye Goatherd Gods" on pages 350–352. It is a double sestina.

ALGERNON CHARLES SWINBURNE (1837–1909)

Sestina

I saw my soul at rest upon a day
    As a bird sleeping in the nest of night,
Among soft leaves that give the starlight way
    To touch its wings but not its eyes with light;
5   So that it knew as one in visions may,
    And knew not as men waking, of delight.

This was the measure of my soul's delight;
    It had no power of joy to fly by day,
Nor part in the large lordship of the light;
10   . But in a secret moon-beholden way
Had all its will of dreams and pleasant night,
    And all the love and life that sleepers may.

But such life's triumph as men waking may
    It might not have to feed its faint delight
15   Between the stars by night and sun by day,
      Shut up with green leaves and a little light;
Because its way was as a lost star's way,
    A world's not wholly known of day or night.

All loves and dreams and sounds and gleams of night
20   Made it all music that such minstrels may,
And all they had they gave it of delight;
    But in the full face of the fire of day
What place shall be for any starry light,
    What part of heaven in all the wide sun's way?

25   Yet the soul woke not, sleeping by the way,
      Watched as a nursling of the large eyed night,
And sought no strength nor knowledge of the day,
    Nor closer touch conclusive of delight,
Nor mightier joy nor truer than dreamers may,
30   Nor more of song than they, nor more of light.

For who sleeps once and sees the secret light
    Whereby sleep shows the soul a fairer way
Between the rise and rest of day and night,
    Shall care no more to fare as all men may,
35   But be his place of pain or of delight,
    There shall he dwell, beholding night as day.

Song, have thy day and take thy fill of light
    Before the night be fallen across thy way;
Sing while he may, man hath no long delight.

Questions

1. Vocabulary: *beholden* (10), *nursling* (26), *conclusive* (28).
2. In what way is Swinburne's sense of spiritual awareness different from Roethke's in these poems?
3. In what way is this a pessimistic poem? In what way does it express the *carpe diem* philosophy (literally, "seize the day") of Marvell's "To His Coy Mistress" (see Chapter 4)?

No poet works in a historical vacuum. The language we use is the product of a long, varied, and chaotic historical process. Out of that process also come different verse forms, whose suitability and vitality have been tested. Just as poets choose the most expressive words, so they choose the most expressive forms in which to work. And just as people have not stopped coining new words, so poets have not stopped fashioning new forms in which to write. In the next chapter we will explore other forms and manners, both recent and ancient, that poets use to shape their language.

Suggestions for Essayists

1. Compare two poems in the same form. How have the poets used the form? Have they treated it differently or in the same way?
2. Some people argue that instead of creating social forms that best express our desires, we are shaped by social forms. For example, some educators believe that schools are not formed around students' needs, but rather that students are shaped by what schools demand. Choose some social event—a dance, a wedding, a lecture—and discuss whether you shape it or it shapes you.

Suggestions for Poets

1. Take an idea and try to write it in two different forms. Observe the changes that happen to the idea as it is given shape.
2. Invent a form of your own and write three poems in it. Do you find that the possibilities of the form are exhausted?

Exercise

Many literary forms have their own traditions—a history, manner, and identity developed over a period of time. A tradition develops in part when writers try to determine how to use a form by looking back at those poets who have used it in the past. One of the longest traditions is the sonnet tradition. The sonnets of Edna St. Vincent Millay look back toward the sonnets of Shakespeare and Spenser. Dante Gabriel Rossetti, who wrote sonnets of his own, also translated the sonnets of the Italian Renaissance, one of which, Cecco Angiolieri's "In Absence from Becchina," is reprinted on pages 172–173. There are many sonnets or sonnetlike poems in this book.

The following is a list of sonnets other than the ones printed in this chapter. Read these sonnets and try to formulate for yourself what sort of tradition these poems create. Then read the sonnetlike poems, and try to determine what they have borrowed from the tradition and how they have deviated from it. Remember, however, that traditions are not laws; traditions change and develop, and each writer contributes to the tradition by affirming, altering, or adding to it.

Sonnets

Cecco Angiolieri, "In Absence from Becchina," p. 172
Elizabeth Barrett Browning, "How Do I Love Thee," p. 367
Samuel Taylor Coleridge, "Pity," p. 189
John Donne, "Death Be Not Proud," p. 354
John Donne, "I Am a Little World Made Cunningly," p. 353
Robert Frost, "The Silken Tent," p. 385
Henry Howard, Earl of Surrey, "The Soote Season," p. 106
John Keats, "When I Have Fears," p. 363
John Milton, "When I Consider How My Light Is Spent," p. 64
Wilfred Owen, "Anthem for Doomed Youth," p. 387
Christina Rossetti, "After Death," p. 376
William Shakespeare, "Let Me Not to the Marriage of True Minds," p. 141
William Shakespeare, "My Mistress' Eyes Are Nothing Like the Sun," p. 313

William Shakespeare, "Shall I Compare Thee to a Summer's Day," p. 133
William Shakespeare, "When, in Disgrace with Fortune and Men's Eyes," p. 52
William Shakespeare, "When Most I Wink, Then Do Mine Eyes Best See," p. 183
Percy Bysshe Shelley, "Ozymandias," p. 363
Edmund Spenser, "One Day as I Unwarily Did Gaze," p. 170
William Wordsworth, "The World Is Too Much with Us," p. 362

Sonnetlike Poems

E. E. Cummings, "the Cambridge ladies who live in furnished souls," p. 388
E. E. Cummings, "next to of course god america i," p. 295
Seamus Heaney, "The Forge," p. 434
Daryl Hine, "The Survivors," p. 428
Gerard Manley Hopkins, "The Windhover," p. 377
John Crowe Ransom, "Piazza Piece," p. 89
Dave Smith, "Picking Cherries," p. 436
Anne Stevenson, "Pregnant," p. 226

13 🌿 The Poem's Shape II

The French and the Italians did not exhaust the formal resources of poetry. Poets, restless for novelty, have sought elsewhere for means of shaping their feelings and expressions. Poets have borrowed forms from many countries and cultures.

The Ode

Because ancient Greece is the seat of Western culture, poets periodically return to it for poetic inspiration and guidance. Poets use Greek forms out of respect for the long Greek tradition and sometimes in the belief that these forms are unmatched vehicles of artistic perfection. Among the most popular forms is the ode. The word *ode* is used broadly in English to refer to any public expression of praise. However, there are three forms to which it more particularly refers: the *Pindaric*, the *Horatian*, and the *irregular* ode.

The oldest of these forms is the Pindaric or regular ode. Pindar lived in the fifth century B.C. and wrote odes celebrating athletic and political victories and often retelling myths in the process. The short ode that follows celebrates the victory of Hagesidamos, son of Archestratos, a boy from western Lokroi who won the laurel in boxing in 476 B.C.

PINDAR (5th century B.C.)

Olympian 11

Turn   Sometimes men need the winds most,
                at other times
                    waters from the sky,
                        rainy descendants of the cloud.

And when a man has triumphed
and put his toil behind,
it is time for melodius song
to arise, laying
the foundation of future glory,
10   a sworn pledge securing proud success.

Counterturn   For Olympian victors, such acclaim
is laid in store
without limit, and I
am eager to tend it with my song.
15   For a man flourishes
in wise understanding,
as in all things,
through a god's favor.
Know now, son of Archestratos,
20   Hagesidamos, because of your boxing victory

Stand   I will sing, and my song will be
an added adornment
to your gold olive crown,
shining with love for Western Lokroi.
25   Go there
and join the revels, Muses.
By my bond,
you will not find a people indifferent to strangers
or blind to beauty, but men of keenest discernment
30   and courage in war.
For the crimson fox
and thunderous lion cannot change their inborn ways.

Translation by Frank J. Nisetich (1942–)

Questions

1. What is the purpose of poetry, according to Pindar?
2. How does the celebration of Hagesidamos's victory become a celebration of western Lokroi?
3. Have the politics of the Olympics changed since Hagesidamos's time?
4. Compare this poem to Housman's "To an Athlete Dying Young" in Chapter 4. What is the relationship between both athletes and their birthplaces?

As you can see, the Pindaric ode is divided into three parts: turn (or *strophe*), counterturn (or *antistrophe*), and stand (or *epode*). Poets can shape the turn however they like. But once the poet has chosen a shape, all the turns and counterturns must share the same stanza form. The stand (or epode) is shaped differently from the turn. However, in longer odes that contain more than one stand, the stands are identically shaped. The Pindaric ode gives poets freedom initially but then holds them to their chosen stanza patterns. In English the stand, or epode, can appear between the turn and counterturn, as in the following poem.

WILLIAM COLLINS (1721–1759)

Ode to Fear

Thou, to whom the World unknown
With all its shadowy Shapes is shown;
Who see'st appal'd th' unreal Scene,
While Fancy lifts the Veil between:
5   Ah Fear! Ah frantic Fear!
   I see, I see Thee near.
I know thy hurried Step, thy haggard Eye!
Like Thee I start, like Thee disorder'd fly,
For lo what Monsters in thy Train appear!
10 Danger, whose Limbs of Giant Mold
What mortal Eye can fix'd behold?
Who stalks his Round, an hideous Form,
Howling amidst the Midnight Storm,
Or throws him on the ridgy Steep
15 Of some loose hanging Rock to sleep:
And with him thousand Phantoms join'd,
Who prompt to Deeds accurs'd the Mind:
And those, the Fiends, who near allied,
O'er Nature's Wounds, and Wrecks preside;
20 Whilst Vengeance, in the lurid Air,
Lifts her red Arm, expos'd and bare:
On whom that rav'ning Brood of Fate,
Who lap the Blood of Sorrow, wait;
Who, Fear, this ghastly Train can see,
25 And look not madly wild, like Thee?

Epode

In earliest Greece to Thee with partial Choice,
 The Grief-full Muse addrest her infant Tongue;
The Maids and Matrons, on her awful Voice,
 Silent and pale in wild Amazement hung.

30 Yet he the Bard who first invok'd thy Name,
 Disdained in Marathon its Pow'r to feel:
For not alone he nurs'd the Poet's flame,
 But reach'd from Virtue's Hand the Patriot's Steel.

But who is He whom later Garlands grace,
35 Who left a-while o'er Hybla's Dews to rove,
With trembling Eyes thy dreary Steps to trace,
 Where Thou and Furies shar'd the baleful Grove?

Wrapt in thy cloudy Veil th' Incestuous Queen
    Sigh'd the sad Call her Son and Husband hear'd,
40 When once alone it broke the silent Scene,
    And He the Wretch of Thebes no more appear'd.

O Fear, I know Thee by my throbbing Heart,
    Thy with'ring Pow'r inspir'd each mournful Line,
Tho' gentle Pity claim her mingled Part,
45   Yet all the Thunders of the Scene are thine!

Antistrophe

Thou who such weary Lengths hast past,
Where wilt thou rest, mad Nymph, at last?
Say, wilt thou shroud in haunted Cell,
Where gloomy Rape and Murder dwell?
50 Or in some hallow'd Seat,
    'Gainst which the big Waves beat,
Hear drowning Sea-men's Cries in Tempests brought!
Dark Pow'r, with shudd'ring meek submitted Thought
    Be mine, to read the Visions old,
55 Which thy awak'ning Bards have told:
And lest thou meet my blasted View,
Hold each strange Tale devoutly true;
Ne'er be I found, by Thee o'eraw'd,
In that thrice-hallowed Eve abroad,
60 When Ghosts, as Cottage-Maids believe,
Their pebbled Beds permitted leave,
And Goblins haunt from Fire, or Fen,
Or Mine, or Flood, the Walks of Men!
    O Thou whose Spirit most possest
65 The sacred Seat of Shakespeare's Breast!
By all that from thy Prophet broke,
In thy Divine Emotions spoke:
Hither again thy Fury deal,
Teach me but once like Him to feel:
70 His Cypress Wreath my Meed decree,
And I, O Fear, will dwell with Thee!

Questions

1. Vocabulary: *haggard* (7), *lurid* (20), *rav'ning* (22), *baleful* (37), *incestuous* (38), *hallowed* (50), *meed* (70).
2. How do the strophe and antistrophe differ from the epode?
3. How does the meter vary within the strophe? What is the basic meter? Which lines are shorter? Which are longer?
4. What is Collins's attitude toward fear? Is it the attitude one might expect from the poem's opening? Where does the attitude change?

5. Collins, a classics scholar, knew that odes celebrate heroic activities. What heroic actions does the poem celebrate? Is fear heroic, according to the poem?
6. According to the poem, when is fear inappropriate?

The Latin poet Horace wrote poems that have also become known as odes. The Horatian or stanzaic ode does away with the epode. Instead, the poet is free to create a stanza form that is repeated throughout the poem. The forms usually employ intricate rhyme and contain lines of varying length. Keats's "Ode to a Nightingale" is a Horatian ode.

JOHN KEATS (1795–1821)

Ode to a Nightingale

I

My heart aches, and a drowsy numbness pains
  My sense, as though of hemlock° I had drunk,   *a poison*
Or emptied some dull opiate to the drains
  One minute past, and Lethe-wards[1] had sunk:
5 'Tis not through envy of thy happy lot,
    But being too happy in thine happiness,—
      That thou, light-winged Dryad° of the trees,   *a tree spirit*
        In some melodious plot
  Of beechen green and shadows numberless,
10   Singest of summer in full-throated ease.

II

O, for a draught of vintage! that hath been
  Cool'd a long age in the deep-delved earth,
Tasting of Flora° and the country green,   *goddess of flowers*
  Dance, and Provençal song, and sunburnt mirth!
15 O for a beaker full of the warm South,
    Full of the true, the blushful Hippocrene,[2]
      With beaded bubbles winking at the brim,
        And purple-stained mouth;
That I might drink, and leave the world unseen,
20   And with thee fade away into the forest dim:

III

Fade far away, dissolve, and quite forget
  What thou among the leaves hast never known,
The weariness, the fever, and the fret
  Here, where men sit and hear each other groan;
25 Where palsy shakes a few, sad, last gray hairs,

---

[1] Lethe is the river that separates the upper world and the underworld. Its waters bring forgetfulness.
[2] Hippocrene is a mythological spring whose waters inspired poetry.

Where youth grows pale, and spectre-thin, and dies;
    Where but to think is to be full of sorrow
      And leaden-eyed despairs,
Where Beauty cannot keep her lustrous eyes,
30   Or new Love pine at them beyond to-morrow.

IV

Away! away! for I will fly to thee,
    Not charioted by Bacchus° and his pards,°   *the god of wine   leopards*
But on the viewless wings of Poesy,
    Though the dull brain perplexes and retards:
35 Already with thee! tender is the night,
    And haply the Queen-Moon is on her throne,
      Cluster'd around by all her starry Fays;°   *fairies, elves*
        But here there is no light,
Save what from heaven is with the breezes blown
40   Through verdurous glooms and winding mossy ways.

V

I cannot see what flowers are at my feet,
    Nor what soft incense hangs upon the boughs,
But, in embalmed darkness, guess each sweet
    Wherewith the seasonable month endows
45 The grass, the thicket, and the fruit-tree wild;
    White hawthorn, and the pastoral eglantine;
      Fast fading violets cover'd up in leaves;
      And mid-May's eldest child,
The coming musk-rose, full of dewy wine,
50   The murmurous haunt of flies on summer eves.

VI

Darkling I listen; and, for many a time
    I have been half in love with easeful Death,
Call'd him soft names in many a mused rhyme,
    To take into the air my quiet breath;
55 Now more than ever seems it rich to die,
    To cease upon the midnight with no pain,
      While thou art pouring forth thy soul abroad
      In such an ecstasy!
Still wouldst thou sing, and I have ears in vain—
60   To thy high requiem become a sod.

VII

Thou wast not born for death, immortal Bird!
    No hungry generations tread thee down;
The voice I hear this passing night was heard
    In ancient days by emperor and clown:
65 Perhaps the self-same song that found a path
    Through the sad heart of Ruth,[3] when, sick for home,

---

[3] In the Bible, Ruth was a Moabite who left her people to stay with her husband, Boaz, and her mother-in-law, Naomi.

She stood in tears amid the alien corn;
  The same that oft-times hath
Charm'd magic casements, opening on the foam
70   Of perilous seas, in faery lands forlorn.

VIII

Forlorn! the very word is like a bell
  To toll me back from thee to my sole self!
Adieu! the fancy cannot cheat so well
  As she is fam'd to do, deceiving elf.
75 Adieu! adieu! thy plaintive anthem fades
  Past the near meadows, over the still stream,
    Up the hill-side; and now 'tis buried deep
      In the next valley-glades:
Was it a vision, or a waking dream?
80   Fled is that music:—Do I wake or sleep?

Questions

1. Vocabulary: *Dryad* (7), *spectre* (26), *verdurous* (40), *eglantine* (46), *requiem* (60), *plaintive* (75).
2. What is the stanza form of Keats's ode?
3. What does the nightingale represent for Keats?
4. Why does he wish to join the nightingale? How does he hope to join him?
5. What is Keats's attitude toward death?
6. Is there anything heroic about this poem?

Many poets no longer call their poems odes, not wishing to force comparison of their poems with those of Keats, Wordsworth, or Shelley. Nevertheless, their basic structure is that of a Horatian or stanzaic ode.

RICHARD WILBUR (1921–)

The Beautiful Changes

One wading a Fall meadow finds on all sides
The Queen Anne's Lace lying like lilies
On water; it glides
So from the walker, it turns
5 Dry grass to a lake, as the slightest shade of you
Valleys my mind in fabulous blue Lucernes.°   *a Swiss lake*

The beautiful changes as a forest is changed
By a chameleon's tuning his skin to it;
As a mantis, arranged
10 On a green leaf, grows
Into it, makes the leaf leafier, and proves
Any greenness is deeper than anyone knows.

Your hands hold roses always in a way that says
They are not only yours; the beautiful changes
15   In such kind ways,
  Wishing ever to sunder
Things and things' selves for a second finding, to lose
For a moment all that it touches back to wonder.

Questions

1. Vocabulary: *sunder* (16).
2. What is the stanza pattern of the poem? Is the shape of the poem appropriate to the subject?
3. To whom is the poem addressed? What is the speaker's attitude toward the listener?
4. Odes celebrate momentous occasions—being victorious at the Olympian Games or first hearing the song of a nightingale. Is a great achievement celebrated in this poem? In what way is the listener heroic?
5. How does the beautiful change?

The last type of ode is the irregular ode. The irregular ode permits the poet the maximum amount of flexibility. It requires that each stanza be different, shaped in a way most appropriate to and expressive of its subject. William Wordsworth's lengthy "Ode: Intimations of Immortality" is perhaps the greatest of irregular odes and appears on pages 331–335. Here is an irregular ode of more modest proportions.

PETER VIERECK (1916–)

Kilroy

Also Ulysses once—that other war.
    (Is it because we find his scrawl
    Today on every privy door
    That we forget his ancient role?)
5 Also was there—he did it for the wages—
When a Cathay-drunk Genoese° set sail.   *Christopher Columbus*
Whenever "longen folk to goon on pilgrimages,"[4]
Kilroy is there;
        he tells The Miller's Tale.

10 At times he seems a paranoic king
Who stamps his crest on walls and says "My Own!"
But in the end he fades like a lost tune,
Tossed here and there, whom all the breezes sing.
"Kilroy was here"; these words sound wanly gay,
15   Haughty yet tired with long marching.

---

[4] This is a line from the prologue of Chaucer's *Canterbury Tales*, in which "The Miller's Tale" also appears.

He is Orestes⁵—guilty of what crime?—
　　For whom the Furies still are searching;
　　When they arrive, they find their prey
(Leaving his name to mock them) went away.
20　Sometimes he does not flee from them in time:
"Kilroy was—"
　　　　with his blood a dying man
　　Wrote half the phrase out in Bataan.

Kilroy, beware. "HOME" is the final trap
25　That lurks for you in many a wily shape:
In pipe-and-slippers plus a Loyal Hound
　　Or fooling around, just fooling around.
Kind to the old (their warm Penelope)⁶
But fierce to boys,
30　　　　thus "home" becomes that sea,
Horribly disguised, where you were always drowned—
　　(How could suburban Crete condone
The yarns you would have V-mailed from the sun?)—
And folksy fishes sip Icarian° tea.　　　　　　　　　　*of or like Icarus*

35　One stab of hopeless wings imprinted your
　　Exultant Kilroy-signature
Upon sheer sky for all the world to stare:
　　"I was there! I was there! I was there!"

God is like Kilroy. He, too, sees it all;
40　That's how He knows of every sparrow's fall;
That's why we prayed each time the tightropes cracked
On which our loveliest clowns contrived their act.
The G. I. Faustus⁷ who was
　　　　everywhere
45　Strolled home again. "What was it like outside?"
Asked Can't, with his good neighbors Ought and But
And pale Perhaps and grave-eyed Better Not;
For "Kilroy" means: the world is very wide.
　　He was there, he was there, he was there!

50　*And in the suburbs Can't sat down and cried.*

Questions

1. Vocabulary: *privy* (3), *wanly* (14), *condone* (32).

---

⁵ Orestes, son of Agamemnon, avenged his father's murder by killing his mother. The Furies then pursued Orestes as punishment.
⁶ Penelope was the patient wife of the long-traveling Ulysses.
⁷ Faustus, or Faust, was a magician or alchemist who sold his soul to the Devil in order to gain supernatural powers, among them the power to move instantaneously from one place to another.

2. In what way is "Kilroy" a celebration of heroic actions?
3. Does the pattern of allusions emphasize the heroic nature? How?
4. Why is "HOME" the final trap?
5. Why does "Can't" sit down and cry in line 50?
6. Compare "Kilroy" to Tennyson's "Ulysses" in Chapter 5.

Basil Bunting's "Ode" does not rhyme; yet it has much in common with traditional odes. After you read it, try to understand Bunting's reason for his title.

BASIL BUNTING (1900–)

Ode

Let them remember Samangan,[8] the bridge and tower
and rutted cobbles and the coppersmith's hammer,
where we looked out from the walls to the marble mountains
ate and lay and were happy an hour and a night;

5   so that the heart never rests from love of the city
without lies or riches, whose old women
straight as girls at the well are beautiful,
its old men and its wineshops gay.

Let them remember Samangan against usurers,
10   cheats and cheapjacks, amongst boasters,
hideous children of cautious marriages,
those who drink in contempt of joy.

Let them remember Samangan, remember
they wept to remember the hour and go.

Questions

1. Is there anything heroic about this poem?
2. How is Samangan compared to the rest of modern society?
3. Does Samangan sound like a dull place to live? Why?

Oriental Forms

Oriental forms have been popular with Western writers since the turn of the century. Poets have admired the economy and clarity of the *haiku* and the *tanka*, two closely related forms. Both the tanka and the haiku are organized by the numbers of syllables per line rather than by rhyme. A haiku is a three-line poem, the lines having five, seven, and five syllables, respectively. The tanka is longer; its first and third lines have five syllables, and the rest contain seven syllables—

---

[8] Samangan (pronounced Sha-măn-gán) was a city-state on the border of the ancient Persian Empire. According to legend, it was in Samangan that the warrior Rustem met the princess and begot a son, Sohrab, whom Rustem killed by mistake many years later in battle, never having learned of his paternity. Thus Samangan represents a condition of innocence that precedes tragic disaster.

thirty-one syllables in all. However, since Oriental languages are so different from English, poets writing in English have freely adapted the forms. Because each syllable in Chinese represents a word, some poets prefer to think of the poems as containing seventeen or thirty-one words. Few poets try to translate these forms by preserving the syllable count. In their native language the haiku and tanka have other rules. Each haiku must contain a seasonal reference. In Japanese, the caesuras must be placed in specific places in the line. See Chapter 6 for more on the haiku.

MATSUO BASHO (1644–1694)

Nine Haiku

The beginning of art—
The depths of the country
And a rice-planting song.

Ailing on my travels,
Yet my dream wandering
Over withered moors.

Spring:
A hill without a name
Veiled in morning mist.

The beginning of autumn:
Sea and emerald paddy
Both the same green.

Silent and still: then
Even sinking into the rocks,
The cicada's screech.

Soon it will die,
Yet no trace of this
In the cicada's screech.

The winds of autumn
Blow: yet still green
The chestnut husks.

You say one word
And lips are chilled
By autumn's wind.

A flash of lightning:
Into the gloom
Goes the heron's cry.

Translation by Geoffrey Bownas and Anthony Thwaite (1930–)

1. Vocabulary: *cicada* (fifth haiku).
2. Is there a seasonal reference in each haiku? Is the reference always obvious?
3. What emotions do the haiku generate? Are they merely objective?
4. With what does art begin, according to Basho? In what way do the poems exemplify his idea of art?

Lady Kasa lived in the eighth century, but little else is known about her. These tanka have been translated into four-line stanzas.

LADY KASA (8th century)

Six Tanka

Like the pearl of dew
On the grass in my garden
In the evening shadows,
I shall be no more.

Even the grains of sand
On a beach eight hundred days wide
Would not be more than my love,
Watchman of the island coast.

The breakers of the Ise Sea
Roar like thunder on the shore.
As fierce as they, as proud as they,
Is he who pounds my heart.

I dreamt of a great sword
Girded to my side.
What does it signify?
That I shall meet you?

The bell has rung, the sign
For all to go to sleep.
Yet thinking of my love
How can I ever sleep?

To love a man without return
Is to offer a prayer
To a devil's back
In a huge temple.[9]

Translation by Geoffrey Bownas and Anthony Thwaite (1930–)

---

[9] Devils were depicted in the back of Japanese temples to warn people that it was pointless to be bad and greedy.

Questions

1. In what way do these tanka trace the relationship between lovers? What is the "plot" of the story?
2. How does the brevity of these poems make them poignant?
3. What is the overall feeling of these tanka? How does each tanka contribute to the feeling?

The influence of Oriental poetry can be observed even in poems that do not strictly obey the forms of either the haiku or the tanka. These poems have small, self-contained units; an emphasis on the direct presentation of sensory experience; and an understated tone.

WALLACE STEVENS (1879–1955)

Thirteen Ways of Looking at a Blackbird

I

Among twenty snowy mountains,
The only moving thing
Was the eye of the blackbird.

II

I was of three minds,
5   Like a tree
In which there are three blackbirds.

III

The blackbird whirled in the autumn winds.
It was a small part of the pantomime.

IV

A man and a woman
10   Are one.
A man and a woman and a blackbird
Are one.

V

I do not know which to prefer,
The beauty of inflections,
15   Or the beauty of innuendoes,
The blackbird whistling
Or just after.

VI

Icicles filled the long window
With barbaric glass.
20   The shadow of the blackbird
Crossed it, to and fro.
The mood
Traced in the shadow
An indecipherable cause.

VII

25   O thin men of Haddam,[10]
Why do you imagine golden birds?
Do you not see how the blackbird
Walks around the feet
Of the women about you?

VIII

30   I know noble accents
And lucid, inescapable rhythms;
But I know, too,
That the blackbird is involved
In what I know.

IX

35   When the blackbird flew out of sight,
It marked the edge
Of one of many circles.

X

At the sight of blackbirds
Flying in a green light,
40   Even the bawds of euphony
Would cry out sharply.

XI

He rode over Connecticut
In a glass coach.
Once, a fear pierced him,
45   In that he mistook
The shadow of his equipage
For blackbirds.

XII

The river is moving.
The blackbird must be flying.

XIII

50   It was evening all afternoon.
It was snowing
And it was going to snow.
The blackbird sat
In the cedar-limbs.

Questions

1. Vocabulary: *inflections* (14), *innuendoes* (15), *bawds* (40), *euphony* (40), *equipage* (46).

---

[10] Haddam is a town in Connecticut. According to Stevens, he chose this town because he liked the sound of its name.

2. Stevens wrote that he meant the poem to be a collection of "sensations" rather than "of epigrams or ideas." What various sensations do you get from the poem?
3. Seasonal references abound in the poem. How are they introduced? How do they function?
4. The poem reinforces what sorts of feelings toward blackbirds? Are they beautiful, common, sexy, ominous, deadly, delicate, wise?
5. In what ways are a "man and a woman and a blackbird/ . . . one"?
6. How is the first section related to the last?

Exercise

Take a common object (like a table) and use it as a focus of attention in a variety of circumstances and perspectives. Follow a tree, a swimming pool, a saltshaker through the course of a year or a day or even an hour.

Comic Forms

Comedy is rarely as freewheeling as it appears. In fact, of all types of expression, comedy is the most formulaic. The punch line must come at the very end, preceded by just the right number of interchanges. Poetry, because of its formal nature, is an excellent medium for comic expression. Poets have developed a number of forms exclusively suited to comedy.

Limericks

Limericks were popularized by Edward Lear after Lear discovered this anonymous example:

> There was an old man of Tobago
> Who lived on rice, gruel, and sago
> Till, much to his bliss
> His physician said this
> To a leg, sir, of mutton you must go.

We can see several important components of the limerick in this example. The first line usually ends in a place or a proper name that has a comic sound, and there is often a dialogue involved. An example of Lear's own work appears in Chapter 12, but here are two modern masters of the form.

OGDEN NASH (1902–1971)

Gervaise

> There was a young belle of old Natchez
> Whose garments were always in patchez.
> When comment arose
> On the state of her clothes,
> 5   She drawled, When Ah itchez, Ah scratchez!

Edouard

A bugler named Dougal MacDougal
Found ingenious ways to be frugal.
He learned how to sneeze
In various keys,
5   Thus saving the price of a bugle.

EDWARD GOREY (1925–)

There Was a Young Woman Named Plunnery

There was a young woman named Plunnery
Who rejoiced in the practice of gunnery,
    Till one day unobservant,
    She blew up a servant,
5   And was forced to retire to a nunnery.

Double Dactyl

Poets have fun playing with words—odd words, long words, words in intricate combination. Anthony Hecht, who is in other respects a very sensible person, developed the double dactyl with a classicist friend. It has many rules: the first line should be nonsense, the second a person's name, the sixth line a single word. The fourth and eighth lines rhyme and are short. The other lines are all two dactyls long. The best way to get a sense of these poems is to read them.

ANTHONY HECHT (1923–)

Vice

Higgledy-piggledy
Thomas Stearns Eliot
Wrote dirty limericks
Under the rose,

5   Using synecdoches,
Paranomasias,
Zeugmas, and rhymes he de-
Plored in his prose.

JOHN HOLLANDER (1929–)

Appearance and Reality

Higgledy-piggledy
Josephine Bonaparte, [11]
Painted by Prud'hon with
Serious mien:

---

[11] Josephine Bonaparte was the wife of Napoleon, the emperor of France.

Sorrow? Oh, hardly. Just
     Cosmetological
     Prudence (her teeth were a
     Carious green.*)

     *Historical.

Shaped Verses and Concrete Poetry
Shaped Verses

Poetry began as a purely oral mode of communication. But as soon as the first scribes began to copy down the poems they heard, poets became interested in the visual component of language. Poets usually write in lines; the line ending is a visual means of indicating rhythm, meaning, and form. It would be improper, therefore, to distinguish between texts that are visually oriented and those that are orally oriented. Once printed, all poems are visual to some degree. However, some poets make greater use of poetry's visual resources.

The simplest way to use the visual component of poetry is to arrange the lines or words in such a way that the poem looks like an object. There is a long tradition of such shaped verses. Perhaps the most famous in English is George Herbert's "Easter Wings."

GEORGE HERBERT (1593–1633)

Easter Wings[12]

Lord, who createdst man in wealth and store,
   Though foolishly he lost the same,
      Decaying   more   and   more
         Till   he   became
5   Most   poor.
         With   thee
       O   let   me   rise
    As   larks,   harmoniously,
  And   sing   this   day   thy   victories:
10 Then   shall   the   fall   further   the   flight   in   me.

My   tender   age   in   sorrow   did   begin:
  And still with sicknesses and shame
    Thou   didst   so   punish   sin,
      That   I   became
15   Most   thin.
        With   thee
     Let me combine,
   And feel this day thy victory;
  For,   if   I   imp°   my   wing   on   thine,   *graft*
20 Affliction   shall   advance   the   flight   in   me.

---

[12] Early editions of Herbert's "Easter Wings" are printed with the lines vertical.

Questions

1. How does the rhyme of the poem reinforce its shape? Is the shape merely super-imposed on the poem?
2. Does the shape of the poem refer only to the Easter wings of the title? Why else do the lines contract and then expand?
3. How does the poem exemplify the concept of the *felix culpa*—the "fortunate fall" from Eden?

Shaped verses are capable of remarkable delicacy and clarity.

MAY SWENSON (1919–)

Unconscious Came a Beauty

Unconscious
came a beauty to my
wrist
and stopped my pencil,
merged its shadow profile with
my hand's ghost
on the page:
Red Spotted Purple or else Mourning
Cloak,
paired thin-as-paper wings, near black,
were edged on the seam side poppy orange,
as were its spots.

UNCONSCIOUS

CAME A BEAUTY

I sat arrested, for its soot-haired
body's worm
shone in the sun.
It bent its tongue long as
a leg
black on my skin
and clung without my
feeling,
while its tomb-stained
duplicate parts of
a window opened.
And then I
moved.

Questions

1. How does the poem reenact its subject?
2. How has Swenson made use of the title?
3. How does the shape of the poem enhance the music of the verse?
4. How does the poem end? How does its shape reinforce that sense of ending?

Shaped poems can become very intricate, especially as poets place restrictions on themselves. John Hollander's shaped verses are composed on a typewriter, and he uses the grid of the typewriter as an instrument of measure. In his shaped poems words are never broken, and he does not add extra spaces between words unless they are on the boundary of the picture.

JOHN HOLLANDER (1929–)

Swan and Shadow

```
                         Dusk
                      Above the
                  water hang the
                          loud
                          flies
                         Here
                         O so
                          gray
                         then
                   What                A pale signal will appear
                   When           Soon before its shadow fades
                   Where          Here in this pool of opened eye
                   In us      No Upon us As at the very edges
                    of where we take shape in the dark air
                    this object bares its image awakening
                       ripples of recognition that will
                          brush darkness up into light
       even after this bird this hour both drift by atop the perfect sad instant now
                          already passing out of sight
                         toward yet-untroubled reflection
                    this image bears its object darkening
                    into memorial shades Scattered bits of
                   Light       No of water Or something across
                   water          Breaking up No Being regathered
                   Soon           Yet by then a swan will have
                   gone               Yes Out of mind into what
                         vast
                         pale
                          hush
                         of a
                         place
                          past
                   sudden dark as
                      if a swan
                         sang
```

Questions

1. In what way does the shape of the poem reflect the concepts expressed in the poem?
2. Why does the poem begin by speaking of the flies?
3. Swans are supposed to sing before they die. Why is this reference appropriate to this poem? What other deaths occur in the poem?

   A good test of a shaped verse is to write out the poem in the traditional way, lining up the lines along the left-hand margin. If the meaning is compromised or diminished, then the poem is strong. There should be an intimate connection between the shape and the content of the poem.

Concrete Poems

Modern poets have experimented with a more radical use of the visual properties of poetry. Shaped verses arrange lines of verse to form a picture; Herbert's poem even rhymes. Concrete poets, however, often will use only a few words. The placement of the letters gives the poem meaning.

The text of the following poem is wholly banal, and is meant to be. It is the placement of the words that is important.

EMMETT WILLIAMS (1925–)

She Loves Me

Questions

1. What shape is suggested by the placement of the words?
2. Why is the final "she" not in the circular configuration of the words?

The next poem uses more words. Not only does the poem picture a forsythia, but it also uses the letters of the forsythia to create a telegraphed message: HOPE INSISTS [on] ACTION. Thus the branches of forsythia suggest also the action that the hope of spring produces.

MARY ELLEN SOLT (1920—)

Forsythia

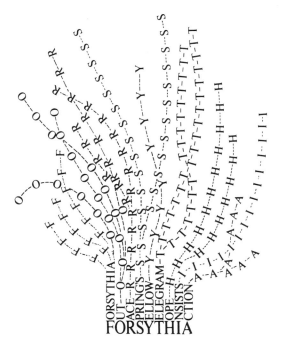

FORSYTHIA

Questions

1. How does a forsythia "telegraph" spring's message?
2. In what ways is all poetry telegraphic? How is this poem telegraphic?
3. Why is spring's message "Hope insists [on] action"? Is this message appropriate for spring?

The Prose Poem

We usually refer to writing other than poetry as *prose*. Prose is considered to be less concentrated and emotional than poetry. This distinction is not always clear-cut, however. In much imaginative literature, such as the novels of James Joyce and Virginia Woolf, prose can become so concentrated and moving that it assumes all the attributes usually associated with poetry except for regular rhythm and versification.

The *prose poem* is a form of poetry that uses imagery and figurative language but forfeits the effects of versification, meter, and line endings. In forfeiting verse rhythms, the prose poem directs more attention to the poets's vision and less to the language itself. The result is an unusually private and ethereal form, more like an interior monologue than an intentional revelation.

The prose poem became highly evolved during the nineteenth century as the French symbolists Rimbaud, Mallarmé, and Baudelaire found it suited to their intimate meditations. Notice how fluidly we follow Baudelaire's thoughts and feelings through the following meditation, without the interruptions of line endings or any self-conscious effects of meter. The poem is like a window into the poet's consciousness.

CHARLES BAUDELAIRE (1821–1867)

Windows

A man looking out of an open window never sees as much as the same man looking directly at a closed window. There is no object more deeply mysterious, no object more pregnant with suggestion, more insidiously sinister, in short more truly dazzling than a window lit up from within by even a single candle. What we can see out in the sunlight is always less interesting than what we can perceive taking place behind a pane of windowglass. In that pit, in that blackness or brightness, life is being lived, life is suffering, life is dreaming. . . .

Above the wave-crests of the rooftops across the way I can see a middle-aged woman, face already wrinkled—a poor woman forever bending over something, who never seems to leave her room. From just her face and her dress, from practically nothing at all, I've re-created this woman's story, or rather her legend; and sometimes I weep while reciting it to myself.

Some poor old man would have sufficed just as well; I could with equal ease have invented a legend for him, too.

And so I go to bed with a certain pride, having lived and suffered for others than myself.

Of course, you may confront me with: "But are you sure your story is really the true and right one?" But what does it really matter what the reality outside myself is, as long as it has helped me to live, to feel that I am alive, to feel the very nature of the creature that I am.

Translation by Michael Benedikt (1935–)

Questions

1. What metaphors can you find in the first paragraph? In the second? How do they reflect Baudelaire's feelings about what he sees?
3. The poet devotes considerable attention to the candle in a window. Does his treatment of the candle amount to poetic imagery, or is it mere prosaic description?
4. Do you appreciate the poet's pride, his exhilaration at feeling alive?
5. What, finally, distinguishes this piece of writing from most prose?

ROBERT BLY (1926–)

A Small Bird's Nest Made of White Reed Fiber

It's a white nest! White as the foam thrown up when the sea hits rocks. Some light comes through it, we get the feeling of those cloudy transoms[13] above Victorian

---

[13] Transoms are windows above doors, meant for ventilation.

doors, or the manless hair of those intense nurses, gray and tangled after long nights in the Crimean wards.[14] It is something made and then forgotten, like our own lives that we will entirely forget in the grave, when we are floating, nearing the shore where we will be reborn, ecstatic and black.

Questions

1. What similes arise from Bly's meditation? What metaphors?
2. What mood is created by the images? Is the poem sad? Depressing?
3. Try casting the poem in verses, regular or free. What does it gain from your alignment? What does it lose?

Suggestions for Essayists

Describe how comedy is formulaic. Use a situation comedy on television as an example. For instance, is the program's opening always the same? Are the situations repetitive? Are the characters predictable?

Many people use shaped language for expressive purpose. Examine the advertisements in a magazine or newspaper. How are the words placed on the page? What is the relationship between the pictures and the words? What sort of type is used? Bold? Italic? Script?

Suggestions for Poets

1. Try your hand at a number of the poetic forms discussed in this chapter.
2. Write a limerick sequence. How quickly do you exhaust its comic narrative potential?

---

[14] The Crimean War (1853–1856) was fought by Britain, France, and Turkey against Russia. The casualties from disease were much greater than those in battle. Thus "Crimean wards" refers to enormous, chaotic, and unsanitary hospitals crammed with dying and wounded soldiers.

14 🌿 Where Language Is Everything

Nonsense and Linguistic Experiment

Poems of Nonsense and Music

Among the many puzzling experiences Alice faces in *Through the Looking Glass* is an incomprehensible poem. She asks Humpty-Dumpty to help her; but alas, despite his lengthy explanation, the poem remains a mystery. Nor has anyone else been of great help. From Alice on, readers have found "Jabberwocky" confounding and delightful.

LEWIS CARROLL (1832–1898)

Jabberwocky

'Twas brillig and the slithy toves
    Did gyre and gimble in the wabe;
All mimsy were the borogroves,
    And the mome raths outgrabe.

5   "Beware the Jabberwock, my son!
    The jaws that bite, the claws that catch!
Beware the Jubjub bird, and shun
    The frumious Bandersnatch!"

He took his vorpal sword in hand:
10   Long time the manxome foe he sought—
So rested he by the Tumtum tree.
    And stood awhile in thought.

And as in uffish thought he stood,
    The Jabberwock, with eyes of flame,
15   Came whiffling through the tulgey wood,
    And burbled as it came!

One, two! One, two! And through and through
    The vorpal blade went snicker-snack!
He left it dead, and with its head
20   He went galumphing back.

"And hast thou slain the Jabberwock?
    Come to my arms, my beamish boy!
O frabjous day! Callooh! Callay!"
    He chortled in his joy.

25   'Twas brillig and the slithy toves
    Did gyre and gimble in the wabe;
All mimsy were the borogroves,
    And the mome raths outgrabe.

We can make out the outlines of the poem easily enough. A father warns his son about a beast called the Jabberwock. To his father's surprise, the son slays the beast. But little of our enjoyment of the poem is derived from this commonplace story. In Carroll's *Through the Looking Glass*, Humpty Dumpty tries to explain the meaning of the poem to Alice:

> "Well, 'slithy' means 'lithe and slimy.' 'Lithe' is the same as 'active.' You see it's like a portmanteau—there are two meanings packed up into one word."
>
> "I see it now," Alice remarked thoughtfully: "and what are 'toves'?"
>
> "Well, 'toves' are something like badgers—they're something like lizards—and they're something like corkscrews."
>
> "They must be very curious creatures."
>
> "They are that," said Humpty Dumpty: "also they make their nests under sundials—also they live on cheese."
>
> "And what's to 'gyre' and to 'gimble'?"
>
> "To 'gyre' is to go round and round like a gyroscope. To 'gimble' is to make holes like a gimlet."

We remember this poem not for what we understand but for what remains delightfully incomprehensible. Many critics say that great poems are never fully understood, that the finest work continues to yield significance. Yet it is one thing to say that a poem is never fully understood and another thing to say it is never understood at all. "Jabberwocky" is one of a special class of poems that resist normal methods of comprehension.

To appreciate "Jabberwocky" and poems like it, we must see how they differ from most writing. A lecture, an advertisement, or a manual of instruction can use figurative language, sound, and rhythm just as poetry does (although in poetry these elements are more apparent). "Jabberwocky," however, has no message; there is no information or wisdom to be derived from it. It exists not as a vehicle to convey ideas, but as a well-crafted—and very amusing—object.

This absence of explicit meaning is not as odd as it may first appear. We do not ask the meaning of a sunset. We appreciate its beauty without question. We do not ask the meaning behind a finely crafted necklace, nor do we question the message behind a landscape painting or a symphony. We enjoy these pieces of art for the beauty, amusement, and excitement they provide, or for any number of other reasons. So, too, we can appreciate a poem even if it presents us with no apparent message.

But if a poem means little or nothing, what is there to enjoy in it? What can a poem do other than convey meaning? These are difficult questions, but if we go back to the origins of language, we may be able to find an answer.

Our first encounters with language are usually devoid of meaning. Children too young to walk will respond with delight to "Patty Cake." They will amuse themselves for hours by jabbering nonsense. As young children, we derive satisfaction from making peculiar sounds. We are pleased when our lips explode with *p*'s or *b*'s, or when our tongues roll with an *r* or an *l*. Later we have fun mastering tongue twisters, for speaking demands the muscular coordination found in many sports. Opera singers train their bodies for years to produce certain sounds that thrill us because they are so difficult to produce. Language, after all, is sound. The printed text, like the score of a musical composition, is a way of noting the sounds of words. Poets who ask us to forget the meaning of words often want us to attend to the sound qualities of language, to return to a childlike delight in its physical nature.

The following poem, "Susie Asado," was written by the American poet Gertrude Stein, who spent most of her life in Paris, where she was the friend of such famous artists and writers as Pablo Picasso, Henri Matisse, and Ernest Hemingway. Stein constantly experimented with the potentials of language. This poem portrays a flamenco dancer. Try to hear in the sound of the poem the insistent rhythms and foot tapping of that Spanish dance.

GERTRUDE STEIN (1874–1946)

Susie Asado

Sweet sweet sweet sweet sweet tea.
    Susie Asado.
Sweet sweet sweet sweet sweet tea.
    Susie Asado.
5   Susie Asado which is a told tray sure.
A lean on the shoe this means slips slips hers.
When the ancient light grey is clean it is yellow, it is a silver seller.
This is a please this is a please there are the saids to jelly.
These are the wets these say the sets to leave a crown to Incy.
10   Incy is short for incubus.
A pot. A pot is a beginning of a rare bit of trees. Trees
tremble, the old vats are in bobbles, bobbles which shade and
shove and render clean, render clean must.
    Drink pups.
15   Drink pups drink pups lease a sash hold, see it shine and
a bobolink has pins. It shows a nail.
    What is a nail. A nail is unison.
    Sweet sweet sweet sweet sweet tea.

Questions

1. Vocabulary: *incubus* (12), *bobolink* (18), *unison* (19).
2. In line 5, what is the noun in the phrase "a told tray sure"? Are there any other words whose part of speech is ambiguous or odd?
3. Do you see any sentences whose structure is clear but whose meaning is unfathomable?
4. Despite the lack of clear meaning, can you detect the speaker's attitude toward Susie Asado? Is this a poem of praise or denunciation? How can you tell?

"Susie Asado" may look like an easy poem to write, but it is the result, according to Stein, "of a strict discipline . . . the absolute refusal of never using a word that was never an exact word." It is much harder than it appears to break language away from meaning and to reveal its full musical properties. Stein employs a number of techniques to achieve these ends. She repeats words, avoids punctuation, uses common words as unusual parts of speech, and telescopes fragmented sentences together. Behind the childlike fun Stein's craft is evident.

"Bantams in Pine-Woods" is another portrait in sound, although Wallace Stevens permits meaning to surface. The title sets the scene: the speaker has encountered a flock of wild roosters in his walk.

WALLACE STEVENS (1879–1955)

Bantams in Pine-Woods

Chieftain Iffucan of Azcan in caftan
Of tan with henna hackles, halt!

Damned universal cock, as if the sun
Was blackamoor to bear your blazing tail.

5   Fat! Fat! Fat! Fat! I am the personal.
Your world is you. I am my world.

You ten-foot poet among inchlings. Fat!
Begone! An inchling bristles in these pines,

Bristles, and points their Appalachian tangs,
10   And fears not portly Azcan nor his hoos.

Questions

1. Vocabulary: *caftan* (1), *henna* (2), *blackamoor* (4).
2. With what techniques has the speaker captured the sound of the roosters?
3. What is the speaker's attitude toward the roosters? How has he conveyed this attitude?
4. "Iffucan" and "Azcan" seem to be words that telescope standard English phrases, "if you can" and "as [you] can." How do these telescoped phrases add to our understanding of the speaker's attitude toward the roosters?

Exercise

Do animals or machines ever make sounds that suggest standard words? Try to translate them. What is a train saying as it chugs along? Or a coffee percolator?

Both Stevens and Stein conceive of the poem as a pattern of sound. We may gain an even better sense of this manner of composition by looking at two translations of the Roman poet Catullus. The first is a fairly standard one by Horace Gregory (1898–1982). Gregory has tried to find the best English equivalent to the meaning of the Latin words. We learn that Catullus is angry because Ameana, an ugly woman with flaring nostrils, has sued him for taking sexual advantage of her. He believes her boyfriend, Mamurra, has put her up to this lie. The second translation is by Louis and Celia Zukofsky. Louis Zukofsky (1904–1978) was an American poet and literary theorist. He defined poetry as occupying a range of sound between speech and music. Zukofsky and his daughter, Celia, decided they would find English words with equivalent *sounds* rather than *meaning* and translate the music of the Latin. First, here is the Gregory translation.

CATULLUS (84?–54 B.C.)

Poem #41

See that girl, Ameana, the one with the big nostrils?
She's the little parasite of that wild boy, Mamurra
and the girl is suing me for a full ten thousand—
personal services of course—
5   someone tell her father,
mother, sister, aunt, or friends to call in a physician,
have him work upon her brain. The poor creature's crazy.
But don't blame me or ask me why or where or how.
A looking-glass must strike her blind—
10   O what a face and what hallucinations!

Now, the Zukofskys' translation:

CATULLUS (84?–54 B.C.)

Poem #41

Ameana pulling, a foot touted high,
touched me for all of ten thousand: and popped scut
is the tour-pickled, low-puling long nosed, ah
decocted heiress of the milked Formiani.
5   Propinquity, quick buss this fuel, cure eye,
amigos, medicos, call convocations:
no nest, *she* is nuts, pulls her neck, rogue harried,
what lies sit solid ice imagine o some.

1. Do you think the Zukofsky poem sounds like English? If not, why not?
2. The Zukofskys use long words such as *propinquity* and *convocations.* Is there anything about the origins of these words that would make them especially appropriate to capture the music of Latin?
3. Although the Zukofskys have not tried to retell the story behind the music, do they leave any traces to suggest the meaning of the poem?

What the Zukofskys have lost in their version is evident. But what, if anything, have they gained? Even if we had *not* read the Gregory translation, we would sense Catullus's outrage. We would hear the brittle *c*'s of line 6 and the hiss of line 8. We can sense the emotion of the poem, like the emotion of orchestral music, by attending to the rise and fall of the sound.

Magical Poems

Some poems are magic spells, curses, or magical invocations; they do not yield their meaning as traditional poems do. In many religions people are forbidden to use the name of God because the name has magic and dangerous powers. One of Adam's first acts in the Garden of Eden was to name all of creation. His names had magical properties, and poets still try to gain power over the world by giving their own private names to things. Here is a "magical" poem that tries to recreate the wonder of Adam's original language.

MICHAEL MOTT (1930–)

Adam Names the Animals

    Ac
    Bez
    Cuf
    Di
5   Eop
    Faw
    Ginzal
    Hut
    Ipoth
10 Ji
    Koz
    Letlak
    Mutal
    Nepsa
15 O
    Petzut
    Quegor Upta
    Rabu

Samsa
20   Tuton Obi
Ul
Vetzma
Wyst
Xtor Aa
25   Yu
Zept

Shakespeare is not averse to casting spells. The following is a short chorus
from *Macbeth*, act 1, scene 3, spoken by the three witches.

WILLIAM SHAKESPEARE (1564–1616)

From Macbeth

The Weird Sisters, hand in hand
Posters° of the sea and land,   *swift travelers*
Thus do go about, about;
Thrice to thine, and thrice to mine
5   and thrice again, to make up nine.
Peace! The charm's wound up.

The following poem is the ritual chant for the sick sung by the Omaha Indians.
It calls on the Aged One to help those who have been obedient.

Ritual Chant for the Sick

He! Aged One, eçka
Thou Rock, eçka
Aged One, eçka
He! I have taught these little ones
5   They obey, eçka
Aged One, eçka
He!
He! Unmoved from time without end, verily
Thou sittest, eçka
10   In the midst of the various paths of the coming winds
In the midst of the winds thou sittest, eçka
Aged One, eçka
He! The small grasses grow about thee, eçka
Thou sittest as though making of them thy dwelling place, eçka
15   He! Verily thou sittest covered with the droppings of birds, eçka
Thy head decked with the downy feathers of the birds, eçka
Aged One, eçka
Thou who standest next in power, eçka
He! thou water, eçka

20 Water that hast been flowing
From time unknown, eçka
He! Of you the little ones have taken
Though thy mysteries remain unrevealed
These little ones crave thy touch, eçka
25 He! Thou that standest as one dwelling place, eçka
Even as one dwelling place, eçka
Ye great animals, eçka
He! Who make for us the covering, eçka
These little ones, thou hast said, let their thoughts reverently dwell on me, eçka
30 He! Thou tent frame, eçka
Thou standest with bent back o'er us
With stooping shoulders, bending over us
Verily, thou standest
Thus my little ones shall speak of me, thou hast said
35 Brushing back the hair from thy forehead, eçka
The hair of thy head
The grass that grows about thee
Thy hairs are whitened, eçka
The hairs that grow upon thy head, eçka
40 O, the paths that the little ones shall take, eçka
Whichever way they may flee from danger, eçka
They shall escape. Their shoulders shall be bent with age as they walk
As they walk on the well-beaten path
Shading their brows now and again with their hands
45 As they walk in their old age, eçka
That of thy strength they shall partake, eçka
Therefore thy little ones desire to walk closely by thy side, eçka
Venerable One, eçka.

Translation by Alice Fletcher (1845–1923)

Questions

1. What is the relationship between the god who is being addressed and the grass? Is it a static relationship?
2. In what way is the god a "tent frame" or "bent . . . / With stooping shoulders"?
3. What arguments or inducements does the chanter use to convince the god to provide health?

The language of magic is special. It often contains invented words or words distorted or borrowed from other languages. According to Jerome Rothenberg, an American poet and critic, magic languages unite "the user . . . with the beings & things he's trying to influence or connect with for a sharing of power, participation in a life beyond his own."

Collage

Some poems also resist expected interpretation because they are collages of words, images, and ideas. *Collage* is a term derived from art and refers to a picture made up of pieces of found objects: scraps of newspaper, bits of old cane backing, a gum wrapper, lengths of string, tin cans. A collage can be made entirely of found objects, or it can be a combination of the objects and the artist's own drawing. Poets perform a similar act. But instead of gathering scraps of newspaper and string, they arrange scattered pieces of language: clichés, phrases they have heard, or quotations.

The following poem by E. E. Cummings is an amalgam of clichés drawn from political oratory.

E. E. CUMMINGS (1894–1962)

• next to of course god america i

"next to of course god america i
love you land of the pilgrims' and so forth oh
say can you see by the dawn's early my
country 'tis of centuries come and go
5   and are no more what of it we should worry
in every language even deafanddumb
thy sons acclaim your glorious name by gorry
by jingo by gee by gosh by gum
why talk of beauty what could be more beaut-
10   iful than these heroic happy dead
who rushed like lions to the roaring slaughter
they did not stop to think they died instead
then shall the voice of liberty be mute?"

He spoke. And drank rapidly a glass of water

Questions

1. Who is the "he" that is speaking? Where is he speaking? Why does he drink a glass of water?
2. What is Cummings's attitude toward the speaker?
3. How many scraps of songs can you find in the poem?
4. Why is line 8 included in the poem? What sort of collection of phrases is it?
5. Is the question in line 13 logically developed? What sort of question is it?

We probably are attuned to the collage of phrases and allusions in the Cummings poem because the phrases and allusions are familiar and because we understand what holds these bits of language together. But the organizing principle behind some collages is less apparent. For example, "Madam Mouse Trots" is one of a group of poems Dame Edith Sitwell collected under the title *Façade*. A facade is the front of a building, but it is also "a false, superficial or artificial appearance or effect." Sitwell is suggesting by her title that the language in the poems is a facade, just as oratorical language is a political facade.

Sitwell incorporates two quotations that open and close the poem. One she acknowledges clearly. The opening two lines are a free translation of the Verlaine poem she quotes as an epigraph. The last line is a misquotation of a Robert Browning poem that all English schoolchildren of Sitwell's generation had to memorize, as familiar to her audience as "The Star Spangled Banner" is to Americans. The French poem was written while Verlaine was in jail. Madam Mouse is the only free creature he sees in prison. The Browning poem concludes this way:

> The lark's on the wing,
> The snail's on the thorn;
> God's in his heaven—
> All's right with the world!
>
> —*"Pippa's Song" from* Pippa Passes

The poem was often viewed as the perfect expression of mindless optimism and satisfaction. At last, you are ready to read the poem.

EDITH SITWELL (1887–1964)

Madam Mouse Trots

"Dame Souris trotte gris dans le noir."

—Verlaine

Madam Mouse trots,
Gray in the black night!
Madam Mouse trots:
Furred is the light.
5   The elephant-trunks
Trumpet from the sea. . . .
Gray in the black night
The mouse trots free.
Hoarse as a dog's bark
10   The heavy leaves are furled. . . .
The cat's in his cradle,
All's well with the world!

Questions

1. How has Sitwell arranged the poem? Do the two quotations agree in feeling with one another?
2. What is Sitwell's attitude toward the quotations? Does she believe that "All's well with the world"?

Edith Sitwell *(Dennis Stock/*
Magnum Photos Inc.)

3. How does the title *Façade* inform the reader's attitude toward the language of the poems? In what way is language a facade? In what way is "Madam Mouse Trots" a facade?

With a poem that assembles and arranges specimens of language, the usual questions one asks about a poem are inapplicable. One cannot ask who is speaking, to whom, and for what reason, because there is typically no persona in a collage poem. However, in such poems, poets act as editors, and one may question their editorial principles:

1. How has the poet selected the material? What criteria were used?
2. How has the poet arranged the material?'
3. What are the poet's feelings toward the material?

E. E. Cummings, for example, selected the most outworn phrases used in political speeches. He has arranged them in the usual order in which they appear in speeches. Thus, "next to of course god america i" is a political speech in miniature. Sitwell has chosen specimens of poetry that discuss serious questions in a naive, childlike way.

Poets have incorporated into their poems not only literary references, but parts of historical documents as well: letters, memos, and papers. Ezra Pound, in the work that occupied most of his life, *The Cantos*, composed poems using numerous languages, anecdotes, Chinese characters, and historical documents. The following portion of *The Cantos* concerns itself with President John Adams and the American political scene in his time.

EZRA POUND (1885–1972)

From Canto LXX

"My situation almost the only one in the world
where firmness and patience are useless"
J. A.[1] vice president and president of the senate

1791

5   Will the french refuse to receive Mr. Pinckney?[2]
             idea of leading Mr. Adams . . .
Blount[3] (senator) has been speculating with the English . . .
surrounded by projecters and swindlers, you will be, Gerry,[4]
            Friendship, Marshall[5] a plain man and the frogs
10   countenance only enemies of our constitution.
             set our seamen ashore at St. Jago de Cuba
till our ships arm . . . office of Secretary as rival of president
in aim to have quintuple directory. . . . Vervennes'[6] friends
dislike the facts laid to his charge.
15   Hamilton[7] no command,
too much intrigue. McHenry[8] was secretary for war, in 98
We shd / have frigates, no European peace can be lasting.
           expedient to recommend war against France?
(presupposing they shall not have declared war against us
20   (thus to Pickering.)[9] "Talleyrand
affects utter ignorance, Mr. Gerry[10] has communicated, although
knowing that Talleyrand had much greater acquaintance
                  with the
said X, Y, Z than has Mr. Gerry.
25   (Signed Gerry)
               Hague 1st July '98
peculators, cd / they be aroused to drive out the French . . .

---

[1] From a letter of John Adams (J.A.) to John Trumbull, January 23, 1791. John Trumbull was a close friend and personal advisor to Adams.

[2] Charles Cotesworth Pinckney was Adams's ambassador to France. However, the French insulted him and would not receive him. The incident, known as the Pinckney Affair, was one of the great international crises of Adams's administration.

[3] William Blount, a senator from Tennessee, conspired with an Englishman, John Chisolm, to invade Spanish territories for the purpose of land speculation. Blount was expelled from the Senate for his actions.

[4] From a letter of John Adams to Elbridge Gerry, July 8, 1797. Gerry was sent by Adams to negotiate the Pinckney affair with France.

[5] John Marshall (1755–1835) was chief justice of the U.S. Supreme Court. He was sent by Adams to help Gerry negotiate with France in the Pinckney Affair.

[6] The Count de Vergennes was a high-ranking French official mentioned in Pinckney's correspondence.

[7] Alexander Hamilton (1754–1804) was one of the Founding Fathers and the first secretary of the treasury. Hamilton was a rival of Adams.

[8] James McHenry was secretary of war under Adams and advisor during the Pinckney Affair.

[9] Timothy Pickering was secretary of state under Adams.

[10] Gerry, John Marshall, and Pinckney tried to negotiate with Talleyrand, the minister of foreign affairs for France. The French wished to be bribed, and Talleyrand sent three ministers—identified in diplomatic communiques only as X, Y, and Z—to obtain these bribes. The insulting negotiations collapsed, ending what has been called ever since the XYZ Affair.

Ezra Pound *(Rollie McKenna)*

Vans M / [11] exhausted all things in enormous bribes" (ciphered)
Talleyrand, leaving however reserves for chicanery,
30   and Murray not yet removed from the Hague
                                 about "peace"
shortly ago were howling for war with Britain,
                             peace, war
aimed at elections. My appointment of Murray
35   has at least laid open characters to me
"you are hereby discharged"
               John Adams, President of the United States
               to Tim Pickering
to execute office so far as to affix seal to enclosed commission
40   John Marshal of Virginia, to be Chief Justice
               and certify your own name *pro bac vice*[12]
Hamilton's total ignorance (or whatever)
               of practice and usage of nations.
eternal neutrality in all wars of Europe.
45   I leave the state with its coffers full
               Dec 28th 1800

Questions

1. Vocabulary: *countenance* (10), *expedient* (18), *peculators* (27), *chicanery* (29).
2. What do these fragments have in common? Why do you think Pound chose them?
3. What is the principle of organization?

---

[11] L. Williams Vans Murray was U.S. ambassador to the Netherlands.
[12] Latin for "in exchange for."

4. Do you get a clear understanding of the historical occurrences, or do you get an impression of the political atmosphere?
5. What do you think Pound felt about the documents? About the history they reveal?
6. Do you have the sense that politics moved slowly, logically, and honestly in Adams's day?
7. Compare Pound's version of Adams's world to today's political conditions. How do they seem different? How do they seem similar?

These collage poems can be very difficult to read. They demand that readers have a wide knowledge of their culture and history and that they be sensitive to subtle shifts in language. You may decide that a poem like *The Cantos* is more difficult than it is informative, beautiful, or interesting. Nevertheless, you should understand that poets who use collage do not merely want to show off and confuse. Pound knew from experience that if he plainly stated his political opinions, people were likely to reject them. But he felt that if reasonable people had the facts, they would eventually draw the same conclusions that he had. The collage method gave Pound the opportunity to give the facts (or near facts) and to arrange them in such a manner that the reader would be led to Pound's conclusions. In other words, Pound lets the reader reenact his poetic and intellectual experience. Collage poems are difficult because readers must do much of the same work the poet has done. They must tie the elements of the poem together. Yet Pound has not given up responsibility or control. He has aided the reader by selecting the most vivid examples and arranging them in the most effective manner.

Poets do not leave readers entirely on their own. Usually they incorporate into the fabric of their poems an indication of the organizing principle or principles. For example, John Ashbery, in "A Man of Words," indicates two ways in which he views language. He tells us that "the snarls [of truth are] ripped out/And spread around." He also writes that there is "Just time to reread this/And the past slips through your fingers." The first passage suggests that truth appears in knotted, isolated scraps of language. The second suggests that words fade away even as they are uttered. Thus Ashbery puts us on guard for two sorts of expressions: those that are short and isolated, and those that are long and loosely flowing.

JOHN ASHBERY (1927–)

A Man of Words

His case inspires interest
But little sympathy; it is smaller
Than at first appeared. Does the first nettle
Make any difference as what grows
5   Becomes a skit? Three sides enclosed,
The fourth open to a wash of the weather,
Exits and entrances, gestures theatrically meant

To punctuate like doubled-over weeds as
The garden fills up with snow?
10 Ah, but this would have been another, quite other
Entertainment, not the metallic taste
In my mouth as I look away, density black as gunpowder
In the angles where the grass writing goes on,
Rose-red in unexpected places like the pressure
15 Of fingers on a book suddenly snapped shut.

Those tangled versions of the truth are
Combed out, the snarls ripped out
And spread around. Behind the mask
Is still a continental appreciation
20 Of what is fine, rarely appears and when it does is already
Dying on the breeze that brought it to the threshold
Of speech. The story worn out from telling.
All diaries are alike, clear and cold, with
The outlook for continued cold. They are placed
25 Horizontal, parallel to the earth,
Like the unencumbering dead. Just time to reread this
And the past slips through your fingers, wishing you were there.

Questions

1. Vocabulary: *continental* (19), *unencumbering* (26).
2. What lines or phrases could be called "tangled versions of the truth"? Which ones seem to flow along? Are they ever combined?
3. How would you describe the tone and diction of the two sorts of expressions?
4. Whose "case inspires interest/But little sympathy" (lines 1–2)?
5. How does the title inform the poem as a whole? Who is a man of words? In what sense is the poem about poetry? In what sense is it autobiographical?

Some poems do not convey their meaning in a traditional manner. These poems use language that is especially charged. Some poets wish to emphasize the music and the magic of words more than their meaning. Others wish to arrange specimens of language. If readers take their time with these poems and concentrate on how the language has been arranged, they will derive much satisfaction from them and will not find them so incomprehensible. One need not feel the frustration of Alice in her journey through Wonderland.

Suggestions for Essayists

1. If you have been to a foreign country where you were unfamiliar with the language, how did you make yourself understood? Discuss the problems of foreign-speaking people visiting this country.
2. Make a collection of strange expressions such as "He went bananas" or "She has a monkey on her back." Discuss what they mean or how they came into use.

Suggestions for Poets

1. Invent a language of your own and write a poem using it.
2. Select the most beautiful words you know and combine them into musical phrases.
3. Select a topic. Construct a poem about it by weaving together lines taken from the poems in this book.

❧ Poems for Further Study

EDWARD LEAR (1812–1888)

There Was an Old Man of the Coast

There was an Old Man of the Coast,
Who placidly sat on a post;
But when it was cold he relinquished his hold,
And called for some hot buttered toast.

MARIANNE MOORE (1887–1972)

The Monkey Puzzle[13]

A kind of monkey or pine lemur
not of interest to the monkey,
in a kind of Flaubert's Carthage, it defies one—[14]
this "Paduan cat with lizard," this "tiger in a bamboo thicket."
5   "An interwoven somewhat," it will not come out.
Ignore the Foo dog and it is forthwith more than a dog,
its tail superimposed upon itself in a complacent half spiral,
this pine tree—this pine tiger, is a tiger, not a dog.
It knows that if a nomad may have dignity,
10   Gibraltar has had more—
that "it is better to be lonely than unhappy."
A conifer contrived in imitation of the glyptic work of jade and hard-stone cutters,
a true curio in this bypath of curio-collecting,
it is worth its weight in gold, but no one takes it
15   from these woods in which society's not knowing is colossal,
the lion's ferocious chrysanthemum head seeming kind by comparison.
This porcupine-quilled, complicated starkness—
this is beauty—"a certain proportion in the skeleton which gives the best results."[15]
One is at a loss, however, to know why it should be here,
20   in this morose part of the earth—
to account for its origin at all;
but we prove, we do not explain our birth.

---

[13] The poem may be read as a riddle. The monkey puzzle is the common name of the Chile pine (*Araucana Imbricata*), a strangely twisted tree.

[14] Gustav Flaubert (1821–1880) was a French novelist.

[15] From Lafcadio Hearn, *Talks to Writers* (1920).

JOHN BERRYMAN (1914–1972)

Young Woman's Song

The round and smooth, my body in my bath,
If someone else would like it too.—I did,
I wanted T. to think "How interesting"
Although I hate his voice and face, hate both.
5   I hate this something like a bobbing cork
Not going. I want something to hang to.—

A fierce wind roaring high up in the bare
Branches of trees,—I suppose it was lust
But it was holy and awful. All day I thought
10   I am a bobbing cork, irresponsible child
Loose on the waters.—What have you done at last?
A little work, a little vague chat.

I want that £3.10 hat terribly.—
What I am looking for (*I am*) may be
15   Happening in the gaps of what I know.
The full moon docs go with you as yóu go.
Where am I going? I am not afraid . .
Only I would be lifted lost in the flood.

JAMES SCHUYLER (1923–)

An Almanac

Shops take down their awnings;
women go south;
few street lamp leaners;
children run with leaves running at their backs.
5   In cedar chests sheers and seersuckers displace flannels and wools.

Sere leaves of the Scotch marigolds;
crystals of earth melt;
the thorn apple shows its thorns;
a dog tracks the kitchen porch;
10   wino-hobos attempt surrender to warm asylums.

Caged mink claw;
gulls become pigeons;
snow bends the snow fence.
Heavy food;
15   rumbling snowplows.

Seats in the examination hall are staggered.
The stars gleam like ice;
a fragment of bone;
in the woods matted leaves;
20   a yellowish shoot.
A lost key is found;
storm windows are stacked on the beams of the garage.

CHARLES SIMIC (1938–)

The Place

They were talking about the war
The table still uncleared in front of them.
Across the way, the first window
Of the evening was already lit.
5   He sat, hunched over, quiet,
The old fear coming over him . . .
It grew darker. She got up to take the plate—
Now unpleasantly white—to the kitchen.
Outside in the fields, in the woods
10   A bird spoke in proverbs,
A Pope went out to meet Attila,
The ditch was ready for its squad.

DAVID SHAPIRO (1947–)

I Haven't

Do you have a lion in your house?
Do you have a serpent in your house?
No fortunately I do not have a lion in my house.

Do you have a woman leaning slightly past the spirals in your house?
5   No I do not have the edge of her dress in my house.
Do you have a lion in your house?

No I do not have the outline of her body in my house.
Do you have a trouvaille° in your house?   *a lucky find*
No fortunately I do not have a lion in my house.

10   Do you have the goddess Hygeia° headless as a house?   *goddess of health*
No I do not have her right hand casting a shadow on my house.
Do you have a lion in your house?

No I do not have her light peplos° folds full of life in   *a Grecian garment*
    my house.
Do you have "truth is the consequences" in your house?
15   No fortunately I do not have a lion in my house.

What do you have in your high heavy house?
Do you have a rendering of her brilliant pitiless hair falling on your house?
Do you have a lion in your house?
No fortunately I do not have a lion in my house.

E. E. CUMMINGS (1894–1962)

from the cognoscenti

bingbongwhom chewchoo
laugh dingle nails personally

bung loamhome picpac
obviously scratches tomorrowlobs

5 wholeagainst you gringlehow
exudes thursday fasters
by button of whisper sum blinked
he belowtry eye nowbrow

sangsung née whitermuch grab
10 sicksilk soak sulksuck whim
poke if inch dimmer twist on
permament and slap tremendous

sorrydaze bog triperight
election who so thumb o'clock
15 asters miggle dim a ram
flat hombre sin bangaroom

slim guesser goose pin yessir wheel
no sendwisp ben jiffyclaus
bug fainarain wee celibate
20 amaranth clutch owch

so chuck slop hight evolute
my eerily oh gargle
to jip hug behemoth
truly pseudo yours podia

25 of radarw leschin

JUDITH JOHNSON SHERWIN (1936–)

Dr. Potatohead Talks to Mothers

when you put on the feet be sure
the claws are attached long
three-toed   when we landed
 on the wetgreen planet in libra
5 the *three-toed* chef broke out
 a gourmet spread frogs' legs
 that had made the hop frozen
 from baltimore / mushrooms
 champagne /
10   *when you put on*
the hands   that same day
the thumbs should not necessarily
oppose   the dominant life forms
 great big black buck mushrooms
15 undulated their velvet
 blackribbed mouths flowed open
 closed on us sucked our juices
 and the monster frogs big as tanks

```
                 ripped off our navigator's
20               legs sautéed them in melted
                 rumpfat /
                                   when you put on
        the arms push in the pegs
        deep so they can't be ripped
25      off                     in alpha centauri[16] minced
                 frozen to fatten their giant
                 cats god we fought them
                 napalm and h-bomb blasted nine
                 planets and all the influences
30               out of the starry night
                 shivered
                                  when you put on
        the head when you put on
        the head be very sure
35      the hat doesn't cover   more
                 of them came when we landed we
                 landed half the universe
                                      the hat should cover
        the hair shelter the brain
40      from being baked powdered the ears
        frozen                   we signed
                 treaties /       what
                 to eat
                                              but the eyes
45                                            uncovered
                 potatoes we died
                 of boredom last week          but the eyes
                                               left open to spot what
                 we landed on x-37
50               in gemini[17] giant potatos rolled
                 out riding fantastic tractors
                 of an unmeltable alloy
                 peeled off                    but the eyes
                                               bare, freezing, spied out
55               our jackets
                 of skin dropped us flayed
        and the teeth should be firmly planted
                 in hot water and boiled
                 yesterday when the dust
60               had settled we signed the treaty
                 we looked for something legal
                 to eat
                                  and the teeth
        there the mouth
65      open
```

---

[16] The nearest star to our sun.
[17] The thirty-seventh planet of the star *x* in the constellation Gemini.

15 🌿 The Well-Made Poem

Judging a work of art is difficult and often frustrating. Many people avoid the practice or argue that it is useless. "Since beauty is in the eye of the beholder," they reason, "any object I find pleasing must be good." Others refuse to form any opinions at all: "Who am I to judge a work of art?" they modestly ask.

There are important reasons for developing a critical faculty, however. One of the chief aims of education is to help people recognize excellence so that they may cultivate what is excellent in themselves. Sloppy, fuzzy writing breeds sloppy, fuzzy thinking. Mawkish, sentimental literature breeds vague, undifferentiated feeling. Good literature puts us into better contact with our thoughts and feelings and helps us distinguish the genuine and appropriate from the false and ill-fitting.

Part of the problem in developing critical skills is that poems are a lot like people: one has difficulty recognizing the truly worthwhile. Placed among strangers, we often gravitate to whoever seems at first the friendliest, kindest person. Often our first impressions are wrong. Later we may discover that bright spot to be merely a flash; the person we thought so interesting, clever, and kind may really be dull, slow, and mean. At the same time we may discover that someone we overlooked, a quiet person who spoke softly and with few words, really has the qualities we seek in a lasting friend.

Literary judgments, like personal ones, are best made over a period of time. Clearly, people who have been reading poems for a while have an advantage over the beginner: they have had time to test their first impressions. Similarly, older poems of merit are more easily recognized than contemporary works because they have had time to show their power. The best way to become a seasoned critic is to start reading now and take the suggestions of your teachers.

One must also be careful not to confuse *taste* with *excellence*. For example, we may like animals and enjoy having pictures of animals around us. Our taste for animal pictures may cloud our appreciation of nonanimal pictures, or it may cause us to overpraise a badly executed animal drawing. Similarly, people have moral or religious beliefs that may color their appreciation of certain works. Experienced readers will be able to recognize excellence even in works they do not particularly like, just as we can recognize that an unpleasant person may be an excellent athlete.

Taste and excellence can be confused in another way. Imagine eating a meal of some exotic cuisine for the first time. You are served course after course of foods you do not recognize, whose names you cannot even pronounce. Nevertheless, you find the food delicious. Can you say the food was well prepared? Not with any authority. To make such a judgment, you would have to have eaten several different versions of each dish. All you can honestly say is that you liked what you ate. People who are beginning to read poetry should acknowledge what they like and explore the experiences that please them. But it will take time to develop the knowledge of what is truly well prepared. What seems innovative may in fact be well worn. What appears dull may actually be subtle. Works we like may not necessarily be those of lasting excellence.

Overall Effectiveness

How then does one evaluate a poem? The principal test is whether each part of the poem contributes to its overall effectiveness. A poem is like a superbly integrated organism whose every feature contributes to the health and success of the body as a whole. The limbs of such a creature are neither too large nor too small. It does not carry an ounce more or less of weight than it needs. It is able to respond appropriately to circumstances, and its every action is animated by liveliness and a keen sense of intelligence. The healthy organism knows how and when to enjoy itself but can be tough and efficient when necessary.

No poem, as no person, is ever perfect. Paul Valéry, the great French poet, remarked that a poem is never completed, only abandoned. Thus the responsible judge balances a work's strengths against its weaknesses. A poem can contain many faults and still be good. Another work may contain no glaring errors, yet seem generally lifeless and unsatisfactory. Critics often disagree not about a poem's faults, but about the impact of those faults on the work's overall effectiveness.

Although the components of a good poem are all interrelated, it is easier to evaluate poems by looking at their various aspects separately. These aspects or areas of judgment will overlap, but for now it is useful to consider them as isolated.

Economy

The best poetry is noted for its concentration of expression and feeling. Poets try to use as few words as possible to gain their end. Thus each word must bear its part of the load and serve as many functions as possible. Bad poetry is marked by (1) looseness of expression, (2) redundancy, and (3) padding for rhyme or meter. The following quatrain exhibits all three weaknesses.

The Frog

The frog he sits upon the bank
　　And catches bugs and flies
And after he gets tired of that
　　He just jumps in and dives.

—*James K. Elmore*

The first line should read simply "The frog sits upon the bank." The superfluous "he" is added to pad the rhythm. Lines 2 and 4 contain redundant expressions. "Jumps in" and "dives" are synonymous, and flies are a kind of bug, not a different type of creature. Line 3 is wordy: "gets tired" means the same as "tires." "The Frog" suffers more than most poems from uneconomical language. Indeed, it is an example of the worst sort of poetry, *doggerel*. Doggerel is language that has rhyme and meter but contains neither feeling nor thought nor music.

Here is a poem for your evaluation.

CLAUDE MacKAY (1814–1889)

Only a Thought

'Twas only a passing thought, my love,
　　Only a passing thought,
That came o'er my mind like a ray of the sun
　　In the ripples of waters caught;
5　　And it seemed to me, and I say to thee,
　　That sorrow and shame and sin
Might disappear from our happy sphere,
　　If we knew but to begin;
If we knew but how to profit
10　　By wisdom dearly bought:
'Twas only a passing thought, my love,
　　Only a passing thought.

Questions

1. Is the "passing thought" original or clear enough to warrant the refrain of lines 1–2 and lines 11–12?
2. Is the "passing thought" buried in all the language used to introduce it?
3. Are there any redundant expressions in the poem? Does a thought pass anywhere but "o'er my mind"?
4. Do you find any padding in the poem? Is line 5 necessary to the poem?
5. Is it clear what we are to "begin" in line 9?
6. How would you evaluate this poem?

Coherence and Consistency

Another test of a poem is whether it is consistent. Careless poets make one statement at the outset and contradict themselves later on. More often, poets may express incompatible attitudes, seeming to approve and disapprove of the same object or person.

But before we accuse a poet of being contradictory, we must be careful. Often, a poet is tracing the evolution of feelings. Matthew Arnold's "Dover Beach," for instance, begins with a quiet, beautiful description of the English Channel but ends with the recognition that the world "Hath really neither joy, nor love, nor light, / Nor certitude, nor peace." The inconsistency is not a poetic fault; rather, it is the most direct and effective means of showing Arnold's evolving realizations. (For a longer discussion of "Dover Beach," see Chapter 6.) The contradictions in the following poem, however, cannot be justified in the same manner.

CHARLES KINGSLEY (1819–1875)

I Once Had a Sweet Little Doll, Dears

I once had a sweet little doll, dears,
    The prettiest doll in the world;
Her cheeks were so red and so white, dears,
    And her hair was so charmingly curled.
5 But I lost my poor little doll, dears,
    As I played in the heath one day;
And I cried for her more than a week, dears,
    But I never could find where she lay.

I found my poor little doll, dears,
10   As I played in the heath one day.
Folks say she is terribly changed, dears,
    For her paint is all washed away,
And her arm trodden off by the cows, dears,
    And her hair not the least bit curled:
15 Yet for old sakes' sake she is still, dears,
    The prettiest doll in the world.

Questions

1. Vocabulary: *heath* (10), *trodden* (13).
2. Is there any redundancy?
3. Are the repeated lines effective in creating unity, or are they merely repetitious?
4. Do you find that the "dears" that end alternate lines are well integrated in the poem? Do they add to the poem's overall effectiveness?
5. Do you believe that the doll is the prettiest one in the world?

This poem contains one glaring contradiction. In line 8 the speaker claims she *never* could find the doll; line 9 says that she found it. Are we to believe that the two stanzas are divided by time? If so, there is nothing to indicate that stanza 1 was written while the doll was still lost and stanza 2 after its recovery. This contradiction may not be enough to spoil this poem, but it is certainly a blemish.

A more difficult aesthetic problem than consistency is *coherence*. Because poetry is so condensed, often a poem will remain unclear after a first, second, or even third reading. Moreover, as discussed in Chapter 14, some poems are intentionally nonsensical or are organized as verbal collages. These poems do not yield their meanings in a conventional way. Third, there are poems whose worlds are drawn from dreams and fantasies. Things occur in them that could not happen in the normal world. Wise readers do not blame a poem for not doing what it never intended to do or for lacking what it never was meant to possess; they do not have rigid expectations of what a poem ought to be. Poems do not need to rhyme, but there are still people who consider a poem defective that doesn't. Conversely, there are those who regard with suspicion a poem that *does* rhyme. A good reader must decide whether a work is coherent within its own rules of composition.

Erasmus Darwin, the author of "Eliza," was a physician, inventor, and poet, and the grandfather of Charles Darwin, whose theory of evolution so revolutionized scientific thinking. "Eliza" is no fantasy; it is meant to be a somewhat romanticized and stylized account of an actual woman killed while impatiently watching for her husband's safety in battle. It should be noted that in the eighteenth century wives would follow their husbands to campsites close to the battlefields.

ERASMUS DARWIN (1731–1802)

Eliza

Now stood Eliza on the wood-crown'd height
O'er Minden's plains spectatress of the fight;
Sought with bold eye amid the bloody strife
Her dearer self, the partner of her life;
5   From hill to hill the rushing host pursued,
And view'd his banner, or believed she view'd.
Pleased with the distant roar, with quicker tread,
Fast by his hand one lisping boy she led;
And one fair girl, amid the loud alarm,
10   Slept on her kerchief, cradled on her arm:
While round her brows bright beams of honour dart,
And love's warm eddies circle round her heart.
—Near and more near th'intrepid beauty press'd,
Saw through the driving smoke his dancing crest,
15   Heard the exulting shout—"They run!—they run!"
"He's safe!" she cried, "he's safe! the battle's won!"
—A ball now hisses through the airy tides
(Some Fury wings it, and some Demon guides),
Parts the fine locks her graceful head that deck,

20   Wounds her fair ear, and sinks into her neck;
      The red stream issuing from her azure veins
      Dyes her white veil, her ivory bosom stains.
      —"Ah me!" she cried, and sinking on the ground,
      Kiss'd her dear babes, regardless of the wound:
25   "Oh, cease not yet to beat, thou vital urn,
      Wait, gushing life, oh! wait my love's return!"—
      Hoarse barks the wolf, the vulture screams from far,
      The angel, Pity, shuns the walks of war;—
      "Oh spare, ye war-hounds, spare their tender age!
30   On me, on me," she cried, "exhaust your rage!"
      Then with weak arms, her weeping babes caress'd,
      And sighing, hid them in her blood-stain'd vest.

        From tent to tent th'impatient warrior flies,
      Fear in his heart, and frenzy in his eyes:
35   Eliza's name along the camp he calls,
      Eliza echoes through the canvas walls;
      Quick through the murmuring gloom his footsteps tread,
      O'er groaning heaps, the dying and the dead,
      Vault o'er the plain,—and in the tangled wood,—
40   Lo! dead Eliza—weltering in her blood!
      Soon hears his listening son the welcome sounds,
      With open arms and sparkling eyes he bounds:
      "Speak low," he cries, and gives his little hand,
      "Mamma's asleep upon the dew-cold sand;
45   Alas! we both with cold and hunger quake—
      Why do you weep? Mamma will soon awake."
      —"She'll wake no more!" the hopeless mourner cried,
      Upturn'd his eyes, and clasp'd his hands, and sigh'd;
      Stretch'd on the ground, awhile entranced he lay,
50   And press'd warm kisses on the lifeless clay:
      And then upsprung with wild convulsive start,
      And all the father kindled in his heart:
      "Oh Heaven!" he cried, "my first rash vow forgive!
      These bind to earth, for these I pray to live."
55   Round his chill babes he wrapp'd his crimson vest,
      And clasp'd them sobbing, to his aching breast.

Questions

1. Vocabulary: *spectatress* (2), *eddies* (12), *intrepid* (13), *convulsive* (51).
2. Does it seem reasonable or possible that a bullet could part her hair, wound her ear, and sink into her neck? From what direction would such a bullet have to come? Does this seem probable since Eliza is in a "tangled wood"?
3. How far away is Eliza from the battlefield? She is close enough to see "through the driving smoke [her husband's] dancing crest"—how is she then in a "tangled wood"?
4. What is the "first rash vow" mentioned in line 53?
5. Who does the listening in line 41? Who does the bounding in line 42?

6. Is it consistent for the son to cry for his father to "Speak low"?
7. Is it logical that a mother anxious for her husband's safety would risk the lives of her children by taking them to a battle?
8. Is the language economical? Do you find any redundancy, padding, or ambiguous pronouns?
9. How would you evaluate this poem overall?

Naturalness

Poetry does not merely transcribe the speech of ordinary people. The language of poetry is shaped, altered, concentrated, and often heightened. Yet the language of a poem should usually be natural—that is, obey the laws of common word order and diction, and avoid rhythms and sounds that are difficult or ugly to pronounce. Of course, poets often create odd or unnatural effects in their poetry for specific expressive purposes. Each case of unnatural language must be judged on its own merits. One must determine whether a passage is justified by expressive power, economy, or variety, or whether it is merely the result of incompetence, haste, or insensitivity.

The following is one of Shakespeare's sonnets. Notice that the opening quatrain is in very plain, natural English. The word order is simple and ordinary. Indeed, the tone of the opening is blunt.

WILLIAM SHAKESPEARE (1564–1616)

My Mistress' Eyes Are Nothing like the Sun

My Mistress' eyes are nothing like the Sun,
Coral is far more red, than her lips red,
If snow be white, why then her breasts are dun:
If hairs be wires, black wires grow on her head:
5   I have seen Roses damasked, red and white,
But no such Roses see I in her cheeks,
And in some perfumes is there more delight,
Then in the breath that from my Mistress reeks.
I love to hear her speak; yet well I know,
10   That Music hath a far more pleasing sound:
I grant I never saw a goddess go,
My Mistress when she walks treads on the ground.
    And yet by heaven I think my love as rare,
    As any she belied with false compare.

Questions

1. Vocabulary: *damasked* (5), *belied* (14).
2. Besides "reeks," are there any other comic words used for rhymes?
3. Shakespeare calls the woman "my love"; yet he lists her defects. Does he resolve this contradiction? Is the poem contradictory?
4. Are any lines padded for rhythm?

5. Is there any redundancy, vague pronoun usage, or verbal looseness?
6. How would you evaluate the poem overall?

Despite the straightforward opening, lines 5 and 6 are in a slightly unusual order. Normally one would say, "I have seen Roses damasked, red and white,/But I see no such Roses in her cheeks." Shakespeare did not order this line for the sake of rhyme or meter, since the more natural line both rhymes and scans. Why, then, did Shakespeare order the words as he did?

First we must recognize that the line is a *chiasmus*, which means "crossing." In a chiasmus the word order of one phrase or clause is inverted in the next. For example, Samuel Johnson wrote, "For we that live to please, must please to live." We can see how these terms cross in this diagram.

We that live to please

must please to live

In Shakespeare's line there is a similar crossing or chiasmus.

I have seen Roses . . .

But no such Roses see I . . .

The chiasmus is an elegant but not too unusual variation that gives art to the poem. More important, it shows that the speaker is not being crude in the opening lines out of ignorance. Clearly, he can construct a line with elegance. He is blunt because he wishes to be brutally honest.

Lines 7 and 8 are also unusually ordered. One normally would say, "The breath that reeks from my mistress is not as delightful as some perfumes." However, such a sentence loses all the humor. "Reeks" is the harshest, most insulting word in the poem. Shakespeare wishes to delay it and emphasize it by locating it not only at the end of the line but also at the conclusion of the quatrain.

We now see that whenever Shakespeare deviates from normal word order in this poem, he does so deliberately, for expressive purposes. Moreover, none of these lines is so oddly ordered that it becomes incomprehensible.

The following poem is filled with lines having odd or unnatural word order. Locate each unusual line and try to reword it in a more standard manner. Compare your version with Empson's. Examine what has been lost and gained in the process. See whether Empson's word order is justifiable or unskilled. Are any of the rhymes forced?

WILLIAM EMPSON (1906–)

Villanelle

It is the pain, it is the pain, endures.
Your chemic beauty burned my muscles through.
Poise of my hands reminded me of yours.

What later purge from this deep toxin cures?
5   What kindness now could the old salve renew?
It is the pain, it is the pain, endures.

The infection slept (custom or change inures)
And when pain's secondary phase was due
Poise of my hands reminded me of yours.

10   How safe I felt, whom memory assures,
Rich that your grace safely by heart I knew.
It is the pain, it is the pain, endures.

My stare drank deep beauty that still allures.
My heart pumps yet the poison draught of you.
15   Poise of my hands reminded me of yours.

You are still kind whom the same shape immures.
Kind and beyond adieu. We miss our cue.
It is the pain, it is the pain, endures.
Poise of my hands reminded me of yours.

Questions

1. Vocabulary: *chemic* (2), *inures* (7).
2. Are any of the words difficult to pronounce? Are any of the sounds ineffective or ugly?
3. Are the repeated lines well integrated into the poem, or do they become mechanical and repetitious?
4. Is there any padding for rhythm?
5. Is the poem always comprehensible? If there are muddy places, is there an expressive justification for the muddiness?
6. Are there any ambiguous pronouns?
7. From what branch of knowledge is most of the language drawn? Is the theatrical term "cue" in line 17 out of place?
8. What is your overall evaluation of the poem?

Rhyme is not the only cause of forced, odd, or inexpressive word order. Metrical regularity can produce ineffective or simply bad uses of language. The following is a wholly commonplace observation about the industrious and muscular ant. But the passage is laughable because of its terrible sense of rhythm and awkward word order.

CORNELIUS WHUR (1782–1853)

From Village Musings

The poet questions the ant

Why did you, feeble as you were, attempt
A task so perfectly herculean?
Could it be to rear your tender offspring?

Did your concern touching their welfare
5   So impel? Was aught like conference held
Ere you began to calculate success? . . .
                         Man, physically
Your superior, could not with equal tools
The work have done. He, comparatively,
10   Might as soon this ponderous earth divide.

Questions

1. Vocabulary: *herculean* (2), *ponderous* (10).
2. Which lines are awkwardly ordered? Is there any expressive justification for the order?
3. What is the meaning of "comparatively" in line 9? Is this a standard use of the word?
4. Is there any padding, redundancy, or looseness of language?
5. What is your overall estimation of the passage?

Tone: Sentimentality and Coldness

Poetry, as we have said, is the language of emotion. A good poem effectively conveys emotion to the reader. Readers do not merely understand the emotion the poet wishes to convey, but feel the emotion themselves. A good elegy, for example, does not merely tell us about grief, but puts us through the process of grieving. Readers who set themselves against a poem will never be able to experience it; thus a poem is a partnership between the skilled writer and the responsive reader. As Walt Whitman said, in order to have great poetry there must be great audiences.

We should not, however, judge a poem simply by the intensity with which it conveys emotion. Of greater importance are subtlety, honesty, and depth of feeling. As any seasoned moviegoer knows, horror and suspense are more easily and intensely conveyed than is the confusion of grief or the disenchantment of youth. We may be thrilled as the latest monster destroys downtown Tokyo, but we are often more profoundly touched by some less spectacular event.

Most readers have a sense of what is an appropriate response to a situation and will reject a feeling that seems unsuitable. Most readers will sympathize with a poet who expresses annoyance at ruining a new coat. They will empathize with a poet depressed over having ruined a car. They will be moved by a poet desperate over the loss of a loved one. But readers will be amused or disgusted by the poet wailing over a ruined coat. "What a crybaby," they will complain— and rightly. Such emotional overreaction is called *sentimentality*. Sentimentality occurs when a poet attempts to bestow on an experience more emotion than it can reasonably sustain.

Sentimentality is any excessive emotion, but it usually takes the form of excessive tenderness. A good test of sentimentality is whether the poem accurately depicts the object or experience. Sentimental people are usually blind to the true nature of their love object. They see the world through "rose-colored glasses."

For example, we may cling to objects long after their usefulness, beauty, and worth are exhausted. The following poem is an example of such a sentimental attachment.

ELIZA COOK (1818–1889)

The Old Arm Chair

I love it! I love it! And who shall dare
To chide me for loving that old arm-chair?
I've treasured it long as a sainted prize;
I've bedewed it with tears, and embalmed it with sighs.
5   'Tis bound by a thousand bands to my heart;
Not a tie will break, not a link will start.
Would ye learn the spell?—a mother sat there;
And a sacred thing is that old arm-chair.

In childhood's hour I lingered near
10   The hallowed seat with list'ning ear;
And gentle words that mother would give,
To fit me to die, and teach me to live.
She told me shame would never betide
With truth for my creed, and God for my guide;
15   She taught me to lisp my earliest prayer,
As I knelt beside that old arm-chair.

I sat and watched her many a day,
When her eyes grew dim, and her locks were grey;
And I almost worshipped her when she smiled,
20   And turned from her Bible to bless her child.
Years rolled on; but the last one sped—
My idol was shattered; my earth-star fled.
I learnt how much the heart can bear,
When I saw her die in that old arm-chair.

25   'Tis past! 'tis past! But I gaze on it now
With quivering breath and sobbing brow:
'Twas there she nursed me; 'twas there she died:
And memory flows with lava tide.
Say it is folly, and deem me weak,
30   While the scalding drops start down my cheek;
But I love it! I love it! and cannot tear
My soul from a mother's old arm-chair.

Questions

1. Do we ever get to see the armchair? What does it look like? Is it in good condition?
2. Does the speaker really value the armchair for itself? Why is it valuable?
3. In what sense is the poem an example of metonymy?

4. Cook calls the chair "a sainted prize," "a sacred thing," and a "hallowed seat." Is this sort of idolatry suitable to an old armchair? Is it consistent with the religious sentiments she was supposed to have learned?
5. The speaker says she "embalmed" the chair with sighs. Does the word convey the emotion she wishes to convey? She also says her "memory flows with lava tide." Is the violence and destructiveness of lava an appropriate image here? Does it convey the feelings Cook wishes to convey? Do you see any other inappropriate expressions?
6. Does the situation warrant the hyperbole Cook employs?
7. What do we usually mean by a "shattered" idol? How does Cook use the idea in line 22? Is it appropriate?
8. How would you evaluate this poem overall?

Some people believe that certain situations are inherently sentimental. Although it is true that some situations lend themselves to sentimental treatment, a good poet can render a potentially sentimental situation with depth, perception, and toughness. The two poems that follow portray poor old women who have fallen on hard times. The subject lends itself to a sentimental treatment, but it can also be handled with conviction.

THOMAS ASHE (1836–1889)

Old Jane

I love old women best, I think:
    She knows a friend in me,—
Old Jane, who totters on the brink
    Of God's Eternity;
5   Whose limbs are stiff, whose cheek is lean,
    Whose eyes look up, afraid;
Though you may gather she has been
    A little laughing maid.

Once had she with her doll what times,
10   And with her skipping-rope!
Her head was full of lovers' rhymes,
    Once, and her heart of hope;
Who, now, with eyes as sad as sweet—
    I love to look on her,—
15   At corner of the gusty street,
    Asks, "Buy a pencil, Sir?"

Her smile is as the litten West,
    Nigh-while the sun is gone;
She is more fain to be at rest
20   Than here to linger on:
Beneath her lids the pictures flit
    Of memories far-away:
Her look has not a hint in it
    Of what she sees to-day.

Questions

1. Vocabulary: *litten* (17).
2. Are there any phrases or sentences whose meaning is obscure?
3. Do the last two lines contradict anything in the poem? Is there really no hint of old Jane's present condition?
4. Are any lines forced? Do the rhymes come naturally? Whose eyes are "as sad as sweet"?
5. Does Ashe provide any clues to how old Jane came to sell pencils on street corners? Do the memories of her past seem an accurate picture of the complexities of youth? Has Jane always been poor? Has she slipped from a better economic condition?
6. Is it reasonable to think that Jane thinks only about dolls, jump rope, and lovers' rhymes?
7. What is Ashe's attitude toward Jane? Can one reasonably share his attitude given the facts he has supplied?
8. Is this poem sentimental? Why?

ROBERT FROST (1874–1963)

Provide, Provide

The witch that came (the withered hag)
To wash the steps with pail and rag,
Was once the beauty Abishag,[1]

The picture pride of Hollywood.
5   Too many fall from great and good
For you to doubt the likelihood.

Die early and avoid the fate.
Or if predestined to die late,
Make up your mind to die in state.

10   Make the whole stock exchange your own!
If need be occupy a throne,
Where nobody can call *you* crone.

Some have relied on what they knew;
Others on being simply true.
15   What worked for them might work for you.

No memory of having starred
Atones for later disregard
Or keeps the end from being hard.

Better to go down dignified
20   With boughten friendship at your side.
Than none at all. Provide, provide!

---

[1] Abishag was a beautiful young woman who nursed King David in his old age.

Questions

1. Vocabulary: *atones* (17).
2. Do you understand the meaning of each phrase? Does the poem contain any contradictions? Is there any padding or redundancy? If so, is there any reason for it?
3. Do the lines seem forced? Are the rhymes natural? If any seem comic, is that intended or the result of artistic miscalculation?
4. Does Frost provide enough background on the scrubwoman to make her seem realistic? Is all the information good?
5. What is Frost's attitude toward the old woman? Can you reasonably share his attitude?
6. Is this poem sentimental?

Exercise

The foregoing two poems develop their subject in very different ways. One tries to be coldhearted; the other is extremely sentimental. The three poems that follow all take as their subject women who are struggling to survive. Try to place them on the scale between indifference and sentimentality. Then try to determine which poems are successful and which are less finely crafted.

WILLIAM BUTLER YEATS (1865–1939)

• Crazy Jane Talks with the Bishop

I met the Bishop on the road
And much said he and I.
"Those breasts are flat and fallen now,
Those veins must soon be dry;
5   Live in a heavenly mansion,
Not in some foul sty."

"Fair and foul are near of kin,
And fair needs foul," I cried.
"My friends are gone, but that's a truth
10   Nor grave nor bed denied,
Learned in bodily lowliness
And in the heart's pride.

"A woman can be proud and stiff
When on love intent;
15   But Love has pitched his mansion in
The place of excrement;
For nothing can be sole or whole
That has not been rent."

PATRICK KAVANAGH (1904–1967)

Tinker's Wife

I saw her amid the dunghill debris
Looking for things

Such as an old pair of shoes or gaiters.
She was a young woman,
5   A tinker's wife.
Her face had streaks of care
Like wires across it,
But she was supple
As a young goat
10   On a windy hill.
She searched on the dunghill debris,
Tripping gingerly
Over tin canisters
And sharp-broken
15   Dinner plates.

GREGORY CORSO (1930–)

The Vestal Lady on Brattle

Within a delicate grey ruin
the vestal lady on Brattle°   *street in Cambridge, Mass.*
is up at dawn, as is her custom,
with the raise of a shade.

5   Swan-boned slippers revamp her aging feet;
she glides within an outer room . . .
pours old milk for an old cat.

Full-bodied and randomly young she clings,
peers down; hovers over a wine-filled vat,
10   and with outstretched arms like wings,
revels in the forming image of child below.

Despaired, she ripples a sunless finger
across the liquid eyes; in darkness
the child spirals down; drowns.
15   Pain leans her forward—face absorbing all—
mouth upon broken mouth, she drinks . . .

Within a delicate grey ruin
the vestal lady on Brattle
is up and about, as is her custom,
20   drunk with child.

Sentimentality is a form of emotional exaggeration. In the best poems each element is in proportion to the others. Thus sentimentality can distort a poem that is in other respects well made. In judging a poem, one should examine each element of the poem to see how and why it is functioning. Only then can one decide whether each element best serves the poem as a whole or whether it is a defect in the poem's overall design.

Coldness is a problem closely related to sentimentality. Instead of overreacting emotionally, a poet may underreact. This coldness often appears in official or public poetry. Poets may be asked to write for a specific occasion that may not engage them emotionally. Or, sometimes, poets will moralize on a public event that they have failed to grasp emotionally. In the following poem Robert Service used the occasion of Dylan Thomas's death from alcoholism to moralize about the evils of drink. Dylan Thomas was a poet, and several of his poems are included in this book. Service seems less moved by the human and poetic loss of Thomas than by the opportunity to sermonize.

ROBERT SERVICE (1876–1958)

Dylan

And is it not a gesture grand
  To drink oneself to death?
Oh sure 'tis I can understand,
  Being of sober breath.
5 And so I do not sing success,
  But dirge the damned who fall,
And who contempt for life express
    Through alcohol.

Of Stephen Foster and of Poe,
10   Of Burns and Wilde[2] I think;
And weary men who dared to go
  The wanton way of drink.
Strange mortals blind to bitter blame,
  And deaf to loud delight,
15 Who from the shades of sin and shame
    Enstar our night.

Among those dupes of destiny
  Add D.T.[3] to my list,
Although his verse you may agree
20   Leaves one in mental mist . . .
Oh ye mad poets, loth of life,
  Who peace in death divine,
Pass not by pistol, poison, knife,—
  Drown, drown in wine!

Questions

1. Vocabulary: *dirge* (6), *wanton* (12), *dupes* (17).

---

[2] Stephen Foster, Edgar Allan Poe, Robert Burns, and Oscar Wilde are all noted for alcoholic tendencies.
[3] The Welsh poet Dylan Thomas (1914–1953).

2. Service may have shortened the last line to suggest the way Thomas's life had been unnaturally shortened. However, does this feeling come across? Do the rhythm and sound of line 8 suggest the seriousness of the subject?
3. "D.T." in line 18 refers to Dylan Thomas but also suggests *delirium tremens*, commonly known as the D.T.'s, the horrifying hallucinations of alcoholics. Is such a pun appropriate in a serious elegy?
4. Is "although" in line 19 the proper connective? Is "sober breath" (line 4) a logical or natural expression? Does it mean anything other than sober?
5. What is the tone of lines 21–24? Is it consistent with the rest of the poem?
6. Do you sense that Service is deeply saddened by Thomas's death? Is he more concerned about Thomas or about the evils of alcohol?

The following is a poem that Dr. Sprat, bishop of Rochester, wrote on the death of a lady friend. Although he expresses the extremes of grief, try to determine, as you are reading, how sincere those expressions are.

THOMAS SPRAT (1635–1713)

On His Mistress Drowned

Sweet stream, that dost with equal pace
Both thyself fly, and thyself chase,
  Forbear awhile to flow,
  And listen to my woe.
5 Then go, and tell the sea that all its brine
    Is fresh, compar'd to mine;
Inform it that the gentle dame,
Who was the life of all my flame,
  In th' glory of her bud
10 Has pass'd the fatal flood.

Death by this only stroke triumphs above
    The greatest power of love:
  Alas, alas! I must give o'er,
  My sighs will let me add no more.

15 Go on, sweet stream, and henceforth rest
  No more than does my troubled breast;
And if my sad complaints have made thee stay,
  These tears, these tears shall mend thy way.

Questions

1. Does the speaker want the stream to flow? Is there any contradiction in his attitude?
2. What evidence does the speaker give that "the gentle dame . . . was the life of all [his] flame"?
3. Does he give you a picture of the woman? Was she young, old, rich, poor, well educated, innocent, a relative?

4. How has death triumphed over love in lines 11–12? Do we know? Did the speaker do anything to save his mistress?

Sentimentality may be laughable, but such cold-bloodedness seems far more offensive.

Completeness

Like any organism, a poem must be complete in order for it to function at maximum effectiveness. We must come to understand what motivates speakers to talk as they do, and what is the significance of their words. Without this knowledge, the poem will seem incomplete. The poet is not obliged to tell us everything; some details are insignificant, and readers should be prepared to make important inferences on their own. If essentials are left out, however, readers will be unable to respond emotionally or intellectually to the poem.

In the following poem the author has failed to give important information that would help us empathize with the speaker's plight. The general outlines are clear, however. A parent—we do not know whether it is a mother or father—grieves over the death of a child—we cannot tell whether it is a son or daughter. The child had apparently been a good one, who had not wished to worry the parent. Yet it is difficult to understand the speaker's guilt and self-mockery. When the speaker says, "It is not true that Love will do no wrong," he or she is apparently referring to some bad act mistakenly committed out of love. But what is the action? Who perpetrated it? Did this action lead to the child's death? We do not and can never know; and without this knowledge, we readers will remain distanced from the speaker and cut off from the poem's potential power.

COVENTRY PATMORE (1823–1896)

If I Were Dead

"If I were dead, you'd sometimes say, Poor Child!"
The dear lips quiver'd as they spake,
And the tears brake
From eyes which, not to grieve me, brightly smiled.
5   Poor Child, poor Child!
I seem to hear your laugh, your talk, your song.
It is not true that Love will do no wrong.
Poor Child!
And did you think, when you so cried and smiled,
10   How I, in lonely nights, should lie awake,
And of those words your full avengers make?
Poor Child, poor Child!
And now unless it be
That sweet amends thrice told are come to thee,
15   O God, have Thou *no* mercy upon me!
Poor Child!

Questions

1. Is it clear why the child says, "If I were dead, you'd sometimes say, Poor Child!"? What did the child mean? Was the child angry, frightened, spiteful, or tender in saying this line?
2. How old is the child? Of what does the child die?
3. What evidence is there in the poem that God has shown the speaker "*no* mercy"?
4. Does the rhyme contribute to the overall effectiveness of the poem?
5. Is the poem sentimental?
6. Is the language natural? Are there any ambiguities without purpose?
7. How would you rate this poem?

The purpose of criticism is to increase a reader's awareness of excellence and the variety of his or her responses to literature. Mature critical judgments are never simple or clear. As we have seen, they are based on a number of different criteria whose relative importance must constantly be reevaluated. Good critics understand the limitations of their views and are prepared to consider alternatives, to reexamine their judgments, to be more open and varied. W. H. Auden, the great poet and critic, once wrote:

> As readers, we remain in the nursery stage so long as we cannot distinguish between taste and judgments, so long, that is, as the only possible verdicts we can pass on a book are two: this I like; this I don't like.
>
> For an adult reader, the possible verdicts are five: I can see this is good and I like it; I can see this is good but I don't like it; I can see this is good and, though at present I don't like it, I believe that with perseverance I shall come to like it; I can see that this is trash but I like it; I can see that this is trash and I don't like it.

Mature critics, rather than limiting their response to literature, have learned to increase their responses and appreciations.

The Good and the Great

A poem is considered great not because it is better made than other poems but for a variety of other reasons. Usually great poems have greater scope or emotional intensity than other poems. As we all know, some subjects and conditions are more easily articulated than others. Great poems explore the most difficult areas of human experience or express concerns in the subtlest, most original ways.

Poems can also become great for other reasons. Some are considered great because they are the first of their kind; they break new artistic ground. Other works articulate the spirit of their age so clearly and succinctly that they become a touchstone for their time. Byron's *Childe Harold's Pilgrimage* is an example of a poem whose fame may well be greater than its craftsmanship. It was the most widely read work of its time.

Works can also become especially valued because they represent a pivotal period in the artistic output of a great poet. As Shakespeare wrote, "Some are

born great, some achieve greatness, and some have greatness thrust upon them."
Likewise, greatness is something that comes mysteriously to a work. It is a quality
so elusive, so special to each great work, that no criteria can be formulated to
describe how it works. We may be able to analyze why a work is excellent, but
we can do no more than recognize when a work is truly great.

We have chosen six poems that are almost universally regarded as great works.
They come from different periods and nations; there are two by Americans, one
by an Irishman, two by Englishmen, and one by an American who became a
British citizen. These poems are somewhat longer than most of the poems in
the book. Great poems often have wider scope and more ambitious subject
matter. Take your time with them as you would with all the other poems in this
book. These poems continue to pose emotional and intellectual challenges even
to the most sophisticated reader.

JOHN MILTON (1608–1674)

Lycidas

*In this monody[4] the author bewails a learned friend, unfortunately
drowned in his passage from Chester on the Irish seas, 1637. And
by occasion foretells the ruin of our corrupted clergy, then in their
height.*

    Yet once more, O ye laurels, and once more
Yet myrtles brown, with ivy never sere,[5]
I come to pluck your berries harsh and crude,°   *unripe*
And with forced fingers rude,
5 Shatter your leaves before the mellowing year.
Bitter constraint, and sad occasion dear,
Compels me to disturb your season due;
For Lycidas is dead, dead ere his prime,
Young Lycidas, and hath not left his peer.
10 Who would not sing for Lycidas? He knew
Himself to sing, and build the lofty rhyme.
He must not float upon his watery bier
Unwept, and welter to the parching wind,
Without the meed° of some melodious tear.   *reward*
15   Begin then, sisters of the sacred well[6]
That from beneath the seat of Jove doth spring,
Begin, and somewhat loudly sweep the string.
Hence with denial vain, and coy excuse;
So may some gentle Muse
20 With lucky words favor my destined urn,

---

[4] A solo song in Greek drama.
[5] Laurel, myrtle, and ivy are plants associated with poetic inspiration. Laurel is given by Apollo,
the god of poetry; myrtle by Venus, the goddess of love; and ivy is associated with Bacchus, the
god of wine.
[6] The muses inspire the arts.

And as he passes turn,
And bid fair peace be to my sable shroud.
For we were nursed upon the selfsame hill,
Fed the same flock, by fountain, shade, and rill.
25   Together both, ere the high lawns appeared
Under the opening eyelids of the morn,
We drove afield, and both together heard
What time the grayfly winds her sultry horn.[7]
Battening° our flocks with the fresh dews of night,   *feeding*
30   Oft till the star that rose at evening bright
Toward Heaven's descent had sloped his westering wheel.
Meanwhile the rural ditties were not mute,
Tempered to th' oaten flute,
Rough satyrs danced, and fauns with cloven heel
35   From the glad sound would not be absent long,
And old Damoetas[8] loved to hear our song.
       But O the heavy change, now thou art gone,
Now thou art gone, and never must return!
Thee, shepherd, thee the woods and desert caves,
40   With wild thyme and the gadding° vine o'ergrown,   *straggling*
And all their echoes mourn.
The willows and the hazel copses green
Shall now no more be seen,
Fanning their joyous leaves to thy soft lays.
45   As killing as the canker° to the rose,   *cankerworm*
Or taint-worm to the weanling° herds that graze,   *newly weaned*
Or frost to flowers that their gay wardrobe wear,
When first the white thorn blows,°   *blossoms*
Such, Lycidas, thy loss to shepherd's ear.
50   Where were ye, nymphs, when the remorseless deep
Closed o'er the head of your loved Lycidas?
For neither were ye playing on the steep,
Where your old Bards, the famous Druids[9] lie,
Nor on the shaggy top of Mona high,
55   Nor yet where Deva spreads her wizard stream:[10]
Ay me! I fondly° dream—   *foolishly*
Had ye been there—for what could that have done?
What could the Muse herself that Orpheus bore,
The Muse herself, for her inchanting[11] son
60   Whom universal Nature did lament,
When by the rout° that made the hideous roar,   *mob*
His gory visage down the stream was sent,

---

[7] That is, buzzes.
[8] A typical shepherd's name.
[9] Druids were the ancient priestly poets of Britain.
[10] "Mona" is the island of Anglesey, a center of Druid activity. "Deva" is the river Dee in Cheshire.
[11] Orpheus, the great poet-singer of Greek mythology, was torn to pieces by Thracian women, who
    threw his head into the river Hebrus.

Down the swift Hebrus to the Lesbian shore?
Alas! What boots° it with incessant care   *profits*
65 To tend the homely slighted shepherd's trade,
And strictly meditate the thankless Muse?
Were it not better done as others use,
To sport with Amaryllis in the shade,
Or with the tangles of Neaera's hair?¹²
70 Fame is the spur that the clear spirit doth raise
(That last infirmity of noble mind)
To scorn delights, and live laborious days;
But the fair guerdon° when we hope to find,   *reward*
And think to burst out into sudden blaze,
75 Comes the blind Fury with th' abhorréd shears,¹³
And slits the thin spun life. "But not the praise,"
Phoebus¹⁴ replied, and touched my trembling ears;
"Fame is no plant that grows on mortal soil,
Not in the glistering foil¹⁵
80 Set off to th' world, nor in broad rumor lies,
But lives and spreads aloft by those pure eyes,
And perfect witness of all-judging Jove;
As he pronounces lastly on each deed,
Of so much fame in Heaven expect thy meed."
85   O fountain Arethuse, and thou honored flood,
Smooth-sliding Mincius, crowned with vocal reeds,¹⁶
That strain I heard was of a higher mood.
But now my oat° proceeds,   *flute song*
And listens to the herald of the sea
90 That came in Neptune's¹⁷ plea.
He asked the waves, and asked the felon° winds,   *whipping*
"What hard mishap hath doomed this gentle swain?"
And questioned every gust of rugged wings
That blows from off each beakéd promontory;
95 They knew not of his story,
And sage Hippotades¹⁸ their answer brings,
That not a blast was from his dungeon strayed,
The air was calm, and on the level brine,
Sleek Panope¹⁹ with all her sisters played.
100 It was that fatal and perfidious bark
Built in th' eclipse, and rigged with curses dark,
That sunk so low that sacred head of thine.

---

¹² Amaryllis and Neaera were typical names for nymphs.
¹³ A fury is an avenging spirit.
¹⁴ Phoebus Apollo, the god of poetic inspiration.
¹⁵ A glistering foil was a thin metal backing used to give sparkle to glass gems.
¹⁶ Arethusa was a fountain in Sicily; Mincius, a river in Lombardy.
¹⁷ Neptune is the Roman god of the sea.
¹⁸ Hippotades is the god of winds.
¹⁹ The most important sea nymph, or nereid.

Next Camus,[20] reverend sire, went footing slow,
His mantle hairy, and his bonnet sedge,
105 Inwrought with figures dim, and on the edge
Like to that sanguine flower° inscribed with woe.   *hyacinth*
"Ah! who hath reft," quoth he, "my dearest pledge?"
Last came and last did go
The pilot of the Galilean lake,°   *St. Peter*
110 Two massy keys he bore of metals twain
(The golden opes, the iron shuts amain).
He shook his mitered locks, and stern bespake:
"How well could I have spared for thee, young swain,
Enow° of such as for their bellie's sake,   *enough*
115 Creep and intrude, and climb into the fold!
Of other care they little reckoning make,
Than how to scramble at the shearers' feast,
And shove away the worthy bidden guest.
Blind mouths! That scarce themselves know how to hold
120 A sheep-hook, or have learned aught else the least
That to the faithful herdsman's art belongs!
What recks it° them? What need they? They are sped;   *does it matter to*
And when they list,° their lean and flashy songs   *choose*
Grate on their scrannel° pipes of wretched straw.   *harsh, meager*
125 The hungry sheep look up, and are not fed,
But swoln with wind, and the rank mist they draw,
Rot inwardly, and foul contagion spread,
Besides what the grim wolf with privy paw
Daily devours apace, and nothing said.
130 But that two-handed engine at the door
Stands ready to smite once, and smite no more."
Return, Alpheus, the dread voice is past,
That shrunk thy streams; return, Sicilian muse,
And call the vales, and bid them hither cast
135 Their bells and flowerets of a thousand hues.
Ye valleys low where the mild whispers use,
Of shades and wanton winds, and gushing brooks,
On whose fresh lap the swart star[21] sparely looks,
Throw hither all your quaint enameled° eyes,   *adorned*
140 That on the green turf suck the honeyed showers,
And purple all the ground with vernal flowers.
Bring the rathe° primrose that foresaken dies.   *early*
The tufted crow-toe, and pale jessamine,
The white pink, and the pansy freaked° with jet,   *flecked*
145 The glowing violet,
The musk-rose, and the well attired woodbine.
With cowslips wan that hang the pensive head,
And every flower that sad embroidery wears:

---

[20] The god of the river Cam.
[21] The Dog Star, Sirius.

Bid amaranthus[22] all his beauty shed,

150 And daffadillies fill their cups with tears,
To strew the laureate hearse where Lycid lies.
For so to interpose a little ease,
Let our frail thoughts dally with false surmise.
Ay me! Whilst thee the shores and sounding seas

155 Wash far away, where'er thy bones are hurled,
Whether beyond the stormy Hebrides,[23]
Where thou perhaps under the whelming tide
Visit'st the bottom of the monstrous world;
Or whether thou, to our moist vows denied,

160 Sleep'st by the fable of Bellerus old,[24]
Where the great vision of the guarded mount
Looks toward Namancos and Bayona's hold;[25]
Look homeward angel now, and melt with ruth:°   *grief and pity*
And, O ye dolphins, waft the hapless youth.

165   Weep no more, woeful shepherds, weep no more,
For Lycidas your sorrow is not dead,
Sunk though he be beneath the watery floor,
So sinks the day-star in the ocean bed,
And yet anon repairs his drooping head,

170 And tricks° his beams, and with new-spangled ore,   *dresses, adorns*
Flames in the forehead of the morning sky:
So Lycidas sunk low, but mounted high,
Through the dear might of him that walked the waves,
Where other groves, and other streams along,

175 With nectar pure his oozy locks he laves,
And hears the unexpressive nuptial song,
In the blest kingdoms meek of joy and love.
There entertain him all the saints above,
In solemn troops and sweet societies

180 That sing, and singing in their glory move,
And wipe the tears forever from his eyes.
Now, Lycidas, the shepherds weep no more;
Henceforth thou art the genius of the shore,
In thy large recompense, and shalt be good

185 To all that wander in that perilous flood.
    Thus sang the uncouth swain to th' oaks and rills,
While the still morn went out with sandals gray;
He touched the tender stops of various quills,
With eager thought warbling his Doric lay:

190 And now the sun had stretched out all the hills,
And now was dropped into the western bay;
At last he rose, and twitched his mantle blue:
Tomorrow to fresh woods, and pastures new.

---

[22] Amaranth is a mythical flower that never fades.
[23] Islands off the coast of Scotland.
[24] A giant who, according to fable, is buried in Cornwall.
[25] Bayona and Namancos are places in northern Spain.

WILLIAM WORDSWORTH (1770–1850)

Ode

Intimations of Immortality from Recollections of Early Childhood

The Child is father of the Man;
And I could wish my days to be
Bound each to each by natural piety.[26]

1

There was a time when meadow, grove, and stream,
The earth, and every common sight,
   To me did seem
   Appareled in celestial light,
5 The glory and the freshness of a dream.
It is not now as it hath been of yore—
   Turn whereso'er I may,
   By night or day,
The things which I have seen I now can see no more.

2

10   The Rainbow comes and goes,
   And lovely is the Rose,
   The Moon doth with delight,
Look round her when the heavens are bare,
   Waters on a starry night
15   Are beautiful and fair;
  The sunshine is a glorious birth;
  But yet I know, where'er I go,
That there hath passed away a glory from the earth.

3

Now, while the birds thus sing a joyous song,
20 And while the young lambs bound
   As the tabor's° sound,   *a small drum*
To me alone there came a thought of grief:
A timely utterance gave that thought relief,
   And I again am strong:
25 The cataracts blow their trumpets from the steep;
No more shall grief of mine the season wrong;
I hear the Echoes through the mountains throng,
The Winds come to me from the fields of sleep,
   And all the earth is gay;
30   Land and sea
  Give themselves up to jollity,
   And with the heart of May
  Doth every Beast keep holiday—
   Thou Child of Joy,
35 Shout round me, let me hear thy shouts, thou happy
   Shepherd-boy!

---

[26] The conclusion of Wordsworth's "My Heart Leaps Up."

4

Ye blessed Creatures, I have heard the call
    Ye to each other make; I see
The heavens laugh with you in your jubilee;
40   My heart is at your festival,
        My head hath its coronal,[27]
The fullness of your bliss, I feel—I feel it all.
      Oh, evil day! if I were sullen
      While Earth herself is adorning,
45   This sweet May morning,
      And the Children are culling°   *gathering*
        On every side,
    In a thousand valleys far and wide,
    Fresh flowers; while the sun shines warm,
50 And the Babe leaps up on his Mother's arm—
      I hear, I hear, with joy I hear!
     —But there's a Tree, of many, one,
A single Field which I have looked upon,
Both of them speak of something that is gone:
55   The Pansy at my feet
        Doth the same tale repeat:
Whither is fled the visionary gleam?
Where is it now, the glory and the dream?

5

Our birth is but a sleep and a forgetting:
60 The Soul that rises with us, our life's Star,
      Hath had elsewhere its setting,
        And cometh from afar:
      Not in entire forgetfulness,
      And not in utter nakedness,
65 But trailing clouds of glory do we come
      From God, who is our home:
Heaven lies about us in our infancy!
Shades of the prison-house begin to close
      Upon the growing Boy
70   But he
Beholds the light, and whence it flows,
      He sees it in his joy;
The Youth, who daily farther from the east
      Must travel, still is Nature's Priest,
75   And by the vision splendid
      Is on his way attended;
At length the Man perceives it die away,
And fade into the light of common day.

6

Earth fills her lap with pleasures of her own;
80 Yearnings she hath in her own natural kind,

---

[27] A coronal is a crown—in this case, it is a crown of flowers.

And, even with something of a Mother's mind,
     And no unworthy aim,
     The homely° Nurse doth all she can   *domestic*
To make her foster child, her Inmate Man,
85   Forget the glories he hath known,
And that imperial palace whence he came.

7

Behold the Child among his newborn blisses,
A six-years' Darling of a pygmy size!
See, where 'mid work of his own hand he lies,
90   Fretted° by sallies of his mother's kisses,   *decorated*
With light upon him from his father's eyes!
See, at his feet, some little plan or chart,
Some fragment from his dream of human life,
Shaped by himself with newly-learned art;
95   A wedding or a festival,
       A mourning or a funeral;
         And this hath now his heart,
         And unto this he frames his song;
          Then will he fit his tongue
100 To dialogues of business, love, or strife;
        But it will not be long
        Ere this be thrown aside,
        And with new joy and pride
The little Actor cons another part;
105 Filling from time to time his "humorous stage"[28]
With all the Persons, down to palsied Age,
That Life brings with her in her equipage;
        As if his whole vocation
        Were endless imitation.

8

110 Thou, whose exterior semblance doth belie
        Thy Soul's immensity;
Thou best Philosopher, who yet dost keep
Thy heritage, thou Eye among the blind,
That, deaf and silent, read'st the eternal deep,
115 Haunted forever by the eternal mind—
        Mighty Prophet! Seer blest!
         On whom those truths do rest,
Which we are toiling all our lives to find,
In darkness lost, the darkness of the grave;
120 Thou, over whom thy Immortality
Broods like the Day, a Master o'er a Slave,
A Presence which is not to be put by;
Thou little Child, yet glorious in the might
Of heaven-born freedom on thy being's height,
125 Why with such earnest pains dost thou provoke

---

[28] Wordsworth is quoting Samuel Daniel, an Elizabethan poet. *Humorous* refers to taking on the roles of various characters.

The years to bring the inevitable yoke,
Thus blindly with thy blessedness at strife?
Full soon thy Soul shall have her earthly freight,
And custom lie upon thee with a weight,
130 Heavy as frost, and deep almost as life!

9

O joy! that in our embers
Is something that doth live,
That nature yet remembers
What was so fugitive!
135 The thought of our past years in me doth breed
Perpetual benediction: not indeed
For that which is most worthy to be blest;
Delight and liberty, the simple creed
Of Childhood, whether busy or at rest,
140 With new-fledged hope still fluttering in his breast—
Not for these I raise
The song of thanks and praise;
But for those obstinate questionings
Of sense and outward things,
145 Fallings from us, vanishings;
Blank misgivings of a Creature
Moving about in worlds not realized,
High instincts before which our mortal Nature
Did tremble like a guilty Thing surprised;
150 But for those first affections,
Those shadowy recollections,
Which, be they what they may,
Are yet the fountain light of all our day,
Are yet a master light of all our seeing;
155 Uphold us, cherish, and have power to make
Our noisy years seem moments in the being
Of the eternal Silence: truths that wake,
To perish never;
Which neither listlessness, nor mad endeavor,
160 Nor Man nor Boy,
Nor all that is at enmity with joy,
Can utterly abolish or destroy!
Hence in a season of calm weather
Though inland far we be,
165 Our Souls have sight of that immortal sea
Which brought us hither,
Can in a moment travel thither,
And see the Children sport upon the shore,
And hear the mighty waters rolling evermore.

10

170 Then sing, ye Birds, sing, sing a joyous song!
And let the young Lambs bound
As to the tabor's sound!

We in thought will join your throng,
    Ye that pipe and ye that play,
175   Ye that through your hearts today
    Feel the gladness of the May!
What though the radiance which was once so bright
Be now forever taken from my sight,
    Though nothing can bring back the hour
180 Of splendor in the grass, of glory in the flower;
    We will grieve not, rather find
    Strength in what remains behind;
    In the primal sympathy
    Which having been must ever be;
185   In the soothing thoughts that spring
    Out of human suffering;
    In the faith that looks through death,
In years that bring the philosophic mind.

11

And O, ye Fountains, Meadows, Hills, and Groves,
190 Forebode not any severing of our loves!
Yet in my heart of hearts I feel your might;
I only have relinquished one delight
To live beneath your more habitual sway.
I love the Brooks which down their channels fret,
195 Even more than when I tripped lightly as they;
The innocent brightness of a newborn Day
      Is lovely yet;
The clouds that gather round the setting sun
Do take a sober coloring from an eye
200 That hath kept watch o'er man's mortality;
Another race hath been, and other palms are won.
Thanks to the human heart by which we live,
Thanks to its tenderness, its joys, and fears,
To me the meanest flower that blows can give
205 Thoughts that do often lie too deep for tears.

MARIANNE MOORE (1887–1972)

The Steeple-Jack

(Revised, 1961)

Dürer would have seen a reason for living
    in a town like this, with eight stranded whales
to look at; with the sweet air coming into your house
on a fine day, from water etched
5   with waves as formal as the scales
on a fish.

One by one in two's and three's, the seagulls keep
    flying back and forth over the town clock,

or sailing around the lighthouse without moving their wings—
10 rising steadily with a slight
        quiver of the body—or flock
mewing where

a sea the purple of the peacock's neck is
        paled to greenish azure as Dürer changed
15 the pine green of the Tyrol to peacock blue and guinea
gray. You can see a twenty-five-
        pound lobster; and fishnets arranged
to dry. The

whirlwind fife-and-drum of the storm bends the salt
20   marsh grass, disturbs stars in the sky and the
star on the steeple; it is a privilege to see so
much confusion. Disguised by what
        might seem the opposite, the sea-
side flowers and

25 trees are favored by the fog so that you have
        the tropics at first hand: the trumpet-vine,
fox-glove, giant snap-dragon, a salpiglossis that has
spots and stripes; morning-glories, gourds,
        or moon-vines trained on fishing-twine
30 at the back

door; cat-tails, flags, blueberries and spiderwort,
        stripped grass, lichens, sunflowers, asters, daisies—
yellow and crab-claw ragged sailors with green bracts—toad-plant,
petunias, ferns; pink lilies, blue
35   ones, tigers; poppies; black sweet-peas.
The climate

is not right for the banyan, frangipani, or
        jack-fruit trees; or an exotic serpent
life. Ring lizard and snake-skin for the foot, if you see fit;
40 but here they've cats, not cobras, to
        keep down the rats. The diffident
little newt

with white pin-dots on black horizontal spaced
        out bands lives here; yet there is nothing that
45 ambition can buy or take away. The college student
named Ambrose sits on the hillside
        with his not-native books and hat
and sees boats

at sea progress white and rigid as if in
50   a groove. Liking an elegance of which
the source is not bravado, he knows by heart the antique
sugar-bowl shaped summer-house of
        interlacing slats, and the pitch
of the church

55   spire, not true, from which a man in scarlet lets
       down a rope as a spider spins a thread;
   he might be part of a novel, but on the sidewalk a
   sign says C. J. Poole, Steeple Jack,
       in black and white; and one in red
60   and white says

   Danger. The church portico has four fluted
       columns, each a single piece of stone, made
   modester by white-wash. This would be a fit haven for
   waifs, children, animals, prisoners,
65   and presidents who have repaid
   sin-driven

   senators by not thinking about them. The
       place has a school-house, a post-office in a
   store, fish-houses, hen-houses, a three-masted
70   schooner on
   the stocks. The hero, the student,
       the steeple-jack, each in his way,
   is at home.

   It could not be dangerous to be living
75   in a town like this, of simple people,
   who have a steeple-jack placing danger-signs by the church
   while he is gilding the solid-
       pointed star, which on a steeple
   stands for hope.

WILLIAM BUTLER YEATS (1865–1939)

· Sailing to Byzantium[29]

I

That is no country for old men. The young
In one another's arms, birds in the trees
—Those dying generations—at their song,
The salmon-falls, the mackerel-crowded seas,
5   Fish, flesh, or fowl, commend all summer long
Whatever is begotten, born, and dies.
Caught in that sensual music all neglect
Monuments of unageing intellect.

II

An aged man is but a paltry thing,
10 A tattered coat upon a stick, unless
Soul clap its hands and sing, and louder sing
For every tatter in its mortal dress,
Nor is there singing school but studying

---

[29] The ancient name for Istanbul. Yeats viewed the civilization of Byzantium as the height of art and artifice.

Monuments of its own magnificence;
15 And therefore I have sailed the seas and come
To the holy city of Byzantium.

III

O sages standing in God's holy fire
As in the gold mosaic of a wall,
Come from the holy fire, perne in a gyre, [30]
20 And be the singing-masters of my soul.
Consume my heart away; sick with desire
And fastened to a dying animal
It knows not what it is; and gather me
Into the artifice of eternity.

IV

25 Once out of nature I shall never take
My bodily form from any natural thing,
But such a form as Grecian goldsmiths make
Of hammered gold and gold enamelling
To keep a drowsy Emperor awake;
30 Or set upon a golden bough to sing
To lords and ladies of Byzantium
Of what is past, or passing, or to come.

T. S. ELIOT (1888–1965)

• The Love Song of J. Alfred Prufrock

S'io credesse che mia risposta fosse
a persona che mai tornasse al mondo,
questa fiamma staria senza più scosse.
Ma per ciò che giammai di questo fondo
non tornò vivo alcun, s'i'odo il vero,
senza tema d'infamia ti rispond. [31]

Let us go then, you and I,
When the evening is spread out against the sky
Like a patient etherised upon a table;
Let us go, through certain half-deserted streets,
5 The muttering retreats
Of restless nights in one-night cheap hotels

---

[30] The gyre symbolizes for Yeats the spinning of the soul.

[31] From Dante's *Inferno*, XXVII, 61–66. These lines are the words of Guido da Montefeltro, a distinguished Florentine who gave bad counsel. They mean:

> If I believe that my reply were made
> To one who would revisit earth, the flame
> Would be at rest, and its commotion laid.
> But seeing that alive none ever came
> Back from this deep, if it be truth I hear,
> I answer without dread of injured fame.

And sawdust restaurants with oyster-shells:
Streets that follow like a tedious argument
Of insidious intent
10 To lead you to an overwhelming question. . .
Oh, do not ask, "What is it?"
Let us go and make our visit.

In the room the women come and go
Talking of Michelangelo.[32]

15 The yellow fog that rubs its back upon the window-panes,
The yellow smoke that rubs its muzzle on the window-panes,
Licked its tongue into the corners of the evening,
Lingered upon the pools that stand in drains,
Let fall upon its back the soot that falls from chimneys,
20 Slipped by the terrace, made a sudden leap,
And seeing that it was a soft October night,
Curled once about the house, and fell asleep.

And indeed there will be time
For the yellow smoke that slides along the street
25 Rubbing its back upon the window-panes;
There will be time, there will be time
To prepare a face to meet the faces that you meet;
There will be time to murder and create,
And time for all the works and days of hands
.30 That lift and drop a question on your plate;
Time for you and time for me,
And time yet for a hundred indecisions,
And for a hundred visions and revisions,
Before the taking of a toast and tea.

35 In the room the women come and go
Talking of Michelangelo.

And indeed there will be time
To wonder, "Do I dare?" and, "Do I dare?"
Time to turn back and descend the stair,
40 With a bald spot in the middle of my hair—
(They will say: "How his hair is growing thin!")
My morning coat, my collar mounting firmly to the chin,
My necktie rich and modest, but asserted by a simple pin—
(They will say: "But how his arms and legs are thin!")
45 Do I dare
Disturb the universe?
In a minute there is time
For decisions and revisions which a minute will reverse.

---

[32] Michelangelo (1475–1564) was one of the greatest painters of the Italian Renaissance, as well as a poet. He never married and had no children.

For I have known them all already, known them all—
50 Have known the evenings, mornings, afternoons,
I have measured out my life with coffee spoons;
I know the voices dying with a dying fall
Beneath the music from a farther room.
        So how should I presume?

55 And I have known the eyes already, known them all—
The eyes that fix you in a formulated phrase,
And when I am formulated, sprawling on a pin,
When I am pinned and wriggling on the wall,
Then how should I begin
60 To spit out all the butt-ends of my days and ways?
        And how should I presume?

And I have known the arms already, known them all—
Arms that are braceleted and white and bare
(But in the lamplight, downed with light brown hair!)
65 Is it perfume from a dress
That makes me so digress?
Arms that lie along a table, or wrap about a shawl.
        And should I then presume?
        And how should I begin?
            *   *   *   *   *

70 Shall I say, I have gone at dusk through narrow streets
And watched the smoke that rises from the pipes
Of lonely men in shirt-sleeves, leaning out of windows? . . .

T. S. Eliot (*National Portrait Gallery, Smithsonian
Institution, Washington, D.C.*)

I should have been a pair of ragged claws
Scuttling across the floors of silent seas. [33]

* * * * *

75 And the afternoon, the evening, sleeps so peacefully!
Smoothed by long fingers,
Asleep . . . tired . . . or it malingers,
Stretched on the floor, here beside you and me.
Should I, after tea and cakes and ices,
80 Have the strength to force the moment to its crisis?
But though I have wept and fasted, wept and prayed,
Though I have seen my head (grown slightly bald) brought in upon a platter, [34]
I am no prophet—and here's no great matter;
I have seen the moment of my greatness flicker,
85 And I have seen the eternal Footman hold my coat, and snicker,
And in short, I was afraid.

And would it have been worth it, after all,
After the cups, the marmalade, the tea,
Among the porcelain, among some talk of you and me,
90 Would it have been worth while,
To have bitten off the matter with a smile,
To have squeezed the universe into a ball
To roll it towards some overwhelming question,
To say: "I am Lazarus, come from the dead, [35]
95 Come back to tell you all, I shall tell you all"—
If one, settling a pillow by her head,
    Should say: "That is not what I meant at all.
    That is not it, at all."

And would it have been worth it, after all,
100 Would it have been worth while,
After the sunsets and the dooryards and the sprinkled streets,
After the novels, after the teacups, after the skirts that trail along the floor—
And this, and so much more?—
It is impossible to say just what I mean!
105 But as if a magic lantern threw the nerves in patterns on a screen:
Would it have been worth while
If one, settling a pillow or throwing off a shawl,
And turning toward the window, should say:
    "That is not it at all,
110   That is not what I meant, at all."

* * * * *

No! I am not Prince Hamlet, nor was meant to be;
Am an attendant lord, one that will do
To swell a progress, start a scene or two,
Advise the prince; no doubt, an easy tool,

---

[33] The crab travels backward. Eliot is alluding to Hamlet's words (act 2, scene 2, lines 205–206), "for you . . . should be old as I am, if, like a crab, you could go backward."
[34] Salome, the daughter of King Herod, had John the Baptist's head brought to her on a platter.
[35] Jesus raised Lazarus from the dead.

115   Deferential, glad to be of use,
       Politic, cautious, and meticulous;
       Full of high sentence, but a bit obtuse;
       At times, indeed, almost ridiculous—
       Almost, at times, the Fool.

120   I grow old . . . I grow old . . .
       I shall wear the bottoms of my trousers rolled.

       Shall I part my hair behind? Do I dare to eat a peach?
       I shall wear white flannel trousers, and walk upon the beach.
       I have heard the mermaids singing, each to each.

125   I do not think that they will sing to me.

       I have seen them riding seaward on the waves
       Combing the white hair of the waves blown back
       When the wind blows the water white and black.

       We have lingered in the chambers of the sea
130   By sea-girls wreathed with seaweed red and brown
       Till human voices wake us, and we drown.

WALLACE STEVENS (1879–1955)

Sunday Morning

I

       Complacencies of the peignoir, and late
       Coffee and oranges in a sunny chair,
       And the green freedom of a cockatoo
       Upon a rug mingle to dissipate
5   The holy hush of ancient sacrifice.
       She dreams a little, and she feels the dark
       Encroachment of that old catastrophe,
       As a calm darkens among water-lights.
       The pungent oranges and bright, green wings
10   Seem things in some procession of the dead,
       Winding across wide water, without sound.
       The day is like wide water, without sound,
       Stilled for the passing of her dreaming feet
       Over the seas, to silent Palestine,
15   Dominion of the blood and sepulchre.

II

       Why should she give her bounty to the dead?
       What is divinity if it can come
       Only in silent shadows and in dreams?
       Shall she not find in comforts of the sun,
20   In pungent fruit and bright, green wings, or else
       In any balm or beauty of the earth,
       Things to be cherished like the thought of heaven?

Divinity must live within herself:
Passions of rain, or moods in falling snow;
25   Grievings in loneliness, or unsubdued
Elations when the forest blooms; gusty
Emotions on wet roads on autumn nights;
All pleasures and all pains, remembering
The bough of summer and the winter branch.
30   These are the measures destined for her soul.

III

Jove in the clouds had his inhuman birth.
No mother suckled him, no sweet land gave
Large-mannered motions to his mythy mind
He moved among us, as a muttering king,
35   Magnificent, would move among his hinds,
Until our blood, commingling, virginal,
With heaven, brought such requital to desire
The very hinds discerned it, in a star.
Shall our blood fail? Or shall it come to be
40   The blood of paradise? And shall the earth
Seem all of paradise that we shall know?
The sky will be much friendlier then than now,
A part of labor and a part of pain,
And next in glory to enduring love,
45   Not this dividing and indifferent blue.

IV

She says, "I am content when wakened birds,
Before they fly, test the reality
Of misty fields, by their sweet questionings;
But when the birds are gone, and their warm fields
50   Return no more, where, then, is paradise?"
There is not any haunt of prophecy,
Nor any old chimera of the grave,
Neither the golden underground, nor isle
Melodious, where spirits gat° them home,   get
55   Nor visionary south, nor cloudy palm
Remote on heaven's hill, that has endured
As April's green endures; or will endure
Like her remembrance of awakened birds,
Or her desire for June and evening, tipped
60   By the consummation of the swallow's wings.

V

She says, "But in contentment I still feel
The need of some imperishable bliss."
Death is the mother of beauty; hence from her,
Alone, shall come fulfilment to our dreams
65   And our desires. Although she strews the leaves
Of sure obliteration on our paths,
The path sick sorrow took, the many paths

Where triumph rang its brassy phrase, or love
Whispered a little out of tenderness,
70 She makes the willow shiver in the sun
For maidens who were wont to sit and gaze
Upon the grass, relinquished to their feet.
She causes boys to pile new plums and pears
On disregarded plate. The maidens taste
75 And stray impassioned in the littering leaves.

VI

Is there no change of death in paradise?
Does ripe fruit never fall? Or do the boughs
Hang always heavy in that perfect sky,
Unchanging, yet so like our perishing earth,
80 With rivers like our own that seek for seas
They never find, the same receding shores
That never touch with inarticulate pang?
Why set the pear upon those river-banks
Or spice the shores with odors of the plum?
85 Alas, that they should wear our colors there,
The silken weavings of our afternoons,
And pick the strings of our insipid lutes!
Death is the mother of beauty, mystical,
Within whose burning bosom we devise
90 Our earthly mothers waiting, sleeplessly.

VII

Supple and turbulent, a ring of men
Shall chant in orgy on a summer morn
Their boisterous devotion to the sun,
Not as a god, but as a god might be,
95 Naked among them, like a savage source.
Their chant shall be a chant of paradise,
Out of their blood, returning to the sky;
And in their chant shall enter, voice by voice,
The windy lake wherein their lord delights,
100 The trees, like serafin, and echoing hills,
That choir among themselves long afterward.
They shall know well the heavenly fellowship
Of men that perish and of summer morn.
And whence they came and whither they shall go
105 The dew upon their feet shall manifest.

VIII

She hears, upon that water without sound,
A voice that cries, "The tomb in Palestine
Is not the porch of spirits lingering.
It is the grave of Jesus, where he lay."
110 We live in an old chaos of the sun,
Or old dependency of day and night,
Or island solitude, unsponsored, free,

Of that wide water, inescapable.
Deer walk upon our mountains, and the quail
115 Whistle about us their spontaneous cries;
Sweet berries ripen in the wilderness;
And, in the isolation of the sky,
At evening, casual flocks of pigeons make
Ambiguous undulations as they sink,
120 Downward to darkness, on extended wings.

A Checklist of Questions for Evaluating Poetry

A list of questions follows that should help you evaluate poetry. Because each poem is different, no list can be complete, and you will need to supplement this list with other questions. Moreover, many great poems defy simple explanation. A poem may break many norms and yet remain a compelling and coherent expression.

Economy

1. Are there any repeated expressions or words? Is this repetition necessary or effective?
2. If the poem has a refrain, is the refrain well integrated, or is it mechanical?
3. Is any line padded to keep the rhythm regular?

Coherence and Consistency

1. Are all the ideas and attitudes consistent? If they are paradoxical, do they reflect a more subtle philosophical or psychological position? Are any inconsistencies part of the poetic development?
2. Are any expressions vague? Can the vagueness be justified by the context of the poem?
3. Are the images comprehensible? Is any oddness the result of dreamlike concentration, or is it the result of thoughtlessness?
4. If the poem seems nonsensical, is it the case that it is not supposed to be comprehensible in a traditional way?

Naturalness

1. Is the order of the language unnatural? Where it is unnatural, has the language been altered for expressive purposes?
2. Are the rhymes forced?
3. Is the diction natural? Where the word choice seems odd, is there some special reason?
4. Can the poem be read easily? Do the sounds fit the subject?
5. Do the rhythms seem appropriate to the subject and mood? Are they boring and mechanical?

Tone

1. Does the tone seem appropriate to the poem's subject and the speaker's attitude?
2. Is the poem sentimental?
3. Is the poem unfeeling?
4. Does the tone vary naturally, or is it mechanical and constant?

Completeness

1. Has the poet provided all the details necessary for the reader's full emotional and intellectual response? If not, is there a good reason?

2. Does the poem conclude or does it merely end?
3. Has the poet satisfied your expectations? If not, has the poet made an acceptable substitute?

Suggestions for Essayists

1. Compare two poems on a similar subject.
2. Select any object (e.g., a car, a house) and describe the criteria by which you decide whether it is good or bad.
3. Discuss the necessity of making critical evaluations.

Suggestions for Poets

1. Find a poem that you think is especially poor and rewrite it.
2. Take a poem you think is especially good and, by using redundancy, inconsistency, and rhythmic alterations, make it bad.

Anthology

Poems for Further Study

DANTE ALIGHIERI (1265–1321)

Ulysses' Speech *from* Inferno (Canto XXVI)

"When I From Circe had departed, who concealed me
    More than a year there near unto Gaëta,
    Or ever yet Æneas° named it so,   *Trojan hero*
Nor fondness for my son, nor reverence
5   For my old father, nor the due affection
    Which joyous should have made Penelope,
Could overcome within me the desire
    I had to be experienced of the world,
    And of the vice and virtue of mankind;
10   But I put forth on the high open sea
    With one sole ship, and that small company
    By which I never had deserted been.
Both of the shores I saw as far as Spain,
    Far as Morocco, and the isle of Sardes,
15   And the others which that sea bathes round about.
I and my company were old and slow
    When at that narrow passage we arrived
    Where Hercules his landmarks set as signals,°   *Straits of Gibraltar*
That man no farther onward should adventure.
20   On the right hand behind me left I Seville,
    And on the other already had left Ceuta.
'O brothers, who amid a hundred thousand
    Perils,' I said, 'have come unto the West,
    To this so inconsiderable vigil
25   Which is remaining of your senses still,
    Be ye unwilling to deny the knowledge,

Following the sun, of the unpeopled world.
Consider ye the seed from which ye sprang;
    Ye were not made to live like unto brutes,
30   But for pursuit of virtue and of knowledge.'
So eager did I render my companions,
    With this brief exhortation, for the voyage,
    That then I hardly could have held them back.
And having turned our stern unto the morning,
35   We of the oars made wings for our mad flight,
    Evermore gaining on the larboard side.
Already all the stars of the other pole
    The night beheld, and ours so very low
    It did not rise above the ocean floor.
40 Five times rekindled and as many quenched
    Had been the splendor underneath the moon,
    Since we had entered into the deep pass,
When there appeared to us a mountain, dim
    From distance, and it seemed to me so high
45   As I had never any one beheld.
Joyful were we, and soon it turned to weeping;
    For out of the new land a whirlwind rose,
    And smote upon the fore part of the ship.
Three times it made it whirl with all the waters,
50   At the fourth time it made the stern uplift,
    And the prow downward go, as pleased Another,
Until the sea above us closed again."

Translation by Henry Wadsworth Longfellow (1807–1882)

JOHN SKELTON (c. 1460–1529)

To Mistress Margaret Hussey

Merry Margaret,
    As midsummer flower,
Gentle as falcon
Or hawk of the tower,[1]
5 With solace and gladness,
Much mirth and no madness,
All good and no badness;
    So joyously,
    So maidenly,
10   So womanly
    Her demeaning
    In every thing,
    Far, far passing

---

[1] *Falcon-gentle* is a hawking term used to denote a young or female hawk; "hawk of the tower" refers to a high-flying hawk looking for prey.

	That I can endite°	*compose*
15	Or suffice to write	
	Of merry Margaret	
	As midsummer flower,	
	Gentle as falcon	
	Or hawk of the tower.	
20	As patient and as still	
	And as full of good will	
	As fair Isaphill[2]	
	Colyander,	
	Sweet pomander°	*coriander*
25	Good Cassander[3]	
	Steadfast of thought,	
	Well made, well wrought,	
	Far may be sought	
	Ere that ye can find	
30	So courteous, so kind	
	As merry Margaret,	
	This midsummer flower,	
	Gentle as falcon	
	Or hawk of the tower.	

SIR THOMAS WYATT (1503–1542)

• They Flee from Me[4]

They flee from me, that sometime did me seek,
With naked foot stalking in my chamber.
I have seen them, gentle, tame, and meek,
That now are wild, and do not remember
5   That sometime they put themselves in danger
To take bread at my hand; and now they range,
Busily seeking with a continual change.

Thankéd be fortune it hath been otherwise.
Twenty times better; but once in special,
10   In thin array, after a pleasant guise,
When her loose gown from her shoulders did fall,
And she me caught in her arms long and small,°   *thin*
Therewithall sweetly did me kiss
And softly said, "Dear heart, how like you this?"

15   It was no dream, I lay broad waking.
But all is turned, thorough my gentleness,
Into a strange fashion of forsaking;
And I have leave to go, of her goodness,

---

[2] Hypsipyle (or Isaphill) was the Queen of Lemnos and the model of a faithful daughter.
[3] Cassandra, daughter of Priam, King of Troy, was famous for her gift of prophecy.
[4] This poem is discussed at length in the Appendix, pages 457–458.

And she also to use newfangleness[5]
20 But since that I so kindely am servéd,
I fain would know what she hath deservéd.

SIR WALTER RALEIGH (1552–1618)

The Nymph's Reply to the Shepherd

If all the world and love were young,
And truth in every shepherd's tongue,
These pretty pleasures might me move
To live with thee and be thy love.

5 Time drives the flocks from field to fold
When rivers rage and rocks grow cold,
And Philomel° becometh dumb;   *the nightingale*
The rest complains of cares to come.

The flowers do fade, and wanton fields
10 To wayward winter reckoning yields;
A honey tongue, a heart of gall,
Is fancy's spring, but sorrow's fall.

Thy gowns, thy shoes, thy beds of roses,
Thy cap, thy kirtle°, and thy posies   *dress*
15 Soon break, soon wither, soon forgotten—
In folly ripe, in reason rotten.

Thy belt of straw and ivy buds,
Thy coral clasps and amber studs,
All these in me no means can move
20 To come to thee and be thy love.

But could youth last and love still breed,
Had joys no date° nor age no need,   *conclusion*
Then these delights my mind might move
To live with thee and be thy love.

Compare "The Nymph's Reply to the Shepherd" with Christopher Marlowe's "The Passionate Shepherd to His Love" on pages 5–6.

SIR PHILIP SIDNEY (1554–1586)

Ye Goatherd Gods

Strephon. Ye goatherd gods, that love the grassy mountains,
Ye nymphs which haunt the springs in pleasant valleys,
Ye satyrs joyed with free and quiet forests.
Vouchsafe your silent ears to plaining° music,   *plaintive, sad*
5 Which to my woes gives still an early morning,
And draws the dolor on till weary evening.

---

[5] "To use newfangleness" means to explore new things—that is, to be fickle.

	Klaius.	O Mercury,[6] foregoer to the evening,
		O heavenly huntress[7] of the savage mountains,
		O lovely star, entitled of the morning,
10		While that my voice doth fill these woeful valleys,
		Vouchsafe your silent ears to plaining music,
		Which oft hath Echo tired in secret forests.

	Strephon.	I, that was once free burgess° of the forests.	*inhabitant*
		Where shade from sun, and sport I sought in evening,	
15		I, that was once esteemed for pleasant music,	
		Am banished now among the monstrous mountains	
		Of huge despair, and foul affliction's valleys,	
		Am grown a screech owl to myself each morning.	

	Klaius.	I, that was once delighted every morning,
20		Hunting the wild inhabiters of forests,
		I, that was once the music of these valleys,
		So darkened am that all my day is evening,
		Heartbroken so that molehills seem high mountains
		And fill the vales with cries instead of music.

25	Strephon.	Long since, alas, my deadly swannish° music	*swanlike*
		Hath made itself a crier of the morning,	
		And hath with wailing strength climbéd highest mountains;	
		Long since my thoughts more desert be than forests,	
		Long since I see my joys come to their evening,	
30		And state thrown down to overtrodden valleys.	

	Klaius.	Long since the happy dwellers of these valleys
		Have prayed me leave my strange exclaiming music
		Which troubles their day's work and joys of evening;
		Long since I hate the night, more hate the morning;
35		Long since my thoughts chase me like beasts in forests
		And make me wish myself laid under mountains.

	Strephon.	Meseems° I see the high and stately mountains	*It seems to me*
		Transform themselves to low dejected valleys;	
		Meseems I hear in these ill-changéd forests	
40		The nightingales do learn of owls their music;	
		Meseems I feel the comfort of the morning	
		Turned to the mortal serene[8] of an evening.	

	Klaius.	Meseems I see a filthy cloudy evening
		As soon as sun begins to climb the mountains;
45		Meseems I feel a noisome° scent, the morning	*offensive*
		When I do smell the flowers of these valleys;
		Meseems I hear, when I do hear sweet music,
		The dreadful cries of murdered men in forests.

---

[6] Mercury is the evening star, the first star to shine at night.
[7] Diana, the moon, depicted as a huntress.
[8] Serene, a deadly dew.

<table>
<tr><td>Strephon.</td><td>I wish to fire the trees of all these forests;</td><td></td></tr>
<tr><td>50</td><td>I give the sun a last farewell each evening;
I curse the fiddling finders-out of music;
With envy I do hate the lofty mountains
And with despite despise the humble valleys;
I do detest night, evening, day, and morning.</td><td></td></tr>
<tr><td>55   Klaius.</td><td>Curse to myself my prayer is, the morning;
My fire is more than can be made with forests,
My state more base than are the basest valleys.
I wish no evenings more to see, each evening;
Shaméd, I hate myself in sight of mountains</td><td></td></tr>
<tr><td>60</td><td>And stop mine ears, lest I grow mad with music.</td><td></td></tr>
<tr><td>Strephon.</td><td>For she whose parts maintained a perfect music,
Whose beauties shined more than the blushing morning,
Who much did pass° in state the stately mountains</td><td>surpass</td></tr>
<tr><td>65</td><td>In straightness passed the cedars of the forests,
Hath cast me, wretch, into eternal evening
By taking her two suns from these dark valleys.</td><td></td></tr>
<tr><td>Klaius.</td><td>For she, with whom compared, the Alps are valleys,
She, whose least word brings from the spheres their music,
At whose approach the sun rose in the evening,</td><td></td></tr>
<tr><td>70</td><td>Who where she went bare in her forehead morning,
Is gone, is gone, from these our spoiléd forests,
Turning to deserts our best pastured mountains.</td><td></td></tr>
<tr><td>Strephon.</td><td>These mountains witness shall, so shall these valleys,</td><td></td></tr>
<tr><td>Klaius.</td><td>These forests eke,° made wretched by our music,</td><td>also</td></tr>
<tr><td>75</td><td>Our morning hymn this is, and song at evening.</td><td></td></tr>
</table>

WILLIAM SHAKESPEARE (1564–1616)

Fear No More[9]

Fear no more the heat o' the sun,
   Nor the furious winter's rages;
Thou thy worldly task hast done,
   Home art gone, and ta'en thy wages.
5 Golden lads and girls all must,
As chimney-sweepers, come to dust.

Fear no more the frown o' the great;
   Thou art past the tyrant's stroke;
Care no more to clothe and eat;
10   To thee the reed is as the oak.
The scepter, learning, physic,° must   *medicine*
All follow this, and come to dust.

Fear no more the lightning-flash,
   Nor the all-dreaded thunder-stone;°   *thunderbolt*

---

[9] The lines are from *Cymbeline*. They are a dirge for the supposedly dead heroine, Imogen.

15   Fear not slander, censure rash;
        Thou hast finished joy and moan.
    All lovers young, all lovers must
    Consign° to thee, and come to dust.   *Give themselves over*

THOMAS CAMPION (1567–1620)

There Is a Garden in Her Face

    There is a garden in her face
Where roses and white lilies grow;
    A heav'nly paradise is that place
Wherein all pleasant fruits do flow.
5   There cherries grow which none may buy
        Till "Cherry-ripe" themselves do cry.[10]

    Those cherries fairly do enclose
Of orient pearl a double row,
    Which when her lovely laughter shows,
10   They look like rose-buds filled with snow;
        Yet them nor peer nor prince can buy,
        Till "Cherry-ripe" themselves do cry.

    Her eyes like angels watch them still;
    Her brows like bended bows do stand,
15   Threat'ning with piercing frowns to kill
All that attempt, with eye or hand
        Those sacred cherries to come nigh
        Till "Cherry-ripe" themselves do cry.

Consider "There Is a Garden in Her Face" as an example of metaphor or allegory.

JOHN DONNE (1572–1631)

I Am a Little World Made Cunningly

I am a little world made cunningly
Of elements, and an angelic sprite;[11]
But black sin hath betrayed to endless night
My world's both parts, and O, both parts must die.
5   You which beyond that heaven which was most high
Have found new spheres, and of new lands can write,[12]
Pour new seas in mine eyes, that so I might
Drown my world with my weeping earnestly,
Or wash it if it must be drowned no more.[13]
10   But O, it must be burnt! Alas, the fire
Of lust and envy have burnt it heretofore,

---

[10] "Cherry-ripe" was the cry of a London fruit seller.
[11] Donne conceives of humanity as being made of both spirit and matter.
[12] Donne alludes to new astronomic and geographic discoveries.
[13] God promised Noah He would not bring another flood to cover the world (Genesis 60:11).

And made it fouler; let their flames retire,
And burn me, O Lord, with a fiery zeal
Of Thee and Thy house, which doth in eating heal.

JOHN DONNE (1572–1631)

Death Be Not Proud

Death, be not proud, though some have calléd thee
Mighty and dreadful, for thou art not so;
For those whom thou think'st thou dost overthrow
Die not, poor Death, nor yet canst thou kill me.
5   From rest and sleep, which but thy pictures be,
Much pleasure; then from thee much more must flow,
And soonest our best men with thee do go,
Rest of their bones, and soul's delivery.
Thou art slave to fate, chance, kings, and desperate men,
10   And dost with poison, war, and sickness dwell,
And poppy[14] or charms can make us sleep as well
And better than thy stroke; why swell'st thou then?
One short sleep past, we wake eternally
And death shall be no more; Death, thou shalt die.

Consider "Death Be Not Proud" as an example of personification.

ROBERT HERRICK (1591–1674)

Delight in Disorder

A sweet disorder in the dress
Kindles in clothes a wantonness.
A lawn° about the shoulders thrown   *fine shawl*
Into a fine distractión;
5   An erring° lace, which here and there   *wandering*
Enthralls the crimson stomacher;°   *bodice*
A cuff neglectful, and thereby
Ribbons to flow confusedly;
A winning wave, deserving note,
10   In the tempestuous petticoat;
A careless shoestring, in whose tie
I see a wild civility;
Do more bewitch me than when art
Is too precise in every part.

---

[14] Poppies are the raw ingredient for opium, which can produce sleep and ease pain as well as cause death.

ROBERT HERRICK (1591–1674)

Upon Julia's Clothes

Whenas in silks my Julia goes,
Then, then, methinks, how sweetly flows
That liquefaction[15] of her clothes.

Next, when I cast mine eyes, and see
5   That brave vibration, each way free,
O, how that glittering taketh me!

WILLIAM DAVENANT (1606–1668)

The Philosopher and the Lover: To a Mistress Dying

Lover
Your beauty, ripe and calm, and fresh
    As eastern summers are,
Must now, forsaking time and flesh,
    Add light to some small star.

Philosopher
5   Whilst she yet lives, were stars decayed,
    Their light by hers relief might find;
But death will lead her to a shade
    Where love is cold, and beauty blind.

Lover
Lovers, whose priests all poets are,
10   Think ev'ry mistress when she dies
Is changed at least into a star;
    And who dares doubt the poet wise?

Philosopher
But ask not bodies doomed to die
    To what abode they go;
15   Since knowledge is but sorrow's spy,
    It is not safe to know.

Compare "The Philosopher and the Lover" with John Crowe Ransom's "Here Lies a Lady" on pages 73–74.

ANNE BRADSTREET (1612?–1672)

To My Dear and Loving Husband

If ever two were one, then surely we.
If ever man were lov'd by wife, then thee;

---

[15] *Liquefaction* is the act of making a liquid, especially from a solid.

If ever wife was happy in a man,
Compare with me ye women if you can.
5   I prize thy love more then whole Mines of gold,
Or all the riches that the East doth hold.
My love is such that Rivers cannot quench,
Nor ought but love from thee, give recompence.
Thy love is such I can no way repay,
10   The heavens reward thee manifold I pray.
Then while we live, in love lets so persever,
That when we live no more, we may live ever.

EDWARD TAYLOR (1645?–1729)

Upon a Spider Catching a Fly

Thou sorrow, venom Elfe:
    Is this thy play,
To spin a web out of thyselfe
    To Catch a Fly?
5   For Why?

I saw a pettish° wasp   *peevish*
    Fall foule therein.
Whom yet thy Whorle[16] pins did not clasp
    Lest he should fling
10   His sting.

But as affraid, remote
    Didst stand hereat
And with thy little fingers stroke
    And gently tap
15   His back.

Thus gently him didst treate
    Lest he should pet,
And in a froppish,° waspish heate   *fretful*
    Should greatly fret
20   Thy net.

Whereas the silly Fly,
    Caught by its leg
Thou by the throate tookst hastily
    And 'hinde the head
25   Bite Dead.

This goes to pot, that not
    Nature doth call.
Strive not above what strength hath got
    Lest in the brawle
30   Thou fall.

---

[16] A "whorle" is the flywheel of a spindle.

This Frey° seems thus to us.   *fray, fight*
     Hells Spider gets
His intrails spun to whip Cords thus
     And wove to nets
35   And sets.

To tangle Adams race
     In's stratigems
To their Destructions, spoil'd, made base
     By venom things
40   Damn'd Sins.

But mighty, Gracious Lord
     Communicate
Thy Grace to breake the Cord, afford
     Us Glorys Gate
45   And State.

We'l Nightingaile sing like
     When pearcht on high
In Glories Cage, thy glory, bright,
     And thankfully,
50   For joy.

Compare "Upon a Spider Catching a Fly" with Walt Whitman's "A Noiseless Patient Spider" on page 371.

JONATHAN SWIFT (1667–1745)

A Description of the Morning

Now hardly here and there a hackney-coach
Appearing showed the ruddy morn's approach.
Now Betty from her master's bed had flown,
And softly stole to discompose her own;
5   The slipshod 'prentice from his master's door
Had pared the dirt and sprinkled around the floor.
Now Moll had whirled her mop with dexterous airs,
Prepared to scrub the entry and the stairs.
The youth with broomy stumps began to trace
10 The kennel-edge,° where wheels had worn the place.   *gutter*
The small-coal man was heard with cadence deep,
Till drowned in shriller notes of chimney-sweep:
Duns[17] at his lordship's gate began to meet;
And brickdust Moll had screamed through half the street.
15 The turnkey° now his flock returning sees,   *prison guard*
Duly let out a-nights to steal for fees:
The watchful bailiffs take their silent stands,
And schoolboys lag with satchels in their hands.

---

[17] "Duns" are people requesting money.

ALEXANDER POPE (1688–1744)

Epistle to a Young Lady, on Her Leaving the Town After the Coronation[18]

As some fond° virgin, whom her mother's care   *foolish*
Drags from the town to wholesome country air,
Just when she learns to roll a melting eye,
And hear a spark,° yet think no danger nigh—   *young admirer*
5   From the dear man unwilling she must sever,
Yet takes one kiss before she parts forever—
Thus from the world fair Zephalinda flew,
Saw others happy, and with sighs withdrew;
Not that their pleasures caused her discontent:
10 She sighed not that they stayed, but that she went.
     She went—to plain-work and to purling brooks,
Old-fashioned halls, dull aunts, and croaking rooks;
She went from opera, park, assembly, play,
To morning walks, and prayers three hours a day;
15 To part her time 'twixt reading and bohea,°   *black tea*
To muse, and spill her solitary tea;
Or o'er cold coffee trifle with the spoon,
Count the slow clock, and dine exact at noon;
Divert her eyes with pictures in the fire,
20 Hum half a tune, tell stories to the squire;
Up to her godly garret after seven,
There starve and pray, for that's the way to heaven.
     Some squire, perhaps, you take delight to rack,
Whose game is "whisk,"° whose treat a toast in sack;   *whist*
25 Who visits with a gun, presents you birds,
Then gives a smacking buss,° and cries, "No words!"   *kiss*
Or with his hound comes hollowing from the stable,
Makes love with nods, and knees beneath a table;
Whose laughs are hearty, though his jests are coarse,
30 And loves you best of all things—but his horse.
     In some fair evening, on your elbow laid,
You dream of triumphs in the rural shade;
In pensive thought recall the fancied scene,
See coronations rise on every green:
35 Before you pass the imaginary sights
Of Lords, and Earls, and Dukes, and gartered Knights,[19]
While the spread fan o'ershades your closing eyes,
Then gives one flirt, and all the vision flies.
Thus vanish sceptres, coronets, and balls,
40 And leave you in lone woods, or empty walls!
     So when your slave, at some dear idle time
(Not plagued with headaches, or the want of rhyme)

---

[18] Pope wrote this poem after the coronation of George I in 1714. Zephalinda and Parthenia are names he has invented for actual friends.

[19] "Gartered Knights" refers to persons honored with the Order of the Garter, one of the highest distinctions the king may grant a British citizen.

Stands in the streets, abstracted from the crew,
And while he seems to study, thinks of you;
45 Just when his fancy paints your sprightly eyes,
Or sees the blush of soft Parthenia rise,
Gay[20] pats my shoulder, and you vanish quite,
Streets, chairs, and coxcombs rush upon my sight.
Vexed to be still in town, I knit my brow,
50 Look sour, and hum a tune—as you may now.

THOMAS GRAY (1716–1771)

• Ode on the Death of a Favorite Cat[21]

Drowned in a tub of goldfishes

'Twas on a lofty vase's side,
Where China's gayest art had dyed
 The azure flowers that blow;
Demurest of the tabby kind,
5 The pensive Selima reclined,
 Gazed on the lake below.

Her conscious tail her joy declared;
The fair round face, the snowy beard,
 The velvet of her paws,
10 Her coat, that with the tortoise vies,
Her ears of jet,° and emerald eyes,   *black*
 She saw; and purred applause.

Still had she gazed; but 'midst the tide
Two angel forms were seen to glide,
15 The genii[22] of the stream:
Their scaly armor's Tyrian° hue   *purple*
Through richest purple to the view
 Betrayed a golden gleam.

The hapless nymph with wonder saw:
20 A whisker first and then a claw,
 With many an ardent wish,
She stretched in vain to reach the prize.
What female heart can gold despise?
 What cat's averse to fish?

25 Presumptuous maid! with looks intent
Again she stretched, again she bent,
 Nor knew the gulf between.
(Malignant Fate sat by and smiled)

---

[20] The poet John Gay, whose poetic fable "The Lion, the Fox, and Geese" may be found on page 154.
[21] Gray wrote this elegy at the request of Horace Walpole (1717–1797), the author. Walpole's cat, Selima, died by drowning in a cistern.
[22] Genii, the plural of genius. They are the protecting spirits of a place or person.

The slippery verge her feet beguiled,
30   She tumbled headlong in.

Eight times emerging from the flood
She mewed to every watery god,
      Some speedy aid to send.
No dolphin came,[23] no nereid° stirred: *sea nymph*
35   Nor cruel Tom, nor Susan heard.
      A favorite has no friend!

From hence, ye beauties, undeceived,
Know, one false step is ne'er retrieved,
      And be with caution bold.
40   Not all that tempts your wandering eyes
And heedless hearts is lawful prize;
      Nor all that glisters gold.

WILLIAM BLAKE (1757–1827)

The Tyger

Tyger! Tyger! burning bright,
In the forests of the night;
What immortal hand or eye,
Could frame thy fearful symmetry?

5   In what distant deeps or skies
Burnt the fire of thine eyes!
On what wings dare he aspire?
What the hand, dare seize the fire?

And what shoulder, & what art,
10   Could twist the sinews of thy heart?
And when thy heart began to beat,
What dread hand? & what dread feet?

What the hammer? what the chain,
In what furnace was thy brain?
15   What the anvil? what dread grasp,
Dare its deadly terrors clasp?

When the stars threw down their spears
And water'd heaven with their tears:
Did he smile his work to see?
20   Did he who made the Lamb make thee?

Tyger! Tyger! burning bright,
In the forests of the night:
What immortal hand or eye,
Dare frame thy fearful symmetry?

---

[23] Dolphins have the reputation for saving people in distress. Tom and Susan are typical names for servants.

ROBERT BURNS (1759–1796)

A Red, Red Rose

O My Luve's like a red, red rose,
    That's newly sprung in June;
O My Luve's like the melodie
    That's sweetly played in tune.

5   As fair art thou, my bonnie lass,
    So deep in luve am I;
And I will luve thee still, my dear,
    Till a' the seas gang° dry.   *go*

Till a' the seas gang dry, my dear,
10   And the rocks melt wi' the sun:
O I will love thee still, my dear,
    While the sands o' life shall run.

And fare thee weel, my only luve,
    And fare thee weel awhile!
15   And I will come again, my luve,
    Though it were ten thousand mile.

WILLIAM WORDSWORTH (1770–1850)

I Wandered Lonely as a Cloud

I wandered lonely as a cloud
    That floats on high o'er vales and hills,
When all at once I saw a crowd,
    A host, of golden daffodils,
5   Beside the lake, beneath the trees,
Fluttering and dancing in the breeze.

Continuous as the stars that shine
    And twinkle on the milky way,
They stretched in never-ending line
10   Along the margin of a bay:
Ten thousand saw I at a glance,
Tossing their heads in sprightly dance.

The waves beside them danced; but they
    Out-did the sparkling waves in glee;
15   A poet could not but be gay,
    In such a jocund company;
I gazed—and gazed—but little thought
What wealth the show to me had brought:

For oft, when on my couch I lie
20   In vacant or in pensive mood,
They flash upon that inward eye
    Which is the bliss of solitude;
And then my heart with pleasure fills,
And dances with the daffodils.

WILLIAM WORDSWORTH (1770–1850)

• The World Is Too Much with Us

The world is too much with us; late and soon,
Getting and spending, we lay waste our powers:
Little we see in Nature that is ours;
We have given our hearts away, a sordid boon![24]
5   This Sea that bares her bosom to the moon,
The winds that will be howling at all hours,
And are up-gathered now like sleeping flowers,
For this, for everything, we are out of tune;
It moves us not.—Great God! I'd rather be
10 A Pagan suckled in a creed outworn;
So might I, standing on this pleasant lea,
Have glimpses that would make me less forlorn;
Have sight of Proteus[25] rising from the sea;
Or hear old Triton° blow his wreathéd horn.   *a sea god*

WALTER SAVAGE LANDOR (1775–1864)

On His Seventy-fifth Birthday[26]

I strove with none; for none was worth my strife,[27]
    Nature I loved, and next to Nature, Art;
I warmed both hands before the fire of life,
    It sinks, and I am ready to depart.

Discuss "On His Seventy-fifth Birthday" as an epigram.

GEORGE GORDON, LORD BYRON (1788–1824)

• She Walks in Beauty[28]

1

She walks in beauty, like the night
    Of cloudless climes and starry skies;
And all that's best of dark and bright
    Meet in her aspect and her eyes:
5   Thus mellowed to that tender light
    Which heaven to gaudy day denies.

---

[24] We have given our hearts away to the sordid gift of "getting and spending"—that is, commercial enterprise.
[25] The old man of the sea, sometimes described as the son of Poseidon.
[26] Landor lived into his ninetieth year.
[27] Landor was constantly in litigation and was forced into exile because of court battles.
[28] This poem was written for Mrs. Robert John Wilmot, Byron's cousin. When Byron first met her, she was wearing a black dress with spangles because she was in mourning.

2

One shade the more, one ray the less,
    Had half impaired the nameless grace
Which waves in every raven tress,
10   Or softly lightens o'er her face;
Where thoughts serenely sweet express
    How pure, how dear their dwelling place.

3

And on that cheek, and o'er that brow,
    So soft, so calm, yet eloquent,
15 The smiles that win, the tints that glow,
    But tell of days in goodness spent,
A mind at peace with all below,
    A heart whose love is innocent!

PERCY BYSSHE SHELLEY (1792–1822)

Ozymandias[29]

I met a traveler from an antique° land   *ancient*
Who said: Two vast and trunkless legs of stone
Stand in the desert. Near them, on the sand,
Half sunk, a shattered visage lies, whose frown,
5 And wrinkled lip, and sneer of cold command,
Tell that its sculptor well those passions read
Which yet survive, stamped on these lifeless things,
The hand that mocked° them and the heart that fed;   *carved and ridiculed*
And on the pedestal these words appear:
10 "My name is Ozymandias, king of kings:
Look on my works, ye Mighty, and despair!"
Nothing beside remains. Round the decay
Of that colossal wreck, boundless and bare
The lone and level sands stretch far away.

JOHN KEATS (1795–1821)

• When I Have Fears

When I have fears that I may cease to be
    Before my pen has gleaned my teeming brain,
Before high-pilèd books, in charact'ry,°   *print*
    Hold like rich garners the full-ripened grain;
5 When I behold, upon the night's starred face,
    Huge cloudy symbols of a high romance,
And think that I may never live to trace
    Their shadows, with the magic hand of chance;
And when I feel, fair creature of an hour,

---

[29] Ozymandias, or Ramses II, was pharaoh of Egypt in the thirteenth century B.C.

10   That I shall never look upon thee more,
        Never have relish in the faery power
            Of unreflecting love!—then on the shore
        Of the wide world I stand alone, and think
        Till Love and Fame to nothingness do sink.

JOHN KEATS (1795–1821)

• To Autumn

1

        Season of mists and mellow fruitfulness,
            Close bosom-friend of the maturing sun;
        Conspiring with him how to load and bless
            With fruit the vines that round the thatch-eaves run;
5   To bend with apples the mossed cottage-trees,
            And fill all fruit with ripeness to the core;
                To swell the gourd, and plump the hazel shells
            With a sweet kernel; to set budding more,
        And still more, later flowers for the bees,
10   Until they think warm days will never cease,
                For Summer has o'er-brimmed their clammy cells.

2

        Who hath not seen thee oft amid thy store?
            Sometimes whoever seeks abroad may find
        Thee sitting careless on a granary floor,
15   Thy hair soft-lifted by the winnowing[30] wind;
        Or on a half-reaped furrow sound asleep,
            Drowsed with the fume of poppies, while thy hook°   scythe
                Spares the next swath and all its twinéd flowers:
        And sometimes like a gleaner[31] thou dost keep
20   Steady thy laden head across a brook;
            Or by a cider-press, with patient look,
                Thou watchest the last oozings hours by hours.

3

        Where are the songs of Spring? Aye, where are they?
            Think not of them, thou hast thy music too—
25   While barred clouds bloom the soft-dying day,
            And touch the stubble-plains with rosy hue;
        Then in a wailful choir the small gnats mourn
            Among the river sallows,° borne aloft   willows
                Or sinking as the light wind lives or dies;
30   And full-grown lambs loud bleat from hilly bourn;°   region

---

[30] The process by which the chaff or husk is separated from the grain, usually by the wind.
[31] One who gathers the remains of a crop after it has been harvested.

Hedge crickets sing; and now with treble soft
The redbreast whistles from a garden croft;[32]
And gathering swallows twitter in the skies.

Discuss "To Autumn" as an example of personification.

THOMAS LOVELL BEDDOES (1803–1849)

Song: How Many Times Do I Love Thee, Dear?

How many times do I love thee, dear?
    Tell me how many thoughts there be
        In the atmosphere
        Of a new-fall'n year,
5   Whose white and sable hours appear
        The latest flake of Eternity—
So many times do I love thee, dear.

How many times do I love again?
    Tell me how many beads there are
10   In a silver chain
            Of evening rain,
Unraveled from the tumbling main,
    And threading the eye of a yellow star—
So many times do I love again.

Compare Beddoes's "Song" with Elizabeth Barrett Browning's "How Do I Love Thee"
on page 367.

HENRY WADSWORTH LONGFELLOW (1807–1882)

The Jewish Cemetery at Newport[33]

How strange it seems! These Hebrews in their graves,
    Close by the street of this fair seaport town,
Silent beside the never-silent waves,
    At rest in all this moving up and down!

5   The trees are white with dust, that o'er their sleep
        Wave their broad curtains in the south-wind's breath,
While underneath these leafy tents they keep
        The long, mysterious Exodus of Death.[34]

And these sepulchral stones, so old and brown,
10   That pave with level flags their burial-place,

---

[32] An enclosed farm plot.
[33] The oldest Jewish synagogue in the United States is located in Newport, Rhode Island.
[34] Exodus, the second book of the Old Testament, records the expulsion of the Jews from Egypt and
their subsequent wanderings. During their travels they made their homes in tents.

Seem like the tablets of the Law, thrown down
　　And broken by Moses at the mountain's base.[35]

The very names recorded here are strange,
　　Of foreign accent, and of different climes;
15　　Alvares and Rivera interchange
　　With Abraham and Jacob of old times.[36]

"Blessed be God, for he created Death!"
　　The mourners said, "and Death is rest and peace;"
Then added, in the certainty of faith,
20　　"And giveth Life that nevermore shall cease."

Closed are the portals of their Synagogue,
　　No Psalms of David now the silence break,
No Rabbi reads the ancient Decalogue°　　　　　　　　　*the Ten Commandments*
　　In the grand dialect the Prophets spake.

25　Gone are the living, but the dead remain,
　　And not neglected; for a hand unseen,
Scattering its bounty, like a summer rain,
　　Still keeps their graves and their remembrance green.

How came they here? What burst of Christian hate,
30　　What persecution, merciless and blind,
Drove o'er the sea—that desert desolate—
　　These Ishmaels and Hagars of mankind?[37]

They lived in narrow streets and lanes obscure,
　　Ghetto and Judenstrass,[38] in mirk and mire;
35　Taught in the school of patience to endure
　　The life of anguish and the death of fire.

All their lives long, with the unleavened bread
　　And bitter herbs of exile and its fears,
The wasting famine of the heart they fed,
40　　And slaked its thirst with marah of their tears.[39]

Anathema maranatha![40] was the cry
　　That rang from town to town, from street to street;
At every gate the accursed Mordecai[41]
　　Was mocked and jeered, and spurned by Christian feet.

45　Pride and humiliation hand in hand
　　Walked with them through the world where'er they went;
Trampled and beaten were they as the sand,
　　And yet unshaken as the continent.

---

[35] The incident is recorded in Exodus 32:19.
[36] The Jews of Newport were of mostly Spanish and Portuguese descent.
[37] Two exiles whose stories are told in the Bible.
[38] In German, literally "Jew Street."
[39] *Marah* means bitterness in Hebrew. During Passover, the Jewish celebration of the Exodus, Jews eat unleavened bread (matzoh) and bitter herbs in commemoration of that bitter time.
[40] St. Paul's epithet for those who did not believe in Christ; it became a phrase applied only to Jews.
[41] Mordecai was a famous Persian Jew. Here the word is used as a synonym for "Jew."

For in the background figures vague and vast
50   Of patriarchs and of prophets rose sublime,
And all the great traditions of the Past
        They saw reflected in the coming time.

And thus forever with reverted look
        The mystic volume of the world they read,
55   Spelling it backward, like a Hebrew book,[42]
        Till life became a Legend of the Dead.

But ah! what once has been shall be no more!
        The groaning earth in travail and in pain
Brings forth its races, but does not restore,
60   And the dead nations never rise again.

ELIZABETH BARRETT BROWNING (1809–1861)

How Do I Love Thee?

How do I love thee? Let me count the ways.
I love thee to the depth and breadth and height
My soul can reach, when feeling out of sight
For the ends of Being and ideal Grace.
5   I love thee to the level of everyday's
Most quiet need, by sun and candle-light.
I love thee freely, as men strive for Right;
I love thee purely, as they turn from Praise.
I love thee with the passion put to use
10   In my old griefs, and with my childhood's faith.
I love thee with a love I seemed to lose
With my lost saints,—I love thee with the breath,
Smiles, tears, of all my life!—and, if God choose,
I shall but love thee better after death.

Compare "How Do I Love Thee" with Thomas Lovell Beddoes's "Song" on page 365.

OLIVER WENDELL HOLMES (1809–1894)

My Aunt

My aunt! my dear unmarried aunt!
        Long years have o'er her flown;
Yet still she strains the aching clasp
        That binds her virgin zone;
5   I know it hurts her,—though she looks
        As cheerful as she can;

---

[42] Hebrew is written from right to left—in Longfellow's mind, backward.

Her waist is ampler than her life,
    For life is but a span.

My aunt! my poor deluded aunt!
10   Her hair is almost gray;
Why will she train that winter curl
    In such a spring-like way?
How can she lay her glasses down,
    And say she reads as well,
15   When through a double convex lens
    She just makes out to spell?

Her father—grandpapa! forgive
    This erring lip its smiles—
Vowed she should make the finest girl
20   Within a hundred miles;
He sent her to a stylish school;
    'T was in her thirteenth June;
And with her, as the rules required,
    "Two towels and a spoon."

25   They braced my aunt against a board,
    To make her straight and tall;
They laced her up, they starved her down,
    To make her light and small;°   *thin*
They pinched her feet, they singed her hair,
30   They screwed it up with pins;—
Oh, never mortal suffered more
    In penance for her sins.

So, when my precious aunt was done,
    My grandsire brought her back
35   (By daylight, lest some rabid youth
    Might follow on the track);
"Ah!" said my grandsire, as he shook
    Some powder in his pan;[43]
"What could this lovely creature do
40   Against a desperate man!"

Alas! nor chariot, nor barouche,[44]
    Nor bandit cavalcade,
Tore from the trembling father's arms
    His all-accomplished maid.
45   For her how happy had it been!
    And Heaven had spared to me
To see one sad, ungathered rose
    On my ancestral tree.

---

[43] The grandfather is loading a flintlock rifle.
[44] A fashionable carriage.

Compare "My Aunt" with T. S. Eliot's "Aunt Helen" on page 174, E. E. Cummings's "the Cambridge ladies who live in furnished souls" on page 388, and Gwendolyn Brooks's "Sadie and Maud" on pages 401–402.

ROBERT BROWNING (1812–1889)

Meeting at Night

1

The gray sea and the long black land;
And the yellow half-moon large and low;
And the startled little waves that leap

In fiery ringlets from their sleep,
5   As I gain the cove with pushing prow,
And quench its speed i' the slushy sand.

2

Then a mile of warm sea-scented beach;
Three fields to cross till a farm appears;
A tap at the pane, the quick sharp scratch
10   And blue spurt of a lighted match,
And a voice less loud, through its joys and fears,
Than the two hearts beating each to each!

Parting at Morning

Round the cape of a sudden came the sea,
And the sun looked over the mountain's rim:
And straight was a path of gold for him,
And the need of a world of men for me.

Robert Browning; paint-
ing by F. Talfond (Na-
tional Portrait Gallery,
London)

EMILY BRONTË (1818–1848)

The Sun Has Set

The sun has set, and the long grass now
    Waves dreamily in the evening wind;
And the wild bird has flown from that old gray stone
    In some warm nook a couch to find.

5   In all the lonely landscape round
    I see no light and hear no sound,
    Except the wind that far away
    Come sighing o'er the heathy sea.

Compare "The Sun Has Set" with James Joyce's "All Day I Hear the Noise of Waters" on page 386.

HERMAN MELVILLE (1819–1891)

On the Photograph of a Corps Commander

Ay, man is manly. Here you see
    The warrior-carriage of the head,
And brave dilation of the frame;
    And lighting all, the soul that led
5 In Spottsylvania's[45] charge to victory,
    Which justifies his fame.

A cheering picture. It is good
    To look upon a Chief like this,
In whom the spirit moulds the form.
10   Here favoring Nature, oft remiss,
With eagle mien expressive has endued
    A man to kindle strains that warm.

Trace back his lineage, and his sires,
    Yeoman or noble, you shall find
15 Enrolled with men of Agincourt,[46]
    Heroes who shared great Harry's mind.
Down to us come the knightly Norman fires,
    And front the Templars bore.[47]

Nothing can lift the heart of man
20   Like manhood in a fellow-man.
The thought of heaven's great King afar
But humbles us—too weak to scan;
But manly greatness men can span,
    And feel the bonds that draw.

---

[45] A Civil War battleground where the Confederate army inflicted severe losses on the Union forces.
[46] The scene of Henry V's victory over the French in 1415. King Henry was also called Harry.
[47] The Templars are one of the three great orders of knighthood founded at the time of the Crusades.

WALT WHITMAN (1819–1892)

A Noiseless Patient Spider

A noiseless patient spider,
I marked where on a little promontory it stood isolated,
Marked how to explore the vacant vast surrounding,
It launched forth filament, filament, filament, out of itself,
5   Ever unreeling them, ever tirelessly speeding them.

And you O my soul where you stand,
Surrounded, detached, in measureless oceans of space,
Ceaselessly musing, venturing, throwing, seeking the spheres to connect them,
Till the bridge you will need be formed, till the ductile anchor hold,
10   Till the gossamer thread you fling catch somewhere, O my soul.

Compare "A Noiseless Patient Spider" with Edward Taylor's "Upon a Spider Catching a Fly" on pages 356–357.

MATTHEW ARNOLD (1822–1888)

The Buried Life

Light flows our war of mocking words, and yet,
Behold, with tears mine eyes are wet!
I feel a nameless sadness o'er me roll.
Yes, yes, we know that we can jest,
5   We know, we know that we can smile!
But there's a something in this breast,
To which thy light words bring no rest,
And thy gay smiles no anodyne.°   *painkiller*
Give me thy hand, and hush awhile,
10   And turn those limpid eyes on mine,
And let me read there, love! thy inmost soul.

Alas! is even love too weak
To unlock the heart, and let it speak?
Are even lovers powerless to reveal
15   To one another what indeed they feel?
I knew the mass of men concealed
Their thoughts, for fear that if revealed
They would by other men be met
With blank indifference, or with blame reproved;
20   I knew they lived and moved
Tricked in disguises, alien to the rest
Of men, and alien to themselves—and yet
The same heart beats in every human breast!

But we, my love!—doth a like spell benumb
25   Our hearts, our voices?—must we too be dumb?

Ah! well for us, if even we,
Even for a moment, can get free
Our heart, and have our lips unchained;
For that which seals them hath been deep-ordained!

30 Fate, which foresaw
How frivolous a baby man would be—
By what distractions he would be possessed,
How he would pour himself in every strife,
And well-nigh change his own identity—
35 That it might keep from his capricious play
His genuine self, and force him to obey
Even in his own despite his being's law,
Bade through the deep recesses of our breast
The unregarded river of our life
40 Pursue with indiscernible flow its way;
And that we should not see
The buried stream, and seem to be
Eddying at large in blind uncertainty,
Though driving on with it eternally.

45 But often, in the world's most crowded streets,
But often, in the din of strife,
There rises an unspeakable desire
After the knowledge of our buried life;
A thirst to spend our fire and restless force
50 In tracking out our true, original course;
A longing to inquire
Into the mystery of this heart which beats
So wild, so deep in us—to know
Whence our lives come and where they go.
55 And many a man in his own breast then delves,
But deep enough, alas! none ever mines.
And we have been on many thousand lines,
And we have shown, on each, spirit and power;
But hardly have we, for one little hour,
60 Been on our own line, have we been ourselves—
Hardly had skill to utter one of all
The nameless feelings that course through our breast,
But they course on forever unexpressed.
And long we try in vain to speak and act
65 Our hidden self, and what we say and do
Is eloquent, is well—but 'tis not true!
And then we will no more be racked
With inward striving, and demand
Of all the thousand nothings of the hour
70 Their stupefying power;
Ah yes, and they benumb us at our call!
Yet still, from time to time, vague and forlorn,

From the soul's subterranean depth upborne
As from an infinitely distant land,
75   Come airs, and floating echoes, and convey
A melancholy into all our day.

Only—but this is rare—
When a beloved hand is laid in ours,
When, jaded with the rush and glare
80   Of the interminable hours,
Our eyes can in another's eyes read clear,
When our world-deafened ear
Is by the tones of a loved voice caressed—
A bolt is shot back somewhere in our breast,
85   And a lost pulse of feeling stirs again.
The eye sinks inward, and the heart lies plain,
And what we mean, we say, and what we would, we know.
A man becomes aware of his life's flow,
And hears its winding murmur; and he sees
90   The meadows where it glides, the sun, the breeze.

And there arrives a lull in the hot race
Wherein he doth forever chase
That flying and elusive shadow, rest.
An air of coolness plays upon his face,
95   And an unwonted calm pervades his breast.
And then he thinks he knows
The hills where his life rose,
And the sea where it goes.

Compare "The Buried Life" with Matthew Arnold's "Dover Beach" on pages 108–109.

FRANCES E. W. HARPER (1825–1911)

The Slave Auction

The sale began—young girls were there,
    Defenceless in their wretchedness,
Whose stifled sobs of deep despair
    Revealed their anguish and distress.

5   And mothers stood with streaming eyes,
    And saw their dearest children sold;
Unheeded rose their bitter cries,
    While tyrants bartered them for gold.

And woman, with her love and truth—
10   For these in sable° forms may dwell—   *black*
Gaz'd on the husband of her youth,
    With anguish none may paint or tell.

And men, whose sole crime was their hue,
    The impress of their Maker's hand,
15 And frail and shrinking children, too,
    Were gathered in that mournful band.

Ye who have laid your love to rest,
    And wept above their lifeless clay,
Know not the anguish of that breast,
20   Whose lov'd are rudely torn away.

Ye may not know how desolate
    Are bosoms rudely forced to part,
And how a dull and heavy weight
    Will press the life-drops from the heart.

EMILY DICKINSON (1830–1886)

My Life Had Stood, a Loaded Gun

My life had stood, a loaded gun,
In corners, till a day
The owner passed, identified,
And carried me away.

5 And now we roam in sovereign woods,
And now we hunt the doe,
And every time I speak for him,
The mountains straight reply.

And do I smile, such cordial light
10 Upon the valley glow,
It is as a Vesuvian face[48]
Had let its pleasure through.

And when at night, our good day done,
  I guard my master's head,
15 'Tis better than the eider-duck's[49]
Deep pillow, to have shared.

To foe of his I'm deadly foe:
None stir the second time
On whom I lay a yellow eye
20 Or an emphatic thumb.

Though I than he may longer live,
He longer must than I,
For I have but the power to kill,
Without the power to die.

---

[48] Vesuvius is an active volcano in Italy, overlooking the Bay of Naples.
[49] The down of the eider is particularly suited for stuffing pillows and quilts.

Discuss "My Life Had Stood, a Loaded Gun" as an example of metaphor.

EMILY DICKINSON (1830–1886)

Apparently with No Surprise

Apparently with no surprise
To any happy flower,
The frost beheads it at its play
In accidental power.

5   The blond assassin passes on,
The sun proceeds unmoved
To measure off another day
For an approving God.

Discuss "Apparently, with No Surprise" as an example of personification.

EMILY DICKINSON (1830–1886)

I Heard a Fly Buzz—When I Died

I heard a Fly buzz—when I died—
The Stillness in the Room
Was like the Stillness in the Air—
Between the Heaves of Storm—

5   The Eyes around—had wrung them dry—
And Breaths were gathering firm
For that last Onset—when the King
Be witnessed—in the Room—

I willed my Keepsakes—Signed away
10   What portion of me be
Assignable—and then it was
There interposed a Fly—

With Blue—uncertain stumbling Buzz—
Between the light—and me—
15   And then the Windows failed—and then
I could not see to see—

EMILY DICKINSON (1830–1886)

After Great Pain, a Formal Feeling Comes

After great pain, a formal feeling comes—
The Nerves sit ceremonious, like Tombs—
The stiff Heart questions was it He, that bore,
And Yesterday, or Centuries before?

<ol start="5">
<li>The Feet, mechanical, go round—</li>
</ol>

Of Ground, or Air, or Ought—
A Wooden way
Regardless grown,
A Quartz contentment, like a stone—

<ol start="10">
<li>This is the Hour of Lead—</li>
</ol>

Remembered, if outlived,
As Freezing persons, recollect the Snow—
First—Chill—then Stupor—then the letting go—

CHRISTINA ROSSETTI (1830–1894)

After Death

The curtains were half drawn; the floor was swept
    And strewn with rushes; rosemary and may
    Lay thick upon the bed on which I lay,
Where, through the lattice, ivy-shadows crept.

<ol start="5">
<li>He leaned above me, thinking that I slept</li>
</ol>

    And could not hear him; but I heard him say,
    "Poor child, poor child"; and as he turned away
Came a deep silence, and I knew he wept.
He did not touch the shroud, or raise the fold

<ol start="10">
<li>   That hid my face, or take my hand in his,</li>
</ol>

        Or ruffle the smooth pillows for my head.
        He did not love me living: but once dead
    He pitied me; and very sweet it is
To know he still is warm though I am cold.

Compare "After Death" with Coventry Patmore's "If I Were Dead" on page 324.

GERARD MANLEY HOPKINS (1844–1889)

· Spring and Fall

To a young child

Márgarét, are you gríeving
Over Goldengrove unleaving?
Leáves, líke the things of man, you
With your fresh thoughts care for, can you?

<ol start="5">
<li>Áh! ás the heart grows older</li>
</ol>

It will come to such sights colder
By and by, nor spare a sigh
Though worlds of wanwood leafmeal[50] lie;

---

[50] Wanwood and leafmeal are two *portmanteau words.* Wan + wood is meant to suggest bloodless limbs, and leaf + (piece) meal suggests the random pattern of the fallen leaves.

And yet you will weep and know why.
10   Now no matter, child, the name:
     Sórrow's spríngs áre the same.
     Nor mouth had, no nor mind, expressed
     What heart heard of, ghost° guessed: *spirit*
     It ís the blight man was born for,
15   It is Margaret you mourn for.

GERARD MANLEY HOPKINS (1844–1889)

• The Windhover[51]

To Christ Our Lord

I caught this morning morning's minion,° king-   *darling*
    dom of daylight's dauphin,° dapple-dawn-drawn Falcon, in his riding   *prince*
    Of the rolling level underneath him steady air, and striding
High there, how he rung upon the rein of a wimpling° wing   *rippling as a veil*
In his ecstasy! then off, off forth on swing,
5   As a skate's heel sweeps smooth on a bow-bend: the hurl and gliding
        Rebuffed the big wind. My heart in hiding
Stirred for a bird,—the achieve of, the mastery of the thing!

Brute beauty and valour and act, oh, air, pride, plume, here
    Buckle! AND the fire that breaks from thee then, a billion
10   Times told lovelier, more dangerous, O my chevalier!°   *knight*

    No wonder of it: shéer plód makes plough down sillion[52]
Shine, and blue-bleak embers, ah my dear,
    Fall, gall themselves, and gash gold-vermilion.

ALICE MEYNELL (1847–1922)

The Threshing-Machine

No "fan[53] is in his hand" for these
Young villagers beneath the trees,
    Watching the wheels. But I recall
    The rhythm of rods° that rise and fall,   *scythes*
5   Purging the harvest, over-seas.

---

[51] The windhover is the common name for the kestrel, a European falcon that flies with its head
   into the wind.
[52] The ridge between two plowed furrows.
[53] A *fan* is a basket used to winnow grain.

No fan, no flail, no threshing-floor!
And all their symbols evermore
    Forgone in England now—the sign,
    The visible pledge, the threat divine.
10   The chaff° dispersed, the wheat in store.   *husk*

The unbreathing engine marks no tune,
Steady at sunrise, steady at noon.
    Inhuman, perfect, saving time,
    And saving measure, and saving rhyme.
15   And did our Ruskin speak too soon?[54]

"No noble strength on earth" he sees
"Save Hercules' arm"[55] His grave decrees
    Curse wheel and steam. As the wheels ran
    I saw the other strength of man.
20   I knew the brain of Hercules.

OSCAR WILDE (1856–1900)

The Harlot's House

We caught the tread of dancing feet,
We loitered down the moonlit street,
And stopped beneath the harlot's house.

Inside, above the din and fray,
5   We heard the loud musicians play
The "Treues Liebes Herz" of Strauss.[56]

Like strange mechanical grotesques,
Making fantastic arabesques,
The shadows raced across the blind.

10   We watched the ghostly dancers spin
To sound of horn and violin,
Like black leaves wheeling in the wind.

Like wire-pulled automatons,
Slim silhouetted skeletons
15   Went sidling through the slow quadrille.

They took each other by the hand,
And danced a stately saraband;
Their laughter echoed thin and shrill.

Sometimes a clockwork puppet pressed
20   A phantom lover to her breast,
Sometimes they seemed to try to sing.

---

[54] John Ruskin (1819–1900) was an English essayist and critic who believed that by following agricultural pursuits, people could avoid the horrors of industrialism.
[55] Hercules was a mythical strong man.
[56] In German, "love's true heart."

Sometimes a horrible marionette
Came out, and smoked its cigarette
Upon the steps like a live thing.

25 Then, turning to my love, I said,
"The dead are dancing with the dead,
The dust is whirling with the dust."

But she—she heard the violin,
And left my side, and entered in:
30 Love passed into the house of lust.

Then suddenly the tune went false,
The dancers wearied of the waltz,
The shadows ceased to wheel and whirl.

And down the long and silent street,
35 The dawn, with silver-sandaled feet,
Crept like a frightened girl.

A. E. HOUSMAN (1859–1936)

Loveliest of Trees

Loveliest of trees, the cherry now
Is hung with bloom along the bough,
And stands about the woodland ride
Wearing white for Eastertide.

5 Now, of my threescore years and ten,
Twenty will not come again,
And take from seventy springs a score,
It only leaves me fifty more.

And since to look at things in bloom
10 Fifty springs are little room,
About the woodlands I will go
To see the cherry hung with snow.

A. E. HOUSMAN (1859–1936)

When I Was One-and-Twenty

When I was one-and-twenty
    I heard a wise man say,
"Give crowns and pounds and guineas
    But not your heart away;
5 Give pearls away and rubies
    But keep your fancy free."
But I was one-and-twenty,
    No use to talk to me.

When I was one-and-twenty
10   I heard him say again,
"The heart out of the bosom
      Was never given in vain:
'Tis paid with sighs a plenty
      And sold for endless rue."
15   And I am two-and-twenty,
      And oh, 'tis true, 'tis true.

Compare "When I Was One-and-Twenty" with John Crowe Ransom's "Piazza Piece" on pages 89–90.

W. E. B. DuBOIS (1868–1963)

The Song of the Smoke

I am the smoke king,
I am black.
I am swinging in the sky,
I am ringing worlds on high:
5   I am the thought of the throbbing mills,
I am the soul toil kills,
I am the ripple of trading rills.

Up I'm curling from the sod,
I am whirling home to God.
10 I am the smoke king,
I am black.

I am the smoke king,
I am black.
I am wreathing broken hearts,
15 I am sheathing devils' darts;
Dark inspiration of iron times,
Wedding the toil of toiling climes
Shedding the blood of bloodless crimes.

Down I lower in the blue,
20 Up I tower toward the true,
I am the smoke king,
I am black.

I am the smoke king,
I am black.

25 I am darkening with song,
I am hearkening to wrong;
I will be black as blackness can,
The blacker the mantle the mightier the man,
My purpl'ing midnights no day dawn may ban.

30   I am carving God in night,
    I am painting hell in white.
    I am the smoke king,
    I am black.

Compare "The Song of the Smoke" with N. Scott Momaday's "The Delight Song of Tsoai-Talee" on pages 138–139.

EDWIN ARLINGTON ROBINSON (1869–1935)

Mr. Flood's Party

Old Eben Flood, climbing alone one night
Over the hill between the town below
And the forsaken upland hermitage
That held as much as he should ever know
5   On earth again of home, paused warily.
The road was his with not a native near;
And Eben, having leisure, said aloud,
For no man else in Tilbury Town to hear:

"Well, Mr. Flood, we have the harvest moon
10   Again, and we may not have many more;
The bird is on the wing, the poet says,
And you and I have said it here before.
Drink to the bird."[57] He raised up to the light
The jug that he had gone so far to fill,
15   And answered huskily: "Well, Mr. Flood,
Since you propose it, I believe I will."

Alone, as if enduring to the end
A valiant armor of scarred hopes outworn,
He stood there in the middle of the road
20   Like Roland's ghost winding° a silent horn.[58]   *blowing*
Below him, in the town among the trees,
Where friends of other days had honored him,
A phantom salutation of the dead
Rang thinly till old Eben's eyes were dim.

25   Then, as a mother lays her sleeping child
Down tenderly, fearing it may awake,
He set the jug down slowly at his feet
With trembling care, knowing that most things break;
And only when assured that on firm earth
30   It stood, as the uncertain lives of men
Assuredly did not, he paced away,
And with his hand extended paused again:

---

[57] From the *Rubaiyat of Omar Khayyam*. The bird referred to is the bird of time.
[58] Roland was a knight who delayed calling for help with his horn at the Battle of Roncesvalles (A.D. 778) until the situation was hopeless.

"Well, Mr. Flood, we have not met like this
In a long time; and many a change has come
35   To both of us, I fear, since last it was
We had a drop together. Welcome home!"
Convivially returning with himself,
Again he raised the jug up to the light;
And with an acquiescent quaver said:
40   "Well, Mr. Flood, if you insist, I might.

"Only a very little, Mr. Flood—
For auld lang syne. [59] No more, sir; that will do."
So, for the time, apparently it did,
And Eben evidently thought so too;
45   For soon amid the silver loneliness
Of night he lifted up his voice and sang,
Secure, with only two moons listening,
Until the whole harmonious landscape rang—

"For auld lang syne." The weary throat gave out,
50   The last word wavered; and the song being done,
He raised again the jug regretfully
And shook his head, and was again alone.
There was not much that was ahead of him,
And there was nothing in the town below—
55   Where strangers would have shut the many doors
That many friends had opened long ago.

STEPHEN CRANE (1871–1900)

A Man Adrift on a Slim Spar

A man adrift on a slim spar
A horizon smaller than the rim of a bottle
Tented waves rearing lashy dark points
The near whine of froth in circles.
5   God is cold.

The incessant raise and swing of the sea
And growl after growl of crest
The sinkings, green, seething, endless
The upheaval half-completed.
10   God is cold.

The seas are in the hollow of The Hand;
Oceans may be turned to a spray
Raining down through the stars
Because of a gesture of pity toward a babe.
15   Oceans may become grey ashes,
Die with a long moan and a roar

---

[59] The good old times.

Amid the tumult of the fishes
And the cries of the ships,
Because The Hand beckons the mice.

20 A horizon smaller than a doomed assassin's cap,
Inky, surging tumults
A reeling, drunken sky and no sky
A pale hand sliding from a polished spar.
          God is cold.

25 The puff of a coat imprisoning air:
A face kissing the water-death
A weary slow sway of a lost hand
And the sea, the moving sea, the sea.
          God is cold.

ROBERT FROST (1874–1963)

Mending Wall

Something there is that doesn't love a wall,
That sends the frozen-ground-swell under it
And spills the upper boulders in the sun,
And makes gaps even two can pass abreast.
5   The work of hunters is another thing:
I have come after them and made repair
Where they have left not one stone on a stone,
But they would have the rabbit out of hiding,
To please the yelping dogs. The gaps I mean,
10   No one has seen them made or heard them made,
But at spring mending-time we find them there.
I let my neighbor know beyond the hill;
And on a day we meet to walk the line
And set the wall between us once again.
15   We keep the wall between us as we go.
To each the boulders that have fallen to each.
And some are loaves and some so nearly balls
We have to use a spell to make them balance:
"Stay where you are until our backs are turned!"
20   We wear our fingers rough with handling them.
Oh, just another kind of outdoor game,
One on a side. It comes to little more:
There where it is we do not need the wall:
He is all pine and I am apple orchard.
25   My apple trees will never get across
And eat the cones under his pines, I tell him.
He only says, "Good fences make good neighbors."
Spring is the mischief in me, and I wonder
If I could put a notion in his head:
30   "Why do they make good neighbors? Isn't it

Where there are cows? But here there are no cows.
Before I built a wall I'd ask to know
What I was walling in or walling out,
And to whom I was like to give offense.
35   Something there is that doesn't love a wall,
That wants it down." I could say "Elves" to him,
But it's not elves exactly, and I'd rather
He said it for himself. I see him there
Bringing a stone grasped firmly by the top
40   In each hand, like an old-stone savage armed.
He moves in darkness as it seems to me,
Not of woods only and the shade of trees.
He will not go behind his father's saying,
And he likes having thought of it so well
45   He says again, "Good fences make good neighbors."

ROBERT FROST (1874–1963)

After Apple-Picking

My long two-pointed ladder's sticking through a tree
Toward heaven still,
And there's a barrel that I didn't fill
Beside it, and there may be two or three
5   Apples I didn't pick upon some bough.
But I am done with apple-picking now.
Essence of winter sleep is on the night,
The scent of apples: I am drowsing off.
I cannot rub the strangeness from my sight
10   I got from looking through a pane of glass
I skimmed this morning from the drinking trough
And held against the world of hoary grass.
It melted, and I let it fall and break.
But I was well
15   Upon my way to sleep before it fell,
And I could tell
What form my dreaming was about to take.
Magnified apples appear and disappear,
Stem end and blossom end,
20   And every fleck of russet showing clear.
My instep arch not only keeps the ache,
It keeps the pressure of a ladder-round.
I feel the ladder sway as the boughs bend.
And I keep hearing from the cellar bin
25   The rumbling sound
Of load on load of apples coming in.
For I have had too much
Of apple-picking: I am overtired
Of the great harvest I myself desired.

30   There were ten thousand thousand fruit to touch,
    Cherish in hand, lift down, and not let fall.
    For all
    That struck the earth,
    No matter if not bruised or spiked with stubble,
35   Went surely to the cider-apple heap
    As of no worth.
    One can see what will trouble
    This sleep of mine, whatever sleep it is.
    Were he not gone,
40   The woodchuck could say whether it's like his
    Long sleep, as I describe its coming on,
    Or just some human sleep.

Compare "After Apple-Picking" with Dave Smith's "Picking Cherries" on page 436.

ROBERT FROST (1874–1963)

A Peck of Gold[60]

Dust always blowing about the town,
Except when sea-fog laid it down,
And I was one of the children told
Some of the blowing dust was gold.

5   All the dust the wind blew high
Appeared like gold in the sunset sky,
But I was one of the children told
Some of the dust was really gold.

Such was life in the Golden Gate:
10   Gold dusted all we drank and ate,
And I was one of the children told,
"We all must eat our peck of gold."

ROBERT FROST (1874–1963)

The Silken Tent

She is as in a field a silken tent
At midday when a sunny summer breeze
Has dried the dew and all its ropes relent,
So that in guys° it gently sways at ease,   *ropes*
5   And its supporting central cedar pole,
That is its pinnacle to heavenward
And signifies the sureness of the soul,
Seems to owe naught to any single cord,

---

[60] Although Frost is associated with Vermont and New Hampshire, he was born in San Francisco and lived there until the age of eleven. This poem is about his California childhood.

But strictly held by none, is loosely bound
10   By countless silken ties of love and thought
To everything on earth the compass round,
And only by one's going slightly taut
In the capriciousness of summer air
Is of the slightest bondage made aware.

Show how "The Silken Tent" is an allegory.

JAMES JOYCE (1880–1941)

All Day I Hear the Noise of Waters

All day I hear the noise of waters
        Making moan,
Sad as the sea-bird is, when going
        Forth alone,
5   He hears the winds cry to the waters'
        Monotone.

The grey winds, the cold winds are blowing
        Where I go.
I hear the noise of many waters
10   Far below.
All day, all night, I hear them flowing
        To and fro.

Compare "All Day I Hear the Noise of Waters" with Emily Brontë's "The Sun Has Set" on page 370.

ARCHIBALD MacLEISH (1892–1982)

Ars Poetica[61]

A poem should be palpable and mute
As a globed fruit,

Dumb
As old medallions to the thumb,

5   Silent as the sleeve-worn stone
Of casement ledges where the moss has grown—

A poem should be wordless
As the flight of birds.

A poem should be motionless in time
10   As the moon climbs,

---

[61] Latin for "the art of poetry."

Leaving, as the moon releases
Twig by twig the night-entangled trees,

Leaving, as the moon behind the winter leaves,
Memory by memory the mind—

15 A poem should be motionless in time
As the moon climbs.

A poem should be equal to:
Not true.

For all the history of grief
20 An empty doorway and a maple leaf.

For love
The leaning grasses and two lights above the sea—

A poem should not mean
But be.

WILFRED OWEN (1893–1918)

Anthem for Doomed Youth

What passing-bells for these who die as cattle?
Only the monstrous anger of the guns.
Only the stuttering rifles' rapid rattle
Can patter out their hasty orisons.
5 No mockeries for them from prayers or bells,
Nor any voice of mourning save the choirs—
The shrill, demented choirs of wailing shells;
And bugles calling for them from sad shires.

What candles may be held to speed them all?
10 Not in the hands of boys, but in their eyes
Shall shine the holy glimmers of good-byes.
The pallor of girls' brows shall be their pall;
Their flowers the tenderness of patient minds,
And each slow dusk a drawing-down of blinds.

Compare "Anthem for Doomed Youth" with A. E. Housman's "To an Athlete Dying Young" on pages 60–61 and Randall Jarrell's "The Death of the Ball Turret Gunner" on page 91.

E. E. CUMMINGS (1894–1962)

in Just-

in Just-
spring   when the world is mud-
luscious the little
lame balloonman

whistles   far   and wee

and eddieandbill come
running from marbles and
piracies and it's
spring

10   when the world is puddle-wonderful

the queer
old balloonman whistles
far   and   wee
and bettyandisbel come dancing

15   from hop-scotch and jump-rope and

it's
spring
and
      the
20   goat-footed[62]

balloonMan   whistles
far
and
wee

E. E. CUMMINGS (1894–1962)

the Cambridge[63] ladies who live in furnished souls

the Cambridge ladies who live in furnished souls
are unbeautiful and have comfortable minds
(also, with the church's protestant blessings
daughters, unscented shapeless spirited)
5   they believe in Christ and Longfellow,[64] both dead,
are invariably interested in so many things—
at the present writing one still finds
delighted fingers knitting for the is it Poles?
perhaps. While permanent faces coyly bandy
10   scandal of Mrs. N and Professor D
. . . . the Cambridge ladies do not care, above
Cambridge if sometimes in its box of
sky lavender and cornerless, the
moon rattles like a fragment of angry candy

---

[62] The word *goat-footed* suggests that the "balloonman" resembles Pan, the Greek god of flocks and pastures, who is depicted as having the ears and hooves of a goat.

[63] Cambridge, Massachusetts, is the home of Harvard University, where Cummings's father taught and where Cummings himself was educated.

[64] Henry Wadsworth Longfellow, the American poet, made his home in Cambridge. One of Longfellow's poems may be found on pages 365–367.

Compare "the Cambridge ladies who live in furnished souls" with Gwendolyn Brooks's "Sadie and Maud" on pages 401–402, T. S. Eliot's "Aunt Helen" on page 174, and Oliver Wendell Holmes's "My Aunt" on pages 367–368.

ROBERT GRAVES (1895–)

Dialogue on the Headland

She: You'll not forget these rocks and what I told you?
He: How could I? Never: whatever happens.
She: What do you think might happen?
        Might you fall out of love?—did you mean that?
5   *He:*   Never, never! "Whatever" was a sop
        For jealous listeners in the shadows.
She: You haven't answered me. I asked:
        "What do you think might happen?"
He: Whatever happens: though the skies should fall
10   Raining their larks and vultures in our laps—
She: "Though the seas turn to slime"—say that—
        "Though water-snakes be hatched with six heads."
He: Though the seas turn to slime, or tower
        In an arching wave above us, three miles high—
15 *She:* "Though she should break with you,"—dare you say that?—
        "Though she deny her words on oath."
He: I had that in my mind to say, or nearly;
        It hurt so much I choked it back.
She: How many other days can't you forget?
20   How many other loves and landscapes?
He: You are jealous?
She: Damnably.
He: The past is past.
She: And this?
He: Whatever happens, this goes on.
She: Without a future? Sweetheart, tell me now:
        What do you want of me? I must know that.
25 *He:*   Nothing that isn't freely mine already.
She: Say what is freely yours and you shall have it.
He: Nothing that, loving you, I could dare take.
She: O, for an answer with no "nothing" in it!
He: Then give me everything that's left.
30 *She:* Left after what?
He: After whatever happens:
        Skies have already fallen, seas are slime,
        Water-snakes poke and peer six-headedly—
She: And I lie snugly in the Devil's arms.
He: I said: "Whatever happens." Are you crying?
35 *She:* You'll not forget me—ever, ever, ever?

Discuss "Dialogue on the Headland" as an example of hyperbole, as a problem of sincerity, or as an example of dramatic poetry.

LOUISE BOGAN (1897–1970)

Night

The cold remote islands
And the blue estuaries
Where what breathes, breathes
The restless wind of the inlets,
5   And what drinks, drinks
The incoming tide;

Where shell and weed
Wait upon the salt of the sea,
And the clear nights of stars
10   Swing their lights westward
To set behind the land;

Where the pulse clinging to the rocks
Renews itself forever;
Where, again on cloudless nights,
15   The water reflects
The firmament's partial setting;

—O remember
In your narrowing dark hours
That more things move
20   Than blood in the heart.

Compare "Night" with Emily Brontë's "The Sun Has Set" on page 370 and James Joyce's "All Day I Hear the Noise of Waters" on page 386.

ARNA BONTEMPS (1902–)

Southern Mansion

Poplars are standing there still as death
And ghosts of dead men
Meet their ladies walking
Two by two beneath the shade
5   And standing on the marble steps.

There is a sound of music echoing
Through the open door
And in the field there is
Another sound tinkling in the cotton:
10   Chains of bondmen dragging on the ground.

The years go back with an iron clank,
A hand is on the gate,
A dry leaf trembles on the wall.
Ghosts are walking.
15   They have broken roses down
And poplars stand there still as death.

STEVIE SMITH (1902–1971)

Not Waving but Drowning

Nobody heard him, the dead man,
But still he lay moaning:
I was much further out than you thought
And not waving but drowning.

5   Poor chap, he always loved larking
And now he's dead
It must have been too cold for him his heart gave way.
They said.

Oh, no no no, it was too cold always
10   (Still the dead one lay moaning)
I was much too far out all my life
And not waving but drowning.

STANLEY KUNITZ (1905–)

The Portrait

My mother never forgave my father
for killing himself,
especially at such an awkward time
and in a public park,
5   that spring
when I was waiting to be born.
She locked his name
in her deepest cabinet
and would not let him out,
10   though I could hear him thumping.
When I came down from the attic
with the pastel portrait in my hand
of a long-lipped stranger
with a brave moustache
15   and deep brown level eyes,
she ripped it into shreds
without a single word
and slapped me hard.
In my sixty-fourth year
20   I can feel my cheek
still burning.

W. H. AUDEN (1907–1973)

Lay Your Sleeping Head, My Love

Lay your sleeping head, my love,
Human on my faithless arm;
Time and fevers burn away
Individual beauty from
5   Thoughtful children, and the grave
Proves the child ephemeral:
But in my arms till break of day
Let the living creature lie,
Mortal, guilty, but to me
10   The entirely beautiful.

Soul and body have no bounds:
To lovers as they lie upon
Her tolerant enchanted slope
In their ordinary swoon,
15   Grave the vision Venus[65] sends
Of supernatural sympathy,
Universal love and hope;
While an abstract insight wakes
Among the glaciers and the rocks
20   The hermit's sensual ecstasy.

Certainty, fidelity
On the stroke of midnight pass
Like vibrations of a bell,
And fashionable madmen raise
25   Their pedantic boring cry:
Every farthing° of the cost,   *quarter of a penny*
All the dreaded cards foretell,
Shall be paid, but from this night
Not a whisper, not a thought,
30   Not a kiss nor look be lost.

Beauty, midnight, vision dies:
Let the winds of dawn that blow
Softly round your dreaming head
Such a day of sweetness show
35   Eye and knocking heart may bless,
Find the mortal world enough;
Noons of dryness see you fed
By the involuntary powers,
Nights of insult let you pass
40   Watched by every human love.

---

[65] Venus is the goddess of love.

W. H. AUDEN (1907–1973)

As I Walked Out One Evening

As I walked out one evening,
    Walking down Bristol Street,
The crowds upon the pavement
    Were fields of harvest wheat.

5   And down by the brimming river
    I heard a lover sing
Under an arch of the railway:
    "Love has no ending.

"I'll love you, dear, I'll love you
10   Till China and Africa meet,
And the river jumps over the mountain
    And the salmon sing in the street,

"I'll love you till the ocean
    Is folded and hung up to dry
15   And the seven stars go squawking
    Like geese about the sky.

"The years shall run like rabbits,
    For in my arms I hold
The Flower of the Ages,
20   And the first love of the world."

But all the clocks in the city
    Began to whirr and chime:
"O let not Time deceive you,
    You cannot conquer Time.

25   "In the burrows of the Nightmare
    Where Justice naked is,
Time watches from the shadow
    And coughs when you would kiss.

"In headaches and in worry
30   Vaguely life leaks away,
And Time will have his fancy
    Tomorrow or today.

"Into many a green valley
    Drifts the appalling snow;
35   Time breaks the threaded dances
    And the diver's brilliant bow.

"O plunge your hands in water,
    Plunge them in up to the wrist;
Stare, stare in the basin
40   And wonder what you've missed.

"The glacier knocks in the cupboard,
    The desert sighs in the bed,

And the crack in the teacup opens
    A lane to the land of the dead.

45   "Where the beggars raffle the banknotes
      And the Giant is enchanting to Jack,
    And the Lily-white Boy is a Roarer,°   *noisy reveler*
      And Jill goes down on her back.

    "O look, look in the mirror,
50   O look in your distress;
    Life remains a blessing
      Although you cannot bless.

    "O stand, stand at the window
      As the tears scald and start;
55   You shall love your crooked neighbor
      With your crooked heart."

    It was late, late in the evening,
      The lovers they were gone;
    The clocks had ceased their chiming,
60   And the deep river ran on.

Discuss "As I Walked Out One Evening" as an example of a ballad.

THEODORE ROETHKE (1908–1963)

My Papa's Waltz

The whiskey on your breath
Could make a small boy dizzy;
But I hung on like death:
Such waltzing was not easy.

5   We romped until the pans
Slid from the kitchen shelf;
My mother's countenance
Could not unfrown itself.

The hand that held my wrist
10   Was battered on one knuckle;
At every step you missed
My right ear scraped a buckle.

You beat time on my head
With a palm caked hard by dirt,
15   Then waltzed me off to bed
Still clinging to your shirt.

Compare "My Papa's Waltz" with Lucille Clifton's "Good Times" on page 428.

THEODORE ROETHKE (1908–1963)

I Knew a Woman

I knew a woman, lovely in her bones,
When small birds sighed, she would sigh back at them;
Ah, when she moved, she moved more ways than one:
The shapes a bright container can contain!
5   Of her choice virtues only gods should speak,
Or English poets who grew up on Greek
(I'd have them sing in chorus, cheek to cheek).

How well her wishes went! She stroked my chin,
She taught me Turn, and Counter-turn, and Stand,
10   She taught me Touch, that undulant white skin;
I nibbled meekly from her proffered hand;
She was the sickle; I, poor I, the rake,
Coming behind her for her pretty sake
(But what prodigious mowing we did make).

15   Love likes a gander, and adores a goose:
Her full lips pursed, the errant note to seize;
She played it quick, she played it light and loose;
My eyes, they dazzled at her flowing knees;
Her several parts could keep a pure repose,
20   Or one hip quiver with a mobile nose
(She moved in circles, and those circles moved).

Let seed be grass, and grass turn into hay:
I'm martyr to a motion not my own;
What's freedom for? To know eternity.
25   I swear she cast a shadow white as stone.
But who would count eternity in days?
These old bones live to learn her wanton ways:
(I measure time by how a body sways).

RICHARD WRIGHT (1908–1960)

Four Haiku

A balmy spring wind
Reminding me of something
   I cannot recall.

The green cockleburrs
Caught in the thick wooly hair
   Of the black boy's head.

Standing in the field,
I hear the whispering of
   Snowflake to snowflake.

It is September
The month in which I was born,
And I have no thoughts.

CHARLES OLSON (1910–1970)

Maximus, to Himself

I have had to learn the simplest things
last. Which made for difficulties.
Even at sea I was slow, to get the hand out, or to cross
a wet deck.
5   The sea was not, finally, my trade.
But even my trade, at it, I stood estranged
from that which was most familiar. Was delayed,
and not content with the man's argument
that such postponement
10 is now the nature of
obedience,
         that we are all late
         in a slow time,
         that we grow up many
15   And the single
         is not easily
         known

It could be, though the sharpness (the *achiote*)°   *a peppery seed*
I note in others,
20 makes more sense
than my own distances. The agilities
         they show daily
         who do the world's
         businesses
25   And who do nature's
         as I have no sense
         I have done either

I have made dialogues,
have discussed ancient texts,
30 have thrown what light I could, offered
what pleasures
doceat° allows   *teaching*

         But the known?
This, I have had to be given,
35 a life, love, and from one man
the world

         Tokens.
         But sitting here
         I look out as a wind

40   and water man, testing
    And missing
    some proof

  I know the quarters
  of the weather, where it comes from,
45 where it goes. But the stem of me,
  this I took from their welcome,
  or their rejection, of me

    And my arrogance
    was neither diminished
50   nor increased,
    by the communication

     2
  It is undone business
  I speak of, this morning,
  with the sea
55 stretching out
  from my feet

IRVING LAYTON (1912–)

Cain[66]

  Taking the air rifle from my son's hand
  I measured back five paces, the Hebrew
  In me, narcissist, father of children
  Laid to rest. From there I took aim and fired.
5 The silent ball hit the frog's back an inch
  Below the head. He jumped at the surprise
  Of it, suddenly tickled or startled
  (He must have thought) and leaped from the wet sand
  Into the surrounding brown water. But
10 The ball had done its mischief. His next spring
  Was a miserable flop, the thrust all gone
  Out of his legs. He tried—like Bruce—again,
  Throwing out his sensitive pianist's
  Hands as a dwarf might or a helpless child.
15 His splash disturbed the quiet pondwater
  And one old frog behind his weedy moat
  Blinking, looking self-complacently on.
  The lin's° surface at once became closing   *pond*
  Eyelids and bubbles like notes of music
20 Liquid, luminous, dropping from the page
  White, white-bearded, a rapid crescendo[67]
  Of inaudible sounds and a crones' whispering

---

[66] In the Bible, Cain is the son of Adam and the brother of Abel, whom Cain kills. Thus Cain is the prototypical murderer.
[67] *Crescendo* is the musical term for increasing volume.

Backstage among the reeds and bullrushes
As for an expiring Lear or Oedipus.[68]

25   But Death makes us all look ridiculous.
Consider this frog (dog, hog, what you will)
Sprawling, his absurd corpse rocked by the tides
That his last vain spring had set in movement.
Like a retired oldster, I couldn't help sneer,
30   Living off the last of his insurance:
Billows—now crumbling—the premiums paid.
Absurd, how absurd. I wanted to kill
At the mockery of it. Kill and kill
Again—the self-infatuate frog, dog, hog,
35   Anything with the stir of life in it,
Seeing that dead leaper, Chaplin-footed,[69]
Rocked and cradled in this afternoon
Of tranquil water, reeds, and blazing sun,
The hole in his back clearly visible
40   And the torn skin a blob of shadow
Moving when the quiet poolwater moved.
O Egypt, marbled Greece, resplendent Rome,
Did you also finally perish from a small bore
In your back you could not scratch? And would
45   Your mouths open ghostily, gasping out
Among the murky reeds, the hidden frogs,
We climb with crushed spines toward the heavens?
When the next morning I came the same way
The frog was on his back, one delicate
50   Hand on his belly, and his white shirt front
Spotless. He looked as if he might have been
A comic; tap dancer apologizing
For a fall, or an Emcee, his wide grin
Coaxing a laugh from us for an aside
55   Or perhaps a joke we didn't quite hear.

Compare "Cain" with Richard Wilbur's "The Death of a Toad" on pages 233–234.

MAY SARTON (1912–)

Lady with a Falcon

Flemish tapestry, fifteenth century

Gentleness and starvation tame
The falcon to this lady's wrist,

---

[68] Oedipus and Lear are both tragic heroes—the former in Sophocles' *Oedipus Rex*, the latter in Shakespeare's *King Lear*.
[69] Charlie Chaplin, the silent screen comic actor, had a distinctive waddling walk.

Natural flight hooded from blame
By what ironic fate or twist?

5   For now the hunched bird's contained flight
Pounces upon her inward air,
To plunder that mysterious night
Of poems blooded as the hare.

Heavy becomes the lady's hand,
10   And heavy bends the gentle head
Over her hunched and brooding bird
Until it is she who seems hooded.

Lady, your falcon is a peril,
Is starved, is mastered, but not kind.
15   The bird who sits your hand so gentle,
The captured hunter hunts your mind.

Better to starve the senseless wind
Than wrist a falcon's stop and start:
The bolt of flight you thought to bend
20   Plummets into your inmost heart.

Compare "Lady with a Falcon" with Robert Duncan's "My Mother Would Be a Falconress" on pages 402–403 and Ted Hughes's "Hawk Roosting" on page 421.

RANDALL JARRELL (1914–1965)

The Woman at the Washington Zoo

The saris go by me from the embassies.

Cloth from the moon. Cloth from another planet.
They look back at the leopard like the leopard.

And I. . . .
5   this print of mine, that has kept its color
Alive through so many cleanings; this dull null
Navy I wear to work, and wear from work, and so
To my bed, so to my grave, with no
Complaints, no comment: neither from my chief,
10   The Deputy Chief Assistant, nor his chief—
Only I complain. . . . this serviceable
Body that no sunlight dyes, no hand suffuses
But, dome-shadowed, withering among columns,
Wavy beneath fountains—small, far-off, shining
15   In the eyes of animals, these beings trapped
As I am trapped but not, themselves, the trap,
Aging, but without knowledge of their age,
Kept safe here, knowing not of death, for death—
Oh, bars of my own body, open, open!

20 The world goes by my cage and never sees me.
    And there come not to me, as come to these,
    The wild beast, sparrows pecking the llamas' grain,
    Pigeons settling on the bears' bread, buzzards
    Tearing the meat the flies have clouded. . . .
25   Vulture,
    When you come for the white rat that the foxes left,
    Take off the red helmet of your head, the black
    Wings that have shadowed me, and step to me as man:
    The wild brother at whose feet the white wolves fawn,
30 To whose hand of power the great lioness
    Stalks, purring. . . .
            You know what I was,
    You see what I am: change me, change me!

HENRY REED (1914–)

Naming of Parts

    Today we have naming of parts. Yesterday,
    We had daily cleaning. And tomorrow morning,
    We shall have what to do after firing. But today,
    Today we have naming of parts. Japonica
5   Glistens like coral in all of the neighboring gardens,
          And today we have naming of parts.

    This is the lower sling swivel. And this
    Is the upper sling swivel, whose use you will see,
    When you are given your slings. And this is the piling swivel,
10 Which in your case you have not got. The branches
    Hold in the gardens their silent, eloquent gestures,
          Which in our case we have not got.

    This is the safety-catch, which is always released
    With an easy flick of the thumb. And please do not let me
15 See anyone using his finger. You can do it quite easy
    If you have any strength in your thumb. The blossoms
    Are fragile and motionless, never letting anyone see
          Any of them using their finger.

    And this you can see is the bolt. The purpose of this
20 Is to open the breech, as you see. We can slide it
    Rapidly backwards and forwards: we call this
    Easing the spring. And rapidly backwards and forwards
    The early bees are assaulting and fumbling the flowers:
          They call it easing the Spring.

25 They call it easing the Spring: it is perfectly easy
    If you have any strength in your thumb: like the bolt,
    And the breech, and the cocking-piece, and the point of balance,
    Which in our case we have not got; and the almond-blossom

Silent in all of the gardens and the bees going backwards and forwards,
30   For today we have naming of parts.

WILLIAM STAFFORD (1914–)

Traveling Through the Dark

Traveling through the dark I found a deer
dead on the edge of the Wilson River road.
It is usually best to roll them into the canyon:
that road is narrow; to swerve might make more dead.

5 By glow of the tail-light I stumbled back of the car
and stood by the heap, a doe, a recent killing;
she had stiffened already, almost cold.
I dragged her off; she was large in the belly.

My fingers touching her side brought me the reason—
10 her side was warm; her fawn lay there waiting,
alive, still, never to be born.
Beside that mountain road I hesitated.

The car aimed ahead its lowered parking lights;
under the hood purred the steady engine.
15 I stood in the glare of the warm exhaust turning red;
around our group I could hear the wilderness listen.

I thought hard for us all—my only swerving—
then pushed her over the edge into the river.

GWENDOLYN BROOKS (1917–)

• Sadie and Maud

Maud went to college.
Sadie stayed at home.
Sadie scraped life
With a fine-tooth comb.

5 She didn't leave a tangle in.
Her comb found every strand.
Sadie was one of the livingest chits°   *young girls*
In all the land.

Sadie bore two babies
10 Under her maiden name.
Maud and Ma and Papa
Nearly died of shame.

When Sadie said her last so-long
Her girls struck out from home.
15 (Sadie had left as heritage
Her fine-tooth comb.)

Maud, who went to college,
Is a thin brown mouse.
She is living all alone
20   In this old house.

Compare "Sadie and Maud" with Oliver Wendell Holmes's "My Aunt" on pages 367–368 and T. S. Eliot's "Aunt Helen" on page 174.

ROBERT DUNCAN (1919–)

My Mother Would Be a Falconress

My mother would be a falconress,
And I, her gay falcon treading her wrist,
would fly to bring back
from the blue of the sky to her, bleeding, a prize,
5   where I dream in my little hood with many bells
jangling when I'd turn my head.

My mother would be a falconress,
and she sends me as far as her will goes.
She lets me ride to the end of her curb
10   where I fall back in anguish.
I dread that she will cast me away,
for I fall, I mis-take, I fail in her mission.

She would bring down the little birds.
And I would bring down the little birds.
15   When will she let me bring down the little birds,
pierced from their flight with their necks broken,
their heads like flowers limp from the stem?

I tread my mother's wrist and would draw blood.
Behind the little hood my eyes are hooded.
20   I have gone back into my hooded silence,
talking to myself and dropping off to sleep.

For she has muffled my dreams in the hood she has made me,
sewn round with bells, jangling when I move.
She rides with her little falcon upon her wrist.
25   She uses a barb that brings me to cower.
She sends me abroad to try my wings
and I come back to her. I would bring down
the little birds to her
I may not tear into, I must bring back perfectly.

30   I tear at her wrist with my beak to draw blood,
and her eye holds me, anguisht, terrifying.
She draws a limit to my flight.
Never beyond my sight, she says.

She trains me to fetch and to limit myself in fetching.
35 She rewards me with meat for my dinner.
But I must never eat what she sends me to bring her.

Yet it would have been beautiful, if she would have carried me,
always, in a little hood with the bells ringing,
at her wrist, and her riding
40 to the great falcon hunt, and me
flying up to the curb of my heart from her heart
to bring down the skylark from the blue to her feet,
straining, and then released for the flight.

My mother would be a falconress,
45 and I her gerfalcon,° raised at her will,   *large Arctic falcon*
from her wrist sent flying, as if I were her own
pride, as if her pride
knew no limits, as if her mind
sought in me flight beyond the horizon.

50 Ah, but high, high in the air I flew.
And far, far beyond the curb of her will,
were the blue hills where the falcons nest.
And then I saw west to the dying sun—
it seemed my human soul went down in flames.

55 I tore at her wrist, at the hold she had for me,
until the blood ran hot and I heard her cry out,
far, far beyond the curb of her will •

to horizons of stars beyond the ringing hills of the world where the falcons nest
I saw, and I tore at her wrist with my savage beak.
60 I flew, as if sight flew from the anguish in her eye beyond her sight,
sent from my striking loose, from the cruel strike at her wrist,
striking out from the blood to be free of her.

My mother would be a falconress,
and even now, years after this,
65 when the wounds I left her had surely heald,
and the woman is dead,
her fierce eyes closed, and if her heart
were broken, it is stilld •

I would be a falcon and go free.
70 I tread her wrist and wear the hood,
talking to myself, and would draw blood.

Compare "My Mother Would Be a Falconress" with May Sarton's "Lady with a Falcon"
on pages 398–399 and Ted Hughes's "Hawk Roosting" on page 421.

With or Without Reason, from the *Disasters of War*, by Francisco Goya
(Courtesy of the Museum of Fine Arts, Boston, William A. Sargent Bequest)

LAWRENCE FERLINGHETTI (1919–)

[In Goya's Greatest Scenes We Seem to See]

In Goya's greatest scenes[70] we seem to see
                       the people of the world
       exactly at the moment when
         they first attained the title of
5   "suffering humanity"
        They writhe upon the page
                  in a veritable rage
                      of adversity
    Heaped up
10   groaning with babies and bayonets
                    under cement skies
      in an abstract landscape of blasted trees
       bent statues bats wings and beaks
          slippery gibbets°   *gallows*
15   cadavers and carnivorous cocks
    and all the final hollering monsters
        of the
            "imagination of disaster"
    they are so bloody real
20   it is as if they really still existed

[70] Francisco Goya (1746–1828) was a Spanish painter and etcher. His *Disasters of War* series of
etchings depicted the horrors of warfare.

And they do

Only the landscape is changed

They still are ranged along the roads
plagued by legionaires
25   false windmills and demented roosters

They are the same people
only further from home
on freeways fifty lanes wide
on a concrete continent
30   spaced with bland billboards
illustrating imbecile illusions of happiness

Compare "[In Goya's Greatest Scenes We Seem to See]" with W. H. Auden's "Musée des Beaux Arts" on pages 12–13.

MONA VAN DUYN (1921–)

In the Cold Kingdom

"The younger brother roasted a breast of Pishiboro's elephant wife and handed Pishiboro some, which he presently ate. Then the younger brother said in a voice full of scorn, 'Oh you fool. You lazy man. You were married to meat and you thought it was a wife.' "

—*From a myth of the Bushmen*

Poised upside down on his duncecap,
a shrunken purple head,
True Blueberry,
enters its tightening frame of orange lip,
5   and the cream of a child's cheek is daubed with
Zanzibar Cocoa, while
        Here at the Martha Washington
        Ice Cream Store
        we outdo the Symbolistes. [71]
10   a fine green trickle—
Pistachio? Mint Julep?
        Words have colors,
        and colors are tasty.
sweetens his chin.
15   In front of me Licorice teeters like a lump of coal
on its pinkish base of Pumpkin.
        A Rauschenberg [72] *tongue*
        fondles this rich donnée,°   *a given, a premise*
        then begins to erase it.

---

[71] *Symbolistes* were members of a group of artists in nineteenth-century France who cultivated symbols and emblems in their work.
[72] Robert Rauschenberg is an American painter.

20   Turning from all that is present
        in the flesh, so to speak,
        let the eye wander off to a menu,
        where it can start to ingest
        "Quite Sour Lemon sherbet,
25   topped with a stem cherry and chocolate sprinkles
                Swilling in language,
        all floating in bubbly cherry phosphate
                the bloated imagination
                is urged to open still wider
30   *and shovel it in,*
        and served with a twist of pretzel."
        In this world "Creamy Vanilla and
        Smooth Swiss Chocolate ice creams"
        can be "blended with chopped pineapple,
35   dark fudge sauce, ripe bananas, whipped topping,
        cookies, roasted nutmeats and nippy chopped cherries."
                the Unconscious, that old hog,
                being in charge here of the
                creative act.

40   At about the moment my tastebuds
        receive a last tickle of Gingersnap
        and begin to respond to
        Orange Fudge, I look at you
        who have bought my ice cream cones for twenty years,
45   *Moving another new ice to the mouth*
                we needn't remember
        and look away
                it is always the same mouth
                that melts it.
50   My mind assembles a ribald tower
        of sherbet dips, all on one cone,
        Apricot, Apple, Tangerine, Peach, Prune, Lime,
        and then it topples.
        You are steadier than I.
55   You order one dip always,
        or, in a dish, two dips of the same flavor.

        In this hysterical brilliance of neon
                Come on, consumers,
                we've got to keep scooping
60   it is twelve or fifteen of us
        to thirty ice creams.
                so that the creams shall not rise
                like cold lava out of their bins,
                numbing our feet, our knees,
65   *freezing our chests, our chins, our eyes,*
        Open the door, quick,
        and let in two handholding adolescents.

Coping with all those glands
makes them good and hungry.
70   *so that, flying out of their cannisters,*
        the chopped nuts
        shall not top off our Technicolor grave
        with their oily ashes.

Listen! All around us toothsome cones
75   are suffering demolition
down to the last, nipple-like tip.
How do we know where to stop?
Perhaps the glasses and dishes
are moulded of candy, and the counters and windows . . .
80   *Over your half-eaten serving of Italian Delight,*
        why are you looking at **me**
        the way you are looking at me?

Discuss "In the Cold Kingdom" as an example of symbolism. Compare it with Judith
Johnson Sherwin's "Dr. Potatohead Talks to Mothers" on pages 305–306.

RICHARD WILBUR (1921–)

Love Calls Us to the Things of This World[73]

The eyes open to a cry of pulleys,
And spirited from sleep, the astounded soul
Hangs for a moment bodiless and simple
As false dawn.
                    Outside the open window
5   The morning air is all awash with angels.

Some are in bed-sheets, some are in blouses,
Some are in smocks: but truly there they are.
Now they are rising together in calm swells
Of halcyon feeling, filling whatever they wear
10   With the deep joy of their impersonal breathing;

Now they are flying in place, conveying
The terrible speed of their omnipresence, moving
And staying like white water; and now of a sudden
They swoon down into so rapt a quiet
That nobody seems to be there.
15   The soul shrinks

From all that it is about to remember,
From the punctual rape of every blessèd day,
And cries,
                "Oh, let there be nothing on earth but laundry,

---

[73] The title is taken from the words of St. Augustine.

Nothing but rosy hands in the rising steam
20 And clear dances done in the sight of heaven."

      Yet, as the sun acknowledges
With a warm look the world's hunks and colors,
The soul descends once more in bitter love
To accept the waking body, saying now
25 In a changed voice as the man yawns and rises,

      "Bring them down from their ruddy gallows;
Let there be clean linen for the backs of thieves;
Let lovers go fresh and sweet to be undone,
And the heaviest nuns walk in a pure floating
Of dark habits,
30   keeping their difficult balance."

PHILIP LARKIN (1922–)

Faith Healing

Slowly the women file to where he stands
Upright in rimless glasses, silver hair,
Dark suit, white collar. Stewards tirelessly
Persuade them onwards to his voice and hands,
5 Within whose warm spring rain of loving care
Each dwells some twenty seconds. *Now, dear child,
What's wrong*, the deep American voice demands,
And, scarcely pausing, goes into a prayer
Directing God about this eye, that knee.
10 Their heads are clasped abruptly; then, exiled

Like losing thoughts, they go in silence; some
Sheepishly stray, not back into their lives
Just yet; but some stay stiff, twitching and loud
With deep hoarse tears, as if a kind of dumb
15 And idiot child within them still survives
To re-awake at kindness, thinking a voice
At last calls them alone, that hands have come
To lift and lighten; and such joy arrives
Their thick tongues blort, their eyes squeeze grief, a crowd
20 Of huge unheard answers jam and rejoice—

What's wrong! Moustached in flowered frocks they shake:
By now, all's wrong. In everyone there sleeps
A sense of life lived according to love.
To some it means the difference they could make
25 By loving others, but across most it sweeps
As all they might have done had they been loved.
That nothing cures. An immense slackening ache,
As when, thawing, the rigid landscape weeps,
Spreads slowly through them—that, and the voice above
30 Saying *Dear child*, and all time has disproved.

HOWARD MOSS (1922–)

Water Island[74]

To the memory of a friend,
drowned off Water Island, April, 1960

Finally, from your house, there is no view;
The bay's blind mirror shattered over you
And Patchogue[75] took your body like a log
The wind rolled up to shore. The senseless drowned
5   Have faces nobody would care to see,
But water loves those gradual erasures
Of flesh and shoreline, greenery and glass,
And you belonged to water, it to you,
Having built, on a hillock, above the bay,
10   Your house, the bay giving you reason to,
Where now, if seasons still are running straight,
The horseshoe crabs clank armor night and day,
Their couplings far more ancient than the eyes
That watched them from your porch. I saw one once
15   Whose back was a history of how we live;
Grown onto every inch of plate, except
Where the hinges let it move, were living things,
Barnacles, mussels, water weeds—and one
Blue bit of polished glass, glued there by time:
20   The origins of art. It carried them
With pride, it seemed, as if endurance only
Matters in the end. Or so I thought.
Skimming traffic lights, starboard and port,
Steer through planted poles that mark the way,
25   And other lights, across the bay, faint stars
Lining the border of Long Island's shore,
Come on at night, they still come on at night,
Though who can see them now I do not know.
Wild roses, at your back porch, break their blood,
30   And bud to test surprises of sea air,
And the birds fly over, gliding down to feed
At the two feeding stations you set out with seed,
Or splash themselves in a big bowl of rain
You used to fill with water. Going across
35   That night, too fast, too dark, no one will know,
Maybe you heard, the last you'll ever hear,
The cry of the savage and endemic gull
Which shakes the blood and always brings to mind
The thought that death, the scavenger, is blind,

---

[74] A community on Fire Island, an island at the end of Long Island, New York.
[75] The body of water that surrounds Fire Island.

40   Blunders and is stupid, and the end
      Comes with ironies so fine the seed
      Falters in the marsh and the heron stops
      Hunting in the weeds below your landing stairs,
      Standing in a stillness that now is yours.

ANTHONY HECHT (1923–)

The Dover Bitch, A Criticism of Life

For Andrews Wanning

      So there stood Matthew Arnold and this girl
      With the cliffs of England crumbling away behind them,
      And he said to her, "Try to be true to me,
      And I'll do the same for you, for things are bad
5   All over, etc., etc."
      Well now, I knew this girl. It's true she had read
      Sophocles in a fairly good translation
      And caught that bitter allusion to the sea,
      But all the time he was talking she had in mind
10   The notion of what his whiskers would feel like
      On the back of her neck. She told me later on
      That after a while she got to looking out
      At the lights across the channel, and really felt sad,
      Thinking of all the wine and enormous beds
15   And blandishments in French and the perfumes.
      And then she got really angry. To have been brought
      All the way down from London, and then be addressed
      As a sort of mournful cosmic last resort
      Is really tough on a girl, and she was pretty.
20   Anyway, she watched him pace the room
      And finger his watch-chain and seem to sweat a bit,
      And then she said one or two unprintable things.
      But you mustn't judge her by that. What I mean to say is,
      She's really all right. I still see her once in a while
25   And she always treats me right. We have a drink
      And I give her a good time, and perhaps it's a year
      Before I see her again, but there she is,
      Running to fat, but dependable as they come.
      And sometimes I bring her a bottle of *Nuit d'Amour*.[76]

Compare "The Dover Bitch" with Matthew Arnold's "Dover Beach" on pages 108–109.

---

[76] *Nuit d'Amour* is French for "night of love."

RICHARD HUGO (1923–)

Driving Montana

The day is a woman who loves you. Open.
Deer drink close to the road and magpies
spray from your car. Miles from any town
your radio comes in strong, unlikely
5   Mozart from Belgrade, rock and roll
from Butte. Whatever the next number,
you want to hear it. Never has your Buick
found this forward a gear. Even
the tuna salad in Reedpoint is good.

10   Towns arrive ahead of imagined schedule.
Absorakee at one. Or arrive so late—
Silesia at nine—you recreate the day.
Where did you stop along the road
and have fun? Was there a runaway horse?
15   Did you park at that house, the one
alone in a void of grain, white with green
trim and red fence, where you know you lived
once? You remembered the ringing creek,
the soft brown forms of far off bison.
20   You must have stayed hours, then drove on.
In the motel you know you'd never seen it before.

Tomorrow will open again, the sky wide
as the mouth of a wild girl, friable
clouds you lose yourself to. You are lost
25   in miles of land without people, without
one fear of being found, in the dash
of rabbits, soar of antelope, swirl
merge and clatter of streams.

KENNETH KOCH (1925–)

Mending Sump

"Hiram, I think the sump is backing up.
The bathroom floor boards for above two weeks
Have seemed soaked through. A little bird, I think,
Has wandered in the pipes, and all's gone wrong."
5   "Something there is that doesn't hump a sump,"
He said; and through his head she saw a cloud
That seemed to twinkle. "Hiram, well," she said,
"Smith is come home! I saw his face just now
While looking through your head. He's come to die
10   Or else to laugh, for hay is dried-up grass
When you're alone." He rose, and sniffed the air.
"We'd better leave him in the sump," he said.

Compare "Mending Sump" with Robert Frost's "Mending Wall" on pages 383–384.

MAXINE KUMIN (1925–)

For a Shetland Pony Brood Mare[77]
Who Died in Her Barren Year

After bringing forth eighteen
foals in as many Mays
you might, old Trinket girl,
have let yourself be lulled
5   this spring into the green days
of pasture and first curl
of timothy.° Instead,   *a kind of grass*
your milk bag swelled again,
an obstinate machine.
10   Your long pale tongue
waggled in every feed box.
You slicked your ears back
to scatter other mares
from the salt lick.[78]
15   You were full of winter burdocks
and false pregnancy.

By midsummer all the foals
had breached, except the ghost
you carried. In the bog
20   where you came down each noon
to ease your deer-thin hoofs in mud,
a jack-in-the-pulpit cocked
his overhang like a question mark.
We saw some autumn soon
25   that botflies would take your skin
and bloodworms settle
inside the cords and bands
that laced your belly,
your church of folded hands.

30   But all in good time, Trinket!
Was it something you understood?
Full of false pride
you lay down and died
in the sun,
35   all silken on one side,
all mud on the other one.

Compare "For a Shetland Pony Brood Mare" with Anne Sexton's "Pain for a Daughter" on pages 416–417.

---

[77] A brood mare is a female horse kept for breeding purposes.
[78] A salt lick is a place on the earth where salt is found on the surface.

Visit

It is not far to my place:
you can come smallboat,
pausing under shade in the eddies
    or going ashore
5   to rest, regard the leaves

    or talk with birds and
shore weeds: hire a full-grown man not
late in years to oar you
    and choose a canoe-like thin ship;
10   (a dumb man is better and no

costlier; he will attract
the reflections and silences under leaves:)
travel light: a single book, some twine:
    the river is muscled at rapids with trout
15   and a laurel limb

will make a suitable spit: if you
leave in the forenoon, you will arrive
with plenty of light
    the afternoon of the third day: I will
20   come down to the landing

(tell your man to look for it,
the dumb have clear sight and are free of
visions) to greet you with some made
    wine and a special verse:
25   or you can come by shore:

choose the right: there the rocks
cascade less frequently, the grade more gradual:
treat yourself gently: the ascent thins both
    mind and blood and you must
30   keep still a dense reserve

of silence we can poise against
conversation: there is little news:
I found last month a root with shape and
    have heard a new sound among
35   the insects: come.

A Supermarket in California

What thoughts I have of you tonight, Walt Whitman, for
I walked down the sidestreets under the trees with a headache
self-conscious looking at the full moon.

In my hungry fatigue, and shopping for images, I went

5   into the neon fruit supermarket, dreaming of your enumerations!

        What peaches and what penumbras! Whole families shopping
at night! Aisles full of husbands! Wives in the avocados,
babies in the tomatoes!—and you, Garcia Lorca,[79] what were you
doing down by the watermelons?

10   I saw you, Walt Whitman, childless, lonely old grubber,
poking among the meats in the refrigerator and eyeing the
grocery boys.

        I heard you asking questions of each: Who killed the
pork chops? What price bananas? Are you my Angel?

15   I wandered in and out of the brilliant stacks of cans
following you, and followed in my imagination by the store
detective.

        We strode down the open corridors together in our
solitary fancy tasting artichokes, possessing every frozen
20   delicacy, and never passing the cashier.

        Where are we going, Walt Whitman? The doors close in
an hour. Which way does your beard point tonight?

        (I touch your book and dream of our odyssey in the
supermarket and feel absurd.)

25   Will we walk all night through solitary streets? The trees
add shade to shade, lights out in the houses, we'll both be
lonely.

        Will we stroll dreaming of the lost America of love past
blue automobiles in driveways, home to our silent cottage?

30   Ah, dear father, graybeard, lonely old courage-teacher,
what America did you have when Charon[80] quit poling his ferry
and you got out on a smoking bank and stood watching the
boat disappear on the black waters of Lethe?

ALLEN GINSBERG (1926–)

My Sad Self

To Frank O'Hara[81]

Sometimes when my eyes are red
I go up on top of the RCA Building
     and gaze at my world, Manhattan—
          my buildings, streets I've done feats in,
5   lofts, beds, coldwater flats
—on Fifth Ave below which I also bear in mind,
     its ant cars, little yellow taxis, men
        walking the size of specks of wool—
Panorama of the bridges, sunrise over Brooklyn machine,

---

[79] Garcia Lorca (1899–1936) was a Spanish poet and playwright noted for his haunting imagery.
[80] In Greek mythology Charon ferried dead souls across the river Lethe to the underworld.
[81] Frank O'Hara (1926–1966) was an American poet, playwright, and art critic. One of his poems
appears on pages 96–97.

10   sun go down over New Jersey where I was born
                & Paterson where I played with ants—
my later loves on 15th Street,
                my greater loves of Lower East Side,
                        my once fabulous amours in the Bronx
15   faraway—
paths crossing in these hidden streets,
        my history summed up, my absences
                and ecstasies in Harlem—
        —sun shining down on all I own
20   in one eyeblink to the horizon
                        in my last eternity—

                                matter is water.

        Sad,
                I take the elevator and go
25   down, pondering,
and walk on the pavements staring into all man's
                                plateglass, faces,
                questioning after who loves,
        and stop, bemused
30   in front of an automobile shopwindow
        standing lost in calm thought,
                        traffic moving up & down 5th Avenue blocks
                                behind me
                        waiting for a moment when. . . .
35   Time to go home & cook supper & listen to
                the romantic war news on the radio

                                . . . all movement stops
& I walk in the timeless sadness of existence,
        tenderness flowing thru the buildings,
40   my fingertips touching reality's face,
        my own face streaked with tears in the mirror
                of some window—at dusk—
                                where I have no desire—
        for bonbons—or to own the dresses or Japanese
45   lampshades of intellection—

        Confused by the spectacle around me,
                Man struggling up the street
                        with packages, newspapers,
                                ties, beautiful suits
50   toward his desire
                Man, woman, streaming over the pavements
                        red lights clocking hurried watches &
                                movements at the curb—

        And all these streets leading
55   so crosswise, honking, lengthily,
                        by avenues

stalked by high buildings or crusted into slums
thru such halting traffic
screaming cars and engines
60   so painfully to this
countryside, this graveyard
this stillness
on deathbed or mountain
once seen
65   never regained or desired
in the mind to come
where all Manhattan that I've seen must disappear.

Compare "My Sad Self" with June Jordan's "My Sadness Sits Around Me" on page 429.

W. S. MERWIN (1927–)

For the Anniversary of My Death

Every year without knowing it I have passed the day
When the last fires will wave to me
And the silence will set out
Tireless traveller
5   Like the beam of a lightless star

Then I will no longer
Find myself in life as in a strange garment
Surprised at the earth
And the love of one woman
10   And then shamelessness of men
As today writing after three days of rain
Hearing the wren sing and the falling cease
And bowing not knowing to what

ANNE SEXTON (1928–1974)

Pain for a Daughter

Blind with love, my daughter
has cried nightly for horses,
those long-necked marchers and churners
that she has mastered, any and all,
5   reigning them in like a circus hand—
the excitable muscles and the ripe neck;
tending this summer, a pony and a foal.
She who is too squeamish to pull
a thorn from the dog's paw,
10   watched her pony blossom with distemper,
the underside of the jaw swelling
like an enormous grape.

Gritting her teeth with love,
she drained the boil and scoured it
15 with hydrogen peroxide until pus
ran like milk on the barn floor.

Blind with loss all winter,
in dungarees, a ski jacket and a hard hat,
she visits the neighbors' stable,
20 our acreage not zoned for barns;
they who own the flaming horses
and the swan-whipped thoroughbred
that she tugs at and cajoles,
thinking it will burn like a furnace
25 under her small-hipped English seat. [82]

Blind with pain she limps home.
The thoroughbred has stood on her foot.
He rested there like a building.
He grew into her foot until they were one.
30 The marks of the horseshoe printed
into her flesh, the tips of her toes
ripped off like pieces of leather,
three toenails swirled like shells
and left to float in blood in her riding boot.

35 Blind with fear, she sits on the toilet,
her foot balanced over the washbasin,
her father, hydrogen peroxide in hand,
performing the rites of the cleansing.
She bites on a towel, sucked in breath,
40 sucked in and arched against the pain,
her eyes glancing off me where
I stand at the door, eyes locked
on the ceiling, eyes of a stranger,
and then she cries . . .
45 *Oh my God, help me!*
Where a child would have cried *Mama!*
Where a child would have believed *Mama!*
she bit the towel and called on God
and I saw her life stretch out . . .
50 I saw her torn in childbirth,
and I saw her, at that moment,
in her own death and I knew that she
knew.

Compare "Pain for a Daughter" with Maxine Kumin's "For a Shetland Pony Brood Mare
Who Died in Her Barren Year" on page 412.

---

[82] An English seat is a type of riding saddle.

RICHARD HOWARD (1929–)

Giovanni Da Fiesole on the Sublime, or Fra Angelico's Last Judgment[83]

For Adrienne Rich[84]

How to behold what cannot be held?
Start from the center and from all that
lies or flies or merely rises left
of center. You may have noticed how
5   Hell, in these affairs, is on the right
invariably (though for an inside Judge,
of course, that would be the left. And we
are not inside.) I have no doctrine
intricate enough for Hell, which I leave
10   in its own right, where it will be left.

Right down the center, then, in two rows,
run nineteen black holes, their square lids off;
also one sarcophagus, up front.
Out of these has come the world; out of
15   that coffin, I guess, the Judge above
the world. Nor is my doctrine liable
to smooth itself out for the blue ease
of Heaven outlining one low hill
against the sky at the graveyard's end
20   like a woman's body—a hill like Eve.

Some of us stand, still, at the margin
of this cemetery, marvelling
that no more than a mortared pavement can
separate us from the Other Side
25   which numbers as many nuns and priests
(even Popes and Empresses!) as ours.
The rest, though, stirring to a music
that our startled blood remembers now,
embrace each other or the Angels
30   of this green place: the dancing begins.

We dance in a circle of bushes,
red and yellow roses, round a pool
of green water. There is one lily,
gold as a lantern in the dark grass,
35   and all the trees accompany us
with gestures of fruition. We stop!

---

[83] Giovanni da Fiesole, also known as Fra Angelico, was born as Guido di Pietro (c. 1400–1455). He was one of the greatest painters of the Italian Renaissance. This poem describes his painting *The Last Judgment* in the Convento degli Angioli, Florence.

[84] Adrienne Rich is an American poet. A poem by Adrienne Rich may be found on page 420.

The ring of bodies opens where a last
Angel, in scarlet, hands us on. Now
we go, we are leaving this garden
40   of colors and gowns. We walk into

a light falling upon us, falling
out of the great rose gate upon us,
light so thick we cannot trust our eyes
to walk into it so. We lift up
45   our hands then and walk into the light.
How to behold what cannot be held?
Make believe you hold it, no longer
lighting but light, and walk into that
gold success. The world must be its own
50   *witness, we judge ourselves, raise your hands.*

Compare "Giovanni Da Fiesole" with W. H. Auden's "Musée des Beaux Arts" on
pages 12–13.

CYNTHIA MacDONALD (1929–)

It Is Dangerous to Be the Conductor

Then, early on in Act III, he [Sir Georg Solti] stabbed himself in
the temple with the point of his third baton. Blood poured down
into his right eye, dripping onto the score and music desk.

TIME MAGAZINE, *September 20, 1976*

Lightning does strike twice. Lully[85] thumping the floor with
His staff, beating time for the Paris Opera, beat it to
Death when he hit his foot instead of board:
Gangrene. But beyond the self-inflicted dangers:
5   What about the second-row cellist with angina pectoris?[86]
The oboist with the wife in Payne Whitney?[87]
And even beyond these, the more familiar:
What about your son who announces he would murder for
Money, who figures prices and vice versa in
10   The margins of *Ellery Queen's Mystery Magazine?*
What about your daughter who spends
All her time on scrapbooks for orphans,
Combing antique stores for a dessert menu from
The Ritz so she can place *Pêche Melba*[88] next to

---

[85] Jean Baptiste Lully (1632–1687) was a French court and operatic composer who died from blood
poisoning when his baton punctured his foot.
[86] A heart condition.
[87] A mental hospital in New York City.
[88] A dessert named after the opera singer Dame Nelly Melba (1881–1931), who also lent her name
to Melba toast.

15   The rotogravure diva who, costumed for Tosca,[89]
       Is pasted on the page emerging from the pouch of a kangaroo?
       As you pound yourself on the foot or stab yourself
       In the temple, do you think of Radames[90] suffocating
       In the tomb, before he ever had children to settle the score?

ADRIENNE RICH (1929–)

A Woman Mourned by Daughters

     Now, not a tear begun,
     we sit here in your kitchen,
     spent, you see, already.
     You are swollen till you strain
5   this house and the whole sky.
     You, whom we so often
     succeeded in ignoring!
     You are puffed up in death
     like a corpse pulled from the sea;
10   we groan beneath your weight.
     And yet you were a leaf,
     a straw blown on the bed,
     you had long since become
     crisp as a dead insect.
15   What is it, if not you,
     that settles on us now
     like satin you pulled down
     over our bridal heads?
     What rises in our throats
20   like food you prodded in?
     Nothing could be enough.
     You breathe upon us now
     through solid assertions
     of yourself: teaspoons, goblets,
25   seas of carpet, a forest
     of old plants to be watered,
     an old man in an adjoining
     room to be touched and fed.
     And all this universe
30   dares us to lay a finger
     anywhere, save exactly
     as you would wish it done.

Compare "A Woman Mourned by Daughters" with Sonia Sanchez's "summer words of a sistuh addict" on pages 427–428.

---

[89] The title role of Giacomo Puccini's opera.
[90] A character in Giuseppi Verdi's opera *Aida*.

TED HUGHES (1930–)

• Hawk Roosting

I sit in the top of the wood, my eyes closed.
Inaction, no falsifying dream
Between my hooked head and hooked feet:
Or in sleep rehearse perfect kills and eat.

5 The convenience of the high trees!
The air's buoyancy and the sun's ray
Are of advantage to me;
And the earth's face upward for my inspection.

My feet are locked upon the rough bark.
10 It took the whole of Creation
To produce my foot, my each feather:
Now I hold Creation in my foot

Or fly up, and revolve it all slowly—
I kill where I please because it is all mine.
15 There is no sophistry in my body:
My manners are tearing off heads—

The allotment of death.
For the one path of my flight is direct
Through the bones of the living.
20 No arguments assert my right:

The sun is behind me.
Nothing has changed since I began.
My eye has permitted no change.
I am going to keep things like this.

Compare "Hawk Roosting" with Robert Duncan's "My Mother Would Be a Falconress" on pages 402–403 and May Sarton's "Lady with a Falcon" on pages 398–399.

DEREK WALCOTT (1930–)

Sea Grapes

That sail in cloudless light
which tires of islands,
a schooner beating up the Caribbean

for home, could be Odysseus[91]
5 home-bound through the Aegean,
just as that husband's

---

[91] Odysseus, or Ulysses, is the hero of Homer's the *Odyssey*, a section of which may be found on pages 42–48.

sorrow under the sea-grapes, repeats
the adulterer's hearing Nausicaa's name
in every gull's outcry.

10   But whom does this bring peace? The classic war
between a passion and responsibility
is never finished, and has been the same

to the sea-wanderer and the one on shore,
now wriggling on his sandals to walk home,
15   since Troy sighed its last flame,

and the blind giant's boulder heaved the trough[92]
from which The Odyssey's hexameters come[93]
to finish up as Caribbean surf.

The classics can console. But not enough.

COLETTE INEZ (1931–)

Spanish Heaven

My heaven is Hispanic ladies in satin tube dresses,
their hair like a chocolate sundae melts into waves.
They are giving me transparent nightgowns
and kisses on my face.
5   Lotteria tickets bulging in my purse.
They are saying *que bonita*[94] in the house
of their throats
and we all eat mangoes and fritos d'amor
selling Avon products to each other forever.

10   And damning Fidel, Trujillo,[95] what bums.
But Evita,[96] what heart and Elizabeth Taylor
there in her shrine,
Monacos of pleasure as Grace takes our hand.[97]
Eyepads of freedom, Avons of love.

15   Mascara of angels, hairspray of God,
they are teasing my hair like a heavenly cloud
while the acid of husbands eating alone
rumbles Dolores, *putas*[98] and rape
in the hell of machismo.

---

[92] An allusion to Odysseus' fight with the Cyclops (see pages 47–48).

[93] The *Odyssey* is in dactylic hexameter.

[94] *Qué bonita* is Spanish for "how beautiful."

[95] Fidel Castro and Rafael Trujillo Molina, two Caribbean dictators, Castro in Cuba and Trujillo in the Dominican Republic until his assassination in 1961.

[96] Eva (Evita) Perón, wife of Juan Perón. Both were dictators of Argentina. Evita Perón was known for her great beauty, among other things.

[97] Elizabeth Taylor and Grace Kelly, American screen actresses. Grace Kelly later became Princess Grace of Monaco.

[98] *Putas* is the Spanish word for prostitutes.

Sylvia Plath *(Rollie McKenna)*

SYLVIA PLATH (1932–1963)

Lady Lazarus[99]

I have done it again.[100]
One year in every ten
I manage it—

A sort of walking miracle, my skin
5   Bright as a Nazi lampshade,[101]
My right foot

A paperweight,
My face a featureless, fine
Jew linen.

10   Peel off the napkin
O my enemy.
Do I terrify?—

The nose, the eye pits, the full set of teeth?
The sour breath
15   Will vanish in a day.

---

[99] Jesus raised Lazarus from the dead (John 11:44)
[100] Plath repeatedly attempted suicide and finally died by her own hand in 1963.
[101] The Nazis sometimes used the skins of Jews they had killed in the concentration camps for lamp shades.

Soon, soon the flesh
The grave cave ate will be
At home on me

And I a smiling woman.
20 I am only thirty.
And like the cat I have nine times to die.

This is Number Three.
What a trash
To annihilate each decade.

25 What a million filaments.
The peanut-crunching crowd
Shoves in to see

Them unwrap me hand and foot—
The big strip tease.
30 Gentleman, ladies,

These are my hands,
My knees.
I may be skin and bone,

Nevertheless, I am the same, identical woman.
35 The first time it happened I was ten.
It was an accident.

The second time I meant
To last it out and not come back at all.
I rocked shut

40 As a seashell.
They had to call and call
And pick the worms off me like sticky pearls.

Dying
Is an art, like everything else.
45 I do it exceptionally well.

I do it so it feels like hell.
I do it so it feels real.
I guess you could say I've a call.

It's easy enough to do it in a cell.
50 It's easy enough to do it and stay put.
It's the theatrical

Comeback in broad day
To the same place, the same face, the same brute
Amused shout:

55 "A miracle!"
That knocks me out.
There is a charge

For the eyeing of my scars, there is a charge
For the hearing of my heart—
60   It really goes.

And there is a charge, a very large charge
For a word or a touch
Or a bit of blood

Or a piece of my hair or my clothes.
65   So, so, Herr Doktor.
So, Herr Enemy.

I am your opus,°   *work, composition*
I am your valuable,
The pure gold baby

70   That melts to a shriek.
I turn and burn.
Do not think I underestimate your great concern.

Ash, ash—
You poke and stir.
75   Flesh, bone, there is nothing there—

A cake of soap,
A wedding ring,
A gold filling.

Herr God, Herr Lucifer,
80   Beware
Beware.

Out of the ash
I rise with my red hair
And I eat men like air.

WENDELL BERRY (1934–)

The Old Elm Tree by the River

Shrugging in the flight of its leaves,
it is dying. Death is slowly
standing up in its trunk and branches
like a camouflaged hunter. In the night
5   I am wakened by one of its branches
crashing down, heavy as a wall, and then
lie sleepless, the world changed.
That is a life I know the country by.
Mine is a life I know the country by.
10   Willing to live and die, we stand here,
timely and at home, neighborly as two men.
Our place is changing in us as we stand,
and we hold up the weight that will bring us down.

In us the land enacts its history.
15 When we stood it was beneath us, and was
the strength by which we held to it
and stood, the daylight over it
a mighty blessing we cannot bear for long.

Compare "The Old Elm Tree by the River" with James Wright's "A Blessing" on page 2.

AUDRE LORDE (1934–)

Now That I Am Forever with Child

How the days went
while you were blooming within me
I remember each upon each—
the swelling changed planes of my body
5 and how you first fluttered, then jumped
and I thought it was my heart.

How the days wound down
and the turning of winter
I recall, with you growing heavy
10 against the wind. I thought
now her hands
are formed, and her hair
has started to curl
now her teeth are done
15 now she sneezes.
Then the seed opened
I bore you one morning just before spring
My head rang like a fiery piston
my legs were towers between which
20 A new world was passing.

Since then
I can only distinguish
one thread within running hours
You, flowing through selves
25 toward You.

Compare "Now That I Am Forever with Child" with Erica Jong's "How You Get Born" on pages 435–436.

N. SCOTT MOMADAY (1934–)

Earth and I Gave You Turquoise

Earth and I gave you turquoise
    when you walked singing

We lived laughing in my house
        and told old stories
5   You grew ill when the owl cried
    We will meet on Black Mountain

    I will bring you corn for planting
        and we will make fire
    Children will come to your breast
10   You will heal my heart
    I speak your name many times
    The wild cane remembers you

    My young brother's house is filled
        I go there to sing
15   We have not spoken of you
        but our songs are sad
    When the Moon Woman goes to you
    I will follow her white way

    Tonight they dance near Chinle
20   by the seven elms
    There your loom whispered beauty
        They will eat mutton
    and drink coffee till morning
    You and I will not be there

25   I saw a crow by Red Rock
        standing on one leg
    It was the black of your hair
        The years are heavy
    I will ride the swiftest horse
30   You will hear the drumming of hooves

SONIA SANCHEZ (1935–)

summer words of a sistuh addict

    the first day i shot dope
    was on a sunday.
                    i had just come
    home from church
5   got mad at my motha
    cuz she got mad at me.   u dig?
                    went out.   shot up
    behind a feelen gainst her.
                        it felt good.
10   gooder than dooing it.   yeah.
                            it was nice.
    i did it.   uh.   huh.   i did it.   uh.   huh.
    i want to do it again.   it felt so gooooood.
                        and as the sistuh
15   sits in her silent/

remembered/high
someone leans for
ward gently asks her:
           sistuh.
20   did u
           finally
learn how to hold yo/mother?
and the music of the day
          drifts in the room
25 to mingle with the sistuh's young tears.
    and we all sing.

Compare "summer words of a sistuh addict" with Adrienne Rich's "A Woman Mourned by Daughters" on page 420.

LUCILLE CLIFTON (1936–)

Good Times

My Daddy has paid the rent
and the insurance man is gone
and the lights is back on
and my uncle Brud has hit
5   for one dollar straight
and they is good times
good times
good times

My Mama has made bread
10 and Grampaw has come

and everybody is drunk
and dancing in the kitchen
and singing in the kitchen
oh these is good times
15 good times
good times

oh children think about the
good times

DARYL HINE (1936–)

The Survivors

Nowadays the mess is everywhere
And getting worse. Earth after all
Is a battlefield. Through the static
We used to call the music of the spheres

5 Someone, a survivor, sends this message:
"When it happened I was reading Homer.

Sing—will nobody sing?—the wrath,
Rats and tanks and radioactive rain."

That was before rationing was enforced
10   On words, of course. Particles went first,
Then substantives. Now only verbs abide
The law, and the odd anarchistic scrawl

How above the crumbling horizon
Brightly shine our neighbours, Venus, Mars.

Compare "The Survivors" with Edwin Muir's "The Horses" on pages 27–28.

JUNE JORDAN (1936–)

My Sadness Sits Around Me

My sadness sits around me
    not on haunches not in any
    placement near a move
and the tired roll-on
5   of a boredom without grief

If there were war
I would watch the hunting
I would chase the dogs
and blow the horn
10   *because blood is commonplace*

As I walk in peace
    unencountered unmolested
    unimpinging unbelieving unrevealing
    undesired under every O
15   My sadness sits around me

Compare "My Sadness Sits Around Me" with Allen Ginsberg's "My Sad Self" on pages 414–416.

DIANE WAKOSKI (1937–)

I Have Had to Learn to Live with My Face

You see me alone tonight.
My face has betrayed me again,
    the garage mechanic who promises to fix my car
    and never does.

5   My face
that my friends tell me is so full of character;
my face
I have hated for so many years;
my face

10 I have made an angry contract to live with
    though no one could love it;
    my face that I wish you would bruise and batter
    and destroy, napalm it,[102] throw acid in it,
    so that I might have another
15 or be rid of it at last.

    I drag peacock feathers behind me
    to erase the trail of the moon. Those tears
    I shed for myself,
    sometimes in anger.
20 There is no pretense in my life. The man who lives with me
    must see something beautiful,

    like a dark snake coming out of my mouth,
    or love the tapestry of my actions, my life/ this body, this
    face, they have nothing to offer
25 but angry insistence, their presence.
    I hate them,
    want my life to be more.
    Hate their shadow on even my words.

    I sell my soul for good plumbing
30 and hot water,
                      I tell everyone;
    and my face is soft,
    opal,
    a feathering of snow
35 against the
                  cold black leather coat
    which is night.
                      You,
                      night,
40   my face against the chilly
                      expanse
                      of your back.
    Learning to live with what you're born with
    is the process,
45 the involvement,
    the making of a life.
    And I have not learned happily
    to live with my face,
    that Diane which always looks better on film
50 than in life.
    I sternly accept this plain face,
    and hate every moment of that sternness.

    I want to laugh at this ridiculous face
                  of lemon rinds

---

[102] Napalm is a defoliant that was used especially during the Vietnam War.

55   and vinegar cruets
        of unpaved roads
        and dusty file cabinets
        of the loneliness of Wall Street at night
        and the desert of school on a holiday
60 but I would have to laugh alone in a cold room
    Prefer the anger
    that at least for a moment gives me a proud profile.

    Always, I've envied
            the rich
65   the beautiful
                the talented
                    the go-getters
                        of the world. I've watched
    myself
70 remain
    alone
    isolated
    a fish that swam through the net
    because I was too small
75   but remained alone
            in deep water because the others were caught
            taken away

    It is so painful for me to think now,
    to talk about this; I want to go to sleep and never wake up.
80 The only warmth I ever feel is wool covers on a bed.
    But self-pity could trail us all, drag us around on the bottom of
    shoes like squashed snails so that
    we might never fight/ and it is anger I want now, fury,
    to direct at my face and its author,
85 to tell it how much I hate what it's done to me,
    to contemptuously, sternly, brutally even, make it live with itself,
    look at itself every day,
    and remind itself
    that reality is
90 learning to live with what you're born with,
    noble to have been anything but defeated,
    that pride and anger and silence will hold us above beauty,
    though we bend down often with so much anguish for
    a little beauty,
95 a word, like the blue night,
            the night of rings covering the floor and glinting
            into the fire, the water, the wet earth, the age of songs,
            guitars, angry busloads of etched tile faces, old gnarled
            tree trunks, anything with the beauty of wood, teak, lemon,
100   cherry
    I lost my children because I had no money, no husband,
    I lost my husband because I was not beautiful,

I lost everything a woman needs, wants,
almost
before I became a woman,
my face shimmering and flat as the moon
with no features.

I look at pictures of myself as a child.
I looked lumpy, unformed, like a piece of dough,
and it has been my task as a human being
to carve out a mind, carve out a face,
carve out a shape with arms & legs, to put a voice inside,
and to make a person from a presence.
And I don't think I'm unique.
I think a thousand of you, at least, can look at those old photos,
reflect on your life
and see your own sculpture at work.

I have made my face as articulate as I can,
and it turns out to be a peculiar face with too much
bone in the bridge of the nose, small eyes, pale lashes,
thin lips, wide cheeks, a rocky chin,
But it's almost beautiful compared to the sodden mass of dough I started out with.

I wonder how we learn to live
with our faces?
They must hide so much pain,
so many deep trenches of blood,
so much that would terrorize and drive others away, if they
could see it. The struggle to control it
articulates the face.
And what about those people
With elegant noses and rich lips?

What do they spend their lives struggling for?

Am I wrong I constantly ask myself
to value the struggle
more than the results?
Or only to accept a beautiful face
if it has been toiled for?

Tonight I move alone in my face;
want to forgive all the men whom I've loved
who've betrayed me.
After all, the great betrayer is that one I carry around each day,
which I sleep with at night. My own face,
angry building I've fought to restore
imbued with arrogance, pride, anger and scorn.
To love this face
would be to love a desert mountain,
a killer, rocky, water hard to find, no trees anywhere/
perhaps I do not expect anyone

to be strange enough to love it;
150   but you.

                  /

ISHMAEL REED (1938–)

beware :   do not read this poem

tonite, thriller was
abt an ol woman, so vain she
surrounded herself w /
        many mirrors

5   it got so bad that finally she
locked herself indoors & her
whole life became the
              mirrors

one day the villagers broke
10   into her house , but she was too
swift for them . she disappeared
        into a mirror
each tenant who bought the house
after that , lost a loved one to

15   the ol woman in the mirror :
        first a little girl
        then a young woman
        then the young woman/s husband

the hunger of this poem is legendary
20   it has taken in many victims
back off from this poem
it has drawn in yr feet
back off from this poem
it has drawn in yr legs

25   back off from this poem
it is a greedy mirror
you are into this poem . from
        the waist down
nobody can hear you can they ?
30   this poem has had you up to here
        belch
this poem aint got no manners
you cant call out frm this poem
relax now & go w / this poem

35   move & roll on to this poem
do not resist this poem
this poem has yr eyes
this poem has his head
this poem has his arms

40   this poem has his fingers
this poem has his fingertips

this poem is the reader & the
reader this poem

statistic : the us bureau of missing persons re-
45   ports that in 1968 over 100,000 people
disappeared leaving no solid clues
         nor trace   only
   a space   in the lives of their friends

MARGARET ATWOOD (1939–)

You Are Happy

The water turns
a long way down over the raw stone,
ice crusts around it.

We walk separately
5   along the hill to the open
beach, unused
picnic tables, wind
shoving the brown waves, erosion, gravel
rasping on gravel.

10   In the ditch a deer
carcass, no head. Bird
running across the glaring
road against the low pink sun.

When you are this
15   cold you can think about
nothing but the cold, the images

hitting into your eyes
like needles, crystals, you are happy.

Compare "You Are Happy" with William Stafford's "Traveling Through the Dark" on page 401.

SEAMUS HEANEY (1939–)

The Forge

All I know is a door into the dark.
Outside, old axles and iron hoops rusting;
Inside, the hammered anvil's short-pitched ring,
The unpredictable fantail of sparks
5   Or hiss when a new shoe toughens in water.
The anvil must be somewhere in the centre,

Horned as a unicorn, at one end square,
Set there immovable: an altar
Where he expends himself in shape and music.
10   Sometimes, leather-aproned, hairs in his nose,
He leans out on the jamb, recalls a clatter
Of hoofs where traffic is flashing in rows;
Then grunts and goes in, with a slam and flick
To beat real iron out, to work the bellows.

MARILYN HACKER (1942–)

Villanelle

For D.G.B.

Every day our bodies separate,
exploded torn and dazed.
Not understanding what we celebrate

we grope through languages and hesitate
5   and touch each other, speechless and amazed;
and every day our bodies separate

us farther from our planned, deliberate
ironic lives. I am afraid, disphased,
not understanding what we celebrate

10   when our fused limbs and lips communicate
the unlettered power we have raised.
Every day our bodies' separate

routines are harder to perpetuate.
In wordless darkness we learn wordless praise,
15   not understanding what we celebrate;

wake to ourselves, exhausted, in the late
morning as the wind tears off the haze,
not understanding how we celebrate
our bodies. Every day we separate.

ERICA JONG (1942–)

How You Get Born

One night, your mother is listening to the walls.
The clock whirrs like insect wings.
The ticking says lonely lonely lonely.

In the living room, the black couch swallows her.
5   She trusts it more than men,
but no one will ever love her
enough.

She doesn't yet know you
so how can she love you?
10 She loves you like God or Shakespeare.
She loves you like Mozart.

You are trembling in the walls like music.
You cross the ceiling in a phantom car of light.

Meanwhile unborn,
15 You wait in a heavy rainsoaked cloud
for your father's thunderbolt.
Your mother lies in the living room dreaming your hands.
Your mother lies in the living room dreaming your eyes.

She awakens & a shudder shakes her teeth.
20 The world is beginning again after the flood.

She slides into bed beside that gray-faced man,
your father.
She opens her legs to your coming.

Compare "How You Get Born" with Audre Lorde's "Now That I Am Forever with Child" on page 426.

DAVE SMITH (1942–)

Picking Cherries

The ladder quakes and sways under me, old wood
I put too much faith in, like ancestors strained.
You circle me, cradling the baby, sun guttering
in your face, parading through the leaves, glad.
5   If I looked down I would see your calm fear, see
in your narrowed eyes my bones chipped, useless.
The bucket hangs from my belt, pulling obscenely
at my pants, but the cherries drop in and grow
one by one. I keep reaching higher than I need
10   because I want the one that tickles your tongue.
When I come down we will both be older, slower,
but what of that? Haven't we loved this climbing?
If the ladder gives way I still believe I can
catch one branch, drop the bucket and ease down.

Compare "Picking Cherries" with Robert Frost's "After Apple-Picking" on pages 384–385.

ALFRED CORN (1943–)

Fifty-Seventh Street and Fifth[103]

Hard-edged buildings; cloudless blue enamel;
Lapidary hours—and that numerous woman,

---

[103] Cross streets of New York City's famed retail district.

Put-together, in many a smashing
Suit or dress is somehow what it's, well,
5 All about. A city designed by *Halston*:[104]
Clean lines, tans, grays, expense; no sentiment.
Off the mirrored boxes the afternoon
Glare fires an instant in her sunglasses
And reflects some of the armored ambition
10 Controlling deed here; plus the byword
That "only the best really counts." Awful
And awe-inspiring. How hard the task,
Keeping up to the mark: opinions, output,
Presentation—strong on every front. So?
15 Life is strife, the city says, a theory
That tastes of iron and demands assent.

A big lump of iron that's been magnetized.
All the faces I see are—Believers,
Pilgrims immigrated from fifty states
20 To discover, to surrender, themselves.
Success. Money. Fame. Insular dreams all,
Begotten of the dream of Manhattan, island
Of the possessed. When a man's tired of New York,
He's tired of life? Or just of possession?
25 A whirlpool animates the terrific
Streets, violence of our praise, blockbuster
Miracles down every vista, scored by
Accords and discords intrinsic to this air.
Concerted mind performs as the genius
30 Of place: competition, a trust in facts
And expense. Who loves or works here assumes,
For better or worse, the ground rules. A fate.

NIKKI GIOVANNI (1943–)

Nikki-Rosa

childhood remembrances are always a drag
if you're Black
you always remember things like living in Woodlawn[105]
with no inside toilet
5 and if you become famous or something
they never talk about how happy you were to have your mother
all to yourself and
how good the water felt when you got your bath from one of those
big tubs that folk in chicago barbecue in
10 and somehow when you talk about home

---

[104] Roy Halston Frowick (1932–), the well-known fashion designer who goes by the name of Halston.
[105] Woodlawn is a suburb of Cincinnati.

it never gets across how much you
understood their feelings
as the whole family attended meetings about Hollydale
and even though you remember
15 your biographers never understand
your father's pain as he sells his stock
and another dream goes
and though you're poor it isn't poverty that
concerns you
20 and though they fought a lot
it isn't your father's drinking that makes any difference
but only that everybody is together and you
and your sister have happy birthdays and very good christmasses
and I really hope no white person ever has cause to write about me
25 because they never understand Black love is Black wealth and they'll
probably talk about my hard childhood and never understand that
all the while I was quite happy

TOM WAYMAN (1945–)

Unemployment

The chrome lid of the coffee pot
twists off, and the glass knob rinsed.
Lift out the assembly, dump
the grounds out. Wash the pot and
5   fill with water, put everything back with
fresh grounds and snap the top down.
Plug in again and wait.

Unemployment is also
a great snow deep around the house
10 choking the street, and the City.
Nothing moves. Newspaper photographs
show the traffic backed up for miles.
Going out to shovel the walk
I think how in a few days the sun will clear this.
15 No one will know I worked here.

This is like whatever I do.
How strange that so magnificent a thing as a body
with its twinges, its aches
should have all that chemistry, that bulk
20 the intricate electrical brain
subjected to something as tiny
as buying a postage stamp.
Or selling it.

Or waiting.

GREGORY ORR (1947–)

All Morning

All morning the dream lingers.
I am like thick grass
in a meadow, still
soaked with dew at noon.

LESLIE MARMON SILKO (1948–)

Love Poem

Rain smell comes with the wind
               out of the southwest.
Smell of the sand dunes
        tall grass glistening
5   in the rain.
Warm raindrops that fall easy
           (this woman)
The summer is born.
Smell of her breathing new life
10   small gray toads on damp sand.
(this woman)
       whispering to dark wide leaves
       white moon blossoms dripping
                tracks in the sand.
15 Rain smell
      I am full of hunger
      deep and longing to touch
wet tall grass, green and strong beneath.
This woman loved a man
20 and she breathed to him
         her damp earth song.
I am haunted by this story
I remember it in cottonwood leaves
         their fragrance in the shade.
25 I remember it in the wide blue sky
when the rain smell comes with the wind.

GARY SOTO (1952–)

History

Grandma lit the stove.
Morning sunlight
Lengthened in spears
Across the linoleum floor.
5 Wrapped in a shawl,

Her eyes small
With sleep,
She sliced papas,
Pounded chiles
10   With a stone
Brought from Guadalajara.[106]

                                  After

Grandpa left for work,
She hosed down
15   The walk her sons paved
And in the shade
Of a chinaberry,
Unearthed her
Secret cigar box
20   Of bright coins
And bills, counted them
In English,
Then in Spanish,
And buried them elsewhere.
25   Later, back
From the market,
Where no one saw her,
She pulled out
Pepper and beet, spines
30   Of asparagus
From her blouse,
Tiny chocolates
From under a paisley bandana,
And smiled.

35   That was the '50s,
And Grandma in her '50s,
A face streaked
From cutting grapes
And boxing plums.
40   I remember her insides
Were washed of tapeworm,
Her arms swelled into knobs
Of small growths—
Her second son
45   Dropped from a ladder
And was dust.
And yet I do not know
The sorrows
That sent her praying
50   In the dark of a closet,
The tear that fell

---

[106] Guadalajara is a city in west-central Mexico.

At night
When she touched
Loose skin
55 Of belly and breasts.
I do not know why
Her face shines
Or what goes beyond this shine,
Only the stories
60 That pulled her
From Taxco[107] to San Joaquin,
Delano to Westside,[108]
The places
In which we all begin.

Compare "History" with Edward Field's "My Polish Grandmother" on pages 20–21.

---

[107] Taxco is an area of Mexico.
[108] Places in California.

Appendix

Writing about Poetry

From time to time most of us will have occasion to write about something we have read. Such an exercise will not be confined to literature courses for which we will compose essays and exams. Businessmen and -women often have to write reports based on other documents. Lawyers must write briefs based on their interpretations of laws and depositions. Although these other sorts of writing may not require precisely the skills required of a literary text, the practice of writing about literature is exceptionally helpful. Indeed, law schools consider the study of literature one of the most valuable preparations for legal training. The care, concentration, and judgment needed to evaluate and write about a literary work is a discipline useful in any number of demanding professions and fields.

Nevertheless, some students balk at writing essays about literature. They feel that literature should be enjoyed and that writing about it dampens their enjoyment. Although it is true that people take a certain degree of pleasure in what comes easily, many readers find that they do not fully appreciate what they read until they force themselves to formulate their responses in writing. Writing about literature, therefore, can aid in a more profound and lasting enjoyment of literature.

Writing about literature is not significantly different from writing on any other subject. A critical essay demands the same clarity and coherence of expression as any other type of writing. For your convenience, however, we have broken down the process into five stages: (1) understanding the work, (2) choosing a thesis, (3) choosing supporting material, (4) organizing the essay, and (5) writing the essay.

Understanding the Work

Before writing anything, you must be certain that you understand the work. You must understand not only each word, but also how the various parts relate to each other. You must understand not only what is present, but also why certain things are excluded from the text. This book has attempted to give you the knowledge and tools needed to analyze poetry, and it would be foolish to attempt to summarize these skills here. We must not concentrate on one or two details and forget the overall pattern of the poem. A good reading of poetry always integrates part and whole.

When assigned to write a paper on a poem or group of poems, you should start by reading the works carefully on your own rather than by reading criticism, biographies, or reader's guides. Your essays should reflect your own emotional and intellectual comprehension of the poem. Outside sources are useful *only* insofar as they enhance your understanding. Repeating critical positions we neither understand nor agree with leads to a muddle of half-formed thoughts and comments.

Moreover, criticism is usually more difficult to understand than the work it discusses. By reading criticism first, you may succeed only in confusing yourself and in making your task harder. Most poems are written for the average literate reader, but most scholarship is written by scholars for scholars. Thus critics tend to assume that their readers have a wide familiarity with history, literary methodology, and other works of literature.

Choosing a Thesis

Before you can write an outline for your essay, you must have a *thesis* or central idea. Every essay contains one thesis. A thesis is a statement that either interprets or evaluates the work under study. It tells your readers what the essay is about, the central point you want them to understand. Consequently, your thesis is the most important sentence in your essay. All other sentences either support it, define it, restrict it, or place it in context. A thesis gives an essay unity and coherence; any sentence that does not clearly relate to it is irrelevant and ought to be rewritten or removed.

Thus, after understanding the poem, your next most important task is to choose a clear, truthful, and interesting thesis. Your job will be easier, of course, if your instructor already has given you one. Usually, however, professors give students more latitude.

Our suggestion for finding a thesis is to ask yourself this question: if I could tell a reader only one thing about this poem, what would that be? The answer to this question ought to be significant, interesting, and helpful to other readers. But remember that you can have only *one* central idea per paper. This central idea will form the basis of your thesis statement.

There are other ways of finding good central ideas. Every good poem has unity; a unifying thread that runs through the poem can also be the central idea of your paper. For example, you may decide that one of the unifying ideas of Tennyson's poem "Ulysses" is Ulysses' search for knowledge. Your thesis could be: "In 'Ulysses' Tennyson explores the hero's obsessive search for knowledge." Here is an idea worthy of development and substantiation.

Many students like to compare two poems. But it is never enough to say that two works are alike or different. A central idea that is so vague and general is sure to lead to a vague and general essay. The more specific your central idea, the more specific your essay will be.

Let us say you are intrigued by two of Shakespeare's sonnets, the ones beginning "Shall I compare thee to a summer's day," and "My mistress' eyes are nothing like the sun." You have read them carefully and have consulted the critics. You are now ready to formulate a thesis. To aid in the process, you may compare them point by point by dividing a piece of paper into two columns, one for each poem. At the end of the process, your paper looks like this:

Summer's day	Nothing like the sun
1. sonnet	1. sonnet
2. compares beloved to nature	2. compares beloved to nature
3. beloved is "fair" (l. 7) golden complexion (l. 6)	3. beloved is dark black hair (l. 4) skin "dun" (l. 3)
4. the beloved's eye is better than the sun (l. 5)	4. beloved's eye inferior to sun (l. 1)
5. the beloved will become the poem in the future (l. 12)	5. the beloved stands beyond the poem (l. 14)
6. beloved's beauty made eternal in poetry (l. 14)	6. beloved's beauty greater than poem can represent (l. 14)
7. beloved possesses more typical beauty	7. beloved has atypical beauty
8. tone: serious throughout, laudatory	8. tone: sometimes comic, insulting; laudatory at end
9. poem emphasizes the lasting condition of poetry and the mutable condition of nature	9. poem emphasizes the false condition of poetry and the indefinable beauty of human beings

This list does not exhaust the points of comparison, but it does give you enough material with which to begin formulating your thesis.

You notice that some of your points are facts about the poems. For example, Shakespeare is writing about two different people, one light, the other dark. Both poems speak of the sun as an eye. Could these facts be the basis of an essay? No. A thesis *must be a statement that needs proof, something controversial or uncertain*. Facts, unless they are revolutionary discoveries, are not sufficiently in need of support to be adequate statements for a thesis.

However, some of the statements are interpretive, and these might be useful for formulating a thesis. For example, the entry under "tone" indicates that both poems end by praising the beloved but that the second poem arrives at its praise in a more complicated manner. One might argue as follows: "Though both poems conclude by praising their subjects, 'My mistress' eyes are nothing like the sun,' approaches the subject in a richer, more complicated way." Because this thesis is both interpretive and evaluative, it needs to be supported. It would make a good thesis.

There are other statements one could use as the basis for a thesis. Entry 9 is interesting. One might argue: "In 'My mistress' eyes,' Shakespeare acknowledges a beauty so peculiarly human that it eludes the criteria of nature and poetry." Or, perhaps, one might wish to argue: "In these two poems Shakespeare suggests that nature is not an adequate measure by which to judge human beauty." Your list of comparisons could lead to a number of interesting theses. Critics and scholars have been studying Shakespeare's sonnets for centuries without exhausting their richness and variety. Clearly you might formulate many different theses comparing these sonnets. You must decide which thesis most interests you and is within your capacity to support.

A good thesis, then, should incorporate a number of characteristics:

1. It should grow out of your understanding of the poem and should not be imposed on a work it may not fit.
2. It should be evaluative or interpretive. It cannot be a statement of fact, unless the fact is not yet accepted.
3. It should be precise. The reader must know what you are trying to prove. Imprecise or vague terms obscure your point and make it difficult to defend your position adequately.
4. It should be restrictive. Think of your thesis as a sort of fort under attack by the skeptical mind of your reader. If you try to protect too wide an area, your supporting forces will be too widely dispersed. A tight defense of a small territory is more likely to succeed. Never argue any point *you* do not thoroughly believe.
5. Finally, your thesis should contain one central idea. One good idea is hard enough to support and defend. More than one compels you to scatter your forces.

Exercise

Of the ten statements that follow, some are good thesis statements, some are poor, and some are not thesis statements at all. Indicate the thesis statements and improve those that seem weak.

1. Auden's "Musée des Beaux Arts" was written in 1939.
2. Written in 1939, "Musée des Beaux Arts" reflects Auden's concern about the coming war.
3. Horace Gregory's and Louis and Celia Zukofsky's translations of Catullus are very different.
4. Dylan Thomas's "Do Not Go Gentle into That Good Night" is a villanelle.
5. "Do Not Go Gentle into That Good Night" is a very moving poem.
6. Love is the subject of many sonnets.

7. Although the couple in George Meredith's *Modern Love* is married, the sequence is typical of Elizabethan sonnet sequences because it traces the dissolution of their love.
8. The comparison between the beloved and nature in Shakespeare's sonnets underscores the supranatural quality of human beauty.
9. Sylvia Plath's "Daddy" is one of my favorite poems.
10. Anne Sexton's "Young Girl in a Maternity Ward" beautifully evokes the confusion, loneliness, and sense of abandonment felt by the teenage mother.

Choosing Supporting Material

Although you have now formulated your thesis, you are not yet ready to start writing. First you must consider the best way to defend and support your thesis.

The best evidence for supporting your thesis is the text of the poem itself. This may seem obvious, but it is suprising how easily writers overlook the poem while writing about it. *Never make a statement about a poem that cannot be corroborated by a passage in the poem.* You should quote frequently and extensively from the poem. Before stating any opinion about the poem, you should be aware of the word, line, or passage that led you to that opinion.

One of the chief complaints teachers make about student literary essays is that they are *impressionistic*; that is, they make general comments about the poem without indicating what in the poem gave rise to those ideas, feelings, or evaluations. No matter how true, well worded, or insightful such impressions are, they are nearly worthless if the writer does not connect them to the text. Students concerned about improving their writing should guard against impressionistic writing.

Your second source of support material comes from what other critics and scholars have said about the work. As we cautioned earlier, your essay should not be a collage of other people's thoughts about the poem. A critic's work should be used only when it furthers your own understanding. You should quote or paraphrase a critic or scholar only in three situations:

1. When the critic makes a point so well that it is worthy of repetition. Some critics are especially articulate and polished writers. Make use of their beautifully turned observations.
2. When the critic supplies you with an idea, a fact (not of common knowledge), a method of presentation, or an opinion that is not your own but whose truth you both recognize and need for your own essay. It is any scholar's duty to acknowledge the intellectual debt by quoting the critic and/or noting the source of the observation.
3. When you believe your own evaluation needs support. By quoting a critic, you are saying indirectly, "See, I'm not alone in this belief. X believes it, too!" Such support is especially needed when you are evaluating a poem's literary merit. It is good to have someone on your side when either praising or disparaging someone's work.

In the following paragraph we can observe all three uses of quotation and paraphrase. The passage is part of an essay on John Milton's use of the sonnet. (You will find three of his sonnets in this book.) The author, James G. Mengert, wishes to show that Milton effectively used traditional aspects of the sonnet in his own special way. Mengert's aim is threefold: it is factual, interpretive, and evaluative. First, Mengert must establish the facts of the sonnet tradition. Second, he must interpret Milton's use of the tradition. Third, he must evaluate Milton's use of the tradition. Mengert cannot do all this work in one paragraph, but this excerpt shows how he goes about supporting his thesis.

> It was not until J. S. Smart's edition of the sonnets in 1921 that Milton was fully allowed to have a conception of the sonnet that was in any sense traditional rather than merely or substantially idiosyncratic.[1] The roots of Milton's sonnet form in traditional, especially Italian, practice were further explored by F. T. Prince.[2] Although there have since been refinements or qualifications of the work of these men, their basic contentions still stand; and studies of individual sonnets can now take for granted Milton's firm grasp of the tradition and resources of the sonnet and go on to examine the interaction of his own powerful, reshaping genius with that tradition. Indeed, it is possible to see this very reshaping as itself a participation in a flexible sonnet tradition. Thus Taylor Stroehr introduces his own analysis of the sonnets with this comment: "He chose the form, one supposes, exactly because it was demanding, suited by its brevity to the expression of occasional thoughts and feelings, by its complexity and sinewy movement to the development of powerful emotion and tough logic." And he concludes his essay with the observation that "Milton plays the conventional elements of linguistic structure off against the less flexible conventions of the sonnet form itself, to produce a compelling expression of poetic feeling, beyond the reach of less self-conscious art."[3]

---

[1] John S. Smart, ed., *The Sonnets of Milton* (Glasgow: Maclehose, Jackson, 1921).
[2] F. T. Prince, *The Italian Element in Milton's Verse* (Oxford: Clarendon Press, 1954), esp. pp. 89–107.
[3] Taylor Stroehr, "Syntax and Poetic Form in Milton's Sonnets," *English Studies* 45 (1964), pp. 289, 301.

Mengert refers to the historical work of J. S. Smart and F. T. Prince and summarizes their findings. He then quotes Taylor Stroehr twice, first because Stroehr so beautifully articulates Mengert's position and later to support Mengert's evaluation that Milton's sonnets are great works of art. This passage is more scholarly than the writing you may be called on to produce, but it clearly indicates how the skillful use of quotation, reference, and paraphrase can support and advance an argument.

Biographical information is perhaps the most difficult information to use in an essay. Some professors absolutely forbid it and may go so far as to remove the author's name from the text of the poem. They argue that the reader should be concerned only with the text and that biographical information is merely sophisticated gossip that has no place in serious literary discussion. Other teachers do recognize a place for biographical information. The rule of thumb to use is that *no biographical information should be included unless it illuminates the poem*. For example, it does help the reader to know that Sylvia Plath's father was a German professor in order to understand why there are German words in her poem "Daddy" and why he is associated with fascism. But the poem is not illuminated by the fact that Plath went to Smith College on a scholarship. Thus one biographical fact may be relevant, another irrelevant. Considerate and interesting writers typically do not set aside a paragraph to give a biographical summary of the author. They do not wish to waste precious space or their reader's time with irrelevant information.

Organizing the Essay

The literary essay, like most essays, is generally divided into three basic parts: an introduction, a body, and a conclusion. Each part has its own structure and purpose.

The chief feature of the introduction is the thesis, which typically appears as the last sentence of the introductory paragraph. The rest of the paragraph sets the stage for the thesis by raising the issue the thesis attempts to answer. Indeed, one could say that the opening or introductory paragraph tries to answer the following questions: Why should a reader be interested in the thesis? Does it answer some unsolved problem? Does the thesis assert something unusual?

Like the introduction, the conclusion is usually a single paragraph in smaller essays. Conclusions generally contain no new material. They summarize what has been said in the essay. They can also project from the material discussed to the further issues it raises. But writers should be careful not to let the conclusion be too provocative. Too many threads left hanging leave the reader dissatisfied.

Most of the essay, then, is made up of body paragraphs. A body paragraph contains three parts. It begins with a topic sentence. The topic sentence is followed by supporting material. An optional concluding sentence either summarizes the paragraph or serves as a transition to the next paragraph.

Before writing an essay, you should first prepare an outline. Even a brief outline can be helpful. For example, let us outline a possible essay based on Tennyson's "Ulysses." The thesis we developed earlier was: "In 'Ulysses,' Tennyson explores the hero's obsessive search for knowledge." We might break this down in three ways:

1. Ulysses' earlier wanderings were a quest for new experiences.
2. Ulysses sees life as a constant quest for knowledge.
3. Ulysses' dissatisfaction with his Ithaca is derived from intellectual boredom.

If we go back through the poem, we can find textual evidence to support our contentions.

1. Ulysses' earlier wanderings were a quest for new experiences:
   a. ll. 11–12 speak of "roaming with a hungry heart."
   b. ll. 13–17 speak of the various experiences he has had on his travels.
   c. l. 64 speaks of Achilles, the hero whom he knew.

2. Ulysses sees life as a constant quest for knowledge:
   a. ll. 19–21 speak of "experience as an archway."
   b. ll. 30–33 speak of the desire "to follow knowledge like a sinking star."
   c. ll. 56–57 speak of the wish to "seek a newer world."
   d. l. 70 speaks of wanting "to strive, to seek, to find."
3. Ulysses is dissatisfied with Ithaca because it is intellectually boring:
   a. ll. 35–43 speak of the slow labor of civilizing people.
   b. ll. 4–5 speak of people as crude and uninteresting.
   c. ll. 22–24 speak of the boredom of a life that is not challenging.
   d. l. 3 suggests that his wife does not interest him.

To this basic outline you could add references to critics and scholars who support your interpretation of "Ulysses."

Several things about this outline are noteworthy. Every point you make about the work is directly supported by several key phrases in the text. One could diagram the relationship between the thesis and the text as a pyramid whose footing is the poem.

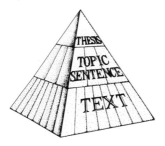

If the text were not there at every point, the entire structure would come crashing to the ground.

Another point you should notice about the outline is that we have chosen quotes from all over the text, but we have not necessarily followed the order of the poem. Under heading 3, we first begin with a quotation from the end of the poem; we then go to a quotation from the beginning, then to one from the middle, and finally to another reference to the opening lines. As a writer, you are busy proving your point. Your essay follows *your* organization, not Tennyson's.

Writing the Essay

Before discussing specific problems of composition, we would like to discuss a general problem with writing literary essays.

An annoying habit in critical writing is speaking of the poem as if the reader has not read the work. In book reviews that appear in newspapers, the writer is obliged to narrate the plot of the story because the reader presumably has *not* read the book. In literary essays, however, *the author should assume that the reader is familiar with the work.* Thus there is no reason to summarize the contents of the poem. Yet time and again, student essays contain such paragraphs as the following:

> Tennyson's "Ulysses" is a dramatic monologue. The poem begins with Ulysses home in Ithaca after traveling ten years. However, Ulysses is not content to remain home. He turns his kingdom over to his son Telemachus, and summons his men back to his ship. Though he admits to being old, Ulysses still believes he can perform "some work of noble note" (l. 52).

Such a summary paragraph is useless and time-consuming. It reveals only the most superficial understanding of the poem. Authors concerned about improving their writing avoid such unnecessary passages.

Introductions

Even professional writers have difficulty deciding where to begin their discussions. Most often, students start the discussion far from their thesis statements and therefore never lead up to them clearly or adequately. Here, for example, is a typical opening of a student paper on "Ulysses."

> Alfred, Lord Tennyson was one of the greatest English poets of the nineteenth century. He was fascinated by Greek epics and mythology. He wrote about the Greeks in such poems as "The Lotus-Eaters," "Tithonus," and "Ulysses." In "Ulysses," Tennyson explores the hero's obsessive search for knowledge.

Notice the jump between the thesis statement and the rest of the paragraph. The opening sentences are very general. They do not discuss Ulysses as either a man or a poem, nor do they mention his quest for knowledge. The key ideas of the thesis are not developed in this poor introductory paragraph. Let us rewrite the opening so that it more suitably prepares for the thesis.

> The Ulysses of Tennyson's poem has a problem understanding his motives, for after struggling ten years to return to Ithaca, he is seized by the desire to go traveling again. He attempts to explain this desire in many ways. He feels useless in Ithaca; he is not a patient administrator; he is misunderstood by his people, who "hoard, and sleep, and feed, and know not me" (l. 5). But the heart of his dissatisfaction is a desire for knowledge. In "Ulysses," Tennyson explores the hero's obsessive desire for knowledge.

Notice how in this second version, the author has gotten straight down to business by eliminating any superfluous discussion of Tennyson in general and focusing immediately on the issue of Ulysses' motives for leaving Ithaca. The thesis, then, is a summary of the discussion in the introduction. Clear and to the point, this new introduction well prepares the reader for the discussion that follows.

Conclusions

Sophisticated writers will attempt to conclude an essay by suggesting the significance of the observations for a wider understanding of life or of the author's work. First, let us look at an adequate conclusion to our paper on "Ulysses."

> Ulysses is not a king satisfied with being an executive, a manager, a bureaucrat. In his past wanderings, Ulysses has accustomed himself to constantly changing experience and ever-increasing knowledge. Ithaca has given him all of the experiences it contains, and now he feels compelled to "seek a newer world " (l. 57). With his band of aging mariners, he determinedly sets out, "to strive, to seek, to find, and not to yield." (l. 70)

Here is another conclusion, one that extends the meaning of the poem while summarizing the argument.

> Through the poem, we come to understand Ulysses' needs better. For Ulysses, power is not enough, comfort is not enough; food, drink, shelter are insufficient for life. Ulysses has become aware of a great human emotion—curiosity, a desire for new knowledge and experience. Once that appetite is developed, it is not forgotten or easily sated. Ulysses' curiosity elevates him above the swashbuckling heroism of his fellow warriors like Achilles, and makes him a new hero for an age yet to come.

Body Paragraphs

Body paragraphs are used to support the thesis. Topic sentences break down the thesis into smaller, defendable units. For example, in the following paragraph Michael Ferber discusses William Blake's poem "London" (the text of which is on page 112). Ferber's thesis is that "London" is basically a political poem, despite the claims of some critics. He hopes to show in part how political the poem is by explaining some of the political implications of the words used in the poem. Here is the paragraph that explains the phrase "charter'd street."

> We meet *charter'd street* right away. I have little to add to the discussions by David Erdman and E. P. Thompson of the connotations of *charter'd* which emerge when we set the poem in its historical context. London had a charter, granting it certain privileges or liberties, and so did many commercial associations in the City such as the East India Company, prominent along the banks of the Thames. Yet one man's charter is another's manacle; charters are exclusive. It was over just this two-sidedness of "charter" and its synonyms that Burke, Paine, and many others fought their pamphlet wars. In Part II of *Rights of Man*, published the year Blake probably wrote his poem (1792), Paine wrote, "It is a perversion of terms to say, that a charter gives rights. It operates by a contrary effect, that of taking rights away." The adjective "chartered" had as it still does the sense of "hired" or "leased," which combines with Paine's pejorative political nuance to suggest the monopolistic and exploitative practices of England's commercial empire. Under the regime of Pitt, as under every regime at least since the Conqueror, all Englishmen are "chartered," and the

second half of the poem is a litany of typical cases: they are sold into slavery as chimney sweepers by their fathers, impressed into the army or navy for a few shillings, hired for a few hours as harlots, or bought and sold on the London marriage market.

Notice how full and yet economical the paragraph is. Ferber does not quote David Erdman and E. P. Thompson directly. He is content merely to refer to their work. His longest quotation is an elegant sentence from Thomas Paine, who perfectly exemplifies both Ferber's and Blake's position.

One difficulty in writing a body paragraph lies in integrating quotations into the flow of your own words. There are two general types of quotations: direct and indirect. An indirect quotation is a paraphrase of the author's words. For example, you might write:

Ulysses says *that* his wife is old.

The word *that* indicates you are not quoting Ulysses' precise words. However, you might have written:

Ulysses complains of being "matched with an aged wife."

This second version is a direct quotation; consequently, the quoted phrase is enclosed by quotation marks. Indirect quotations save both space and explanation. Often one can more easily paraphrase an author than integrate direct quotations. However, indirect quotations are of limited use. Because the words are yours, they are less convincing than the poet's own words. You open yourself to the charge of altering the poet's meaning to suit your own purposes.

Direct quotations may be either short or extensive. Short quotations can be as brief as one word or as long as two lines, and they are placed within the text of the essay. For example, the sentence "Ulysses complains of being 'matched with an aged wife,' " represents a short quotation. Extensive quotations are any that are longer than two lines of poetry or two sentences in length. They are generally isolated from the main text and distinguished from it in some way, as in this example of an essay that discusses Robert Frost's "Out, Out—." (The text of "Out, Out—" can be found on pages 24–25.)

> The most painful of these encounters [with the physical world], of course, takes place in "Out, Out—," where a boy helping some adults work with a power saw loses his right hand to the saw and then, as a result, life itself. The implicit epigraph to this poem is contained in the passage in *Macbeth* that follows the words of the title:
>
> > Out, out, brief candle!
> > Life's . . . a tale
> > Told by an idiot, full of sound and fury,
> > Signifying nothing.
>
> These lines, as I have pointed out in another connection, express not Frost's cynical view of life, but his tacit condemnation of a world in which people

make things go wrong, starting with the refusal of the unnamed "they" to allow the boy an extra half-hour at the end of the day to watch the sunset.

Notice that since the quotation begins in the middle of the poetic line, the quotation is placed in a way that indicates its position. Indeed, a writer is always expected to indicate where each line ends. In short quotations the slash is used to indicate line breaks, as in this discussion of Wordsworth's "The Solitary Reaper."

> The aloneness of the singer is intensified in the second stanza when she is compared to the lone nightingale singing in far-off Arabia and to the solitary cuckoo "Breaking the silence of the seas/Among the farthest Hebrides." The melancholy tone and rhythm established in the first stanza are developed in the third stanza.

The foregoing passage indicates several aspects of quoting. When you quote, you *must* quote the passage exactly as it is written, without making any alterations. In the foregoing passage, the line break is indicated and Wordsworth's punctuation is preserved precisely as it was published.

Occasionally you will want to delete or add words to a quotation. Deletions must be indicated by an *ellipsis*, or three dots. Notice that in the quotation from Shakespeare, the author has deleted several words. The omission is indicated by an ellipsis. One should delete only unimportant words or phrases. You do not want to alter the meaning of the text by eliminating essential words. Additions are indicated by placing the inserted words in brackets. For example, note the addition in this sentence about "Out, Out—":

> The boy in Frost's poem has his life snuffed "out [like a] brief candle."

In quotations one may also replace pronouns with their antecedent nouns. One must be careful to preserve the original meaning, however. For example, in Tennyson's poem, Ulysses always speaks of himself in the first person. Such references may not be clear when quoted. In the following passage, note how a proper name has been substituted for the pronoun *me*.

> The people of Ithaca are lazy, stupid and barely civilized. They "hoard, and sleep, and feed, and know not [Ulysses]."

Deletions and additions are often necessary to integrate quotations into the text. Many writers prefer numerous short quotations over long ones. By quoting frequently, an essayist can constantly refer to the text and keep the poet's words in the reader's mind.

Not all quotations need to be preceded with a comma. A comma is not necessary if the quotation is part of the sentence's flow. Study the punctuation of the following two sentences.

1. Ulysses says, "I cannot rest from travel."
2. Ulysses is a man who "cannot rest from travel."

In the first sentence there is a grammatical break between the sentence and the quotation. In the second the quotation is part of the sentence's flow; thus no commas are needed in sentence 2. Examine how quotations are used in the passages we have studied. You will notice that careful writers try to integrate their quotations into the flow of their sentences.

Citations

Writers should acknowledge the source of whatever ideas or quotations they have borrowed. Borrowings should be noted at the bottom of the page where they occur or at the end of the essay. Normally, at the end of the borrowing and raised above the line, authors place a number that corresponds to the number of the acknowledgment.

Why do authors footnote? The practice may seem tedious, troublesome, and unnecessary, but it does serve important functions.

First, it is a means of maintaining intellectual honesty. We all are indebted to others for ideas, skills, and knowledge, and we acknowledge that debt. Without such acknowledgment we would be claiming as our own what were actually someone else's thoughts; to the educated person, stealing others' ideas is as heinous as stealing their property. Indeed, copyrights and patent laws make it a punishable offense to steal someone's words and ideas without compensation and permission.

A second reason for footnotes is the relative brevity of quotations. Your reader may want to understand the quotation's context or find out more of what the author has to say. Footnotes give readers a means to satisfy their curiosity.

For literary essays, notes must contain the author's name, the title of the book or article, and the page number at the end. In the case of an article, you must also note the name of the journal or book in which it appeared and the volume and date of its appearance. For books, you must note the place of publication, the publisher, and the date of publication.

We cannot give a complete list of all the conditions you may need to footnote. For a complete list, consult the latest *MLA Handbook for Writers of Research Papers, Theses, and Dissertations,* published by the Modern Language Association. The following are three of the major situations that arise: footnoting a poem, a critical article, and a scholarly book.

A poem in a scholarly edition

> [1] Alfred, Lord Tennyson, "Ulysses," in *The Poems of Tennyson*, ed. Christopher Ricks (London: Longman's, Green & Co., 1969), p. 560.

A scholarly article

> [2] James G. Mengert, "The Resistance of Milton's Sonnets," *English Literary Renaissance* 11 (1981), p. 82.

A scholarly book

> [3] Elizabeth Huberman, *The Poetry of Edwin Muir: The Field of Good and Ill* (New York: Oxford University Press, 1971), p. 227.

After the initial citation of a work, you do not need to restate all this information. If you are using only one work by the author, you may merely state his or her name and the page reference.

⁴ Huberman, p. 95.

If you are referring to several works by the same author, after the first citation you may use the author's last name, a shortened title, and the page reference.

⁵ Huberman, *Muir*, p. 97.

If you are writing a paper on a single work (Tennyson's "Ulysses," for example), you may follow a less cumbersome procedure. Your first entry should follow this form:

> ¹ Alfred, Lord Tennyson, "Ulysses," in *The Poems of Tennyson*, ed. Christopher Ricks (London: Longman's, Green & Co., 1969), p. 560, l. 3. All further line references to this work appear in the text.

After this initial reference, you may simply place line numbers in parentheses after quotations.

> Ulysses feels useless in Ithaca; he is not a patient administrator; he is misunderstood by his people, who "hoard, and sleep, and feed, and know not me" (l. 5).

If you are studying a novel or book-length poem, you merely substitute page numbers for line numbers.

Bibliographies

Short essays do not need bibliographies. However, teachers may require bibliographies in order to give students practice in writing them. A bibliography lists alphabetically by the author's last name all the works consulted. Thus our list of books and articles would look like this.

Huberman, Elizabeth. *The Poetry of Edwin Muir: The Field of Good and Evil.* New York: Oxford University Press, 1971.

Mengert, James G. "The Resistance of Milton's Sonnets," *English Literary Renaissance* 11 (1981). 81–95.

Tennyson, Alfred Lord. "Ulysses," in *The Poems of Tennyson*. Ed. Christopher Ricks. London: Longman's, Green & Co., 1969. 560–566.

Two Complete Essays

The following are two discussions of poems. The first is part of a longer essay on Thomas Wyatt's "They Flee from Me." This is a scholarly discussion. The second is an example of a student essay on Robert Lowell's "Skunk Hour." This too is a scholarly discussion. You can find the text of the poems on pages 349–350 for "They Flee from Me" and pages 122–123 for "Skunk Hour." Read the poems first, and then read the essays.

DAVID MATTHEW ROSEN

Time, Identity, and Context in Wyatt's Verse

In reading Thomas Wyatt's poem "They Flee from Me," one is struck by the power of the human voice speaking in its lines. Though a lithe and simple lyric, "They Flee from Me" resonates with nuances of emotion that encompass not only the speaker's distress at the loss of love, but also his distress at the irrevocable passage of time.[1] How does Wyatt create this remarkable voice full of the evanescence of beautiful moments? It is through the layering of time, the juxtaposition of incident in a way that suggests the dissolution of one moment into the next, and so conveys impermanence, frustration, despair.

In "They Flee from Me" each stanza creates a context for the next. In the opening stanza, the poet relates his experience with some ambiguous creatures in an unclear past by juxtaposing their former tameness with their present return to a wilder state. The fragility of their momentary tameness is heightened by its distance in time and by our awareness of its extraordinary character. The preciousness of this experience and the poignancy of its loss serve as the context for our understanding of what follows.

The second stanza recreates a more particular time when unexpectedly the beloved kissed her lover. When the woman embraces the poet, the moment is sweet for being both unexpected and desired. Yet we are aware that, although longed for, the moment is disconnected from what appears to be the natural flow of things—the woman's usual behaviour, her distance. Like the creatures', it is the possibility of the woman's reversion to a wilder state, the sense of her underlying wildness that is brought to the moment, that, in fact, makes the moment precious. The woman and the creatures are so desirable because they can never be fully possessed.[2] They are, like creatures in much of Wyatt's verse, too complex to be contained by any person or any arbitrary set of rules.

The moment of the kiss, nonetheless, remains for the poet a sacred moment, fixed and transcendent, as he exclaims at the beginning of the second stanza. But this transcendent past, this luminous moment—that in religion would begin a new era and order different from the temporal one—remains unfulfilled expectation. In a world pressed forward by time, the kiss is inevitably juxtaposed with events as they actually turn out. Like the past changing to a present with which it is both connected and disconnected, the woman changes. Like time itself, she recognizes her relationship with her lover, but like time, she invites "newfangleness." Although to the poet's idealistic mind the woman's actions seem cruel and unexpected, they are no more cruel and unexpected than the creatures' actions with which they are linked. Only the poet's static position

---

[1] For an amusingly jaundiced review of critical background, see Richard L. Greene, "Wyatt's 'They Flee from Me' and the Busily Seeking Critics," *Bucknell Review* 12, no. 3 (Fall 1964), pp. 17–30. Some have not been intimidated: Leonard E. Nathan, "Tradition and Newfangleness in Wyatt's 'They Flee from Me,' " *ELH* 32, no. 1 (1965), pp. 1–16; Leigh Winser, "The Question of Love Tradition in Wyatt's 'They Flee from Me,' " *Essays in Literature (Western Illinois University)* 2, no. 1 (Spring 1975), pp. 3–9; Carolyn Chiapelli, "A Late Gothic Vein in Wyatt's 'They Flee from Me,' " *Renaissance and Reformation* 1 (New Series), no. 2 (1977), pp. 95–102.

[2] Michael McCanles, "Love and Power in the Poetry of Sir Thomas Wyatt," *Modern Language Quarterly* 29, no. 2 (June 1968), pp. 145–160.

makes them seem unexpected. In terms of the general lesson of the creatures and the poem's special logic, the poet should have anticipated what would happen.

This conflict of expectation and event is the crux of the poem, then. The poet, unlike the changing and complex world about him, remains rigid in his view of things. As a result things out of his control seem to happen to him. His sense of his own helplessness and our sense of it as well is heightened by the awareness that we develop and share as the poem develops, the awareness that time moves, that past and present do not form a pattern, that the world is complex and therefore its moments of simplicity are precious.

This sense of the distance of moments in a continuous time is intensified by the lover's static position, layering the final question of the poem with real emotion: "I would fain know what she has deserved." It is useless to answer, useless to ask. One might as properly inquire what "they" which flee deserve. There is no way for the speaker to ask for judgment, to assume control. By recourse to what system of rules? The question is heavy with emotion, vibrating sadness, cynicism, argumentativeness and more.

Thus when we examine the events of the poem, we find that they lead to complications that result in the poet's despair. And if we look again we will find that even the poet, though he won't admit it, has the same complexities and changeableness; he too is human and affected by time. We see this when he is taken in the woman's arms, for then it is he who is like the creatures who fed at his hand. However, when the woman gives him leave to fly, unlike the creatures and unlike her, he cannot. In spite of, or because of these various poses, the lover exposes his own complexity, a complexity he shares with all creatures. Although the speaker tries to maintain a steadfast position, we can see that his view continuously evolves as it copes with the contexts of past actions. This forced complexity of the lover's view grinds against his static faith and only serves to isolate him further in a world he cannot account for, control, or accept. In this way time past becomes more precious and more hopelessly lost. In the end, his final words are rather unconvincing as a call for justice, unconvincing to himself as well, it seems. Yet they are convincing as an expression of his mixed and authentic emotions. Our appreciation of the emotions that shape these simple words attests to the thickening of experience that the progress of the poem and Wyatt's handling of time have achieved.

From this poem we learn that the past acts like an after-image of a continuous action. The after-image continues to affect our view of the present moment from which it is now disjoined and which it can only partly explain. The progress of the poem is a process of accumulating detail, of accumulating these images that create a context for a present in which it becomes clear how time works and how complex things are. Reading becomes a process of changing or modifying our own viewpoints so that reading resembles the time which it often contemplates and in which it takes place. In other words, our sense of loss develops as the poem develops; as the reader must give up one beautiful word or image to go on to the next, so the poet has given up each moment of his life, savoring it and unwillingly losing it. Our sense of loss when the poem stops is like the poet's own sense of loss. Although the poet can never recover the beautiful moments that he has lost, luckily we may reread the poem and through it reexperience the beauty of Wyatt's own evanescent human voice expressing his poignant sense of loss, beauty and isolation.

Eleanor Lester

Skunk Hour: An Explication

Robert Lowell's poem ''Skunk Hour'' is dedicated to
Elizabeth Bishop, whose poem ''The Armadillo'' Lowell
used as a model.[1] The poems do indeed contain many
similarities. But whereas Miss Bishop concludes her
poem with the armadillo clenching ''a weak mailed fist/
. . . ignorant against the sky,''[2] a sign of impotent
resistance against man's invasion, Lowell's skunk
''jabs her wedge-head in a cup/of sour cream''[3] and will
not be frightened away. The skunk triumphs over both man
and time not by resisting them, but by adapting herself
to them. For Richard Wilbur, ''they stand for stubborn,
unabashed livingness, and for [Lowell's] own refusal
. . . to cease desiring a world of vitality, freedom,
and love.''[4] The skunk may not be the sweetest creature,
but she survives.

The skunk's acceptance is in marked contrast to the
people who inhabit Nautilus Island. The ''heiress'' who
is ''in her dotage''(l. 6) fights the encroachment of
civilization, and thus

>   she buys up all
>   the eyesores facing her shore
>   and lets them fall. [ll. 10–12]

The result does not improve nature but increases the
number of ruins. Like the heiress, the decorator fights
a futile battle to improve the drab world by decorating
his shop. Nevertheless, ''there's no money in the
work,'' and ''he'd rather marry'' (ll. 23–24). The
decorator's resistance achieves nothing.

The people of Nautilus Island are not regenerative.
The decorator is homosexual. The heiress has produced
one child, but he is a bishop with vows of celibacy.
''The summer millionaire/who seemed to leap from an
L. L. Bean/catalogue'' (ll. 14–16) is lost, either
bankrupt or dead. In either case, his holdings are not
passed down to his offspring, but sold off to the
highest bidder. Lowell himself commented that in
''Skunk Hour,'' ''Sterility howls through the
scenery.''[5]

However, the most desperate character of all is the speaker of the poem, Lowell himself. He admits that his ''mind's not right'' (1. 30) and believes that like Milton's Satan, he himself is hell. A Puritan and a peeping Tom, he prowls the local lovers' lane hoping to catch some couple making love. Yet the locale of the lovers' lane is not particularly auspicious; it tops the ''hill's skull'' (1. 26) at the place ''where the graveyard shelves in the town'' (1. 29). In short it is a place not of regeneration but of death, a location which Lowell ghoulishly haunts.

Only the skunks thrive; in fact, they have taken over the town:

> They march on their soles up Main Street,
> white stripes, moonstruck eyes' red fire
> under the chalk-dry and spar spire
> of the Trinitarian Church [ll. 39—42]

There may be something sinister in the ''red fire'' of their eyes, but at least they show more life than the ''chalk-dry'' Trinitarian Church. Indeed, the skunk does not march alone; she leads ''her column of kittens'' (1. 45).

The skunks' triumph is not wholly laudable. They are smelly. They are scavengers; they swill ''the garbage pail'' (1. 45). Their eyes are sinister. But they are not merely bad. They have beautiful ostrich plume tails and ''moonstruck'' eyes. Yet, their survival rests not on their beauty but on their adaptability to the world around them. Unlike the humans, they are not caught up in any of the outdated beliefs, fashions, or hierarchies.

The choice Lowell seems to be giving us is not very attractive. We can either hold on to our cherished beliefs and kill ourselves off, or we can become that somewhat stinky and homely scavenger and flourish. Lowell is trying to frighten us with this choice, but I for one ''will not scare'' (1. 48) and hold out for a better bargain.

Notes

[1] Robert Lowell, ''On 'Skunk Hour,' '' in *The Contemporary Poet as Artist and Critic,* ed. Anthony Ostroff (Boston: Little, Brown, 1964), p. 109.

[2] Elizabeth Bishop, ''The Armadillo,'' in *The Complete Poems* (New York: Farrar, Straus and Giroux, 1969), p. 123.

[3] Robert Lowell, ''Skunk Hour,'' in *Life Studies* (New York: Noonday Press, 1964), p. 90, 11. 46–47. All future line references to this work appear in the text.

[4] Richard Wilbur, ''On Robert Lowell's 'Skunk Hour,' '' in *The Contemporary Poet as Artist and Critic,* ed. Anthony Ostroff (Boston: Little, Brown, 1964), p. 87.

[5] Lowell, ''On 'Skunk Hour,' '', p. 107.

Glossary

Allegory. A literary or dramatic device in which the events of a narrative or an implied narrative obviously and continuously refer to another simultaneous structure of events or ideas, whether historical events, moral or philosophical ideas, or natural phenomena.   149–153

Alliteration. The repetition of an initial consonant sound in two or more words of a line (or line group), to produce a noticeable artistic effect, as in "The sails did sigh like sedge"(Coleridge).   208–212

Allusion. Tacit reference to another literary work, to another art, to history, to contemporary figures, and the like.   180–182

Anapest. A metrical unit of three syllables, of which the first two are unstressed and the last is stressed.   194

Anaphora. Repetition of the initial word in several successive lines of poetry.   58

Antistrophe. See *Pindaric ode.*

Assonance. As distinguished from rhyme, the repetition of vowel sounds preceded by unlike consonants, as in "Be near me when my light is low."   208–212

Ballad. Usually a narrative poem in quatrains in which the second and fourth lines rhyme. In a ballad, the first and third lines are typically four feet long, and the second and fourth lines three feet long.   17–18, 241–242

Ballade. A form that consists of three eight-line stanzas and an envoi.   254–255

Bard. A poet-reciter in a preliterate or semiliterate society; more loosely, a poet or poet-singer.   15, 19

Blank verse. Unrhymed iambic pentameter lines.   193

Caesura. A rhetorical pause within a poetic line, usually in the middle.   201

Note: Page numbers following definitions refer to discussion in the text.

Carpe diem. A theme in many love poems, in which a lover is implored not to be hesitant in affection (Latin for "seize the day").   54, 91, 260

Chiasmus. A rhetorical device in which words initially presented are restated in reverse order. An example is the sentence, "For we that live to please, must please to live."   314

Conceit. An intricate, extended, or farfetched metaphor or simile that arouses a feeling of surprise, shock, or amusement.   133–137

Concrete poem. A poem in which the visual arrangement of the letters and words suggests the meaning.   279–283

Connotative meaning. See *Denotative meaning.*

Couplet. A two-line stanza, usually rhymed.   242–244

Dactyl. A metrical unit of three syllables, of which the first is stressed and the second two are not.   194

Denotative meaning. Literal meaning; the dictionary meaning as opposed to connotative meaning, which is the associations (historical, evaluative, and economic) the word conveys. For example, *car* and *automobile* refer to the same object, but *automobile* is more formal and old-fashioned than *car.*   109

Diction. The writer's choice of words.   233–235

Didactic poetry. Poetry whose purpose is to teach.   226–229

Dimeter. A metrical line with two feet.   193

Doggerel. Rough, poorly constructed verse, characterized by strong and monotonous rhyme and rhythm, cheap sentiment, triviality, and lack of dignity.   204–205, 309

Double dactyl. A complicated comic form of eight lines, the fourth and eighth of which rhyme.   278–279

Dramatic irony. A situation in which the author and the audience share knowledge by which they can recognize the characters' actions as wholly inappropriate, or the characters' words as possessing a significance unknown to the characters themselves.   90–91

Dramatic monologue. A poem in which the poet adopts a fictive or historical voice, or persona, and from which an entire dramatic scene may be inferred.   80–82

Elegy. A lyric, usually formal in tone and diction, suggested either by the death of an actual person or by the poet's contemplation of tragic aspects of life.   55–63

Encomium. A song praising not a god but a hero, sung at the *komos,* the jubilant procession or revels that celebrated the victor in the Olympic games.   54–58

End rhyme. Rhymes at the ends of lines of poetry.   204

End-stopped line. A line that ends where the syntactic unit ends, at a clear pause, or at the end of a sentence.   201

English or Shakespearean sonnet. A fourteen-line poem rhyming *abab cdcd efef gg.* It consists of three quatrains and a closing couplet.   246–248

Enjambment. The employment of run-on lines that carry the sense of statement from one line to another without rhetorical or syntactic pause at the end of the line.   201

Envoi. A short concluding section of a poem that bids the poem farewell or contains concluding remarks.   254–255

Epic. A long narrative poem. Primary epics are passed down orally and have a legendary author (for example, the *Iliad* and the *Odyssey*, which are traditionally ascribed to Homer). A secondary epic is one written by a known author.   19

Epigram. A poem with the qualities of an inscription, and thus short, pointed, and often with a witty or surprising turn of thought.   65

Epistolary poem. A letter in verse.   87–88

Epode. See *Pindaric ode.*   264

Fable. A story in which animals are given human attributes and represent moral, philosophic, psychological, or political postitions. Fables typically have morals as their conclusions.   153–155

Feminine ending. An unstressed syllable at the end of a line.   199

Feminine rhyme. A rhyme in which the similarity of sounds is in both of the last two syllables—for example, *dreary/weary.*   205

Figurative language. Language that uses figures of speech and that cannot be taken literally.   125

Foot. A measurable, patterned unit of poetic rhythm usually consisting of one stressed syllable and one or more unstressed syllables.   193

Formulae. Stock phrases used by poets in reciting oral poems.   15–16

Free verse. Poetry that is both unrhymed and without a regular meter, although it may be more or less rhythmical.   239–241

Haiku. An Oriental lyric form of seventeen syllables in three lines of five, seven, and five syllables, respectively. The haiku must state or imply a season and, except for modern innovations, is almost wholly restricted to natural images.   100, 202, 272–277

Heptameter. A metrical line with seven feet.   193

Heroic couplet. A rhymed couplet in iambic pentameter whose second line is end-stopped.   242–244

Hexameter. A metrical line with six feet.   193

High diction. Formal literary language.   233–235

Horatian ode. An ode that repeats the same irregular stanza pattern throughout. It is personal rather than public, general rather than occasional, tranquil rather than intense, and is intended for the reader in privacy rather than for the spectator in the theater.   263, 267–270

Hyperbole. An exaggeration; a statement that something has either much more or much less of a quality than it truly has.   171–174

Iamb. A metrical unit of two syllables in which the second is stressed.   193

Image. A direct presentation of sensory experience.   99–106

In medias res. Literally, "in the middle of things"—the way in which epics traditionally start.   17

Internal rhyme. Rhyme that occurs in the middle of a line.   206

Irony of situation. See *Dramatic irony*.

Irregular ode. An ode in which each stanza has a different irregular shape.   263, 270–272

Italian or Petrarchan sonnet. A poem fourteen lines long and divided between an opening octet and a closing sestet. The rhyme scheme is *abba abba//cdc cdc*.   245–248

Limerick. A five-line comic form rhyming *aabba*, of which the first, second, and fifth lines are trimeter and the third and fourth dimeter.   277–278

Literary ballad. A ballad intended to be read rather than sung.   241

Low diction. Street language; simple or vulgar words.   233–235

Lyric. A highly concentrated poem of direct personal emotion, most often written in the first person. Lyric poetry is generally considered the most intense genre of poetry, the form that most honors its musical origins. The love poem, the elegy, and the meditation are all forms of lyric poetry.   49–54

Masculine ending. A stressed syllable at the end of a line.   199

Masculine rhyme. A rhyme in which the similarity of sounds is in the final syllables of the words involved.   205

Metaphor. A figure of speech in which a person, an object, or an idea is imaginatively transformed, as in "The grass is itself a child, the produced babe of the vegetation" (Whitman). A metaphor may be suggested by comparison, but it need not be.   125–130, 182

Meter. The measure of stressed and unstressed syllables in lines of poetry. When stresses occur at regular intervals, the poetry is said to have regular meter.   193–198

Metonymy. A figure of speech in which a single name of a person, place, or thing comes to stand for a more complex situation or experience with which the name is associated—for example, *Washington* for the U.S. government, *the press* for the enterprise of journalism.   176–180

Monometer. A metrical line of one foot.   193

Near rhyme. Two words or syllables that have approximate sounds, such as "lids" and "lads."   206

Octave. An eight-line stanza or section; often, the first eight lines of an Italian or Petrarchan sonnet.   245

Octometer. A metrical line with eight feet, rare in English.   193

Ode. The name of the most formal, ceremonious, and complexly organized form of lyric poetry, usually of considerable length. The ode is often used as a poem of praise for a formal occasion such as a marriage, a funeral, or a state ceremonial.   66–70, 263–272

Off rhyme. See *Near rhyme*.

Onomatopoeia. A word whose sound imitates the actual sound to which it refers, such as *pop, sizzle,* and *crash.*   209–212

Oxymoron. A phrase that combines two seemingly contradictory elements, such as *icy heat, loud silence, painful ease.*   183–184

Paradox. A seemingly contradictory statement.   182–184

Partial rhyme. See *Near rhyme.*

Pastoral. An artistic work that contains an urbane nostalgia for the simplicity of the shepherd's life and of country conventions, and which thus depicts rural living in a highly idealized and stylized manner; a classical dialogue between shepherds.   90–92

Pentameter. A metrical line with five feet.   193

Persona. The speaker of the poem, who may or may not be the same as the poet.   10–14

Personification. The granting of human attributes to things that are not human.   147–148

Petrarchan sonnet. See *Italian sonnet.*

Pindaric ode. An ode of three parts—strophe, antistrophe, and epode. The strophe and antistrophe are the same irregularly shaped form, invented by the poet for each ode. The epode contrasts in shape.   66, 263–267

Popular ballad. A ballad passed on orally, with no known author.   16–17

Posthumous monologue. A poem spoken by the dead.   91

Primary epic. See *Epic.*

Prose poem. A form that uses imagery and figurative language but forfeits the effects of versification, meter, and line endings.   283–285

Psalm. A sacred song or hymn, such as any of the sacred songs collected in the Old Testament Book of Psalms. Psalms are organized through a complex series of parallel and opposed ideas.   240

Psychomachia. Literally, "conflict of the soul"; a work in which parts of the personality or mind are in conflict with one another, sometimes depicted as an inner debate or quarrel.   152

Pun. A play on words with similar sounds or on a single word with different meanings.   232–233

Pyrrhic. A metrical unit of two unaccented syllables.   195

Quantitative meter. Meter determined by the duration of syllables rather than by their accents.   213

Quatrain. A stanza of four lines, rhymed or unrhymed.   18, 241

Rhyme. The occurrence of the same stressed vowel sounds in two words, such as in *spring–sing, dies–eyes, day–gray.* This is known as perfect rhyme and assumes that the accented vowel sounds involved are preceded by different consonant sounds. For variations, see *Feminine rhyme, Internal rhyme, Near rhyme,* and *Masculine rhyme.*   203–207

Rhyme scheme. A pattern of rhyme throughout a stanza or poem.   204–205

Scansion. The system of describing more or less conventional poetic rhythms by visual symbols for purposes of metrical analysis and study.   192–193

Secondary epic. See *Epic.*

Sestet. A six-line unit that can stand alone as a stanza or as the concluding six lines of an Italian or Petrarchan sonnet.   245

Sestina. A verse form that consists of six six-line stanzas and a concluding tercet. The end words of each line of the first stanza are repeated in subsequent stanzas.   257–260

Shakespearean sonnet. See *English sonnet.*

Shaped form. A poem whose lines, taken together, form a visual representation of its subject.   279–283

Simile. A comparison of one thing with another, explicitly announced by the word *like* or *as.*   130–133

Soliloquy. A speech to oneself.   79–87

Sonnet. A fourteen-line poem in iambic pentameter whose rhyme scheme has, in practice, been widely varied. Sonnets concern themselves with love, death, politics, and other topics that evoke intense personal feelings.   245–250

Spondee. A metrical unit of two accented syllables.   195

Stanza. A sequence of lines that form a metrical, tonal, or intellectual unit.   18, 51, 241

Stress. Emphasis given to a word or syllable. There are two forms of stress: stress of accent and stress of emphasis. Stress of accent occurs in polysyllabic words. Thus we say beaúty rather than beautý. Stress of emphasis is the stress we give to particular words in a sentence. In the sentence, "I have a bad headache," the word *bad* is stressed.   192–193

Strophe. See *Pindaric ode.*

Syllabic verse. A poem whose line lengths are calculated by the number of syllables in each line rather than the number of feet per line.   202–203

Symbol. An object, person, action, or situation that signifies more than itself and thus may be read both literally and metaphorically.   155–160

Synecdoche. A figure of speech wherein part of a thing is employed to suggest the whole, or a larger concept is used to suggest something specific. *Example:* "All hands were on deck."   174–176

Synesthesia. The manner of speaking about one sense in terms of another. "He wore a *screaming* yellow necktie" is an example of synesthesia because *yellow* is described as if it were a sound.   104

Talon. The last word of the line of a sestina.   258

Tanka. A Japanese lyric form of thirty-one syllables, in lines of five, seven, five, seven, seven. Historically, its diction has been traditional and elevated, and its subjects most often include love, lament, felicitations, travel, and nature.   272–277

Tercet. A three-line stanza.   250

Terza rima. A form of interconnected three-line stanzas that rhyme *aba bcb cdc ded efe.* . . .   250–254

Tetrameter. A metrical line with four feet.   193

Tone. The writer's attitude toward a subject as exhibited through rhythms, sounds, and the selection of words.   221–237

Trimeter. A metrical line with three feet.   193

Triplet. A verse unit of three lines, usually containing rhyme, employed as a stanzaic form, as a variation on the couplet, or occasionally as a complete poem in itself.   242

Trochee. A metrical unit of two syllables in which the first is stressed.   193

Villanelle. A poem made up of five tercets, all rhyming *aba*, and a concluding quatrain, rhyming *abaa*. Lines 6, 12, and 18 repeat line 1; lines 9, 15, and 19 repeat line 3.   255–257

Index of First Lines

Note: For ease of reference, there are three separate indexes—first lines, authors, and titles. The index of authors begins on page 481, and the index of titles on page 489.

Hurrah for revolution and more cannon-shot! 176

I strove with none; for none was worth my strife, 362
It is not far to my place: 413
It is the pain, it is the pain, endures. 314
It little profits that an idle king, 85
I traveled on, seeing the hill where lay, 150
It's a white nest! White as the foam thrown up when the sea hits rocks. Some light, 284
It's too dark to see black, 95
I used to fall, 219
I wake to sleep, and take my waking slow. 257
I wandered lonely as a cloud, 361
I wander thro' each charter'd street, 112
I will arise and go now, and go to Innisfree, 214
I will lift up mine eyes unto the hills: from whence cometh my help. 240
I woke up this mornin' 18

John Anderson my jo, John, 235
Just off the highway to Rochester, Minnesota, 2

Lately, I've become accustomed to the way, 76
Lay your sleeping head, my love, 392
Let me not to the marriage of true minds, 141
Let them remember Samangan, the bridge and tower, 272
Let us go then, you and I, 338
'Lias! 'Lias! Bless de Lawd! 236
Light flows our war of mocking words, and yet, 371
Lightning does strike twice. Lully thumping the floor with, 419
Like the pearl of dew, 274
Look, it's morning, and a little water gurgles in the tap. 225
Look one way and the sun is going down, 173
Lord, who createdst man in wealth and store, 279
Love, 148
Love bade me welcome: yet my soul drew back, 169
Loveliest of trees, the cherry now, 379

Madam Mouse trots, 296
Márgarét, are you gríeving, 376
Marke but this flea, and marke in this, 142
Maud went to college. 401
May he lose his way on the cold sea, 54
Merry Margaret, 348
Morning and evening, 31
Mother, I cannot mind my wheel; 9
"Mother dear, may I go downtown, 23
Much have I traveled in the realms of gold, 245
My aunt! my dear unmarried aunt! 367

Pity me not because the light of day, 247
Poised upside down on his duncecap, 405
"Poor wanderer," said the leaden sky, 160
Poplars are standing there still as death, 390
Pray to what earth does this sweet cold belong, 110

Rain smell comes with the wind, 439
Ray Charles is the black wind of Kilimanjaro, 181
Reading how even the Swiss had thrown the sponge, 177
Robert Frost at midnight, the audience gone, 250
Robinson at cards at the Algonquin; a thin, 189
Rose, harsh rose, 120
Round the cape of a sudden came the sea, 369

Season of mists and mellow fruitfulness, 364
See that girl, Ameana, the one with the big nostrils? 291
Seivers was one of the hardest running backs since, 230
September rain falls on the house. 258
Shall I compare thee to a summer's day? 133
She is as in a field a silken tent, 385
she loves me, 282
She walks in beauty, like the night, 362
Shops take down their awnings; 303
Shouts from the street, spotlights crossfire, 21
Shrugging in the flight of its leaves, 425
Slowly the women file to where he stands, 408
soft rainsqualls on the swells, 111
So I would hear out those lungs, 179
Some say the world will end in fire, 65
Something there is that doesn't love a wall, 383
Sometimes men need the winds most, 263
Sometimes when my eyes are red, 414
somewhere i have never travelled, gladly beyond, 70
so much depends, 120
Sorrow is my own yard, 79
So there stood Matthew Arnold and this girl, 410
Success is counted sweetest, 228
Sweet Mercy! how my very heart has bled, 189
Sweet stream, that dost with equal pace, 323
Sweet sweet sweet sweet sweet tea. 289

Take hand and part with laughter; 199
Taking the air rifle from my son's hand, 397
That is no country for old men. The young, 337
That sail in cloudless light, 421
That's my last Duchess painted on the wall, 93

Index of Authors

Index of Titles

1   2   3   4   5   6   7   8   9   0